BOUNDARIES
OF THE SOUL

BOUNDARIES
OF THE SOUL

· · ·

The Practice of
Jung's Psychology

REVISED
AND UPDATED

JUNE SINGER

Anchor Books
A DIVISION OF
RANDOM HOUSE, INC.

New York

Library of Congress Cataloging-in-Publication Data
Singer, June.
Boundaries of the soul : the practice of Jung's psychology / June Singer.
p. cm.
Includes bibliographical references and index.
1. Psychoanalysis. 2. Jung, C. G. (Carl Gustav), 1875–1961.
I. Title.
BF173.S564 1994
150.19'54—dc20 94-9070
CIP

ISBN 0-385-47529-2

www.anchorbooks.com

Printed in the United States of America

You would not find out the boundaries of the soul, even by travelling along every path: so deep a measure does it have.

—HERACLITUS

I am indebted to the following: to Dr. Werner H. Engel, whose encouragement was present at the conception of this book and helped immeasurably throughout the writing; to Dr. Leland H. Roloff, whose discerning comments helped me to enliven the style; to Dr. Karen Signell and Suzanne Kent for their critiques from the feminine perspective; to James B. Martin, who corrected the final copy; and to Mary Kennedy, who prepared the typescript with care and devotion. Finally, I am grateful to my analysands, who allowed me to share in their experience and so to deepen my own understanding.

June Singer
Palo Alto, California

Contents

Part Four: ANALYSIS AND THE HUMAN SPIRIT

Preface to the
New Edition

A FEW DAYS AGO I received a letter from my publisher congratulating me on the number of copies of *Boundaries of the Soul* now in print, and announcing a plan to reprint once again the book that has for more than twenty years served as an introduction to the psychology of C. G. Jung. The letter coincided with my seventy-fifth birthday. This was a milestone that reminded me of my mortality and demanded that I look at where I was on my life's journey. I had written BOUNDARIES OF THE SOUL after less than a decade of analytic practice. Most of Jung's writings had yet to be translated, so the non-German-speaking reader did not have access to the full body of his thought. Now, more than twenty years later, the world has changed, psychology has changed, and I have changed.

Faced with still another reprinting of BOUNDARIES, I asked myself, Is this the legacy I want to leave behind me? The answer that came to me was this: much of what I have written is still current—in the way that Jung's work is still current—and I can stand up for it. But there is also much of what I wrote that is outdated and no longer represents my present thinking. I suggested to my publisher that BOUNDARIES OF THE SOUL should not simply be reprinted but should undergo a thorough revision to bring it up to date, and she agreed.

Rereading Jung, I found that his basic understanding of the psyche as it operates in our lives endures and provides a solid foundation for inner work. Much of what he wrote is timeless, but there are areas where it is evident that Jung was a product of his cultural setting and his times. Yet throughout his life he continued to evolve his theories, unceasingly attempting to integrate his new insights into the body of his work. My favorite of all the sayings ascribed to Jung is, "I thank God I am Jung and not a Jungian!" By this I understand that he did not want his followers to accept blindly what he wrote as "truth" but to do as he did—be themselves and adapt their insights to evolving situations. So now, a quarter of a century after Jung's death, I feel justified in taking a fresh view of Jung's concepts and considering where they remain applicable to contemporary life and where some revisions may be called for.

I find that people today require new answers to old questions about such matters as the nature of the relationship between analyst and analysand, gender issues, personality typology and the value of objective measures, the interaction between the individual and what Jung called "the collective," the uses of the new freedom our society has claimed to speak about inner experience, and the greater recognition of the intricately interwoven threads of body, mind and soul as related to suffering and to healing. I often think of the legacy left to us by Jung, and how deeply indebted to him I am. Yet with the passing of the years I have found myself beset by more and more questions for which Jung had no answers. Like all disciples, I have had to think for myself and devise new ways to meet changing conditions, and so my practice of Jung's psychology has taken on its own form.

The chapter "Anima and Animus: Will One Sex Ever Understand the Other?" was written before anyone had heard of the "women's movement" and the subsequent revolution in our concepts of gender roles in society. That chapter had to be scrapped and a new one, "Anima and Animus: The Opposites Within," written to replace it. The original chapter, "Psychological Types: Key to Communications," was written before Jung's typology became the basis for important personality inventories that have found wide use both clinically and in the workplace, so that chapter underwent radical revision. In the original edition, a chapter called "Analysis and the Counter-Culture" had the distinct flavor of the sixties. I had to take note of the fact that in the nineties there is no longer an identifiable "counterculture," only "minorities," whose members may one day form the majority in the United States. The counterculture chapter had to go, and I have added a new chapter, "Psyche in the World," which deals with the fact that Jung's psychology and psychology in general have burst out of the consulting room and entered into the mainstream.

Other revisions throughout the text reflect my mature thoughts about the practice of Jung's psychology. They encompass the results of my own reflective life spent working with the psyche in others as well as in myself. For what is psyche, if not soul? Soul is what makes us more than a pile of chemicals and a tangle of neurons; soul is that essence of consciousness that enables us to know ourselves and our world, to recognize what is unique in us as individuals and what each one of us shares with the immense totality of which we are a part.

This new edition of BOUNDARIES OF THE SOUL is an expression of these reflections.

June Singer
Palo Alto, California, 1994

Introduction

THE PURPOSE OF THIS BOOK is twofold: to give an overview of the thought of C. G. Jung as it applies to the growth and development of individual consciousness, and to provide some glimpses into the experience of Jungian analysis. In my early days as a Jungian analyst, Jung's psychology was known to the general public mostly through the writings of Jung's detractors, who objected to his excursions into the uncharted waters of the unconscious as too risky or too speculative. Today thoughtful people recognize that Jung provides a bridge in our time between the scientific-intellectual aspects of life and the religious-nonrational aspects. Jung has faced the apparent dichotomy between abstraction and generalization on one side and the experience of immediate knowing on the other. Our culture, steeped in the principles of Aristotelian logic, finds it difficult to accept paradoxical thinking as valid. Too often it seems necessary to make a choice between the rationalistic-academic way of life or the anti-intellectual camp. Jung's greatness is that he saw both of these as aspects of the same reality, as polar opposites on a single axis. I intend to describe how Jung came to his position, and to explain how Jung's concepts have been integrated into my own work as an analytical psychologist.

One of the comments I heard when I first began attending courses at the C. G. Jung Institute for Analytical Psychology in Zurich in 1960 was, "You cannot really understand the psychology of Jung through merely reading him. You have to assimilate his concepts into yourself and live them actively." While I have come to agree that the most direct way of doing this is through a guided tour, that is to say, through the analytic process, I am convinced that this is not the only way. And it is of course fortunate that it is *not* the only way, for Jung's teachings have much to offer to the troubled world in this last decade of the twentieth century, and there are not nearly enough Jungian analysts to meet the need, the interest, and the demand. There were less than four hundred members of the International Association of Analytical Psychologists in the world and eleven groups training Jungian analysts in 1972, when this book was first published. By the time of the 1992 IAAP Congress there were two thousand members and thirty-two training groups. Still, if we multiply this by the small number of patients any analyst is able to see during a given period of time, it becomes immediately apparent how very few people can be given direct exposure to Jung's ideas through the analytic process.

With the increase in the number of analysts, interest in Jung's ideas mounted proportionately. At first, small study groups composed of lay people who had been in Jungian analysis sprang up around individual analysts or groups of analysts. Everyone who belonged to such a group was required to have had at least fifty hours of Jungian analysis, because Jungian analysis was still considered to be comprehensible only to those who had experienced the process. As far as I know, the first group that opened its membership to anyone who wanted to learn about Jung, whether they were in analysis or not, was the Analytical Psychology Club of Chicago, founded in 1965. Now, almost three decades later, Jungian groups open to all who wish to come have sprung up in nearly every major city in the United States. People meet to learn about and discuss the life and work of Jung, which they attempt to understand in terms of their own personal experience. They attend lectures, workshops and classes, and participate in various creative activities based on the principles of Jung's psychology. Books and articles by Jungian analysts are reaching an ever increasing number of people, and even occasionally find their way to the top of the *New York Times* best-seller list. It is clear enough that Jung has come out of the consulting-room closet.

When Jung's psychology was first taught in universities, the demand often came from the students rather than from faculty members. Typically, students have come across references to Jung in their readings in philosophy or personality psychology, or in the works of such men as Paul Tillich, Erich Fromm, Rollo May, Martin Buber, Mircea Eliade, Claude Lévi-Strauss, Alan Watts, Aldous Huxley, Hermann Hesse or Freud—men who have read Jung or known Jung, and who have never been the same afterward. Remarks these men have made, taking issue with Jung, never quite resolving their differences with him, leave their readers with the misty awareness that Jung had the capacity to touch something essential in the human soul which needs to be touched or needs to be healed, in order to be made whole.

Mentally acquisitive people have been led by their own curiosity to find out what manner of man Jung was, and why he left his imprint upon the work of so many of the great minds of our century, despite the fact that he himself was often put down as too much of a mystic, unscientific, inconsistent, and wordy; and also to question why, on occasion, he has been vilified and discredited by those who needed to deify the gods of rationalism. The students of the sixties are now the professors of the nineties. They have experienced the revolution of the study of consciousness that has occurred over the past thirty or so years, and they recognize the importance of understanding those aspects of the psyche that are not under the control of the rational ego, as well as those that are.

Another reason for the rather late renascence of Jung is the fact that publication of his *Collected Works* in English was not completed until 1979, and the paperback edition until a decade later. A complete index of Jung's works and a bibliography are now available.

Much has been written about this man, in many lands and by many people, scholars and psychologists, poets and playwrights, musicians and nuclear physicists. Some of the best works on the psychology of Jung have been written by Jungian analysts, who have formulated the theoretical approach in terms of their own experiences—as therapists and as human beings—living in an active relationship with the unconscious. It is understandably hard to get at Jung in any methodical way. And, where "methods" have been devised, they tend to schematize the abstractions at which Jung arrived, without maintaining the vitality of the flesh-and-blood experiences from which his theories were generalized. Such writings often lack a real understanding of the struggles of thinking people whose orientation is toward the future, and who rail against a social system which fails to offer sustenance for their spiritual lives while it surfeits them with things and concepts and methodologies.

The one book which has broken through all of this to give the public a glimpse into the private world of the psyche through Jung's eyes is *Memories, Dreams, Reflections.*[1] Jung began it in 1957, when he was already in his eighties. This book has been called Jung's "autobiography" for want of a better designation. But, if an autobiography is a chronicle of a man's life and his impact upon the world, his successes and his failures, then *Memories, Dreams, Reflections* is not an autobiography. It is rather the confession of a man concerning his observations of those aspects of living that may be called the "inner life." All people experience an inner life to greater or lesser degrees, but it is self-understood that they rarely share it with other people. Jung did share these matters shortly before his death with his collaborator, longtime assistant and trusted friend, Aniela Jaffé. While he wrote much of the book himself and approved all of it, Jung talked it through with Mrs. Jaffé, who recorded and edited the material and then submitted it to him for further discussion and clarification before incorporating it into the book. Like all of Jung's work, it bears his unique imprint. It was the product not of his isolation from humanity but rather of his intense interaction with another human being. It reflected the interplay of his consciousness with the unconscious—not "his own" unconscious, but that collective mystery most of which must remain forever hidden from consciousness with only occasional glimpses offered to anyone whose attitude is open enough to receive it.

Close to the beginning of *Memories, Dreams, Reflections* a short passage establishes for the reader the basic attitude with which Jung approached not only his own life but also the phenomenon of *Life* itself. This is what has seized so many readers and refused to let them go until they had lived with Jung for a long enough time to make him the friend of their soul. The passage follows:

> Life has always seemed to me like a plant that lives on its rhizome. Its true life is invisible, hidden in the rhizome. The part that appears above the ground lasts only a single summer. Then it withers away—an ephemeral apparition. When we think of the unending growth and decay of life and civilizations, we cannot escape the impression of absolute nullity. Yet I have never lost a sense of something that lives and endures underneath the eternal flux. What we see is the blossom, which passes. The rhizome remains.[2]

Students in universities today engage too much in the examination and dissection of the blossom. Psychology courses emphasize the diagnosis, evaluation and treatment of mental disorders. In some approaches to treatment, behavior is broken down into operations to be observed, measured, predicted, controlled and manipulated. In others, cognition becomes the focus of treatment; and thoughts, perceptions and attitudes are modified to correspond to socially acceptable standards. Again, in the so-called psychodynamic approaches, an understanding of the causal factors in aberrant behavior or ideation is sought as the potential healing factor.

No one would argue that human behavior is not a matter about which psychology must concern itself. Yet, discouraged by the variety of attempts to "fix" problems that seemed to be at the root of human suffering, many thinking people turned to a more existential approach. But often they, too, were not altogether satisfied with an acceptance of what is the human condition or, to put it more accurately, acceptance of what the human condition appears to be. The bloom of existential psychology has begun to fade, for it is not fulfilling to find all of one's meaning in *this moment* and in the often terrifying experience of *this moment.* We were torn between two extremes: on the one hand was the existential ultimatum that we are here in this frightful or fabulous present, and nowhere else, nor would we ever be anywhere else; and on the other hand was the Freudian dilemma that we are where we are because of where we were and what happened to us in infancy, and all efforts must be devoted to overcoming that past which can never be changed, and which casts its long shadow across the future. Many concerned people became disenchanted with both extremes.

Some sought to escape by not thinking at all. In place of serving the demand to "think" (which has been put upon their heads since ever there were such institutions as universities), they have listened lately to the Pied Pipers who lured them with the cry that "thinking is out," no longer allowable. What you needed to do now was to "feel," to "sense," to "touch," and all that this implied, without bothering to recognize the disciplined partner to the emotional experience that rational thinking provides.

Others have gone beyond sensing, into the various kinds of self-administered drug experiences, in which their perceptive mechanisms are so altered as to distort their impressions of the objective world—thus leading to the dangerous conclusion that, if that world can be changed subjectively through changing the eye that sees it, it need not be changed objectively by correcting the flaws that actually exist "out there."

Meanwhile, tremendous advances have been made in the

field of psychopharmacology, based on study and research of the biochemical aspect of mental health and human behavior. We are more knowledgeable than ever before about the ways in which the psyche is affected by our physical condition, and it is now generally recognized that certain types of mental illness are amenable to alleviation through the use of prescription drugs that regulate body chemistry in ways that can alter moods and compensate psychological imbalance. These medications can often allow persons to become more accessible to psychotherapy than they would be otherwise. All of these approaches to psychological illness are geared toward restoring the ability to function in the world so that a person can carry on the necessary activities to lead a productive life. This is what Jung would have called "tending the blossom."

Nevertheless, and despite all of these practical and technical resources that we have at hand today, there seems to be a renewal of the age-old search for something larger, and perhaps not so well defined. It has to do with an understanding of ourselves and our place in the eternal scheme. For, as we learn more and more about ourselves and our universe from the researches of contemporary biology and physics, we can no longer see ourselves as isolated in our little bags of skin. Who are we? Where have we come from? Where are we going? These are the questions that more and more people are asking. Jung has provided some answers and, more than that, some directions in which to carry on the search. People have become aware that . . . "Yes, the blossom is important, but so is the rhizome." It is not a matter of making a choice: either-or. Both are necessary to the existence of the plant and to its growth. But in today's hurried world, where the blossom is easily seen, enjoyed, and knocked off its stem when it begins to wither and decay, the rhizome is all too often overlooked. We forget that it carries the source of tomorrow's blossom. I admit that Jungian psychology may lay too much emphasis on the rhizome, and not enough on the blossom. Jung has often enough been criticized for that. But just *because* institutional psychology has dealt with the observable phenomena, and dealt with them relatively adequately within the limitations of its methods, it has not been necessary for Jung or for Jungians to dwell overlong upon grounds that have been competently tended by others. Therefore, at the risk of appearing one-sided in my approach, I will follow Jung's way and stress the importance of the unconscious rather than of consciousness, the mysterious rather than the known, the mystical rather than the scientific, the creative rather than the productive, the religious rather than the profane, the meaning of love rather than the techniques of sex.

I have found that this is what many young people are looking for, to round out the one-sided views of life they are fed on most campuses, in most churches, and elsewhere. I have found this out in my own analytic practice, where I listen to the concerns of undergraduate and graduate students, professors, clergymen, and those others who have turned their backs on school and church and have looked for a different way. They have come, not *to* me, but *through* me to Jung, and to what they hope will be a clarification of what they have somewhat dimly understood yet recognized as a great personal value *in potentia* for themselves in Jung's work, and in his life.

By way of introduction to the analytic process, I will review some important moments and motifs of Jung's early life. I will proceed much as a therapist must do with a patient, that is, I will attempt to see the man in the context of his life history, with particular reference to the patterns that were established in youth, and which determine to a large degree his subsequent attitudes and activities.

Born in 1875 in Kesswil, Switzerland, Jung came to manhood just at the turn of the century. His interests had been varied during his student years, but they divided naturally between his philosophical, humanistic and religious concerns, and his fascination with science. To the latter category belonged archaeology, the subject that most intrigued him. He wrote in his autobiography, *Memories, Dreams, Reflections*[3] that he was intensely interested in everything Egyptian and Babylonian. As we know from his later writings and the course of his life, this interest was not in the shards and stones so much as it was in the mysteries that inspired ancient peoples to tell and preserve their myths and legends about how the world was created and the nature of the forces that animated it.

The autobiography reveals Jung's early awareness of two quite distinct aspects of his own personality. Each one held sway over its own sphere of interests, and each one had its own style of functioning. I suppose that a double sense of self exists in many people, especially in childhood when the direction of their lives is not yet focused, and the demands of society and practical necessity have not yet made themselves felt. How many of us in childhood enjoy fantasies of what we will be when we grow up, pursue daydreams in which we imagine ourselves as heroes and conquerors, magicians or scientists or great inventors, and are torn between this or that hero of our secret life until there comes a time when we must decide what role to assume, what may be possible and what impossible in terms of our resources and limitations. Yet in most of us the awareness of these "personalities *in potentia*" is vague and diffuse, and is often disregarded instead of being consciously thought through and resolved.

What was unusual about Jung's "two personalities" was that from early childhood he reflected upon them. Personality No. 1 was the schoolboy of 1890, the one who had to accept what he was taught in school and in the realm of religion, or suffer serious consequences. No. 1 was supposed to be obedient, polite and respectful, and not to ask questions which implied any skepticism. No. 2 lived in quite another realm, as he later wrote, "like a temple in which anyone who entered was transformed and suddenly overpowered by a vision of the whole cosmos, so that he could only marvel and admire, forgetful of himself."[4] Throughout his whole life ran a play and counterplay between these two personalities. He did not regard this as a split or dissociation in the ordinary sense of pathology, but believed that this duality is played out to a greater or lesser degree in every individual. Gradually he came to know each aspect in its uniqueness and watched the development of each from the standpoint of the other. His fine capacity to differentiate the varied, apparently autonomous aspects of the psyche came to him intuitively when he was very young. It is possible to trace back his theory of the structure of the psyche to his early observations about his own functioning from his first experiences of self-awareness. It is interesting to note that Jung has often been criticized because of his lack of interest in the psychology of the child and his alleged exclusive interest in the psychology of the adult. It is true that in his published scientific writings he did not stress the developmental stages of the child, particularly of the infant, as did Freud. He did not theorize about the feelings, the subjective experiences of childhood, from the "objective" stance of the adult. Instead, he found ways to re-enter the delicate web of his childhood. He writes of recollections of his own life beginning with his second or third year. He remembers seeing the sun glittering through the leaves and blossoms of the bushes as he looked upward from his buggy when the hood had been left up one splendid summer day; again, he recalls becoming aware of the pleasant taste and characteristic smell of warm milk as, sitting in his high chair, he spooned it up with bits of bread broken up in it.

He re-experiences "separation anxiety" as he tells of his illness at the age of three, and his dim awareness that it had something to do with a temporary separation of his parents. His mother had to spend several months in a hospital in Basel a few miles from his home. While she was gone he was cared for by an elderly and none too sympathetic aunt and he was deeply troubled by his mother's absence. He wrote that for a long time thereafter he felt distrustful when the word "love" was spoken and he associated a feeling of innate unreliability with women. His father stood for reliability, but he also represented powerlessness. Jung lets us know that these early impressions were revised over the course of time, for he says, "I have trusted men friends and been disappointed by them, and I have mistrusted women and not been disappointed."

He writes of his early fears, particularly fears of the night, when his vivid imagination peopled the blackness of the room with forms that shaped themselves out of nearly invisible patches of light. In the muted roar of the Rhine Falls outside his window were drowned the voices of those unfortunates who had been claimed by the water-swirled rocks. Also, out of the same sound, he sometimes thought he could discern his father's distant clerical voice as he intoned funereal phrases.

In those tense nights of early childhood, dreams became a living myth for Carl Jung and, as with all living myths, he did not recognize their true nature when they first came upon him. His autobiography tells us that the earliest remembered dream occurred when he was between three and four years of age, and that it was to occupy him all his life. Those who have said of Jung that he undervalued the importance of sexual symbolism in the child have not heard of this dream and the tremendous import it had for him.

The dream took place in the big meadow behind the vicarage where he lived with his family. While aimlessly wandering he suddenly discovered a dark, rectangular stone-lined hole in the ground with a stone stairway within, leading down. He descended with fear and hesitation, and found himself standing before a doorway with a round arch closed off by a heavy and sumptuously brocaded curtain. This he pushed aside and, amazed, saw before him a large throne room all of stone with a red carpet leading to a golden throne, a magnificent throne such as would be used by the king in a fairy tale. Something was standing upon the throne which he took at first to be a tree trunk twelve to fifteen feet high and about one-and-a-half to two feet thick, of a curious composition: made of naked flesh and skin. On top was something like a rounded head with no face and no hair but with a single eye on the top, gazing motionlessly upward. Above the head was an aura of brightness. The child was paralyzed with terror, feeling that the thing might crawl off the throne at any moment and creep toward him. Suddenly, in the background, he heard his mother's voice calling out, "That is the man-eater!"

The towering phallus of the dream was a subterranean God, "not to be named," Jung felt. Looking back upon that shattering sight in later years, he came to believe that through that dream he had originally conceived the idea that sexuality is a symbolized form for the creative potency of the Deity. How great a contrast to the classic psychoanalytic view of religion and ideas of Deity as sublimations for qualities of maleness, such as sexuality, fatherhood, authority!

The mysteries implicit in religion held so great a fascination for Jung as a child that his openness to this aspect of life seemed nearly to be predestined. He relates, concerning a time before he was six when he could not yet read, that his mother read aloud to him from *Orbis Pictus*, which contained accounts of exotic religions. He was especially interested in Hinduism, and the illustrations of Brahma, Vishnu and Shiva fascinated him. As his mother later told him, he returned to these particular pictures again and again; but what his mother did not know was that he nourished an obscure feeling for their relatedness to the earlier phallic dream. This was a secret which he kept, knowing that there was something "heathen" about the idea that his mother would never accept.

In the beginning of analysis the analyst usually will ask the analysand to tell him about his dreams. The dream is an important diagnostic tool. It is much more than that, but in the very first sessions the special value of the dream is that it gives the analyst an impression which comes directly from the unconscious and is not modified by any conscious wishes or desires on the part of the analysand. Presented as he is with the image that the analysand puts forth, largely for his own conscious purposes and with certain intentions to create an image, the analyst wants to gain access to a view that takes him beyond this. Often, the patient brings an "initial dream" to the first session or two, a dream which may lay open the whole psychic process as it takes place in the individual. In the absence of such a dream, or even as an adjunct to it, the analyst will frequently ask for a dream that has recurred frequently, or for a dream of early childhood, the earliest that can be recalled. Such a dream, having persisted through many years in some borderline area of consciousness from which it can be snatched back readily, has the import of a personal myth. It carries, in allegorical or metaphorical terms, the story by which a man lives, just as a tribal mythology often presents in symbolic form the way in which a people lives.

For this reason, I have called attention to the phallic-mystery dream of Jung's early childhood. That it remained with Jung into the ninth decade of his life suggests its importance. We will see how threads which have their beginning here will emerge time and again throughout Jung's life, in his *Weltanschauung*, in his writing, and in the practice of Jungian psychotherapy. It was this early (although Jung of course had at the time not the slightest awareness of it) that sexuality and spirituality were unalterably fused together as essential aspects of a single concept of human nature. The image of God and the image of the phallus were no more separate and distinct for Jung than they were for the pre-Hellenic Arcadians who raised ithyphallic shrines to Hermes, the giver of fertility —or to architects of those fabled temples of southern India, with façades depicting the sexuality of the gods as prototypes of the creative power in nature and in humans, who are seen as small fragments of the created and creating world.

Jung had learned early in his childhood that reality had to be discriminated in order that one could separate what could be lived out and talked about, from what had to be reserved and thought about. One ear had to be tuned to an outer world, which might be parents or school or community, and the other to an inner world which has its own way of knowing and growing, based on innate or spontaneously arising images and on individual developmental patterns.

During his school years, the secret, introspective life remained important to Carl Jung. When he was a student, much as it is today, independent thought and fantasy were rarely encouraged in the classroom. The way to get along in school was to accept what you had been taught without questioning it too much and to repeat what you had heard at examination time. This was well and good for Jung when it came to history and languages, because they did not really deal with the direct experience of the learner. But when it came to mathematics, specifically algebra, he could not accept the concepts at all. He enjoyed his studies of flowers and fossils and animals, because these were observable, but he was unable to say what numbers really were; he could not imagine quantities that resulted from merely counting. When it then came to algebra he was unable to recognize that different letters amounted to the same thing; to him "a" and "b" had to be different. He objected to rote learning; an idea was only valid for him when he could discover it himself.

An unhappy incident for Jung, but a fortunate one for posterity, occurred and temporarily resolved the academic problem for the young scholar. One day Carl was given a shove by another boy that knocked him off his feet and against the curbstone, so that he almost lost consciousness and for about a half hour afterward was a little dazed. At that moment the thought that he would now not have to go to school any more flashed through his mind, and he remained lying there on the sidewalk somewhat longer than was necessary contemplating the possibility. After receiving more than his share of solicitous attention from maiden aunts and worried parents, he began to have fainting spells from time to time, especially when he had to return to school or when homework became particularly irksome. He managed to stay away from school for months at a time, happily engaged in pursuing his own interests in the mysterious worlds of trees, stones, shaded pools, and the swamp near his home that teemed with tiny animals and plants. Indoors, his father's library with books on the classics and philosophy often absorbed him for hours. There were times when he busied himself making drawings of whatever amused or interested him, or haunted his fantasies. Although much time passed in loafing, collecting, reading and playing, he was not altogether happy. The vague feeling persisted that he was not really living, but rather escaping from the challenges and excitement of life.

One day a shocking realization came when he overheard his father confiding to a friend his worries about his young son, who might have epilepsy or some other incurable disease and might never be able to earn a living or take care of himself. The boy was at this moment suddenly struck with the import of the results of his malingering. He recognized that the moment had arrived for him to put away his childish games and return to his studies. Again and again fighting the growing tendency to faint, he refused to give in, and within a few weeks he was able to return to school. He writes, "I . . . never suffered another attack, even there. The whole bag of tricks was over and done with! That was when I learned what a neurosis was."⁵

In later life, Jung was to recognize that a neurosis is often a rebellion of an unconscious psyche against forces which it perceives as threatening to its specific individual nature. An unconscious psyche at its deeper levels has little concern with the demands of parents or teachers or society in general—but it seeks its own survival as an entity, as well as the survival of its offspring: thoughts and feelings. It has its particular tendencies, its "genius" in the less common sense of the word, meaning a strong leaning or inclination, a peculiar, distinctive or identifying character or spirit, which is often personified or embodied as "a tutelary spirit." It would seem that Jung's tutelary spirit had been kept reasonably well under control during his primary years, getting enough attention so that it would not intrude itself overmuch into the disciplines of study. His resistance to certain types of study were dealt with by conscious efforts of the will. But when the threshold of consciousness was lowered, as it was when Jung's head hit the curbstone, the "genius" found an opportunity to come forth.

This suggests the classic story of the genie (same root word) who streams out of the bottle when the stopper is released, and performs for the individual his every secret wish. It may be compared to the conduct of the neurotic who responds to every impulse, until at last the consequences of his acts begin to come down upon his head and he cannot cope adequately with them. It is then that he runs with his neurosis to the psychotherapist, as the possessor of the genie in fabled times ran to the magician to ask him to put the genie back into the bottle.

Carl Jung managed to get under control his tendency to function in other ways than those approved by his schoolmasters. It was often a struggle, however, and remained so until he learned to come to terms with it, and to give the genii of the unconscious their due. Throughout his school years, Jung pursued his studies in a wide variety of fields, and he also continued to observe his own developing mind in process. He noted his continuing growth in the two distinct directions which would alternate with one another for dominance. The first was the now industrious schoolboy, deep into the classics and the natural sciences, building up a fund of knowledge through voracious reading. The second concerned itself with the mysteries of ultimate things, was given to questioning the nature of God and of reality, to brooding, to silence and to secrets. He spoke of his number one and his number two "personalities"— one oriented toward the objective world "out there" and the other toward the subjective world of the psyche. No matter which aspect of personality was in the forefront of consciousness, the other was never very far away. This dual experiencing of reality produced at times a rare richness of approach, at other times a gloomy obscurantism, and sometimes confusion and anxiety. This characteristic "divisible" quality of personality exists in varying degrees in everyone and is the basis of many unconscious conflicts, as dynamic psychiatry has well understood. Jung's extraordinary gift was in his willingness to take up these conflicts within himself and to follow them wherever they might lead, despite his feelings of insecurity and his sometime fear, his sometime awe. Thus, almost without knowing it, he committed himself from a very early age to exploring the psyche from its own depths. Only later would the way to do it become clear to him.

After a period of indecision at the end of his student years, Jung made the decision to enter medical school rather quickly. He was still hoping to enter the university to study in the natural sciences, despite the fact that archaeology was his most compelling interest. He had not yet learned what in this science summoned him, although the call was clear. But family finances were such that he could not study anywhere except in nearby Basel, and the University of Basel did not offer the curriculum he wanted. Also, though he had by now grown tall and strong, he had never forgotten his father's fears that poor, sickly Carl would never be able to earn his living. Medicine seemed to be a practical solution, for it provided a number of specialities and the possibility of research, and in the meantime offered the chance of a comfortable livelihood. And so, in the last days before matriculation, he enrolled in the faculty of medicine.

Medical school was difficult and demanded a great deal of concentration. Special training in anatomy and pathology demanded precise attention to objective realities and factual knowledge, and what he called his "number two personality" had little time or occasion to assert itself, until the summer of 1898, when several very curious happenings occurred which were to lead Jung's attention astray into an entirely new direction.

The first of these experiences took place during the summer vacation while Jung was at home poring over his textbooks. His mother was seated in an armchair in the adjoining room, knitting. Suddenly a report like a pistol shot was heard. Jung jumped up from his work and ran to his mother, to find her flabbergasted in her armchair, the knitting fallen from her hands. "It was right beside me!" she cried out, and Jung, following her eyes, saw that the sturdy round table which had come from the dowry of his paternal grandmother and was now about seventy years old, had split from the rim straight through to the center and beyond, not following any joint. He could not understand it—how could a table of solid walnut that had dried out for seventy years now suddenly split on a summer's day in the relatively high humidity of the Swiss climate? He was thinking to himself that it could have been con-

ceivable in winter next to a heating stove but at this time—
what in the world could have caused such an explosion? As if
in answer to the unverbalized question, Jung's mother said,
"Yes, yes, that means something." When Jung related the incident later, he recalled that against his will he was impressed
and annoyed with himself at not having anything to say.

The next very curious happening occurred about two
weeks later. Jung had arrived at his home about six in the
evening to find the household upset and excited. There had
been another shattering noise about an hour earlier. Jung
searched all about for the cause of it and, finding no cracks in
any of the furniture, began to examine the interiors of various
pieces in the room where the sound had been heard. At last he
came upon a cupboard containing a breadbasket with a loaf of
bread in it, and beside it lay the bread knife. The blade had
snapped off into several pieces; the handle lay in one corner of
the rectangular basket and each of the other corners held a
piece of the broken blade. The knife had been used a couple of
hours earlier during afternoon tea and had been replaced in
the cupboard intact, and the cupboard had not been opened
since. The next day Jung took the pieces of the knife to one of
the best cutlers in town who examined them with a magnify-
ing glass. The cutler stated: "There's no fault in the steel.
Someone must have deliberately broken it piece by piece. It
could be done, for instance, by sticking the blade into the
crack of the drawer and breaking off a piece at a time. Or else
it could have been dropped on stone from a great height. But
good steel can't explode."

Again, Jung had no answer. He kept the pieces of the knife
as long as he lived. He had sought to penetrate the mystery,
not necessarily to explain it, and certainly not to explain it
away. As he did not discard the knife, so Jung never did push
away any of the unanswerable problems that beset his life.
Perhaps that was a reason for many of his difficulties, as well
as a cause of his greatness. When faced with the unknowable,
he was never willing to say simply, "That is out of my province, I will not allow myself to be concerned with it or side-

tracked by it." Rather, his attitude was, "I will try to understand it, but if I cannot, I will keep it always near me, and hope that one day the meaning that is concealed in the mystery may be in some measure revealed." Later on, this statement would characterize his attitude toward dreams.

Perhaps something of the uneasy mood still pervaded the atmosphere when, a few weeks later, Jung heard of certain relatives who had been engaged in table-turning, and also about a young medium in the group who was said to be producing some peculiar trance states during which she would relay messages from spirits of departed persons. Jung immediately connected the strange manifestations that had so recently occurred in his house with the conversations he was hearing from members of his family about the fifteen-and-a-half-year-old girl, S.W. Out of curiosity he began attending the regular Saturday evening séances which were held by his relatives. For about two years Jung followed these séances, observing instances of what purported to be communications from the beyond, tapping noises from wall and table, and some highly interesting verbal messages relating to what appeared to be a reconstruction of a long bygone past.

Toward the end of this time Jung was preparing for the examinations which would conclude his formal medical education. He had not found the usual lectures and clinics in psychiatry particularly interesting and so had put off until last his preparations for the examination in that subject. In those days psychiatry was held in contempt rather generally by the medical profession. Insane asylums for the most part were isolated in the country and the doctors lived there with the patients, remote from the rest of the world. Mental illness was considered to be a hopeless and fatal disease, and the psychiatrist a fool to want to devote his life to such a thankless cause. So, when Jung picked up the *Textbook of Psychiatry* by Krafft-Ebing[6] he was not at all prepared for the effect that it would have upon him.

Jung describes in his autobiography the strong impression made on him by these words in the Preface, "It is probably due to the peculiarity of the subject and its incomplete state of development that psychiatric textbooks are stamped with a more or less subjective character." And when, a few lines further on, the author referred to the psychoses as "diseases of the personality," Jung became aware, in what he called later "a flash of illumination," that psychiatry was the only possible goal for him. Here was a field in which the two streams of his interests could run together. It was the one empirical field which encompassed all that was known about the biology of man and also all that was known about his spiritual nature. In psychiatry it could all be combined. The "subjective character" of psychiatric textbooks of which Krafft-Ebing spoke provided a welcome concurrence with Jung's own awareness of the importance of subjective experiential perception as a vital factor in the acquisition of all knowledge. He informed his professor of internal medicine, who had fully expected Jung to follow in his footsteps, that he had made the decision to study psychiatry. No amount of persuasion from his teacher or from colleagues and friends could dissuade him from embarking upon the career that they all assured him would be a bypath to obscurity.

He completed his examinations successfully and on December 10, 1900, took up his post as resident at Burghölzli, the cantonal mental hospital of Zurich. There Jung's attitude took on a quality of profound intention, consciousness, duty and complete responsibility. He became committed to a stern regimen within the walls of the hospital: studying, reading, learning to make diagnoses, observing the patients, observing his colleagues—and reflecting again upon the S.W. notes he had made during the two years in medical school. These notes, which he had laid aside not knowing what to make of them, now took on new meaning in the perspective of a doctor occupied with severely neurotic and psychotic patients. Jung began now to acquire some objectivity as to the meaning of the manifestations which had occurred at the séances. By now he was sufficiently removed from the experience of being present at the séances that he could reflect on the subjective aspects of the phenomena that he had observed: the thoughts and feelings of the medium, S.W., and the way they appeared to Jung as he viewed them from a medical standpoint. Here, at the turn of the century, the breach was widening between the rational thinkers in the emerging science of human behavior and those more interested in the mythic and mysterious aspects of the psyche. Jung's personal individuation moved him toward accepting the challenge of exploring the never-never land between science and mysticism, in order to gain an understanding of how people think and feel and why they behave as they do.

Jung has asserted that his observations of the altered states of consciousness in S.W., and his subsequent interpretative writing about them, wiped out his earlier philosophy and made it possible for him to achieve a psychological point of view. Through this, he became interested in the subjective aspect of experience, that is, the realization that what happens in the objective world is highly colored by the factors present in the individual to whom it is happening. Understanding these subjective factors gives the event a whole new dimension of reality. He did not underestimate this dimension thereafter, for he realized that all that we know comes to us through the agency of the psyche—what is perceived must be seen in the context of the total field of the perceiver before it can have any existential meaning and before it can be given any valid interpretation.

Psychic reality is not the same as objective reality. Psychic reality refers to immediate reality as we experience it, and what we perceive are the psychic contents which crowd into the field of consciousness. In his own words:

> All that I experience is psychic. Even physical pain is a psychic image which I experience; my sense impressions— for all that they force upon me a world of impenetrable objects occupying space—are psychic images, and these alone

constitute my immediate experience, for they alone are the immediate objects of my consciousness. My own psyche even transforms and falsifies reality, and it does this to such a degree that I must resort to artificial means to determine what things are like apart from myself. Then I discover that a sound is a vibration of air of such and such a frequency, or that a colour is a wave of light of such and such a length. We are in truth so wrapped about by psychic images that we cannot penetrate at all to the essence of things external to ourselves. All our knowledge consists of the stuff of the psyche which, because it alone is immediate, is superlatively real.[7]

Interestingly enough, Jung was making these discoveries for himself about the nature of *psychological reality* at just about the same time that important and not unrelated discoveries in the physical world were being formulated and presented to a skeptical public view. It was in the summer of 1900 that the physicist Max Planck entered into the intense theoretical work which led to results so different from anything known in classical physics that Planck himself could hardly believe his own findings. His son tells that his father spoke to him about his new ideas on a long walk through the woods near Berlin, explaining that he had possibly made a discovery of first rank, comparable only to the discoveries of Newton. He must have realized at this time that his formula had touched the foundations of our description of nature, and that these foundations would soon start to move from their traditional location toward a new and as yet unknown position of stability. In December of 1900, Planck published his quantum hypothesis.[8] Werner Heisenberg, in reviewing the history of quantum physics, said of this great advance of Planck's,

In classical physics science started from the belief—or should one say from the illusion?—that we could describe the world or at least parts of the world without any reference to ourselves. . . . It may be said that classical physics is just that idealization in which we can speak about parts of the world without any reference to ourselves. Its success has led to the general ideal of an objective description of the world. Objectivity has become the first criterion for the value of any scientific result. . . . Certainly quantum theory does not contain genuine subjective features, it does not introduce the mind of the physicist as a part of the atomic event. But it starts from the division of the world into "object" and the rest of the world. . . . This division is arbitrary and historically a direct consequence of our scientific method; the use of the classical concepts is finally a consequence of the general human way of thinking. But this is already a reference to ourselves and in so far our description is not completely objective.[9]

But also in the year 1900, another epoch-making event in the exploration into the subjective aspects of man and his world took place: Sigmund Freud published his *Interpretation of Dreams*. In this momentous volume, Freud brought to light the results of his years of study and inquiry into the meaning of dreams, his own and those of his patients. One of his guiding principles was that the dream could not be studied properly apart from the mind of the dreamer, nor the mind of the dreamer apart from his dreams. Subject and object had to be seen in their relationship to one another. And, when the subject was man the dreamer, and the object was the man in the dream, a degree of clarity and differentiation was demanded that presented the analyst with a whole new series of dilemmas.

Jung, the medical student, read the new book *Interpretation of Dreams* by the controversial Viennese doctor when it first came out. He later wrote, "I had laid the book aside, at the time, because I did not yet grasp it."[10] The book, like many of the impressions that were making their mark on the mind of Jung during these crucial years, all but dropped out of consciousness. But all the while these matters were constantly being turned over and over again in the unconscious, mixing with other contents, and gathering power for their emergence at a later time when the ground would be better prepared for them.

In 1900, too, Jung completed his doctoral dissertation *On the Psychology and Pathology of So-Called Occult Phenomena*. In the process of presenting the case of S.W., he made order of the chaotic supply of material he had gathered during the previous year when he had attended the séances. Jung began his dissertation with the traditional scientific approach, reviewing the literature up to the time of his observations that dealt with "certain rare states of consciousness."[11] He identified and defined terms whose meanings had not yet been agreed upon by the various authors: "narcolepsy" (a tendency to fall asleep for no apparent reason), "somnambulism" (activity in a trance state), "lethargy," *"automatisme ambulatoire"* (automatic walking while seeming to be awake), and "periodic amnesia," in which there is no remembrance upon awakening of the strange events which were described during the trance state. He also described a condition called "double-consciousness" in which subjects are at one time aware of the external conditions surrounding them and able to communicate to those present the description of a totally different dimension of awareness, in respect to both time and space. And lastly, he discussed the states of pathological dreaming and pathological lying, in which subjects are not aware of their departure from what seems to be normal for most people.

In all these conditions what interested Jung most was that they did not seem to be limited to any specific set of psychiatric syndromes. He observed that they occur in people who are otherwise quite normal and who carry on their work and their relationships to other people in an unremarkable manner. The peculiar departure from the usual state of consciousness, which occurs in every one of us from time to time, was seen by Jung to stem from a *complex*, which is nothing more than an idea filled with emotionally charged contents, which interrupts our attention and redirects our thinking and often our behavior.

The idea of the complex led Jung to a search through the labyrinthine maze of the human psyche, to seek out those incomprehensible elements which erupt into consciousness from unknown sources and interfere with our plans and hopes, our intentions and desires. The trail of the complex led backward toward its sources in those basic elemental tendencies of the human personality which produce certain specific kinds of thinking patterns common to the entire human species. These Jung named the *archetypes*.

The search for complexes led Jung in another direction also, toward the images which people create or discover—as expressions of the not-yet-known. These he called *symbols*. And so it was that Jung occupied himself for much of his life with the mysteries that everyone senses but only a fascinated few explore.

Because of this intense preoccupation with the unknowable, Jung has been called a mystic by some critics. They point out where he differs from Freud—Freud was intent upon reducing all psychic processes to rational explanations, while Jung was content to let his speculations run free as he entered into the realm of the mysterious without attempting to concretize the ineffable experience. He had many arguments with Freud about this, and most were never resolved. The questions were crucial in bringing about the separation of Freud and Jung—although many, more practical, reasons for their disagreements have been advanced. Yet as Freud grew older, and as his experience deepened and was tempered by his own suffering, his thinking approached closer to Jung's in these matters. The two men influenced each other significantly, in the areas of their disagreement as well as in the areas of their agreement.

It is not my intention to present a study of Jung's life, or of the history of his relationship with Freud. This material has been dealt with fully by others. In this work I will only touch upon such areas of Jung's personal experience and his relationship with Freud as are needed to explain the basic Jungian concepts and how they developed. My primary purpose is to present these concepts as clearly as I can, and to show how they function in the analytic process and also in the course of everyday living.

I have not done extensive research, in the ordinary sense, in the preparation of this book. A good part of what I have come to believe and tried to communicate was distilled in the alembic of my own analytic experience. For this, I am deeply grateful to those analysts with whom I had my training in Zurich, Dr. Liliane Frey and Dr. Heinrich K. Fierz. I returned to them from time to time since I completed the formal program in Zurich, and was privileged to refresh at the springs of their wisdom. With their deaths they have left the world far richer for their presence.

There is another debt to acknowledge, though there are hardly words to express my gratitude for the contributions made by my analysands to my learning experience and to the substance of this book. These men and women have shared with me their sorrows and their desires, their secret shames, their fears, their doubts of self and others, and also some rare moments of understanding and deeply-rooted joy. Their concerns have served to provide the illustrative material which gives depth and meaning to the descriptions of various aspects of analytic practice. I have changed the names and many of the circumstances connected with the incidents described. Sometimes I have used a dream in an entirely different context from that in which it occurred. Certain of the characters are composites rather than individuals. On the whole, the persons who provided these examples expressed their willingness to allow the use of their case material, recognizing that the scientific study of analytical psychology, or any other psychological discipline for that matter, depends on the sharing and communication of the data of experience. In those rare cases where there were objections, the case material has, of course, not been used.

Another source has been my students. They have listened to me, argued with me, forced me to rethink and refine my ideas. They have contributed many ideas of their own. In the process we together have tried to update some of the approaches to psychological understanding to suit the rapidly changing needs and interests of men and women living in the United States.

At all times I have had the sense that an old wise man was standing behind me, meditating with closed eyes, his gold-rimmed glasses perched up on his balding forehead.

I have not agreed with Dr. Jung in all things—and I do not believe he would have wanted that, for he saw as an important goal not slavish imitation, but each person's realization of his own individuality. When I describe what I do in psychotherapy, I am not saying that this is *the Jungian way,* nor is it necessarily representative of what other Jungian analysts do, or ought to do. Because the analytic process is so personal, I can only offer material from my own experience, as examples of possibilities that exist in the practice of analytical psychology. And yet, as Jung taught, there are certain experiences which are common to all mankind, with which we can empathize and from which much can be learned. A blending of individuality and commonality structures the human personality. This constant and ever-changing interplay of the individual psyche and the collective psyche forms the background for the work of the analytic process: the search for self-knowledge, and for knowledge of the wider Self, as carried on in the spirit of C. G. Jung.

Part One

. . .

THE BASICS

. . .

1

Analyst and Analysand

. . .

SCIENTIFIC KNOWLEDGE today commands a vastly different audience for its discoveries than it did only a few years ago. Within a single generation, ordinary people have achieved access to information about new developments in all of the sciences, information that in the past had stayed within the private preserves of researchers until theories were substantiated and facts were established. But with the insatiable hunger for information on the part of the media—which serve like an umbilical cord to nourish the human mind—not the slightest bit of news or rumor escapes the press, the television camera or the computer network. The news of a new medical discovery often reaches the morning paper before it comes out in the professional journal. Secrets almost never exist for long; they bombard the psyche constantly with opinions and advice and the hard sell. Whether the subject matter is a commercial product, a political position or a social activist's plea, our minds are the ready targets and our pocketbooks the ultimate goal. Expert knowledge in the hard sciences and in some technical fields is still relatively rare, but when it comes to the area of psychology most people feel qualified to make judgments about human nature after reading a few articles or watching the interminable sequence of talk shows professing to examine the human condition by presenting sufferers from every possible traumatic injury to the psyche. After all, the viewer may reason, if psychology is what the name implies, the study of the human psyche, that is, the mind as it experiences itself, why should not my view of what is happening or can happen in the psyche be as valid as anyone else's? After all, I have a "mind," whatever that is; I know what I feel and what I experience at least as well as anyone else who may practice psychology on me.

At the same time, we see a current trend toward exposing publicly the most painful wounds that human beings can experience: the traumas of incest, sexual abuse, starvation, ritual torture, psychotic depression, dissociation of the personality, multiple personality disorder, alcoholism and the deterioration resulting from drug abuse, institutionalized rape, and innumerable other indignities assaulting mind, body and spirit. Watching and listening to the suffering victims stirs up memories and unresolved pain in many individuals who may have concealed their own sorrow and shame under a shroud of neuroses. For these people, psychology offers a thread of hope, so fragile that they fear it, and yet so important that they go very far to obtain its help.

Where once the modern treatment of mental and emotional disorders was limited primarily to the behavioral, the cognitive and the psychodynamic approaches, since the consciousness revolution of the sixties, scores of other approaches have developed and have served many people as they have discovered their own affinity to a specific method. For example: all kinds of body-oriented therapies base their approach on the principle that whatever painful or traumatic event occurs to an individual is stored in the structure and tissue of the body and can be released through working directly with the body. Social psychologists look to the conditions surrounding the individual for the source of the difficulties. Self psychologists seek to differentiate the "true self" from any number of "false selves." Object relations theorists see infantile interpersonal relationships as setting the stage for all subsequent relationships. And there is a whole host of group psychologists who work directly with individuals within a special society created for the purpose of utilizing the reflection of others as a person deals with his or her own issues.

Why then should there be still another book about still another approach to the problem of the human psyche, and especially an approach which is not very current, not very popular, and which does not promise a "cure" to anybody—much less to everybody? I refer to the work of the Swiss psychiatrist Carl G. Jung, work which is a "psychology" only in the broadest sense of the word, for it deals with human experience of every kind as it is experienced through that mysterious and hypothetical—if you will—organ which no one has ever seen or weighed or measured: the psyche. Jung's "analytical psychology" (the name he gave to his approach at the time of his break with Freud, in order to distinguish his work from that of the founder of "psychoanalysis") includes and is subject to the discipline of the scientific method, but it is not limited to the traditional methodology of science. It includes and is subject to the insights of religion, but is not limited to the forms of traditional religious expression. Furthermore, analytical psychology concerns itself with the kernel of art which is the functioning of the creative process, but it is not bound by the techniques of any of the arts.

Dealing with such broad and extensive fields of human endeavor, Jung's psychology consequently appears vast and complex. In some of his writings Jung is mercifully clear and direct, but in many of his works he is difficult and abstruse, often seeming to be carried along by his thought processes instead of consciously directing them. It is in this latter type of work that he is at his best in weaving a richly textured and intricately patterned fabric, and yet he is here most difficult to understand. It is said often of certain of Jung's books that the first time you read some of them they seem to be absolutely incomprehensible, except for a few sections of unusual clarity which stand out with more of a promise than an explication. The next time you read him the area of light enlarges, the shadows are not quite so deep. And it is the experience of many who read Jung that with each successive reading a whole new view of his meaning is revealed, so that in time his writing uncovers the living experience of the psyche. The meaning of Jung's life and work and its implications for psychotherapy cannot be grasped easily.

Why then, in these days when our national health care system is committed to providing universal service in the form of basic care, mostly through organizations and agencies of various kinds, and when cost effectiveness is a major criterion for service, is the psychology of Jung rapidly gaining adherents—and this without any special publicity or proselytizing? Why is Jungian analysis attracting more and more people, despite the fact that its appeal is admittedly limited to those who are willing to submit themselves to a long and difficult process which must of necessity disturb the very premises upon which their lives are based? Why are people willing to set aside the equilibrium with which they have lived for many years more or less successfully, and chance a journey through the mysterious realms of the hidden recesses of the psyche, a journey which Jung called "the way of individuation"? Why have they taken this path with all its potential dangers, the agonizing slowness of the process, the requirements for a great investment of time, energy and money, and the absence of the familiar unconditional guarantee of success?

The problem of the multiplicity of psychologies was anticipated by Jung at least as early as 1933 when, in an essay called "Problems of Modern Psychotherapy" he wrote:

> Since the mind is common to mankind it may seem to the layman that there can be only one psychology, and he may therefore suppose the divergences between the schools to be

either a subjective quibbling, or else a commonplace disguise for the efforts of mediocrities who seek to exalt themselves upon a throne. . . . The many-sidedness and variety of psychological opinions in our time is nothing less than astonishing. . . . When we find the most diverse remedies prescribed in a textbook of pathology for a given disease, we may confidently assume that none of these remedies is particularly efficacious. So, when many different ways of approaching the psyche are recommended, we may rest assured that none of them leads with absolute certainty to the goal, least of all those advocated in a fanatical way. The very number of present-day "psychologies" amounts to a confession of perplexity. The difficulty of gaining access to the mind is gradually borne in upon us. . . . It is small wonder therefore, that efforts to attack this elusive riddle are multiplied, first from one side and then from another.[1]

How much more true this is today, sixty years after Jung wrote those words!

Jung believed that the well-being of the psyche is directly connected with our conscious or unconscious philosophy of life, so that our way of looking at things is actually of supreme importance to us and to our mental health. The important fact about a situation or thing, from a psychological standpoint, is not so much *how it objectively is*, as it is *how we see it*. That which is unbearable may become acceptable if we can give up certain prejudices and change our point of view. This philosophy of life—a *Weltanschauung*, as Jung called it—is developed step by step through every increase in experience and knowledge. As a person's image of the world changes, so a person changes. Jung, writing on "Analytical Psychology and *Weltanschauung*," illuminates his entire approach to the human psyche:

A science can never be a *Weltanschauung*, but merely a tool with which to make one. Whether a man takes this tool in hand or not depends on the sort of *Weltanschauung* he

already has. For no one is without a *Weltanschauung* of
some sort. At worst he has at least that *Weltanschauung*
which education and environment have forced upon him. If
this tells him, to quote Goethe, that "the highest joy of man
should be the growth of the personality," he will unhesitatingly seize upon science and its conclusions, and with this as
a tool will build himself a *Weltanschauung* to his own edifi-
cation. But if his inherent convictions tell him that science is
not a tool but an end in itself, he will follow the attitude that
has become more and more prevalent during the last hundred and fifty years and has increasingly shown itself to be
the decisive one. Here and there single individuals have desperately resisted it, for to their way of thinking the meaning
of life culminates in the perfection of the human personality
and not in the differentiation of techniques, which inevitably
leads to an extremely one-sided development of a single instinct, for instance the instinct for knowledge. If science is
an end in itself, man's *raison d'être* lies in being a mere intellect. If art is an end in itself, then its sole value lies in the
imaginative faculty, and the intellect is consigned to the
woodshed. If making money is an end in itself, both science
and art can quietly shut up shop. No one can deny that our
modern consciousness, in pursuing these mutually exclusive
ends, has become hopelessly fragmented. The consequence
is that people are trained to develop one quality only; they
become tools themselves.[2]

The inevitable conclusion is that the many psychological
theories become rationales for psychotherapies, rationales
which are in turn merely tools designed to fashion a certain
type of personality, whatever type is considered valuable by
the originator of the system. Thus for one system the achievement of maturity might be the crowning goal, freedom from
symptoms for another, self-understanding for a third, or adjustment to the norms of society, or realization of potential for
growth, or learning to accept responsibility, or reducing existential *Angst*, or simply "being real," and so on *ad infinitum*.
There are psychological "tools" to open you up, calm you
down, adjust you and readjust you. Each one deals with one

or more aspects of the human personality, and many focus on a single problem or a single type of problem, or seek to reduce all human psychological ills to a single explanation.

While Jung's psychology may be many things to many people, of one thing we may be certain, it is not a "tool." Unlike many other well-known psychologists, Jung never presented a psychological theory in the strict sense of a theory: that is, a body of generalizations and principles developed in association with the practice of psychotherapy and forming its content as an intellectual discipline. Unlike the leaders of most other psychological schools, Jung does not offer a methodology, a technique for procedure, a series of "applications" that the Jungian analyst can use from the insights and formulations of the master. For what is essential in the psychology of Jung is the requirement that each individual develop consciously a unique *Weltanschauung*, a "philosophy of life," if you will, in accordance with the "given" factors of the personality which are present at birth, and unfold according to their genre and in their own time, and also those "acquired" factors which include the environment into which one is born and the circumstances and events of life. I see this philosophy as one which must transcend the fragmentary approaches to the human psyche that are currently subjects of so much literature and discussion. It must envision people as unitary and total beings—encompassing everything that every psychological approach says that we are, even though some of those approaches may be in direct opposition to some others.

Jung has wisely said that if you are able to observe a quality that is characteristic of a person, you may be quite certain that somewhere in that person the opposite is equally true. I believe that the greatness of Jung rested in his ability to accept the paradox as a fact of man's psychological being. And the great paradox of Jung's work is that it is highly individual—it depends very much on the particular nature of the individual who conceived it, while at the same time it reaches into general principles drawn from the history of human consciousness and experience and thus is applicable to a wide spectrum of human nature.

I have observed that my colleagues all function in their individual ways; their analytic training has in no way recast them into a single mold. Some are extremely liberal in dealing with patients, quite permissive in terms of relationships—others have developed a relatively formalized structure. Some, who are physicians, follow the medical model and use drugs as an adjunct to analytic treatment when this is indicated. Others insist that Jung's psychology is a "cure of souls" and properly falls close to, if not actually within, the area of religion. Still others say it is a way of educating a person for a better life, and as such belongs within the purview of academic psychology. And one Jungian analyst has suggested that "Before the work of Jung can be carried further . . . analysts will have to free themselves from those remains of theology, of academic psychology, and especially of medicine which still clutter the ground and which are false markers for an analytical psychology."[3] At the same time, when medication needs to be considered for a patient, Jungian analysts often collaborate with psychiatrists who specialize in psychopharmacology. Thus it is clear why it is so difficult to attempt to explain in a general way exactly how Jungian analysis works. On the other hand, it seems a more practical undertaking to write about Jungian analysis and how it works *for me*. In such an undertaking it will be possible to discuss some of Jung's basic principles, how he discovered them, and how an understanding of what he has illuminated makes it possible for the Jungian analyst, specifically *this* Jungian analyst, to function.

This writing project has been over a dozen years in the deep freeze, and only now begins to thaw out. It had its inception with the first course I attended at the Jung Institute in Zurich, given by Jolande Jacobi, one of the foremost interpreters of Jung. The subject was "Masculine and Feminine Psychology" or, as familiarly called in Jungian circles, "Anima and Animus."[4] I discovered that what Dr. Jacobi had to say had direct reference to me personally, and to problems in my own first marriage which, in part, had grown out of failure to understand some of the basic differences between the ways in which men and women approach one another. Jung's explications of the mysterious unconscious workings which give rise to certain of our sex-oriented attitudes came to me as an overwhelming experience of what seemed to be "prior knowledge," as though somewhere within me I had always been aware of these differences, although I had never been able to formulate them.

At the beginning, I resisted the idea of analysis for myself. I could quite easily see the advantages of this for *other* people because I could see that *they* had obvious psychological problems which required attention. But I could not see that I personally had any such problems. To embark upon the analytic experience would be an admission that there might be something wrong with me, something that needed correction. However, as I began to get some feel for a new attitude toward the psyche, I came to recognize that the best way to experience the transformation about which Jung spoke would be to undergo personal analysis. And so this intensive experience was started.

At the same time, I was reading Jung. I found his work sometimes beautifully and strikingly clear. But in some places it was complicated, convoluted, rambling, and unorganized. Jung made no complete systematic presentation himself, and the interpreters I read who sought to systematize his writing tended toward essays that were overschematized, that somehow failed to capture the spirit of Jung. I asked around, "Why doesn't somebody write a clear, simple book about Jung, explaining how his theories are applied in analytic practice?"

I never received a satisfactory answer. Many "Jungians" would say, "Just wait till you've been around here a while, then you'll understand." Or "Jung can't be explained in simple terms. One has to live Jung, not just read Jung." Or, "It takes the kind of devoted study that these books require to come to a real appreciation." Or "to explain Jung is to destroy Jung." Nevertheless, as I heard the lectures and participated in discussions, and proceeded with my personal analysis, I kept feeling that much of what I was learning could be written about in a clear and non-technical manner, using illustrations from the actual experiences of people in analysis. As time went on, however, I began to have my doubts. The feeling grew in me that it would be necessary to travel Jung's labyrinthine path in order to approach anywhere near the center. The "way of individuation" was described as a lifelong journey, and the more I read of Jung, the more I realized that I would need to devote many years of personal analysis, study and reflection before I could approach the insights of this great man with a true measure of understanding.

At the end of the course of studies, with my head crammed full of information, and a sense of having come to terms with my own personal psychology to the degree that I would now be able to carry on my developmental progress independently of my analyst, I appeared for final examination. I shall never forget what happened to me when I sat before the examiner and the two experts for my oral examination on The Individuation Process, which is the essence of analysis. I had prepared for this in a most elaborate manner, and was ready to show how the analytic process has its parallel in the alchemical literature of the Middle Ages, in Tantric yoga, in the Hebrew Scriptures and elsewhere. I was ready to illustrate and document all statements I would be asked to make. I appeared. I was informed that there would be only one question for this examination, that is, for this section of the six-part examination. The question that was put to me was the following: "If you were asked to explain the Individuation Process to one of the fellows who sweeps the streets of Zurich with a faggot broom, during the time it takes to wait for the tram, what would you tell this man?" I don't need to tell you that I was taken aback by the question!

I cannot recall whether my first reaction was more one of shock or fury. In any case, I flashed to my own background the story of Rabbi Hillel, who had been asked a similar question. The question put to him was, "Can you explain the essence of Judaism while I am standing on one foot?" Hillel had answered, "Do not do unto your neighbor what you would not have your neighbor do unto you. That is the essence of Judaism. All the rest is commentary."

Quieted by this thought, I had a momentary vision of something I had been doing the day before, taking a sailing lesson on the Zürichsee, the Lake of Zurich. It was as though the unconscious had presented me at the right moment with an image of the Process. I began to speak. "It is as though you were sitting in a little sailing boat in the middle of the Zürichsee, and had no idea how to manage a sailboat. If the current was right and the wind was right, you might get to where you were going sooner or later. Or you might bob around indefinitely and get nowhere. Or a storm could come up and you could be overturned and the whole project could end in disaster. But begin the Process, guided by another who has been through it already and coped with the difficulties and found ways to solve them, and it is all different. You learn to take into account the structure of the boat itself, how it is made and how it responds to the water and the wind. The boat is comparable to your own personality. You learn about the currents in the lake; these correspond to the realities of life in which you are situated and which are somewhat predictable. You learn about the winds, which are invisible and less predictable, and these correspond to those spiritual forces which seem to give direction to life without ever showing themselves. In learning to sail you do not change the current of the water nor do you have any effect on the wind, but you learn to hoist your sail and turn it this way and that to utilize the greater forces which surround you. By understanding them, you become one with them, and in doing so are able to find your own direction—so long as it is in harmony with, and does not try to oppose, the greater forces in being. You may still have to face dangers—there may be swift currents or wild winds at times, but somehow you do not feel helpless any longer. In time, you may be able to leave your guide and sail alone, and one day you may even become a guide for others. You are not helpless any more."

I remembered well the first hour of my own analysis. I was not sure why I was there, except that I was no longer young and the hopes and promise of earlier years were still unfulfilled. It seemed to me that my life was narrowing down, closing in, that there were fewer and fewer possibilities open for development with the passing years. I felt that whatever little I had possessed of talent or skill was falling away, but I could not put my finger on what was wrong with me. I could see that plenty was wrong in my daily life, but most of it was "not my fault." My analyst asked me what I hoped to gain personally from analysis. I found that this was a question that had not even occurred to me! But then some thoughts did come up, and I replied that I wished that I were able to express myself better, more articulately, to be able to say what I mean, and not to be afraid to take a strong position. As a child I had been more verbal than most, but over the years I had become more and more inhibited in expressing myself in conversation. Of course I found reasons for it. I could blame it on external circumstances, and I did, without the slightest realization of what the "symptom" of my painful shyness was pointing to, in terms of real need. The analyst took me at my word and we began with my own perception of my situation. She was fully aware of something that I had yet to learn, that the problems which the analysand brings to the analyst in the beginning are not the real problems, though they often contain the real problems in a cryptic form.

The starting point of understanding the analytic process is the concept of the psyche as a self-regulating system in which consciousness and the unconscious are related in a compensatory way.[5] What is seen in the beginning by the analysand and is presented to the analyst as "problems" consists of what is already in consciousness. By consciousness, I mean that level of awareness that is achieved by the individual through the perceptions and understanding of the world and of oneself.

My consciousness consists of myself and my world, and the relationship between them as it appears to me. It is clear enough that the psyche is not identical with consciousness, and that any understanding of the psyche must begin with an understanding of the role of the unconscious and the relations between consciousness and the unconscious.

Anything psychic, that is any experience when it comes into awareness, will take on the quality of consciousness; otherwise it remains unconscious. The organ of awareness is called the ego, and as such the ego functions as the center of consciousness. The field of consciousness then refers to all contents that are related to the ego. A whole other sphere lies outside the ego. This is characterized as the non-ego field, the unconscious. The psyche consists of consciousness and the unconscious, but the critical point is that these are not two separate systems, but rather two aspects of one system, with the exchange of energy between consciousness and the unconscious providing the dynamic for growth and change. This growth and change takes place throughout life in a natural way, with unconscious contents constantly being fed into consciousness and assimilated. At the same time, conscious contents are constantly being repressed, forgotten, or just overlooked and, losing their energic charge, they fall into the unconscious.

The analytic process deals with this constant interplay between consciousness and the unconscious, attempting to improve the nature of the dynamic interchange in the direction of bringing order out of disorder, purpose out of aimlessness, and meaning out of senselessness. Toward this end we need to see the unconscious as potentially constructive, offering an ongoing stream of information to compensate the limitations of conscious awareness. The analytic process is a means of systematically drawing upon the resources of the unconscious and progressively integrating these contents into consciousness; at the same time "letting go" of those conscious contents, attitudes and modes of behavior, that are no longer necessary or desirable.

The goal of treatment, which is rarely understood at the beginning and then only in an intellectual way, is the shift of psychic balance from the area of consciousness with the ego as its center, to the totality of the conscious and unconscious psyche. This "totality" has its own center, which Jung has called the "self," in contradistinction to the "ego." How this shift of balance develops, and what it means in terms of the changes in the lives of individuals undergoing analysis, can best be understood through a discussion of actual situations in analytic practice.

The importance of the analysand's first interview is that it establishes the patterns and expectations for the future analytical work and for the analyst-analysand relationship. To begin with, the attitude of the analyst toward the patient will be immediately apparent to the patient, and will have its effect from the first moment on their relationship. Please note that I am using the word "patient" when I speak of my analysand, to conform with the language used by Jung, for consistency in this book. However, in my analytic practice I prefer to refer to the people with whom I work as "clients," which I understand to mean a different sort of relationship from the doctor-patient relationship in which the doctor is the authority figure and the patient is conceived of as in some way ill. My view of the analysand is that this is a person who comes to me for my expertise in the area of analytical psychology, but that the analysand is the expert with respect to his or her personal history and perceptions. So, with each of us bringing our own part into the process, we work together, more as equals than as though we were in a hierarchical relationship. This said, I will continue to use the term "patient" to be consistent with Jung's writings, with the understanding that I mean to regard the "patient" as a true partner in the healing process.

The Jungian, as psychotherapist, approaches each new patient with interest, curiosity, and wonder. Here is the great mystery of humanity: that every man and woman, though sharing in the evolutionary history of mankind, is yet unique! "In thine own breast dwell the stars of thine own fate," Jung

was fond of quoting. Each person speaks a different language
—although the patient uses the same words that I do, each
means something subtly different by them. Each one's ways of
being, ways of thinking and feeling and perceiving and knowing are distinctly that person's, based on a particular constellation of archetypal foundations, the sum total of the person's
experiences, and the behavior patterns that have been shaped
by the interaction between the internal and external factors.
No one has ever been exactly like this person who sits with me
—I must regard this person well, for there will never be another who is quite the same.

In my experience, I have found that people rarely enter
into analysis with the stated purpose of confirming that individuality which was born in them as a potential, and which
has somehow gotten lost in the pursuit of the practical goals
of their lives. More often they have gone along well enough
until some crisis arose which tested all their abilities and resources and still could not be dealt with in any satisfactory
way. They feel frustrated, hurt, or desperately alone in an
alien or hostile world. If they are young, they may feel blocked
in achieving some career goal; they know they should be able
to get beyond the point where they are stuck, but they cannot.
Or, if they are in the second half of life, they may reflect upon
themselves and find that for all their strivings they have had
precious little satisfaction; life has become empty, meaningless, boring. Success or failure are alike to them. The years
should have brought them a sense of reward, but there is only
a revulsion with overindulgence in the face of spiritual pov-
erty. They ask themselves: "Isn't there more than this?"

Most psychotherapists maintain that people are individuals and that psychotherapy should enable them to fulfill their
individual potential by utilizing more effectively the special
gifts with which they are endowed. I agree, they say so. But I
am not so sure that all really function in complete devotion to
this principle, or that they even believe it is a good thing that
we are all so different, both in terms of our psychological constitution as well as our way of dealing with the world. Too

many believe, or act as if they believed, that the function of
psychotherapy is to smooth off the rough edges of differences
and induce or persuade the individual to adapt to the demands or requirements of the situation. To be "normal" means
to many the same as being able and willing to conform to
some sort of a socially produced "norm," an "accepted" standard of behavior.

This attitude is nowhere so evident as in the question so
often raised by professionals who practice one or another
form of psychotherapy, but who have never themselves completed a successful analysis. In the past it was mostly the popular press that asked the question, How can you evaluate analysis anyway? Today the health maintenance organizations,
managed care providers and government agencies are asking
for evaluation of the cost/benefit ratio in health care and are
applying often gross statistical standards as to "how many
treatments are required" for this or that diagnosis. More and
more, the nature of psychotherapy tends to be determined by
collectively determined criteria that are supposed to characterize the outcomes of "good therapy." It takes only a little
insight to recognize that the goals of many of today's decision
makers in the health care field are to restore mentally disturbed people to a level of functioning in the world that will
enable them to stay out of hospitals and to manage their lives
with a minimum of outpatient therapy, if that is absolutely
necessary.

Different therapists from different schools of thought have
their own ideas as to how this can be accomplished. For the
sake of efficiency, the therapist is often called upon to impose
the method most likely to produce rapid results by relieving
the symptoms of distress. Analytic or "depth" psychotherapy is
usually considered too time-consuming and too expensive for
most health care plans to cover. While some institutions that
train psychotherapists recognize the importance of a personal
and/or training analysis for people who wish to practice psychotherapy, many do not. The danger is that most psychotherapists who have not had analysis themselves tend to get *their*

way confused with *the* way, and consequently in their work they find themselves living out their own unconscious needs *through* the patient to prove their own efficacy as psychotherapists. This is, of course, an ego trip, and precisely what the analytic process is designed to avoid. It is for this reason that prospective analysts, as part of their training, must go through a personal, therapeutic analysis. They must undergo the experience of facing and dealing with the manifestations of their own unconscious through intense involvement with the analyst until, at the end, through disengagement from the analyst-as-a-person they achieve their independence while retaining the meaning of the analytic relationship.

Everything that happens in the course of analysis may be regarded as being of potential importance. Analysts must of course sort out and determine what they will deal with in any given moment and what they will exclude. Otherwise the analysis would never proceed very far, and surely it would never terminate. The patient also will make similar decisions, but often for different reasons. Even at the very start, in that fateful phone call in which a stranger informs the analyst, "I would like to make an appointment to come in and talk with you—or to consider the possibility of undergoing analysis—or simply to discuss a certain problem." Obviously, the analyst will not be able to interview everyone who wants to come in, and so it is important to learn right then whether this may be an individual with whom the analyst may be able to work. In most agencies, the initial contact is with an intake worker. Analysts in private practice often prefer to do their own initial screening of prospective analysands.

I find it helpful to do the initial telephone screening myself. I get a feeling for the level of awareness in individuals with respect to what they are actually seeking, also for the degree of anxiety or urgency, and sometimes even for their capacity for insight. All of this can occur in a very brief conversation, in which I generally try not to get into the nature of the presenting problem itself. This topic is reserved for the initial interview, when analyst and patient meet face to face for the first time, exposed to each other in as near a condition of psychic nakedness as is possible.

A few questions at the time of the initial telephone call can reveal much: "How did you come to call me?" Or, "Did someone refer you to me? Have you ever had psychotherapy or analysis before, or are you now in therapy? If so, when, and with whom? And for how long? What do you hope to gain from coming to see me? Can we talk about some practical matters such as frequency of sessions, fees, location, schedule? What brings you to look for a therapist *at this time?*" And of course these questions may lead to others.

On the phone some people come right to the point. Others begin to ramble, not knowing what to say, and starting off in all directions: "I've heard a lot about you, Dr. Singer," "I was reading this book by Jung," and so on—so I have to help the person focus in—by saying something that brings him directly into the moment—perhaps like, "How did you happen to decide to call me *just now?*" Another may launch into a long and complicated story—"I was an only child and . . ." and on and on. Here again, I must try to see if the person can be brought to some sort of focus out of the diffusion—for instance by saying, and at the same time showing that the person on the other end of the line is a person to me, "And just how do you feel *I* may be of help to *you?*" If these simple attempts to get an idea of at least the precipitating factor fail to work, I may quickly realize that this may be a person who is unable to come into contact with the minimal requirements of a degree of insight, and I will seriously question whether the analytic approach, with its strenuous demands for a concentration of consciousness, is going to serve the needs of this individual. Experience has taught me to determine very quickly whether it makes sense to offer an appointment to the patient, or to suggest that something else may be indicated. Recognizing my own infallibility in this, I always say to the prospective analysand that this appointment will be exploratory to see whether or not psychotherapy or analysis is appropriate for the person at this time. There are many other avenues that might be better for this person, for example, short-term therapy, couple counseling or family therapy, group therapy, a support group where there is sharing with others whose issues are similar. Even if it appears that Jungian analysis might be appropriate, we must explore the question as to whether or not this is the right time, or whether we are suited to work together. I make it clear that neither of us has any obligation to continue after this first exploratory meeting. This often relieves the person's anxiety and, I must say, it's helpful to me as well.

When an appointment has been made, I note the questions that the prospective patient asks or fails to ask. "How do I get to your office?" and "Where can I find a place to park?" are the questions asked in a dependent, helpless way, or in a manner which indicates that the person is cool and efficient and wants to save the time of blundering about. Does the person ask whether anything should be prepared for the initial meeting? If so, I often suggest that if the person has any dreams between now and the appointment, they should be written down and brought in to the initial session. I never speak of the *first* session, because that implies that there is to be a second, a commitment which neither I nor the patient can be prepared to make before an actual meeting, so I speak in terms of an *initial* session. Also, I never tell a beginning patient in which form the dreams should be brought, because the way that is chosen will tell me a great deal about the attitude toward the dreams. It says quite a different thing to me if a patient brings in a dream scrawled on a piece of scratch paper, or typewritten with a few errors, or impeccably typed by an office secretary. Yes, people do that, too, as if they were submitting them for publication! Some bring in a beautifully hand-bound book which they have made, while others write on the backs of pages which were once mimeographed for some other purpose and left over. Such *little* things can tell the therapist a lot. That is, if the therapist is watching what is happening and not busily trying to follow a set of procedures.

The first telephone conversation may also offer clues as to how much the caller knows about what she may be getting into. For instance, if she asks how long it will take, I can be pretty sure she doesn't have much of an idea of what analysis may involve, and I know that it will be necessary to spell everything out very carefully. Other questions will show her reality-orientation and sense of practicality: questions concerning my hours, fees, what happens if she has to cancel the appointment, and so on. Ordinarily these do not come up in the first phone call, but sometimes they do, and I have to be prepared to answer them in a way that will convey my own way of working. All the while I am also learning about the prospective patient from the questions she raises.

Suppose now the appointment has been made and the hour has come. Does the person arrive early, on time, or late? I note this, because as a therapist I will want to find out what this signals. Some people automatically allow themselves an extra few minutes to go to a place where they have never been —"time to get lost." Others invariably come with "I didn't realize the traffic was so heavy at this time of day," or "I couldn't find a place to park"—and then there are the ones who get lost, or who simply didn't leave in time. And always, there are the compulsive ones who push the doorbell at the exact stroke of the hour. They are all telling me something about themselves, whether they realize it or not. And as therapist, I had better get the message.

Sitting in my office, I hear a knock on my door. Is it timid, indecisive? Is there another tentative rap, in case I didn't hear? Or a fast, crisp clack? Or an aggressive bang bang bang? Before I see the patient she has transmitted a signal. I had better hear it. The door is opened and there is the first eye contact. Therapists of some schools believe in stress situations to test out the patient. I do not. Life is stressful enough, in my opinion. I am not there to manipulate the patient, not even "for her own good." I am there to befriend her, and not to antagonize her or deliberately mobilize her defenses. It seems to me that if I am to be privileged to gain access to the dark reaches of the unconscious, it is my role to provide an atmosphere of trust and freedom in which new patients will be helped to face hidden aspects of themselves that they may fear. I am to help open wide the doors that have long been shut, the doors which have long kept out the dangerous and stormy thoughts and feelings which they did not dare to meet alone. Now I am to be fully present; and I must get this fact across. It begins at the threshold of my consulting room.

The quality of attention that the therapist brings to the analytic encounter begins at the very beginning, and must be maintained throughout on many levels. I am always amused when supervisors who are training psychotherapists demand a "verbatim" report on just exactly what is said by the patient and by the therapist during the therapy hour, as if all that mattered were the words. This is only the beginning, and far less important than the non-verbal communication. The tone of the voice, for example, is more important than what is said, for it communicates much, including the emotion and the sincerity or lack of sincerity behind what is said. The eyes, whether they dart about or seem to have an inward focus, or whether they make an easy connection with the therapist, or whether there is terror there, or deep sadness, all this is very important. You can't put this into a verbatim report, nor can you put in the posture, the sureness of the person's walk, the way the person has dressed for the initial interview. Clearly I could cite many pages of what the competent therapist will focus attention upon, but since this changes from moment to moment and also occurs simultaneously on many levels, suffice it to say that not only the ear, but every sense, must be tuned to the total expression of the person who sits before me.

When our eyes meet for the first time, I pronounce her name. She is an individual to me, I look squarely at her so that I will see her as a person, and I let her see me. I introduce myself. I bring the person into my office, my place as I have arranged it; a place which expresses me, my likes and dislikes, my totems and talismans, my pictures, my desk, and my computer. All these are extensions of myself.

One reason I prefer private practice in my own setting to working in an institution is that here I am able to establish my own environment. My office is a place of symbolic separation from the world, which makes it possible to view the world in a special way—outside of its pressures and its immediacy. I believe that the unconscious does not perform well before an audience. Perception of it becomes contaminated with all sorts of cultural values and needs for approval. This is what I try to minimize in my way of being-with a patient, and I can do it less self-consciously if I know that in my work I am not answerable to anyone except to the person who sits with me, and to myself.

I am not unaware of the value of cross-fertilization that comes when one works with other professionals. In a group setting much may be gained in breadth from discussion of cases and sharing experiences and especially problems. Still, it is difficult enough to understand another person and to formulate your ideas and responses concerning him, when you work together with him in intimate communion; how unreasonable then it is to expect that someone who does not know the patient but depends only on selected bits of data in a report could give valid counsel on the handling of a case? While a therapist is being trained there is no question that adequate supervision is necessary, but all the more it must be remembered that the presence of the tape recorder or the one-way mirror, or the patient's knowledge that his case will be discussed in conference cannot help having its effect on what transpires between patient and therapist. It is a calculated risk; perhaps in a training situation the value outweighs the disadvantages, but I am not sure.

The privacy of the analytic hour is offered to the patient in exchange for confidence in and personal commitment to the process. Confidentiality is also promised—that nothing the person tells me will be spoken of outside this office, except where I am bound by law to disclose certain matters. I may cite examples, such as the requirements for insurance coverage, my sense that the person may be endangering self or others, or when there might be legal proceedings—such as in a child custody case. I say that even in such instances extreme discretion would be used. Another thing that my patients are offered is the freedom to say anything that comes to mind. I might not choose to respond to certain questions, but that is my decision—the person is free to say or to ask. Each of us must be free to function within the boundaries we set for ourselves. I reserve for myself the privilege of talking about my own personal life and my feeling reactions only to the point where I feel comfortable with it and where it appears to me to be relevant to the task in which we are mutually engaged.

The initial session begins, and I have been as receptive as I know how to all the non-verbal messages that have come my way: the patient's general appearance indicating her self-image, her voice and posture and her walk. Many such minute matters as these combine to give an impression which will form a base for what will happen later on. Until now, the approach has been consistent with that of most therapists who utilize "depth psychology," that is, psychology in which unconscious material is a primary consideration.

One distinctive feature of the Jungian approach is the analysts' openness about themselves and their own reactions. Their involvement in the process is active. They are not merely observers, nor even participant-observers, but active partners in a mutual endeavor. Receptivity to the patient continues—as they are now in this moment—and to all that they bring to recount as they discuss the details of the situations which have brought them to therapy. The analyst listens attentively in order to understand what the patient is saying and to hear the feeling behind the words. There will be continual checking with the patient to make sure the intended message is getting across. The analyst listens and evaluates the nature of the problem and the patient's motivations and capacity for carrying on therapy or analysis.

Up to this point I have used the words "therapy" and "analytically oriented therapy" and "analysis" more or less interchangeably. "Therapy," an abbreviated form of "psychotherapy," refers to "the use of any psychological technique for the treatment of mental disorder or maladjustment" performed by a professionally trained person.[6] Analysis is a specific form of psychotherapy which deals chiefly with unconscious materials such as dreams, fantasy, visions, creative productions and, in the orthodox psychoanalytic framework, with free association. The analyst will utilize an approach based on his understanding of the unconscious processes, even though he may not in all cases interpret the unconscious material to the patient. Analysis is a specifically dialectical process in which the analyst and analysand are together engaged in attaining an understanding of unconscious material.

Interpretations arise out of the analyst's experience in the personal and training analysis and out of the experience of analyzing others. In the Jungian framework, based as it is upon a familiarity with archetypal material, the analyst needs to have a familiarity with mythology and comparative religions and other fields which contribute to a knowledge of a variety of symbols of the collective unconscious. How far the analyst will go in interpretations depends very much on the analyst's own background, plus the kind of material that appears in individual cases, and the ability of the analysand to deal with this sometimes highly charged matter. Sometimes the symbols have not to be interpreted at all, but rather taken "as is," or for what they evoke, and observed in that spirit. At first the analyst will reserve interpretation for the most part, waiting to see what effect the raising of newly emerged contents to a conscious level will have on the patient, and what the patient will do spontaneously with the material that comes up spontaneously—so that the analyst does not "direct" the process. It is important to let the unconscious have its say.

Two matters have to be dealt with specifically in the first exploratory sessions. One concerns the patient's understanding of his or her role in the analysis, and the second concerns an understanding of the role of the analyst. Patients need to recognize why they have come to analysis: they have found themselves in a conflict situation that appears insoluble, and this discrepancy is between the conscious attitude they hold and unconscious factors which interfere with their carrying through on the intentions which correspond with their conscious attitudes. They need to know, too, that their tasks will be to make themselves accessible to whatever unconscious material may present itself, and to face it as honestly as they can. By unconscious material, I will explain, we mean the dreams, the fantasies, and other expressions of thought and behavior which do not seem to originate with one's own will or awareness—those things which seem to happen to cross one's plans and hopes and prevent one from fulfilling one's commitments. One must realize that the conflict between consciousness and the unconscious cannot be resolved by advice from the analyst or even through the willingness of the patient to co-operate, but only through the patient's trying to understand the unconscious material as it comes up, and moreover to carry away the insights in leaving the consulting room and returning to the field of daily living.

The second matter that needs to be discussed is the attitude of the analyst. Since patients are identified with their own conscious attitudes, it may be necessary at times for the analyst to take up a position on the side of the unconscious, as the advocate for the point of view of the unconscious. This means that the analyst will be charged with helping the patient to uncover material which has either long remained repressed in the unconscious, or material that has not yet come to consciousness and stays "underground" to all intents and purposes, in a state of potentiality. Thus in some ways the role of the analyst becomes adversarial toward certain of the patient's conscious attitudes.

I let the analysand know from the beginning: "you will face the dark, ugly, and tawdry aspects of your life which you have been avoiding, and since these contents are and have long been unacceptable to you, something in you will take every possible means to frustrate their disclosure. As for the positive, developmental trends which up to now have remained unconscious, these by their revolutionary nature have the capacity to disturb the established patterns you currently hold; hence you will resist them too."

The beginning analysand will say, "I understand, and I am willing to go through all this," but in fact most analysands do not yet understand what it will be like, and when it comes to going through it they will fight it with all the intensity of their beings. Yet I will have to warn them about potential resistance. Later in the analysis when they have fought their way through it, they will probably say, "*Now* I understand what you meant by resistance, whereas I did not really understand before." The only possible way to know what is real is to discover, first, what has been unreal.

Sometimes the new analysand will bring a dream to the initial interview; sometimes the first dream does not appear until after the first session, or after several sessions. It is not at all unusual for the initial dream to be a significant one, putting into focus either the condition of the patient or else his feelings about the analysis or the analyst.

Gina, a young woman of Roman Catholic religion, came into analysis in a desperate situation. She was about five months pregnant by the first man with whom she had had sexual relations. He had no intention of marrying her. She was the sort of woman who seemed ideally suited for the role of wife and mother, but circumstances were against it, and she blamed her own impetuousness for not having avoided the pregnancy. Yet she said with conviction that she was unwilling to compound her guilt by adding murder to her crime of carelessness. She would have the child, and she would have to find an attitude toward it that would be consistent with what she understood as the meaning of her life. This did not permit the negation of a life for which she was responsible, her firstborn. Gina brought the following dream to the first analytic session: *I was thinking about coming to you. I had a guide. She said you do all sorts of weird things. She said you told one lady to throw her car into the water. She said you told another lady to jump into the cold icy water of the lake and swim across.*

This dream contained Gina's fears of the analytic process. The whole thing was mysterious to her. She expected to have demands made which would be extremely difficult for her to meet. In the course of our discussion of the dream I asked her what a car meant to her. Her car was her most valuable possession; she had worked very hard to pay for it. It was a source of great pleasure. When I questioned further, the car turned out to be the place where she and her friend had had sexual intercourse. So, evidently, the car represented the treasure (her sexuality) that she felt she had misused, and therefore it would have to be sacrificed. All her guilt was bound up in this painful realization. Her guilt also resulted in her having withdrawn her tender feelings into herself as she had become somewhat hardened to the world. This was understandable in the face of what she expected to find in the attitudes of friends and relatives.

The second lady in the dream represented to her the absence of sensitivity to emotion that she was experiencing. "It is as though all my feelings have gotten turned off and I feel nothing for anyone, I just don't care. And still I miss my feelings, painful as they are, and wish I could get them back." Jumping into the icy water would be a great enough shock, she said, to make her *feel* again. The analyst would demand that from her, and the analysis would be like icy water. The dream shows her attitude: the sacrifice will have to be made, the risk will have to be taken, and the hope is that she will be made whole with her feelings once more.

The beginnings of *transference* are also present in this initial dream. Gina brings into her analysis an unconscious relationship to the analyst, upon whom she had placed the image of a stern task-mistress. Since she had not yet met me, these expectations had to come from within herself; they were reflections of her own unresolved conflicts, unconscious emotions and problems with relationships. These were activated at the prospect of entering a new and intense relationship. Transference means that something from elsewhere is transferred or redirected into the analytic relationship. Thus we have attitudes and behaviors coming up in analysis which carry with them more emotional charge than would seem to belong to the situation being explored. Behind the façade of the analytic dialogue, however, stands the life history of the patient, with all its personalities and conflicts and the feelings associated with them. The experiences of the individual and, more than these, the bases upon which the life experience takes place, namely the archetypal foundations of the personality, all infuse the analytic confrontation. Much of this process happens unconsciously, but it gives rise to feelings and emotions that then become conscious.

I want to return to the first session with Gina not only because it contained an important initial dream, which illustrates how transference can be present even before the analysis begins, but because another very important aspect of analysis entered into this case in an especially dramatic way. This concerned the attitude of the analyst toward the patient, an attitude which, like that of transference, has a strong unconscious aspect. *Countertransference* is the term used to describe the unconscious analyst-analysand relationship as experienced subjectively from the side of the analyst.

Here are some of the countertransferential factors in the case of Gina. I had a very powerful emotional reaction to her the first moment I saw her. Gina's youth and her long straight brown hair, her dark eyes with the mod glasses, reminded me with excruciating sharpness of my only daughter who had died just a few months before. My daughter had been newly married, and had no child, and so my hopes ever to have a grandchild had been demolished. Now Gina's coming, wondering whether to keep her child, hit me very strongly; I felt rising in me a determination that she should not under any circumstances give up her child for adoption. Because I am close enough to my own unconscious, I could feel the "mother-tiger" rising within me. So all the while as I was listening to and speaking with Gina, I was dealing with the uproar in my own unconscious.

I had to recall what I had learned in my own analysis when I had been training, shortly after I had begun to work with my first cases under supervision. I was, like all neophytes, exceedingly eager to achieve a successful outcome, and I tended to become quite active in leading, rather than gently guiding the process. My training analyst had gently tried to restrain me, but when that failed she shocked me one day by saying, "You are not supposed to want the patient to get well!"

At first I could not quite believe this, for I surely did not understand her meaning. But gradually as it sank in I was able to see that if I acted out of my desire to heal the patient, I was setting myself up as the miracle worker. I would be doing it for my own satisfaction, for the joy of success, and possibly for the approval of my training analyst. My own needs would be in the foreground then, and the patient's needs would revert to the secondary position. Besides, the possibility for healing lies in the psyche of the patient, the place where the disunion or split exists. The psyche, as Jung has taught, is a self-regulating system, containing within it all the elements which are necessary both to produce a neurosis and to transform the neurosis into a constructively functioning attitude. If I, as analyst, impose my concepts of the direction into which the analysis should go and what the outcome should be, I am doing violence to the potential unity of the patient's psyche. My task is to use myself as a vehicle for clarifying the patient's dilemmas and for helping her learn to interpret her unconscious production. My task is not to contaminate the analysis with my own problems. And it is for this reason that I constantly need to be aware of my own needs and my own biases.

The twin problems of transference and countertransference in the psychology of Jung are given a position of great importance in the analytic process. In this, analytical psychologists are in full agreement with analysts of other schools. Jung has stated in "The Psychology of the Transference," "that almost all cases requiring lengthy treatment gravitate round the phenomenon of transference, and that the success or failure of the treatment appears to be bound up with it in a very fundamental way."[7]

The nature of the transference in Jungian analysis develops along with the style of the analysis, and especially as fostered by the individuality of the analyst. Jung long ago "took analysis off the couch," with all the meaning that implies, symbolical as well as otherwise. "The couch, with the analyst sitting behind the patient, clearly aims at establishing as far as possible (I don't believe it is very far, in fact) an 'impersonal,' 'objective' analyst figure. That it also forms one of the defense mechanisms used by analysts for self-protection is evident," we are told by a Jungian critic of the couch technique.[8] In the Jungian analysis, the analyst and analysand sit face to face on the same level. This gives greater flexibility to the analytical situation and to the active interchange that goes on between the two participants. I, as analyst, am exposed and I expose myself deliberately to the observing and scrutinizing view of the analysand. This puts us immediately on the same plane, and we are therefore part and parcel of a mutual relationship.

Jung has warned the analyst with respect to countertransference:

> Even the most experienced psychotherapist will discover
> again and again that he is caught up in a bond, a combina-
> tion resting on mutual unconsciousness. And though he may
> believe himself to be in possession of all the necessary
> knowledge concerning the constellated archetypes, he will in
> the end come to realize that there are very many things in-
> deed of which his academic knowledge never dreamed. Each
> new case that requires thorough treatment is pioneer work,
> and every trace of routine then proves to be a blind alley.
> Consequently the higher psychotherapy is a most exacting
> business and sometimes it sets tasks which challenge not
> only our understanding or our sympathy, but the whole
> man. The doctor is inclined to demand this total effort from
> his patient, yet he must realize that this same demand only
> works if he is aware that it also applies to himself.[9]

The analysis of the transference is the crux of the analyst-analysand relationship, for the unconscious patterns come into play here where we can see them directly and do not have to rely on the patient's recital of things past. Transference material is presented spontaneously by dreams, and so in looking at the dreams we can see the outcroppings of unconscious processes, disengaged from any conscious purposes of the analysand. In this way the analysis of the dream has a certain advantage over the analysis of the defenses and resistances; for the latter may be all mixed in with the will and other conscious notions.

In my own experience I have found that the transference material is not necessarily disguised to the degree that it becomes necessary to interpose concepts like that of a "dream censor" who twists the message of the dream into something quite different, even opposite from what appears. Some transference dreams can be taken quite literally, for their meaning is evoked by images and symbols with beautiful clarity.

For example, a male schoolteacher in his late thirties who is bound to his mother by hate and fear, and who occasionally takes a hallucinogenic drug, brought the following dream: *I am visiting the zoo and am in a giant outdoor bird cage there looking at plants and birds. I wander down a steep path and find Dr. S. cooking what smells to be chocolate fudge. There, in an earthen room below the birds, are twelve huge vats of gurgling, bubbling chocolate candy. She tells me that it is a kind of a grain candy, completely non-sugared and very non-habit-forming. She then offers me some and I taste it, remarking that it tastes like regular fudge to me. She says, "See, what did I tell you about drugs?" I leave to walk out of the bird cage, and my mother is there, fat and ugly. She starts wrestling me, saying, "You're going to stay in the cage, you're going to stay in the cage," in a sing-song kind of way. I grab her and begin shaking her. As I shake her I keep saying to myself the same thing I once thought when I really shook a student in my class, hard, "Migod, you're shaking the shit out of this kid!"*

Bill, the dreamer, feels encapsulated. His life is like a big cage, so large that he can go about with apparent freedom, but go too far and he suddenly finds out where the bars are. He feels comfortable enough among pubescent children, partly because in his emotional life he is still stuck somewhere in

that place. He has never been able to enjoy a sexual relationship with a woman, and the few sexual encounters he has had
with males have had a puerile quality. It appeared to me that
his sexual development was retarded, and I was not sure
whether his mild interest in sex with men came from a natural
homosexuality or from an inability to make the necessary
break with the overpowering mother to approach a romantic
encounter with a woman of his own age without being terrified. My impression was that his sexuality was still undifferentiated.

As a young child he had been surrounded by prohibitions
against enjoying any sensual pleasures. He was informed in
no uncertain terms that his body and everything that came out
of it was filthy and untouchable. He recalls his mother standing over him and shaming him when he was two or three, but
can't remember why. He must have repressed suddenly all the
good feelings associated with the "making" of warm, soft, pun-
gent feces. Bill recalled that he was kept at home a great deal
of the time with minor ailments while the other children were
out playing. He had no early experience of body contact or sex
play with other children. It seemed to him that wherever he
went, his mother was watching him, that he was never out of
her sight. He grew extremely shy and, not surprisingly, failed
to form any close attachments outside of the family. Much of
his time was spent in solitary activity: practicing the cello,
reading, and compulsive masturbation surrounded by guilt
feelings and fear of divine retribution. All through his growing
years Bill was dogged by a sense of failure in personal relationships. As a young adult he related to others mostly on a
superficial "talky" level, without any sense of concern about
the other, and without ever feeling that he himself was held in
high regard.

In his analytic "confession" he described his masturbatory
fantasies; they were oriented toward boys and men and full of
unending streams of urine and inundations of feces; there
were all sorts of scenes of sexual abuse being heaped on him,
or performed by him on other people. I listened to it all with-

out much comment, primarily interested in understanding what it meant to him. Since there was no judgment from my side, he had felt freer in going ahead to explore his actual relationships of various kinds. These were brief impersonal homosexual encounters.

My appearance in his dreams showed that he experienced me as being involved with him and committed to the process in which we were both engaged (were we not in the same huge bird cage?). My acceptance and participation in his reliving of his repressed experiences allowed him to convert the disgust he had learned back into its original context of something natural—to him that was sweet and delicious, like "regular fudge." But the old suspicion was not gone from him; he felt that my acceptance of him could not be altogether real, it must carry a moral judgment, perhaps referring to my having questioned the wisdom of his sometime use of LSD or mescaline. He associated me in his mind with the image of the chiding mother. In other words, he had projected that image onto me. So even while consciously and rationally he saw me as myself, on an unconscious level he saw his mother—and he transferred his feelings of fear and distrust of his mother to me. Therefore, in the dream he tried to escape (and in reality this preceded his attempt to flee from analysis because of the tensions it produced), and then we were able to see what it was that he was resisting. I was really his mother after all, it appeared, and he saw any attempt on my part to hold him within the discipline of the process as a ruthless effort to control him, which he must avoid by a counterattack. The aggressive behavior which could not be lived out with his mother, except in dreams, had found its way into his daily life, where he had taken on the mother role himself and found himself "shaking the shit out of this kid." The permissiveness which my activity in the dream symbolizes is something he missed in his childhood and would have liked to attain now, but he was unable to because he could not trust it. It would be a task in the analysis to give him the opportunity to test out freer attitudes and to discover that these attitudes, which appear in his dreams, represent not only elements of unfulfilled wishes or incest fantasies, but a still more important element in them.

The other element of the dream, which we have not yet considered, is that which is suggestive of the potential for future development of the dreamer. In this case the symbol of the cooking provides the clue, for obviously "cooking" here is not the ordinary occupation of whipping up a batch of fudge in the kitchen. The cooking is an extraordinary procedure, taking place on a subterranean level which has to be approached by going down a steep path and entering an earthen room. Here, in the place that symbolizes the depths of the unconscious, twelve huge vats are boiling and gurgling. Cooking means changing or transforming a substance from one form into another to make it edible, that is, assimilable. It is as though the dream were saying, "Look here, there is a tremendous job to be done, but look, this substance has within it all that is needed to produce something valuable and highly desirable!"

Often in the process of analysis the unconscious yields up symbols of transformation, like this one. The appearance of the symbols does not mean that a transformation of the personality is imminent; it only means that it is a possibility. For some individuals, if these symbols appear at a time of psychological readiness, they may be taken as a challenge to advance beyond the stage of concern with neurotic symptoms and their causes, and to begin to consider the deeper meaning of the symptoms, that is, their constructive aspect. A constructive view of a symptom means trying to see what it is that the symptom is symbolically attempting to accomplish—to what psychological need is it responding?

Looking at a symptom in this way corresponds to Jung's "purposive view" of neurosis. Jung accepted first of all the important psychoanalytic precept that neurotic and psychotic symptoms rest on a base of conflict between the instinctive nature of people and the demands imposed upon them by the society in which they live. He then moved on another step. He was not content only to analyze every neurotic and psychotic symptom from the point of view of determining where it came from, why it got started, and how it worked, as he perceived that Freud had done. Jung also wanted to know where the symptoms might be leading the patient, that is, what unconscious purpose might be operating. He believed that the way to uncover meaning in events and developments was to observe the direction in which they were pointing, that is, to look for the purposive aspect of the symptom.

Thus Jung was willing to consider and probe the early history of the child, not as an end in itself, and not even to discover clues leading back to traumatic events that, being repressed, acted to sensitize points in the psyche which would form the grounds for later psychic disturbances. His major interest in infantile experience was to discern patterns in it which, established at a very early age, proceeded to give form to future thought and behavior. His concern was not alone to establish the *causes* of neuroses, but rather to be able to find in them some hint as to the *direction* in which they were leading the patient. The "cure" of the symptoms was not necessarily the most essential matter. In earlier times, and still among some people today, homosexual behavior is regarded as a symptom of an illness that needs to be cured. It seemed to me that cessation of homosexual behavior for Bill at that time would have been anything but a "cure," even if it could have been accomplished. I thought of it as possibly an effort on Bill's part to enter into relationships where he felt relatively safe instead of being isolated from any kind of social life. That he did seek out some relationships seemed to be a positive thing, as it left the way open for whatever sexual orientation might prove to be natural for him when he became less inhibited. In any case, one could say that Bill's neurosis had a purposive aspect, namely to lead him out of his social alienation; therefore it could be allowed to play itself out until such time as it would no longer be needed.

I made the statement earlier that the reasons a person gives for wanting to enter analysis are rarely the true reasons. They are, without a doubt, the conscious reasons, and the would-be analysand is completely sincere in advancing them. Whether he offers marital problems, or coming to terms with the death of a member of his family, or not being able to succeed in his work, or drinking too much, or sexual impotence, or a generalized feeling of anxiety—it all boils down to a truth which seems deceptively simple but is in fact complicated and all-encompassing. It is that he has looked at himself and does not like the person he has become, and that he believes that somewhere in him is rising the possibility of being another sort of person, the one he was meant to be.

That second entity was united with the first at some point in time, perhaps in early childhood, perhaps in adolescence under the aegis of an admired friend or an inspiring teacher. It may have been recognized as a peaceful way of being, or a way of seeing the world that was wide and full of wonder; or it may have been seen in terms of devotion to some idea, some purpose. In the struggle for material possessions, for personal achievement, for social position or for the favors of an entrancing lover, the second entity was sacrificed—the birthright for the mess of pottage. For some this meant the determined putting away of the dreams of youth, and sometimes in that process the unique promise of the personality simply slipped away unnoticed, leaving a sense of quiet despair. Primitive people have termed this "loss of soul." Those people of an ancient tribal culture would try by their own means to call back that mysterious entity that gave life its zest and energy but, failing this, they would seek out the witch-doctor or shaman for help. Such a man or woman was one who had been chosen for a life of dedication to the world of non-corporeal reality—chosen for this not by any group but by some psychic or spiritual manifestation of a particular quality of being that set him or her apart from the other members of the tribe. It could be an illness, a physical impairment, an ability to see visions. The shaman had to be prepared for this vocation by undergoing an arduous period of isolation and personal sacrifice, taking into herself or himself the sufferings of the people and living them through until they could be exorcised or transformed.

Contemporary people experience something very like the feelings of ennui, lowered vitality, being "boxed-in" that sent primitive people in search of the wise one of the tribe to get back their souls. Today, there are many self-proclaimed wise ones, from the Pied Pipers of instant intimacy to the purveyors of instant salvation. Yet how many are willing to involve themselves with one suffering individual for as long as it takes to help that person come together again, and to reunite the splintered fragments?

Besides, the task is not merely to restore what is lost. In becoming lost, the "soul" (I do not know a better word for that central guiding aspect of the unconscious, the nature of which we may have only a dim awareness) has ceased to be the connecting ribbon of a road between the conscious individual and the vast unknown and unknowable. It needs not only to be restored to what it was before, but it needs to serve as a travelers' highway in which a continuous and busy intercourse between the ego and the unconscious may take place. In this active and reciprocal relationship neither the ego nor the unconscious will remain as it was in the past.

The change that may be brought about in the analytic process, the dialectic between the ego and the unconscious, may come close to its true potential; if so, it will result in a transformation of the personality. This transformation is not achieved through the efforts of an outside agent; the analyst, for instance, does not "make it happen." Rather, the analyst is there to help in enabling the self-regulating aspect of the psyche to function. The analyst will take the side of the unconscious when the ego of the analysand is in the foreground attempting to control everything. On the other hand, when the analysand is floundering out of control in the grip of overwhelming unconscious material, the analyst may align on the side of the ego, and offer whatever strength may be needed to enable the totality of the personality to survive.

The intervention of the analyst, however, is a subtle matter, for the analyst may not allow the initiative to be taken from the analysand. The analyst is there, with strength, when the situation demands more than the analysand is able to muster. But, for the most part, the process is carried on by the analysand, and by following the leads provided from the unconscious as well as from the data of the daily living experience. Contrary to what many people believe when they enter analysis, the analysand is encouraged to lead the process. Analysis is not something that an analyst "does to" a person. I am reminded of an initial dream which was brought by a patient to his second analytical session: *I was lying on a huge butcher's block, naked, with my hands tied to the corners above my head and my feet tied to the opposite corners. Someone was standing over me with a great knife, poised to draw and quarter me.* This dream suggests that the would-be analysand conceived of analysis on the medical model, with psychotherapy as a form of treatment—a radical form to say the least!

Another initial dream was more optimistic, yet to the point: *I had bought a new car, but I did not know how to drive it. A woman told me to get behind the wheel and she would show me what to do. At first I was frightened, but she said, "We will go slowly at first until you get used to it, and after a while you will get the feel of it." I followed her instructions until I was convinced that I would soon be in control. After a while she said, "Now it is time for us to look under the hood."*

Gradually throughout the analytic process, analysands learn to recognize the many and varied aspects of themselves that were unconscious before. These vary in their acceptability—those which come from the dark repressed side may be fought intensely, while those which offer promise may be embraced with joy. The excitement of analysis is that one never knows what may be presented—but this fact is sure, the most evil and disgusting images are capable of being redeemed, while the treasures that were hard to attain may easily be lost again to the unconscious. Perhaps this suggests one reason why the analysand at times exerts so much resistance to the analytic process.

Resistance disguises itself behind many masks: they range from minor symptomatic actions such as being late or missing appointments, to raising spurious arguments to rationalize behavior, forgetting to bring dreams or swamping the analyst with dreams, tight-lipped silences or compulsive talking, rejecting the analyst's interpretations out of hand or accepting everything the analyst says like a "good pupil" who is looking for teacher's approval.

Psychotherapists of certain schools confront their patients immediately and excoriate them for their resistance to the therapeutic process. I would hesitate before doing so. I often wonder, when I become aware of resistance in patients and find in myself the tendency to call them to account, whether it is possible that secretly I feel rejected by the patients. Could I, unconsciously of course, be asking myself, "How can this person who is so disturbed and who functions so uncertainly feel anything but eagerness to listen to me and learn from my wisdom? He *has* to be broken of this dastardly habit." I hope I am able to avoid this hubris at all costs, and if I sometimes do, it is only that I am acutely aware that I could easily commit this sin were I to forget for a moment that I am fully capable of it!

It seems to me that I, as analyst, must regard my analysand as though I were an anthropologist, and he a native, exploring the unknown regions of his psyche, where the territory is as yet unmapped. As psychotherapist, I may have a wide variety of experience gained from other expeditions, and I may know in general what sort of equipment to take, and for what kinds of dangers I must be on the lookout. But the person with me is the one who knows, and knows in depth, the terrors of his particular wilderness, and where they may be lurking. Therefore, I as psychotherapist, am open to being led by my patient, to allowing my patient ample opportunities to structure the forays. There will be a preliminary period in which each participant in the search must learn the rudiments of the other's language, in order that we may communicate to each other the ways in which each of us may contribute to the joint endeavor. Sometimes a patient, inexperienced in leading the search, may be reluctant to expose the secret places. I must accept in my own mind the reality that the native has been there a long time, and knows all the paths and the terrain, also all the places to hide. The native may have his own way of doing things, and one day he may not arrive at the appointed time at the anthropologist's hut, with his burden balanced on his head. What then?

A therapist, with this image before her, will ask herself while she is waiting for the knock at the door, why is he still not here when it is so late? Is there something in *his life* which is distracting him from our arranged appointment? Or is it possible that *I* may have done something to put him off? Did I frighten him last time? Did I ask too much from him? Did I in some way insult him? Did I fail to give him credit when he cleared a new path? Did I fail to take his hand when he reached out to me? So then the therapist does not approach the patient next time only with the questions: Why did *you* make yourself late; or dodge an interpretation; or forget to bring your dreams. She will also ask, What could *I* have done to bring this about? She will seek out information from the patient at such times as to how he reacted to the last session, what he took away from it, how he understood what occurred, and what happened in the interim between the sessions.

There is a time in the process of analysis when resistance on the part of the patient may be a welcome sign for the analyst. This is a fact that I did not learn from any book, but from one of my analysands. I was discussing the question of resistance with a perceptive young woman, and I was saying that I did not think the analyst needs to be in a hurry to break down the patient's resistance. To this she heartily agreed, and added: "What the patient often is resisting is a therapist's attempt to get her to give up her independent responsibility for how she conducts her life, and her independent standpoint."

2

Complexes by Day
and
Demons by Night

. . .

I FIND THAT JUNG's "complex theory" and the related ideas concerning psychic energy are not easy to comprehend from an exclusively pragmatic point of view. On the other hand, if one can admit to being open-minded enough to allow for the possible existence of demons, many difficulties in understanding the nature of complexes can be overcome.

What Jung has called *complexes* are certain constellations of psychic elements (ideas, opinions, convictions, etc.) that are grouped around emotionally sensitive areas. I understand the complex as consisting of two factors. First, there is a nuclear element which acts as a magnet, and second, there is a cluster of associations that are attracted to the nucleus. I see the nuclear element itself as made up of two components. One is determined by experience, and so is causally related to the environment. The other is determined by the disposition of the individual in question, and is innate; its foundation is basic to the structure of the psyche. When the disposition of the individual at some point confronts an experiential situation which can in no way be handled, a psychic trauma occurs. It is as though you bump up against an object—most times there is enough resilience so that no harm is done or, if you are temporarily out of balance, your equilibrium is quickly regained. But if the bump is hard enough, and if you were totally unprepared for it, you may be cut or bruised or broken, and the area may remain sensitive. Then every time you touch it, you will feel the hurt; you will favor it and try to protect it by your behavior. If, nevertheless, someone hits you on the same spot, you will cry out in pain. A psychic wound acts in somewhat the same way, but the whole process is largely, if not totally, unconscious. Therefore you feel its effects, even though you do not know the meaning and the cause of the suffering. When in analysis I trace the predisposing factor to its roots, I am likely to discover an elemental characteristic of the individual's nature, a *given*. It is not the superficial psychic jolts and bumps that occur which give rise to the formation of complexes, but only those wounds which lay bare the vital, pattern-forming elements of the psyche, the elements which Jung has called the *archetypes*. Those experiences which threaten our deepest beliefs—in our gods and in ourselves—those are the ones which give rise to complexes.

Jung proposed that the nuclear element of the complex is characterized by its feeling-tone, the emphasis arising from the intensity of the emotion involved. This emphasis, this intensity, can be expressed in terms of energy, a value quantity. In direct relation to the amount of energy, the energic quantity, is the capacity of the nucleus to draw associations to it, thereby forming a complex. The more energic quantity, the more associations, hence the more material from everyday life experiences gets drawn into the complex.

Only when you are experiencing a complex can you evaluate its feeling tone, and then only to the degree that the nuclear element itself is *conscious*. Ordinarily, with some awareness of what in your nature and what in your life experiences have led to this psychic sensitivity, it is possible for you as an individual to make a reasonably good adaptation to a complex. You may either structure your life so as to avoid situations which contribute to the production of excessive psychic tension or, if that is not possible or desirable, you may learn how to deal with the tensions that the complex-laden situation produces. But if, as frequently occurs, the nuclear element is *unconscious*, then it becomes impossible to achieve a subjective awareness of the feeling-tone in the experience through which you as an individual must move.

As a complex becomes conscious, little by little it is possible to disengage its components and so to defuse the bomb, as it were. The bomb is still there, or at least its component parts are there, but it is not now so dangerous. An unconscious complex continues to add more and more to its nucleus and associated contents, thus building up increasing pressure in the volatile bundle. I believe that it is this sense of intolerable pressure that often brings people into psychotherapy, although when they express the feeling-tone of the complex to me it is most likely to come out in terms of a specific problem or symptom.

The concept of the complex was Jung's original contribution to psychotherapy, and Freud acknowledged his debt to his younger colleague. In his 1901 study *The Psychopathology of Everyday Life*, where Freud described the way in which "complexes" interfere with our conscious intent by causing embarrassing slips of the tongue, misreadings, forgetting of people's names and other errors and bungled actions, he used the explanatory expression "circles of thought." The word "complexes," replacing this in the 1907 edition, marks the beginning of Jung's influence on Freud.[1] The primary complex upon which Freud concentrated his efforts throughout his work was the well-known "Oedipus complex," centering around the mother-son relationship. The ramification of this complex is seen in the "castration concept" with which Freud dealt extensively, and the "Elektra complex" which describes the problems in the father-daughter relationship paralleling the Oedipus complex. Alfred Adler, in his use of this concept, focused his attention on the "inferiority complex" with all its associated "power complexes," these latter conceived of as neurotic means of overcoming inferiority feelings. Jung carried the concept of the complex much further than either Freud or Adler, pointing out its damming effects in many and various phases of life. He paid particular attention to the "mother-daughter complexes" which he specifically described in his essay on "Psychological Aspects of the Mother Archetype."[2] He also called attention to the complex of "possession" which often manifests itself in a belief in spirits: "Spirits are complexes of the collective unconscious which appear when the individual loses his adaptation to reality, or which seek to replace the inadequate attitude of a whole people by a new one. They are therefore either pathological fantasies or new but as yet unknown ideas."[3] Other complexes, according to Jung, are ideas with which people identify themselves and their endeavors, hence the "savior complex," the "healer complex," and the "prophet complex," to name only a few. Even the ego, according to Jung, might better be called the "ego complex" as it is a specific and powerful self-concept with which the individual identifies himself and which draws to itself certain very specific ideas. A list of complexes could be extensive, for it would cover every type of feeling-toned idea that tends to create a highly charged atmosphere of thought or behavior.

Some of the more abstruse papers in analytical psychology have been written on the subject of complexes, dealing with principles which, I readily confess, I have found difficult to integrate intellectually. Experiencing the complex is much easier in the analytic session, when you recognize its presence in unconscious material. Dreams often provide access to these apparently split-off portions of the psyche which make their appearance as separate entities, often in some non-human or mythological form. Sometimes they point the way to long-buried experiences which, although forgotten, have retained their power to create neurotic disturbances and interfere with the natural functioning of the psychic life of the individual.

Such was the experience of Cecelia, a bright young college woman. When I began analysis with her she was living with a man who was rather limited in personality and quite immature. Cecelia had been "lost" in the hippie-psychedelic world of the sixties since she dropped out of college two years before in her first semester. Her story was so commonplace in those days that it need not be repeated in detail. She was the daughter of upper-middle-class parents who were themselves unhappy and unloving. The mother was a self-righteous woman who always knew how things should be done and said so, expecting all members of the family to conform to her requirements in everything from what to wear to what political opinions to hold. The father, quiet, introverted, and beaten-down, said little at home, except now and then when he tried impotently to modify the strenuous demands of his wife. With Cecelia he was always patient, permissive, and non-directive.

The year before, a crisis had occurred. Cecelia was caught smoking marijuana by her mother. Her father admitted he had known about it for a long time, that he didn't regard it as terrible. His attitude only infuriated the mother. She severely reprimanded Cecelia, calling her all sorts of degrading names. Soon after this, Cecelia ran away from home, and shortly became involved with an older man who was deep in the drug scene. This man introduced her to acid, mescaline, group sex. Cecelia had some bad trips and became disoriented and paranoid. When her parents finally caught up with her they consigned Cecelia to a private mental hospital. A couple of months later she came out sullen, angry at the world, but convinced that there had to be a better way to live than the way she had been living for the past year.

In the course of the drug experience, by a circuitous route she had found her way to reading Jung. While entranced by the visionary world she had glimpsed under LSD, she had come across the book *The Psychedelic Experience, a manual based on the Tibetan Book of the Dead* by Timothy Leary, Ralph Metzner, and Richard Alpert. The authors included in their introduction tributes to three men: Dr. W. Y. Evans-Wentz,

Tibetan scholar and translator of *The Tibetan Book of the Dead*,
Lama Anagarika Govinda, one of the world's leading interpreters of Tibetan Buddhism, and Carl G. Jung. Cecelia's introduction to the drug world may have provided her with instant
ecstasy, but as time went on she discovered that instant ecstasy is not necessarily followed by instant enlightenment. She
wanted to find out what others had to say about enlightenment. She began to read Jung, and discovered that his way to
a deeper understanding of the mysterious processes of the unconscious was far from instantaneous, but that it offered a
slow and painstaking way of entering into a productive relationship with those processes. She also found in her reading
that not only Jung but also Evans-Wentz and Lama Govinda
were men who had gone through the discipline of academic
study, learning the techniques of discrimination and making
order which are necessary to transform a creative flash into a
creation of substance.

After the "easy way" did not work for Cecelia, she decided
to come into analysis and submit herself to the difficult developmental way. She returned to college, studying, often chafing
at some of the requirements, but expressing her discomfort by
talking about her problems in a *responsible* way (by this I
mean seeking out the facts in the situation rather than bluster-
ing about in generalities and baseless opinions), writing poetry and prose, and doing some interesting painting.

She continued to have paranoid feelings at times, and she
would become angry when her wandering thoughts became
temptations that distracted her from doing what she felt was
necessary to rebuild her life. The young man with whom she
was then living was a fellow student whom she had met recently at the university. He wanted to marry her. On one level
she was all for the marriage, but she would frequently pick
fights with him so that it seemed as though she were trying to
alienate him. Whenever she was encouraged to reflect on the
apparent inconsistency of her behavior, she would insist that
she was doing everything possible to improve the relationship.

Cecelia found his presence supportive at the time, but she was not sure she wanted to live her life with him.

One night she had the following dream: *There is a big black she-bear. She is fighting with a man. The man, with the help of another man, stuffs the bear down in a hole. Then I go and get a gun. One of the men shoots the bear over and over. They drag her out of the hole and she is still a little bit alive, so they shoot her again. There is blood all over the bear. Then there is a large wedding. Everyone is there. The bride comes out. She is very ugly and she is sneezing. Her mother puts a fake fur dress and coat in brown and black over her wedding dress.*

Cecelia's dream expressed her feeling of the heavy and threatening power that constantly opposed her conscious wishes. The power was female and inexorable—whatever you did it could not be done away with. The power of the masculine element in her life was of little use against the dreadful she-bear. Cecelia tried to help by getting a gun. She thought that she could destroy the rough and cruel animal but, since it was a part of her, she could not do so without jeopardizing the totality of herself. Stuffing the bear down a hole was symbolic of trying to get rid of some element in life that could not be tolerated. In this case the she-bear image may have referred on one level to the girl's mother, in her menacing aspect. But over the years the mother-complex had drawn to it so many experiences and feelings and attitudes that it was now well covered over, and the original image that attracted these contents was no longer recognizable. A whole complex of ideas relating to the terrible power, Mother, her cruelty, and her blind-instinctive protectiveness of her young, was represented by this brutal creature. The rebellious aspects of the girl, the runaway who attempted to deal with the problem by avoidance, were symbolized by the men who shot the bear while she was down in the hole.

The effort to drag the bear to the surface suggests the analytic process of bringing up that which is hidden. Here, again, the purpose seemed to be to demolish the destructive complex. Living with the young man, in direct opposition to the mother's wishes was a bloody business, and all the more when we see how the young man's personality resembled in some ways the girl's weak and ineffectual father. In the end of the dream the bride came out and was very ugly and sneezing. The *negative-mother complex* interfered with the expression of that beautiful femininity which is the traditional quality associated with a bride on her wedding day. Sneezing is said to be an age-old tactic for getting rid of devils or demons—which is why we say "God bless you" whenever one of those infernal creatures is supposedly let loose. The mother-complex, as expressed by the image of the mother of the bride, had not been done away with, only transformed into a different image, but she still went about her nefarious business, attempting to hang onto the girl the empty bearskin, trappings of the cruel and dominating female.

After working through the negative-mother-complex with Cecelia for some time, it began to come clear that the bear symbolized that inner aspect of her nature which had never been sufficiently fed with warmth and affection, and therefore continued to demand what it needed in an unreasonable way. The angry devouring quality which had become associated with Cecelia's own personality had to be given what is required—and Cecelia had to learn to pay attention to it. She began to take an interest in her home, making it a very personal expression of her own interests and skills. She renewed her interest in painting and hung her works where she could enjoy them. She designed a beautiful mural for her wall, in the form of a sun-circle which represented to her a new cycle of life, a new day and a new chance every morning. She enjoyed her courses in eastern religions and English literature, and wrote some very good term papers. Now and then she composed a poem, just for herself. The creative-maternal began gradually to overcome the destructive-maternal.

Some may say of her that she was using her art and her craft to sublimate her neurotic tendencies. But I would not tell her that. I cannot imagine that she would settle for that, she who has fought the battle for deliverance from the terrible mother.

Anyone familiar with Freud's *Interpretation of Dreams* will readily see that Cecelia's dream could as easily have been interpreted in the traditional psychoanalytic manner. Her difficulty in relating sexually to her young man could have been seen in purely personal terms, rather than in terms of the devouring mother who negates the creative-maternal aspect of the feminine. Cecelia might have been described as being in a regressed psychosexual stage, still living in a pregenital state and unable to progress beyond an oral dependency on her mother. The details of the interpretation that might be offered are not important here. What is important is the difference in thrust that occurs, depending on whether you emphasize the cause of the complex and so solve the problem of etiology (i.e., origin, especially of a disease), or whether you see the complex as a dynamic indicator pointing toward the potential development of the dreamer.

Jung discovered the complex very early in his career, while he was working at the Burghölzli Clinic in Zurich as a resident in psychiatry. When he arrived at the Clinic in 1900, he was already engaged in the writing of his doctoral dissertation, *On the Psychology and Psychopathology of So-Called Occult Phenomena.*[4] During the day he was engaged in seeing patients and in working on a research project under the direction of his chief, Dr. Eugen Bleuler, whose great contribution to psychiatric history was the monograph *Dementia Praecox or The Group of Schizophrenias.* By night Jung was absorbed in the problems of S.W., the young lady who had produced the amazing séances and the aberrant behavior which had been of such great interest to him in his medical-school years.

As Jung described S.W., she had a pale face with large dark eyes that gave out a peculiar, penetrating look. Although her body was slight and of delicate construction, she appeared to be in good health. Her typical behavior for the most part was quite reserved, but there were times when she would become engulfed in the most exuberant joy or exaltation. Her education was extremely limited. She came from a home where there were few books about and where the members of the family were all artisans or business people with very limited interests. Furthermore, she was of average or slightly below average intelligence, with no special talents. She enjoyed handwork or just sitting around daydreaming, when there were no chores to be done. So, superficially at least, there was nothing remarkable about this teen-ager which would give rise to expectations that she would become a "visionary" living as much in a strange world beyond the ordinary senses as in the usual world.

But there were differences. A pattern existed in her family which would suggest the acceptance as normal of what we would probably call paranormal phenomena. A young child tends to accept as a matter of course the behavior of members of its family, however outlandish that behavior may appear to outsiders. Thus, S.W. had no way of knowing that waking hallucinations were peculiar, to say the least. How could she, when her paternal grandfather, a very intelligent clergyman, frequently recounted his visions in the form of whole dramatic scenes complete with dialogues? Or when her paternal grandmother was subject to fainting fits that were nearly always followed by trance states during which she uttered prophecies? Her father is described by Jung in his case history as "an odd, original person with bizarre ideas," and two of his brothers were much the same. All three had waking hallucinations and were given to premonitions. Her mother was a borderline psychotic, one sister a hysteric and called a "visionary," and another sister had a heart condition that Jung described as having a strong psychosomatic element.

In a household such as S.W.'s, the rational aspects of life must have existed side by side with the non-rational, or even the irrational. Missing—or, at best, faulty—would have been the barriers which early training and education typically erect between fact and fantasy in a child's mind. Inner vision must have been granted at least equal validity with experience in the objective world. No one would say to the child who "saw" shapes in the dark, "Don't worry, darling, they aren't really there, they're *just* imaginary." On the contrary, the images of the night would have been reinforced with great interest by the parents, and perhaps even with the suggestion that they surely belonged to a world of spirit which sometimes became manifest to a chosen few. In S.W.'s family, the possibility of contacting the "spirit world" was looked upon as a very special gift, rather than as potentially dangerous. S.W. was, as I have indicated, a girl of little education or cultural achievement. The intellectual world was fairly closed to her. But the door to the non-rational events of life was wide open. She saw them as events which simply occurred; it did not seem to require any special effort on her part to experience them.

This "spirit world" is one with which many conventionally educated Americans have a great deal of trouble. Most young children have imaginary playmates, look for images in the clouds, are careful not to offend the spirits ("Step on a crack, you break your mother's back"), and have countless other ways of paying respects to the non-rational part of life. But early childhood education is a brainwashing carried on mostly under the influences of child-development experts schooled in watered-down Freudian concepts that seek to explain superstitions as the result of certain unconscious conflicts—as if perhaps on an unconscious level an aggressive, rebellious child sometimes really does want to break his mother's back, while at the same time loving that mother dearly and needing her. The demonic tendency in the unconscious has to be split off from consciousness because the child cannot admit to the conflict within himself. Therefore the spirit would have to be seen on the outside, and it would have to be propitiated.

Our rational parents, having been well indoctrinated with the belief that every event has a cause, believe that they have understood the causes of superstitions and fantasies. These "causes" may be traced back to undesirable tendencies existing in the individual. A rational education roots out these tendencies, exposes them as destructive aspects of the unconscious, as if exposure or even understanding makes an end of them. Freud's essay on "Determinism, Belief in Chance and Superstition," in *The Psychopathology of Everyday Life* was instrumental in promoting the view that it could. Its influence has had a tremendously important effect on the course of childhood education. It translated into psychological terms the voices of the Enlightenment that called for the elimination of the superstitious, the mystical, and the non-rational in the Western intellectual tradition.

S.W. had been exposed to none of this new thought. It is not surprising that when she heard at home and from friends about table turning that she would take an interest in it and ask to be allowed to take part in the experiments. Half jokingly and half seriously, she joined the circle of family and friends, sat in the darkness and felt movement in the table around which they were all seated. In the midst of all this she announced one night that she was receiving communications, and that these were being transmitted to her through the spirit of her grandfather. Those present, and among them the medical student, Carl Jung, were surprised by the clerical tone of the messages, which seemed to be "in character" with the old man. We piece together some of what must have taken place from Jung's dissertation, a psychological analysis based on his notes taken after returning home from the séances.

He described the trance state from which S.W. spoke as "somnambulism," after his first observation in August 1899. He referred to the event as an "attack" and apparently regarded the whole matter as the manifestation of a psychiatric illness. Whatever else it might be, he was unwilling to conjecture at that time.

At the onset of an attack, S.W. would grow pale, slowly sink to the floor or into a chair, and close her eyes. Then she would assume the state of suspended animation with apparent loss of voluntary control, clinically known as catalepsy. When she at last began to speak, she would be generally relaxed, her eyelid reflexes remaining normal, as well as her sense of touch, so that when someone brushed against her unexpectedly she would start as though frightened. At this stage she was no longer aware of her usual personality, as evidenced by her failure to react when called upon by her name. She took the roles of various dead friends and relatives and carried them off with astounding accuracy, according to those present. Gradually, over weeks, her performances built up into whole dramatic scenes full of passion and glowing rhetoric. Sometimes she would even expound with great fluency in literary German, a language which she spoke with hesitation and fumbling in her normal state. Her speeches would be accompanied by grandiloquent gestures. Sometimes they would erupt into ecstatic fervor. Invariably she spoke of herself in the third person, and when she used first person it was only to prophesy another outburst.

S.W.'s mediumistic performances followed a pattern familiar to anyone who has read occult literature. It would not be unexpected that they might occur in a girl of her background. Especially interesting to Jung, however, was the content of certain visionary experiences which she described to him in their private meetings. She told him that between being awake and falling asleep as she lay in bed, she would experience a light flooding the room. Shining white figures would detach themselves from the brightness around them. The women wore flowing robes girdled at the waist and turbans wrapped about their heads. As time went on she had begun to find that the spirits were already there when she went to bed. After that she began seeing them in the daylight, though only for fleeting moments. The visions filled her with a feeling of unearthly bliss. Only on rare occasions, and then at night, did she see terrifying images of a demonic character.

Jung became convinced that S.W.'s visions had a singular reality of their own, the nature of which he could only surmise. As the weird experiences developed she reported that they seemed perfectly natural to her, and she told him, "I do not know if what the spirits say and teach me is true, nor do I know if they really are the people they call themselves; but that my spirits exist is beyond question. I speak to them about everything I wish as naturally as I'm talking to you. They must be real." Yet the young girl who was seeing the apparitions was quite different from the one who lived a normal unremarkable life in between these highly charged times. Jung saw that she was leading a "double life" with two personalities existing side by side or in succession, each continually striving for mastery.[5]

Jung's interpretations of the girl's activities in her trance states were made under scientific conditions which included meticulous observation and classification of data. He described in detail all the symptoms: the headaches that preceded the attacks, the cold pallor associated with them, and lapses of attention suggestive of epileptoid disorder. He also described the various manifestations: in addition to the visions there were automatic writing, glossolalia (speaking in strange incomprehensible tongues) and cryptomnesia (the appearance in consciousness of memory images which are not recognized as such—but which appear as original creations).

Jung felt that he would have to involve himself more fully in order to get a feeling for what was happening. His participation would have to go beyond the objective, scientific approach. He entered into the table turning himself, noting the effect of verbal suggestion on the subject. He also experimented with the even more potent effect of a very slight push or a series of light rhythmical taps of his own. The movement of the table would grow stronger and continue even when he had stopped applying the stimulus. Jung explained this as the induction of a partial hypnotic trance and compared it to methods often used by hypnotists to produce an exhibition of automatism.

He took the factor of suggestibility into account, as well as the questionable mental health of the subject. All of this could explain well enough some aspects of the alteration of the states of consciousness, but he still knew nothing about the sources of the *content* of what S.W. spoke about. As her condition became more extreme, it appeared that she was developing a highly systematized "mystic science." She began to hint that the spirits had revealed to her the nature of strange forces in the world and the Beyond.

She decided that she could trust Jung, and after a while she offered him a sheet of paper upon which she had written numerous names. They were neologisms purporting to describe the nature of the forces which guide the universe, these being both material and spiritual forces acting upon human beings and the physical world. Jung diagramed the entire system according to her instructions, and traced her patterns of word association that may have led to the coining of the words. They included a conglomeration of word fragments from physics, astrology and mythology. At the same time he was interested in the construction of the system itself, as an example of the way unconscious processes lend themselves to an attempt to decipher the mysteries of the creation and functioning of our world. He knew from his classical studies that myths of cosmogony arise in every culture and often lay the basis for the way in which the culture develops. Could his fascination with the communications of S.W. have had to do with his conviction that myths occur not only in a collective setting, but that they can also arise spontaneously in an individual? Perhaps even some of his personal experiences, for example his recollection of his childhood dream of the phallus enthroned, may have prepared him for the emergence of the mythic where the person is not bound by the constraints of a conventional consciousness.

S.W. produced other extravaganzas. One featured a frivolous gentleman with a North German accent who attempted to charm all the ladies present. Another was the report of the instructions of the spirits on the subject of the geography of Mars where, she learned, everyone travels by flying machines which have long been in existence there. (This is especially interesting in view of the fact that this report preceded by several years the Wright brothers' first flight in a power-driven, heavier-than-air machine.) Reincarnation also played its role in the complex systems she related, through a spiritual

being called "Ivenes," who embodied herself periodically
about every two hundred years all the way back to biblical
times. She wove a complicated tapestry of narration which
involved all the members of her family in their present and
previous existences, surprising and baffling Jung and the others with her "amazing aplomb and . . . clever use of details
which S.W. must have heard or picked up from somewhere."[6]

There are hints in Jung's dissertation that while he was
pondering these matters he was beginning to formulate in his
own mind the concept of many-faceted unconscious parts of
the psyche which, when activated, could yield up a wealth of
material which is not to be accounted for solely by a theory of
repression. But then something occurred which inhibited
Jung's tendency to speculate further at that time. After the
productions of S.W. had reached their climax with the description of "Ivenes" and her retinue of relatives and reincar-
nations, a gradual decline in their quality became noticeable.
The ecstasies grew more and more vacuous and the phenomena became shallower, while characters who had formerly
been well differentiated now became confused and amor-
phous. Within a short time the communications became uncertain and cautious, and the rather prosaic adolescent began
to come through the disguises.

It had become noticeable to Jung that S.W. now began
visibly to force her "spirits" to act, and the performances soon
took on the character of a fraud. At this point Jung lost interest and withdrew, much to his subsequent regret.

Jung conjectured that the various personalities which had
emerged, specifically the ones which were clearly defined and
appeared with regularity and continuity, were possibly representations of unconscious aspects which had become disasso-
ciated from the subject's conscious personality. During the séance, the subject in the process of verbalizing is accessible to
suggestion which acts hypnotically to isolate the speech center. For example, the question to the medium, "Who is speaking?" can act as a suggestion for synthesizing the unconscious
personality. He was able to demonstrate how the unconscious

personality gradually builds itself up through suggestion, and how the very formation of unconscious personalities has enormous suggestive power on the development of further unconscious personalities. He conjectured that when the split-off unconscious personalities emerged in a séance, the emotions connected with them had to be transformed into something not seeming to be a part of the subject's own feelings. Could the split-off portion of the psyche, therefore, be finding symbolic expression in the guise of clairvoyants and other remarkable figures long dead? Now for the first time in his writings Jung mentions Freud: "Whether this offers a parallel to the results of Freud's dream investigations must remain unanswered, for we have no means of judging how far the emotion in question may be considered 'repressed.' "[7]

As to the visual hallucinations, Jung looked for a possible basis for S.W.'s visions just as she was dropping off to sleep. Where silence favors auditory hallucinations, darkness favors visual images. The expectation that one *could* see a spirit causes an excitation of the visual sphere. Then appear the "entoptic phenomena," slight amounts of light in apparent darkness which seem to assume shapes, especially in the presence of a vivid imagination.

What is especially important about this initial published work at the beginning of Jung's career is his assumption that the receptivity of the unconscious for strange and mysterious experiences far exceeds that of the conscious mind. Jung achieved this insight in a day when the concept of the unconscious was only beginning to be talked about in the field of psychology (although it had been well known to artists and poets and playwrights and certainly to the romantics of all ages). Jung was probably dealing here with a case of multiple personality disorder, which in those days went unrecognized but which today is understood as a form of dissociative disorder usually initiated by some early traumatic event or situation.

Naturally Jung discussed the progress of his dissertation from time to time with his chief. Eugen Bleuler must have had mixed feelings as he examined the work of the young doctor who seemed drawn to deal with material which was highly questionable in terms of its suitability for a scientific treatise. No doubt he was fully aware of the balance that was needed when he steered Carl Jung into working on the studies in word association at the very time that S.W. and "Ivenes," and the revelations of mystic sciences were consuming a large portion of his attention.

The work on the Association Experiment occupied an enormous amount of Jung's energy while he was at the Burghölzli Clinic. It was as though he were willing to put all the fury of his creative energy into proving that patients' responses to a series of words could be measured and evaluated. Perhaps he was weary of pondering the questions that had been raised for him by S.W., and still more by the mysterious "Ivenes," who arose out of somewhere, certainly not out of the past experiences of the simple-minded, poorly educated fifteen-year-old girl.

The Word Association Experiment was one of the first psychological projective tests ever devised, if not the very first. The term "projective test" was not yet in use at the time, and the word "experiment" was used instead of "test" with reference to this work, for the reason that "test" suggests that there can be only one correct answer to the question or problem posed, while "experiment" suggests that there is no specific answer expected but that the subject is free to respond spontaneously to what is asked of him. Furthermore, an experiment must be open-ended since it is conducted for the purpose of discovering something that was not known before, while the purpose of a test is to find out how close the person being tested can come to giving the response desired by the tester.

In the Association Experiment, the clinic patient was told first of all that this was not a test, there were no right answers or wrong answers, and there was to be no competitive evaluation. The patient was given one hundred words—one by one—and was to respond to each word as quickly as possible with the first word that came to mind. The patient was told that the responses would be noted and the response time would be clocked. After this was done, the list of words was given to the patient a second time, and this time was asked to reply using the same word given the first time if possible. The stated purpose of the experiment was to discover the role of word associations in establishing diagnoses for mental patients.

Professor Bleuler had asserted, "Every psychical activity rests upon the interchange of the material derived from sensation and from memory traces, upon *associations.*" He was convinced that apart from the somewhat questionable capacity to perceive pain and pleasure, which is perhaps inherent in the smallest organism, any psychic activity without association was unthinkable. He had expressed his amazement that "the proposition that our laws of thought are but rules of association is strangely enough still contested." He theorized that the laws of thought and the laws of association must seem almost identical, once it is realized that the laws of association are not so simple as to be exhausted by placing them in a few well-ordered categories (association by similarity, contrast, simultaneity, and so on). He was sure that every association in the thinking process is accompanied by an almost endless number of more or less distinct presentations. Among the associations that might present themselves could come those related to events from the past experiences of the individual. These might include specific events in his life or fantasy experiences which had occupied him at one time or another. Another rich source of associations might be the purposes or intentions of the individual which were too rudimentary to be recognized as thought. The mood of the subject could inhibit or else supply adequate associations. Bleuler concluded: "On the activity of association there is mirrored the whole psychical essence of the past and of the present, with all their experiences and desires. It thus becomes an index of all the psychical processes which we have to decipher in order to understand the complete man."[8]

When questioned by his colleagues as to the possibility that he may have been overemphasizing the importance of the "small matter" of what association a certain word might evoke, Bleuler strained his proposition even further. He went on record as saying that in a certain sense "*every* psychical event, *every* movement, is only possible to that particular man with his particular past, in one definite way. Each single action represents the whole man: the endeavor to deduce the whole man from his handwriting, physiognomy, shape of his hand, his style, even the way he wears his shoes, is not altogether folly."[9]

As far as verifying Bleuler's hypotheses upon which the experiments were based, the work Jung and his associates carried on over a period of several years was a spectacular failure. Types of associations did not correlate in any significant way with various disease entities. There were a few possible exceptions, but on the whole the various types of associations as defined by Bleuler were spread throughout the normal and the patient population. As to reaction times, when these were averaged, it was found that, in general, men tended to respond slightly more quickly than women, and that educated people tended to respond slightly more quickly than the uneducated. But it was not possible to establish that patients' diseases could be diagnosed on the basis of the categories of their associations.

Pondering the disappointing results of his work, it occurred to Jung that he had failed to focus on one unexpected but important factor which had shown up in the experiments, namely, the great variation in response time from one word to another in an individual patient. He found this to be true in normal subjects as well. While most stimulus words given would call forth responses in something between one and two-and-a-half seconds, certain words would produce a prolonged interval before the response, and some words would draw even a complete blank from the subject. Jung's question to himself, "What does this mean?" proved to be the seed for the future development of his complex theory. And so, what had been a descriptive theory of association now suddenly became a dynamic theory of association; the problem was no longer

"What sort of association is this?"—it was now, "How does the process of association work, what promotes it, what interferes with it, and why?"

The keys to the process of association, as Jung understood them, were *intention* and *attention*. The conscious attitude of most of the people most of the time is an intention to associate one bit of information with another. This is what thinking is in its simplest form, putting two and two together, and also it is what thinking is in its more complicated forms. While we intend to relate facts or concepts or ideas one to another, we find that in order to do this successfully we have to direct our attention. To the degree that we are attentive to what we are hearing or reading or seeing, we are able to think about it and draw meaningful inferences from it. In the Association Experiment when the attention was focused in on the word, the intention to respond promptly could be carried out. There were words, however, which when pronounced by the experimenter, brought about an unusual reaction, an interruption of attention. Such unusual reactions, Jung thought, pointed to complexes. In addition to prolonged reaction time, there were other complex indicators. These were first noted by Jung and later became some of the classical diagnostic clues to be used thereafter in the practice of psychotherapy in practically all schools of thought.

Some of the complex indicators were: 1) reaction with more than one word; 2) reaction against the instructions (this could be related to distractions or could indicate limited intelligence); 3) mistakes in reproduction (these could suggest avoidance or memory failure); 4) reaction expressed by a change in facial expression (being caught unaware like a child with his hand in the cookie jar); 5) reaction expressed by laughing (there might be a displacement of affect as in attempting to cover up a painful association); 6) movement of feet, body, or hands (suggestive of uneasiness, discomfort); 7) coughing or stammering (playing for time in order to find a secondary association in lieu of the first which came to mind); 8) insufficient reactions like "yes" or "no" (these could point to

blocks making a genuine association impossible); 9) not reacting to the real meaning of the stimulus word (this would be a
defense of the individual's image of himself); 10) habitual use
of the same word (this too would point to avoidance, and possibly to stereotypical response to pressures); 11) response in a
foreign language (here it would be important to find out what
part the language played in the life of the individual); and
lastly, 12) a total lack of reaction (for this is also a reaction,
and a meaningful one; in psychotherapy "no-thing" is something).

So Jung was off on a whole new track, that of discovering
how the presence of complexes in the mental patients subjected to the experiment interfered with the process of their
associating words to one another. The same difficulty was experienced by other people who were not mental patients; and
while the results were less dramatic than with the patients,
they nevertheless supported the findings that disturbances of
association come from interruptions of attention, which in
turn result from collision with the complex. The pattern of
associations and their interruptions points to the complex.

In the analytic process the trend of the patient's association is followed very closely by the analyst. By stimulating the
process of associations through the asking of well-placed and
open-ended questions, the associations can lead back to the
complex and the complex can be unraveled to disclose its nuclear elements. But the patient does not speak in terms of
complexes to his analyst; he is more likely to disclose his private demons, because that is frequently the way in which complexes appear. Let us take for an example the case of Paul.

Paul was the operator of an independent realty firm. He
had several people working for him, but he was clearly in
charge, and he handled most of the important transactions.
He had made a great deal of money at various times in his life,
often through questionable dealings. In the process he had
lost friends and made important enemies. Now things were
going badly for him, and he began therapy hoping to find an
alternate way of viewing his life. His presenting complaint was

severe depression with an absence of the energy and enthusiasm that had fired him previously. The analysis had been characterized by a series of "true confessions" about all his wrongdoing in the past, punctuated by his expression of a desire to change, and remorse for the sins and errors committed in making his outrageous fortune. With all the ventilation, there was no relief of the depression. I thought that there had to be a great deal more to come before we would begin to see daylight, so I waited for a clue. At last it came, in the form of the following dream: *I am sitting in the living room with my wife, talking about some problems I am trying to work out in my business. A small object is on the table in front of me, near the edge of the table. I think to myself—if this object falls off the table I'll have financial disaster, but if it stays on I'll be successful. If I don't touch it, it will be safe. But if the object were to get to the center of the table, I think, then it will be absolutely foolproof, secure. So I begin to move it gently toward the center of the table, but my thumb catches it and it falls off. Now I am sure that my unconscious controls my conscious mind through this device of making me move the object.*

I asked Paul if he ever had feelings in waking life similar to those that he had in the dream. He replied that he very often had the feeling that certain happenings in his life were omens, that they showed him how things were going to work out, and when they made their predictions there just never was any way out of what they predicted, they always seemed to work out in the way that he had known of beforehand. I asked him if he could recall any other instances, could he perhaps trace back to the first time when something of this nature happened to him?

He thought awhile and then said he thought he knew what might have been the first of this kind of experience. It had happened on a golf course. He had managed to play his way into a tournament by a combination of cheating when he thought he could get away with it, and a run of very good luck. Now he was in for the big money, but this time there was no chance to cheat, and although he was a good player, he was

really outclassed. It would have to be a very lucky day if he
were to have a chance of winning. And he wanted very much
to win. He was in excellent physical shape and his competitive
nature was honed up to its sharpest. He played well. He was,
in fact, playing for all he was worth. Tension mounted. He had
managed to tie his contender for the match on the second to
the last hole. His opponent teed off and set the ball well down
on the fairway. Paul took careful aim, his ball landed near the
other. The opponent had another good shot and landed on the
green. Now Paul swung a little off, his ball dropped in the
rough, and Paul began to pray. He told himself, now I'm really
getting it. This is happening to me because of what I've been
doing lately in my business. If I get out of the rough and win
this hole and the match, I'll straighten out for once and for all,
and stop this dirty business I've been involved in. By the time
he had gotten to where his ball was, the bargain had been
struck. The opponent made a long putt that wavered on the
edge of the cup and stayed out. Paul was feeling relaxed and
easy. He blasted off and came up onto the edge of the green.
He knew now he could do no wrong. Then his opponent
nudged his ball into the hole. Paul made a perfect putt and
sank his own. The score was tied. The last hole was the best
and smoothest Paul had ever played. He won the match by a
single point.

But the next day, of course, at business Paul was back to
his old tricks. The game was far from his thoughts. After that,
though, he was never very good at golf. Whenever the going
got tough, he would mess it up. He would know ahead of time
that he was going to do it, and it always worked out that way.
He knew it was because he had not kept his bargain.

There were quite a few more instances where Paul was
plagued. He revealed to me a series of events in which there
was always some irrational factor that was managing his life
for him in ways that he could not control. Always he saw the
punitive element coming from a source outside himself.

He was reminded of a time when he was playing poker.
Once he had gotten into a game which was really too big for

him. He did not have the courage to admit it to the other men, and so he played with them time and time again, often losing more than he could afford. On one particular day he dropped his hand down on the table, and when he picked it up he found that he had accidentally picked up six cards instead of five. He quickly discarded the one least likely to succeed. Quicker still were the eyes of the men playing with him, and he was thrown out of the game as a cheater. But he "knew" that "something" was forcing him out of a game he didn't belong in, and that he couldn't have stepped out by himself.

Paul had been born and raised a devout Catholic. As a child he had been taught that if he would pray, God would hear his prayers and answer them. But in order to get what he wanted from God he had to obey the rules that were set out by Mother and by the Church; if not, he would surely be punished. Though Mother was a faithful churchgoer, Father preferred to sleep on Sunday morning. Father didn't seem to be too concerned about the rules, he did just about as he pleased. That included staying out late quite often and coming home drunk, and paying very little attention to the needs of Paul and his brothers and sisters. If Paul wanted something he had to find his own ways of getting it. When he wanted money he would take it without asking from his parents' dressing table. When a dime was given to him for the collection plate he would pocket it and later spend it on himself at the candy store. But always with the uneasy feeling that something bad would happen to him for his misdeeds—and when on occasion something bad did happen, he "knew" that it had to happen. He could not escape the all-seeing eye of God. In later life, when he drifted away from the Church, the "eye" lost whatever benevolence it might once have had for him. It became the eye of the demon, with whom he might sometimes bargain but who would always exact his due. The demon would drive him, the demon would get in his way, the demon would watch him.

Jung had described the acute effects of the complex in one of his very early essays, "The Psychology of Dementia Praecox," written while he was still at Burghölzli. Recognizing that his concept of the complex was as yet in a very rudimentary phase, it is nevertheless interesting to see how he has caught the sensation associated with it, and how it comes across with much the same emotional tone as that expressed by Paul in the grip of his obsessional ideas. Jung wrote:

> Reality sees to it that the peaceful cycle of egocentric ideas is constantly interrupted by ideas with a strong feeling-tone, that is, by affects. A situation threatening danger pushes aside the tranquil play of ideas and puts in their place a complex of other ideas with a very strong feeling-tone. The new complex then crowds everything else into the background. For the time being it is the most distinct because it totally inhibits all other ideas; it permits only those egocentric ideas to exist which fit *its* situation, and under certain conditions it can suppress to the point of complete (momentary) unconsciousness all ideas that run counter to it, however strong they may be. It now possesses the strongest attention-tone.[10]

Over the years Jung made many advances in his complex theory. He developed a concept of psychic energy which he thought of as being analogous to the concept of physical energy in physics. "Modern psychology," he wrote in 1934, "has one thing in common with modern physics, that its method enjoys greater recognition than its subject. Its subject, the psyche, is so infinitely diverse in its manifestations, so indefinite and so unbounded, that the definitions given of it are difficult if not impossible to interpret . . ."[11] He goes on to say that the definitions which result from the methods of observation are much easier to derive. Out of his empirical research, observing many clinical cases, Jung recognized that a certain psychic condition interpolates itself between the subject (that is, the psyche) and the experiment, which one could call the "experimental situation." This "situation" could then jeopardize the whole experiment by *assimilating* not only the experimental procedure but also its purpose. By *assimilation*,

Jung meant "an attitude on the part of the subject, who misinterprets the experiment because he has at first an insuperable tendency to assume that it is, shall we say, an intelligence test or an attempt to take an indiscreet look behind the scenes."[12] Such an attitude on the part of the subject brings him to attempt to disguise the very process which the experimenter is trying to observe.

It was, therefore, of utmost importance that Jung's discovery of the complex came not as a result of looking directly for proof of a hypothesis that such a mechanism as the complex did indeed exist. Rather, the complex was discovered inadvertently, as the method of the association experiments was disturbed by the autonomous behavior of the psyche, that is, by assimilation of the apparent purpose of the experiment. Then it was that Jung discovered the *complex*, which had been registered before as a *failure to react*.

The discovery of how the complexes interweave in their nuclei the archetypal roots of the personality and the environmental stimuli, and then draw to themselves associated contents, made it evident to Jung on how weak a footing the old view stood—that it was possible to investigate *isolated* psychic processes. He asserted that there are no isolated psychic processes, just as there are no isolated life processes. "Only with the help of specially trained attention and concentration can the subject isolate a process so that it appears to meet the requirements of the experiment. But this is yet another 'experimental situation,' which differs from the one previously described only because this time the role of the assimilating complex is taken over by the conscious mind, whereas before this was done by more or less unconscious . . . complexes."[13]

Anyone who has become aware of the existence of a complex, and particularly of his own complex, cannot hold to the naïve assumption that consciousness is a unified structure functioning in an orderly manner. For that would mean that there would be no barrier between the will and the act, and that individuals would be able, invariably, to accomplish what they set out to do, unless purely external circumstances intervene. But who among us has not set forth in the morning with a task to do and nothing in the world, apparently, to stop us and returned at the end of the day with the task still undone? The unity of consciousness is frequently disturbed by intruders from the unconscious—they impede the intentions of the will, they disturb the memory, and they play all kinds of tricks, as we have seen.

Jung offers this definition of the feeling-toned complex:

> It is the *image* of a certain psychic situation which is strongly accentuated emotionally and is, moreover, incompatible with the habitual attitude of consciousness. This image has a powerful inner coherence, it has its own wholeness and, in addition, a relatively high degree of autonomy, so that it is subject to the control of the conscious mind to only a limited extent, and therefore behaves like an animated foreign body in the sphere of consciousness. The complex can usually be suppressed with an effort of will, but not argued out of existence, and at the first suitable opportunity it reappears in all its original strength.[14]

Here is an example of how the autonomous complex operates, and how the victim of it attempts by all possible means to escape it. Leroy was a corporation executive who had the responsibility of managing his company so that he would get the maximum possible amount of productivity out of his employees. Leroy was known to his associates as an extremely firm and determined man in his dealings, but still open to advice and counsel from the men in the company to whom he was directly responsible. He was an eminently successful businessman, clearly on his way to becoming the next president of his company. He was, however, constantly in a state of dissatisfaction with his work. He spent most of his spare time reading trade journals, calculating his investments in the stock market, conferring with subordinates, and in general attempting to improve his own abilities to handle his work. In the meantime his wife and family had the leavings of his wearying days.

The estrangement between himself and his wife, which was hardly noticeable to him, was suddenly brought into sharp focus when she told him that she was tired of being disregarded and used as a menial to grease the wheels of his smoothly functioning machine, and that she wanted to leave the marriage.

He hardly knew what had happened to him—after all he had done to provide her with material things, social status, and opportunities to follow her own interests. At the same time, he was vaguely aware that no matter how hard he worked there was always more to be done and no matter how much he studied there was more to be learned. He was running on an ever-faster-moving treadmill, and he was desperately tired. He knew that he needed help, and so he consulted an analyst.

In the first session Leroy told me that he had been extremely upset lately, that he was sleeping poorly and that his nights were full of dreams, and images that he could not be sure were dreams—maybe they were waking visions. He was especially disturbed about the latter. I reassured him that the visions were hypnagogic, which means that they come in the drowsiness that precedes sleep when the conscious defenses against the unconscious are down, and that they are quite common. Leroy had never discussed such matters with anyone, and consequently he was anxious and did not know what to make of them. I suggested that it might be worthwhile for us to talk about these experiences together, and that if he were to have such a vision before the next session, perhaps he would like to make a sketch of it and bring it in. He demurred, saying that he was no good at drawing, and I replied that I was not an art critic, but that his drawing might provide a good way to let me participate in those visions. It could be helpful in the process that we were undertaking, and also he might discover some things about himself that would be surprising. The last remark caught his fancy and when he arrived for the next session he had a picture with him.

Leroy was not sure whether it had been a dream or a vision, but he had sketched the picture. It showed a man high up and clinging to a poorly constructed tower made of loose stones fitted together. It looked as though he were trying to get away from something. But his foot slipped and knocked one of the stones out and it was falling. A woman was sitting at the base of the tower. More than likely the rock would fall on her head.

Since this was only the second session, we did not attempt to understand the dream too much, except that I asked him how he could imagine that the dream represented his life situation. It came out that he was really very worried about his business, and his whole life for that matter, because his business was his major concern. There were many unreliable people working for him; he had not been able to trust some of them. He suspected that many weaknesses and failures had been covered up by his employees for his benefit in order to show a promising balance sheet at the end of each year. He definitely felt that he was in a shaky position, and that the picture depicted what he had been unable to admit to himself. And he saw his wife as a potential victim of his instability.

At this point, I reflected, it might have been possible to have gone into the exploration of the tower as an image of himself and his own development, characterized by uncompleted tasks and haphazard habits. The woman at the bottom may have represented something of the not-yet-conscious other side of himself which was in jeopardy. But I did not know the analysand well enough yet to jump to any such conclusions, so we left the picture as something that we could ponder further, and that would, in the course of the analysis, probably take on deeper shades of meaning. I recognized that the motif of climbing, the one of the shaky foundation, and that of the damsel in distress were all archetypal themes well known in myth and legend, and that any one of them might point to the nucleus of a complex.

The next session with Leroy continued to set the stage for the drama which the analytic process would bring to light. It centered about a significant dream which I will report here with some of Leroy's comments.

The dream begins: *I am made a king. Everyone seems to be quite nice and accepting about it. It is connected with a church.*

Here he broke in to tell me, "I've never wanted to admit it, because it is a bit ugly, but this has always been a key word. My name is Leroy, which comes from *le roi*, which is French for 'king.' Although I was named after my grandfather, I always thought there was something fateful about it. I remember when I was quite young thinking I was going to be someone special. It seems my mother determined that her son was going to grow up to be a 'great man' of some kind. The extreme limit of this, I remember, came one day when I wondered if *I* was the next messiah.

"Maybe the church has something to do with the fact that in trying to be very much my father's son, in trying to be just exactly what he wanted me to be, I went to church with him (my mother was not religious in this sense) and became exceedingly religious at a very early age. I remember one birthday I was given money which I took and went, with my father of course, to a 'religious store' and spent the whole amount on religious items such as a big leather-bound Bible, pictures of Jesus, crosses, and such things. I was going to be a minister in those days."

I asked him if he ever has any feelings today that resemble those early memories he was speaking about.

"This feeling of being 'king' I still get," he replied. "I will be sitting with a group of people, usually strange people, perhaps in a business conference. I am not at ease with them, and I will suddenly notice that all of my attention is focused on myself. It is as if I am too big, or too *there*, as if I expect everybody else in the room to feel as I do, that I am the center of attention. Somehow I connect this feeling, which I find very uncomfortable, with earlier feelings of being the favorite child, destined for great things, admired by all my parents' friends. My parents would always make a big point of telling me when

somebody said what an admirable, outstanding boy I was—
and when I heard this I couldn't have been more pleased. It
seems this was my major goal in life at that time, impressing
upon everybody what a good boy I was: I mean good in every
sense of the word—good-looking, moral, hard-working, devoted to my parents, and so on. Even now, very often, I find
myself expecting to be better than other people." He hesitated,
and I waited. Then he continued, "Even now that I've admitted
I need help from you, I catch myself saying to myself, 'Well, in
the end, you *will* turn out just as you always expected. You will
learn about yourself, get straightened out, and still be a great
man.' "

He went on, "I mentioned the problem I have getting all
my work done the way I want it. When I am going at it too
hard I sometimes get a strange feeling in the pit of my stomach that says, 'You'd better stop right now if you know what's
good for you.' Maybe my work is the ladder by which I try to
climb to the top of the tower to be king."

I thought of the young woman sitting at the bottom of his
tower; and of him, oblivious to the fact that he has kicked
loose the stone that will fall on her head.

The dream continues: *I learn that Jack has secretly conceived a plot to kill me. He seemed nice like the rest but he was
plotting to kill me. He was only prevented from this by being
killed.* Jack is the head of a division in Leroy's business. He
had been rising rapidly. But he was doomed at the start, Leroy
told me, because he, Leroy, was not going to let anybody get
ahead of him, so he had handled this by giving Jack impossible tasks in which he was bound to fall short. Then Leroy
would miss no opportunity to point out these failures in the
company meetings.

I am king of a little principality at Waterford Road. [This is
the street where he grew up.] *It reminds me of a little French
court. I have my subjects and they dress up and have nice parties. I reign for some time and then the time comes for choosing
my successor. My subjects are playing a game whereby they are
trying to shoot me with a bow and arrow. I am trying to escape*

from them. I am afraid of them and I am trying to fly away from them, running behind the house, trying to fly up in the trees, but I am hard pressed.

I asked him about the flying, and he told me: "Ever since I can remember, this 'flying' has been an important part in my dreams. It always takes the same form. I flap my arms up and down as hard as I can, exerting the greatest possible effort, and am always barely able to rise in this fashion. I always make agonizingly slow progress, and I always know that if I stop flapping my arms just as hard as I can, I will fall to earth. Very often when I am doing this with all my effort, I don't move at all. These are the worst moments." He continued relating the dream: *Three of my subjects come after me from different directions. I have to flap my arms like crazy to make any progress. I am having a very hard time keeping clear of them. Finally I realize that the only way to avoid being caught or wounded by them is to disarm them. So taking a risk, I manage to get close enough to them, without getting hit, to disarm them. But others may be coming. I continue trying to fly around in this manner. I am above the front lawn, working at it like crazy, flapping my arms, barely able to keep in the air, only with great effort making any progress. Mitchell* [another executive in the firm] *comes along and I tell him he can be king. It seems there is an end to my confusion about who will be king. Then it seems as if the problem is not really solved. A lot of people want to be king and I haven't yet found anyone who would be really appropriate.*

Until now Leroy has tried to solve his problem in four ways. First he depended on his right of kingship, his authority, to maintain his regal position. Second, threatened, he tried to escape, using whatever resources he had readily at hand. Third, finding progress too slow, he decided to demolish the threatening agency. And fourth, knowing that he could not depend on destroying all opposition everywhere, he decided to maintain his authority by designating his successor. But this, also, did not seem to solve the problem.

The dream is not finished yet. *I fly up in the air with great*

*effort as usual, to the top of the house. I land on it and use it as
a resting place and push off on it on my trip to another section
of the house. There is much less effort to this mode of travel
through the air than trying to go wholly under my own power.*
Leroy now begins to make use of an existing structure, and he
gains some support and impetus from it, as he could not do
when he was isolating himself in mid-air and depending upon
his will alone.

*Then I see some trees in front of me and I decide to pull
them back and allow them to propel me through the air. I will
pull back a few of these locust trees. But their trunks have
thorns on them and as I reach them I am pricked in the right
hand by two thorns. They go into my fingers, through the gloves
I am wearing. For the moment I am chiefly concerned with finding out if the thorns broke off in my fingers (it seems they did
not) and if I am bleeding (not too much, it seems).*

*At this point I realize that there is only five minutes left in a
TV show before the end of which a new king must be chosen. In
a way I am desperate because no appropriate king has turned up
and I have assumed that it was up to me to pick him. The way
the deal works is that he walks up the road, or appears in some
other manner, and my subjects, all of whose attention is directed
to awaiting him and looking for him, would pounce on him and
choose him king.*

*Suddenly there is a big commotion in the yard. Someone has
come in at the last moment and been chosen king. I go down
and, lo and behold, he is quite appropriate though not whom I
had expected. In fact it seems I barely know him. But he will
make a good king.*

When Leroy turns to the trees for help he is actively reaching out beyond the limits of his own capacity, that is, his ego
functioning. No longer has he to find his deliverance all on his
own from "the pursuing demons who threaten his 'superiority'"; there is help from another source. Trees may be understood symbolically, and there is a whole literature on this. But
for our purpose here it is enough to say that the tree, with its
roots underground and its branches rising toward the sky,

symbolizes an upward trend and is therefore related to other symbols, such as the ladder and the tower, which stand for the general relationship between the "three worlds" (the lower world: the underworld, hell; the middle world: earth; the upper world: heaven). The three worlds of tree symbolism reflect the three main portions of the structure of the tree: roots, trunk and foliage. In its most general sense, the symbolism of the tree denotes the life of the cosmos: its consistency, growth, proliferation, generative and regenerative processes. All this, and especially the "three world" symbolism, must have been in the unconscious knowledge of the dreamer, given his religious background and the archetypal basis underlying it.[15]

But the particular tree selected by the dream itself, the locust tree, is significant on several counts. To be sure, the locust tree has spines, which could conceivably wound a person in the way that the dream suggests. The prick of the thorn awakens one to consciousness in many a fairy tale. Locust trees have very hard wood; they are resistant to injury and last a long time. They grow rapidly. They spread by means of suckers that spring from the roots, as well as by scattered seeds. So, like the rhizome that stays alive through the seasons while the blossoms perish, which seemed to Jung to be a metaphor for the continuity of unconscious processes in contrast to the transience of the conscious ones, locusts spread and grow from the activity under the earth's surface. All of this leads to the thought that the locust may be an agent of transformation, and this seems to be suggested in this dream. The idea is not new; it can be found in the Bible. When Moses was leading the children of Israel through the wilderness of Shur they were three days without water. And when they came to Marah they could not drink the waters of Marah for they were bitter, and people murmured against Moses. "And he cried to the Lord and the Lord showed him a tree, *a locust tree*, and he threw it into the waters, and the waters became sweet."[16]

As the dreamer, Leroy, was considering his wound, as he was trying to assess the results of getting help from something beyond his own ego, namely the locust tree, he suddenly realized that his time was nearly up. He was brought with a rush back toward the world of everyday consciousness—the TV show would soon be over, and that was all the time that was allowed. The dreamer was desperate, but only "in a way"—and that meant that his desperation was based on his assumption that he had to be the one man in control, and that nothing good could happen if he did not manage it. Suddenly he found out that this was not the way it was going to work but that destiny has its own way of determining who shall rule and who shall lay down the scepter.

When the time was right, the appropriate person arrived and was chosen king. It was not that Leroy did it, and it was not whom he expected. In fact Leroy hardly knew him. But he did know that he would make a good king.

The complex which had Leroy was clearly delineated by the dream. It was a power-complex, pressing on him the feeling that by reason of his birth—and his name was his birthright—he was entitled to be and expected to be in a controlling position. This nucleus, "the kingship idea," had conditioned much of his behavior from early childhood. As the years went by, in his religious fantasies with their messianic flavor, in his successes in social situations and at school and later in his business, one incident after another supported his tendency to dominate every situation, to relate to others sometimes benevolently, sometimes tyrannically, but inevitably to support his image of himself as the superior man. And all the time, on the unconscious side, he was haunted by the fear that he must be sorely inferior to the expectations he had for himself, and to those he evoked in those who knew him. How difficult life must have become for this man who felt required to carry such heavy burdens!

If the dream points the way to the origin of the complex, it also offers an attitude which could be helpful in coming to terms with the complex. In fact, the dream suggests much that will be worked through in the course of the analysis, for it is one thing to see what needs to be done and quite another to shift lifelong attitudes and alter ways of thinking and consequently ways of behaving. The purposive aspect of the dream is the indication that too often the dreamer attempts to function out of his ego, by his will alone. He must learn that when his ego, his will, is out of harmony with the demands of nature or destiny or biology in the broad sense or, if you will, the cosmic rhythm that some call God; if he is out of harmony with that, he cannot prevail. So, when the feeling comes that what he is doing at tremendous cost and effort is getting him nowhere, then he must respect the nature of things outside his own will and control, and allow them to help him. And finally, when all else fails, he must be willing simply to "let it happen," and then the end which he had formerly pursued in the most energetic and hopeless way now is easily and simply achieved. *I barely know him. But he will make a good king.* This dream helped to show the way for Leroy to trust and pay attention to the wisdom of the unconscious. It was possible, then, for the analysis to move on.

The unconscious contains that portion of the human potential which needs to be actualized in order for individuals to move toward *individuation*, that is, toward becoming whatever they are innately capable of being. As such it is the *Ur-grund* of our being, the *original basis* from which everything valuable may develop. At the same time, its mysterious depths hold strange shapes, which emerge at times to frighten us, as they have done since the dawn of human consciousness. The world of the unconscious, as seen in its collective and mythological dimensions, has long been a theme of Mircea Eliade, historian of religion, and friend of Jung. Eliade explains the mystique so often associated with the unconscious, the unknown, as follows:

> In archaic and traditional societies, the surrounding world is conceived as a microcosm. At the limits of this closed world begins the domain of the unknown, of the formless. On this side there is ordered—because inhabited

and organised—space; on the other, outside this familiar space, there is the unknown and dangerous region of the demons, the ghosts, the dead and of foreigners—in a word, chaos or death or night. This image of an inhabited microcosm, surrounded by desert regions regarded as a chaos or a kingdom of the dead, has survived even in highly evolved civilisations such as those of China, Mesopotamia and Egypt.[17]

Jung would insist that the images of archaic man are much closer to the European and American psyche of the twentieth century even than Eliade had admitted in the preceding paragraph. He tells us in his essay on "Archaic Man"[18] that "it is not only primitive man whose psychology is archaic. It is the psychology also of modern, civilised man. . . . Every civilised human being, however high his conscious development, is still an archaic man at the deeper levels of his psyche."[19] He describes various customs practiced by natives in their rituals and ceremonies, as he observed them in his travels to the interior of the African continent. The aborigines he met disclaimed any awareness of particular significance of their acts, including their intercourse with ghosts, ancestral spirits, and the like. Jung was unwilling to allow that their ways of thinking, their taking for granted what seems so strange to us, are really as foreign as we would like to believe. He illustrates his contention with a hypothetical case:

> Now let us suppose that I am a total stranger in Zurich and have come to this city to explore the customs of the place. First I settle down on the outskirts near some suburban homes, and come into neighbourly contact with their owners. I then say to Messrs. Müller and Meyer: "Please tell me something about your religious customs." Both gentlemen are taken aback. They never go to church, know nothing about it, and emphatically deny that they practise any such customs. It is spring, and Easter is approaching. One morning I surprise Mr. Müller at a curious occupation. He is

busily running about the garden, hiding coloured eggs and
setting up peculiar rabbit idols. I have caught him *in
flagrante.* "Why did you conceal this highly interesting ceremony from me?" I ask him. "What ceremony?" he retorts.
"This is nothing. Everybody does it at Eastertime." "But
what is the meaning of these idols and eggs, and why do you
hide them?" Mr. Müller is stunned. He does not know, any
more than he knows the meaning of the Christmas-tree. And
yet he does these things, just like a primitive..Did the distant
ancestors of the Elgonyi know any better what they were
doing? It is highly improbable. Archaic man everywhere
does what he does, and only civilized man knows what he
does.[20]

It must be added that "archaic man" exists within every
living person today, just as does "civilized man." To the degree
that the non-rational motivates behavior, our functioning is
characterized as archaic, and to the degree that the rational
functions predominate, we are said to be functioning in a civilized way. I hasten to add that I have no intention of placing a
value judgment either on archaism or on civilization with its
material and technological progress. Rather, I am attempting
to differentiate between these two strands in the organization
of the human psyche, which co-exist irrespective of time or
place.

Since psychotherapists are aware of hidden individual differences which may be at the base of psychological disturbances, it is necessary for them to approach patients in terms
of their own ways of being, if the two are to meet on any
common ground at all. The psychotherapist must gently encourage and go along with the patient to seek out the complexes, fully prepared to find in the place of the expected complexes apparitions resembling demons and other strange
spirits. This attitude made it possible for me to share some
strange experiences with a young widow, Matilda.

The first few analytic sessions did not disclose the real
nature of the underlying complexes. Matilda was severely de-

pressed but she was not suicidal; she appeared much too passive for that. Rather, her mood was more one of utter disgust with the world in general. It was a vague, diffuse feeling; she lacked interest in nearly everything she was doing. Matilda was only twenty-three years old. Her husband had been killed in an automobile accident a year ago, after they had been married only four months. She was now about twenty pounds overweight, careless of her appearance, apathetic in manner, presenting a generally unattractive impression, although her features were basically good. She had suffered a great deal and was still suffering over her husband's death. She told me that she regarded it as a completely senseless and horrible accident of fate. She said that there was no way of understanding it or accepting it; that the whole thing was pointless, and it proved to her that life, itself, was utterly pointless.

No, there could not possibly be any sense to it. She could not look to God for help, as some well-meaning friends had advised her to do. She could not believe in God. She could not believe there was anybody up there pulling the strings, determining what would happen to a person. She could not believe that there was any such thing as destiny. Things happened by mere chance. Everything was a kind of random accident. There was no use trying to exert effort or will; you had no control anyhow. Life was a series of aimless events. Such was Matilda's conscious attitude when she came to me.

I let her know that I accepted her attitude as being a reasonable one in the face of what had recently happened to her, also because of earlier events in her life which had led her to reject various forms of authority, including that of the fundamentalist Protestant religion in which she had been reared as a young child. But I asked her if she could see that her attitude must be unconstructive, because it is impossible to build any structure, psychic or otherwise, unless there is purpose, plan and wider view. I suggested that purpose depended on finding some meaning in life, and I suggested, in this connection, that she read a little classic by Viktor Frankl titled *Man's Search for Meaning*. In this book Frankl had written of his experiences as a Jew imprisoned in a Nazi concentration camp. He had observed that some of the internees submitted to their fate and were led without a fight to the gas chambers. Others, however, used every wily device and trick imaginable, and stretched their endurance to the utmost, so that in one amazing way or another a considerable number of these latter managed to survive. Those who lived through the darkness of the abyss were the ones, Frankl observed, who had been able to find some meaning or mission in their lives, some purpose for which they felt they were intended to live. They were impelled by a sense of destiny, and with that sense they would not or could not break faith.

In the particular session that enabled her to bring forth secrets from her hidden depths, Matilda began talking about Frankl's book. It was clear that her feelings were ambivalent. She began by saying that there were some things about the book that she liked very much, but then she quickly switched to a critical attitude toward the author's "faith" in something "supernatural." She said that she could not go along with his attributing the internees' ability to survive to a notion of something moving them outside of their own energies, that is to say, outside of their personal courage and determination. The idea of something being "arranged" ahead of time collided with her "rational" views, namely that all events depended on prior cause. She could not see that there were times when an anticipation of the future could affect events or behavior in the present. She seemed so centered in her pragmatic attitude that I felt the need to ask her whether she had ever had a dream that took her beyond her world of palpable reality. Oh yes, she announced almost with embarrassment, there had been this dream that had recurred several times: *I dream that I am standing in among the trees. There is nothing in sight except fields and trees. I walk up to the top of a hill and as I stand there I look up at the sky and all of a sudden the universe starts parading in front of me. All the planets come within touching distance. The sound of the wind is like choral music.*

It was clear to me that this had been a particularly moving

dream for her, for she brightened in the telling of it. I asked her if she had experienced anything like a sense of awe when the planets had come "within touching distance." She replied that she had had a feeling that it was glorious, but not awe. The gloriousness came from seeing that Saturn was so luminous that she could see it with all the rings around it, and all the other planets, just this tremendous sense of nearness. But *awe*, that was an expression reserved for a fear of God, but she didn't see God in this—she felt that this was nature, that the entire experience was wholly natural and she had felt very good about it, but insisted that any sense of awe was lacking.

There was little more to be said about the dream, and we fell into a period of silence. I sensed that the recollection of this dream had led her thoughts onto something else. She seemed hesitant to speak, she almost began once or twice, and finally, "There was another dream. I dreamed it over a year ago."

The dream occurred shortly after her marriage. At this time she was a child care worker in a home for delinquent children, a job which necessitated her staying overnight at the home once or twice a week. It was on one of those nights at her place of work, she dreamed: *I receive a phone call one night about 10:30. It is a Michigan State policeman. He tells me that Bill has been in an automobile accident, and is dying. He is in a Grand Rapids hospital. The rest of the dream concerns my attempts to get transportation to Grand Rapids in time. There are no commercial planes going, a cab can't take me, and none of the staff that are on duty have cars. I am attempting to rent a private plane when I wake up.*

The dream had upset her so much that she had told her mother about it at the time. The mother could verify what she said.

About two months after this dream, the patient's husband was indeed killed in an automobile accident. She was called by the state police and told that he was dying. She was sleeping in the children's home at the time, and she had great difficulty in getting transportation to the hospital where he had been taken. There were no commercial planes. There were no private cars available where she worked. She had to argue with someone from a taxi company and finally was able to get a driver to take her to the place. The only difference between dream and reality was the location of the accident; the direction was the same but the distance was less.

Matilda told me that this apparently precognitive dream had weighed heavily on her and that she couldn't get it out of her mind. And since then, whenever she had a dream in which a tragedy took place, she got uncontrollably anxious. It was her recurrent anxiety that had led her to seek psychiatric help a short time before she came to me. It hadn't worked out and she had terminated the therapeutic relationship.

I asked her whether any particular event or circumstance had precipitated her getting to the psychiatrist at that time. She answered, "Yes."

"A couple of months after Bill's death," she told me, "I was in the hospital giving blood to replace some of what Bill had needed. While the blood was being taken I realized that something was going wrong. I felt that there had been some kind of interruption, I had the feeling that the blood was coagulating, that a blood clot was forming, and that it was moving toward my heart. I felt that I was going to die, and it seemed very easy just to give up and let go. But I called the nurse and she quickly removed the needle. I felt very faint and shaky. After some black coffee I felt better physically, but the feeling of letting go of life stayed with me. It preyed on my mind so much that I thought I had better see a psychiatrist, and a couple of weeks later I did just that.

"Naturally I told him the dream which had so accurately predicted Bill's death. He questioned me about my relationship with Bill and discovered that, like any marriage, it had had its imperfections. He announced his conclusion, which was that unconsciously I had really wanted to see Bill dead. The dream, according to him, was a manifestation of a death wish. I couldn't accept that," she said most emphatically, "because the dream was too close to what actually happened. His typical Freudian explanation just didn't seem to fit."

"If that doesn't explain it, then what do *you* think may have been behind your experience?" I asked Matilda.

"I allow very much for the possibility of precognition, or ESP." Now it all began to come out. "I don't understand it, but I have studied the experiments of Dr. Rhine at Duke University and I have been forced to recognize that I've had those kinds of experiences too. Ghosts? I don't know if I believe in ghosts, but . . . let me tell you this . . . a week after Bill died, when I was very, very upset, some friends came to visit. As I was talking with them I began to get really involved emotionally. All of a sudden a stack of dishes rattled loudly. There was no physical reason for the rattling. The stack had been sitting in the sink all evening, but at this particular moment they rattled. I don't know what to make of it."

Getting all wound up now in her narrative, Matilda continued. She talked about an old lady who had been a neighbor of hers, who had been sickly, and whom she had visited from time to time in her home. A few months before the incident, this old lady had been taken to a nursing home, which was on the road that Matilda took each day as she drove to work. For several days she had been thinking that she ought to stop by and see the woman, but she was always in a hurry, or had errands to do, and so kept putting it off. Suddenly one morning as she passed the nursing home she felt the strongest impulse pulling at her and saying, "I must go and see her, I have to go and see her." She had already gone by the nursing home, but now she backed up, stopped the car, went up and knocked on the door. There she was told, when she asked for her friend, that she was too late, the old lady had died that very night.

Then she recounted another experience—Bill had once said to her, out of the blue, "You know, Cartwright is dead." Cartwright had been a good friend in another city whom they had not seen or heard from in several months. A few days after that they learned that Cartwright had suffered a fatal heart attack, and at almost exactly the time Bill had felt like saying, "Cartwright is dead."

I have not yet found any explanation for these kinds of experiences that satisfies me, and therefore I had no easy answers for Matilda. I found it particularly interesting that all of this came out after she had firmly declared herself against any explanations of behavior or experience that could not be tested and validated biologically or physically. She had, in reading Frankl's book, attributed to him a belief in "supernatural forces," although the book had not actually made any such assertion. I had to understand her "disbelief" as being her way of avoiding dealing with something that she knew was of a certain kind of reality, even though she did not know the nature of that reality. I could see that she had left her Freudian therapist very much as Jung had left Freud long ago, when Jung had brought his "mystical speculations" to Freud and Freud had refused to take them seriously, in fact, had gone to great lengths to explain them away.

Jung did not feel that everything had either to be explained or else left outside the boundaries of scientific investigation. He preferred to deal with the mysteries in whatever way he could, and often his way was to speak in metaphors, to take psychic experiences as though they were palpable realities, and speak of them "as though." He was able "to image" concepts, and if this is imagination then it is out of imagination that reality emerges. William Blake tells us in one of his Proverbs: "What is now true was once only imagin'd."

The imagination, the ability to form an image of something one has not yet seen, appears to be a universal quality which may be enjoyed by everyone. Unwilling to recognize the possibility of perceiving what does not stem directly from the senses, Matilda had become a victim of a complex centered around a deification of rationality and the conscious will. She could not go beyond the limit of sense perception; she could not risk the belief that some things were not only beyond her understanding, but even beyond the possibility of understanding. In her effort to sustain her faith in faithlessness, she had constantly repressed the awareness of the non-rational in her life. And so the denial-of-the-mystical complex had grown, drawing to itself more and more inexplicable contents with which she refused to deal. Far from being forgotten, they acted as magnets, attracting her energies and keeping them from more productive channels. Hence the deepening depression, the sensation of loss of energy, the absence of any enthusiasm for life. All this was expressed by her statement, "It's not that I want to die, it's just that I see no reason to go on living."

For me, Jung's explication of the complex makes the cases of Matilda and the others more comprehensible. He also clarified the correspondence between complexes and demons:

> The personal unconscious . . . contains complexes that belong to the individual and form an intrinsic part of his psychic life. When any complex which ought to be associated with the ego becomes unconscious, either by being repressed or by sinking below the threshold, the individual experiences a sense of loss. Conversely, when a lost complex is made conscious again, for instance through psychotherapeutic treatment, he experiences an increase of power. Many neuroses are cured in this way.[21]

So far, Jung and Freud were in agreement in their view of the complex. But here is where Jung entered unfamiliar territory:

> . . . when, on the other hand, a complex of the collective unconscious becomes associated with the ego, i.e., becomes conscious, it is felt as strange, uncanny, and at the same time fascinating. At all events the conscious mind falls under its spell, either feeling it as something pathological, or else being alienated by it from normal life. The association of a collective content with the ego always produces a state of alienation, because something is added to the individual's consciousness which ought really to remain unconscious, that is, separated from the ego. . . . The irruption of these

alien contents is a characteristic symptom marking the onset of many mental illnesses. The patients are seized by weird and monstrous thoughts, the whole world seems changed, people have horrible, distorted faces, and so on.[22]

To this Jung added the following qualifying footnote:

Those who are familiar with this material will object that my description is one-sided, because they know that the archetype, the autonomous collective content, does not have only the negative aspect described here. I have merely restricted myself to the common symptomatology that can be found in every text-book of psychiatry, and to the equally common defensive attitude toward anything extraordinary. Naturally the archetype also has a positive numinosity . . .

He went on to differentiate personal complexes from collective complexes:

While the contents of the personal unconscious are felt as belonging to one's own psyche, the contents of the collective unconscious seem alien, as if they came from outside. The reintegration of a personal complex has the effect of release and often of healing, whereas the invasion of a complex from the collective unconscious is a very disagreeable and even dangerous phenomenon. The parallel with the primitive belief in souls and spirits is obvious: souls correspond to the autonomous complexes of the personal unconscious, and spirits to those of the collective unconscious. We, from the scientific standpoint, prosaically call the awful beings that dwell in the shadows of the primeval forests "psychic complexes." Yet if we consider the extraordinary role played by the belief in souls and spirits in the history of mankind, we cannot be content with merely establishing the existence of such complexes, but must go rather more deeply into their nature.[23]

The cases I have used as examples of complexes and their effects on behavior illustrate the contemporary importance of going more deeply into the ramifications of Jung's complex theory. These examples show how the complex works in the life of the individual. The complexes of the collective unconscious have far-reaching effects which go beyond the experience of the individual, affecting groups of all kinds within a given society. All social movements could probably be understood from the standpoint of the factor which Jung has called "the autonomous complex arising out of the collective unconscious."

3

From Associations to Archetypes

...

WHEN JUNG EXPLORED the implications of his discoveries about the complex, he often was able to trace its origin to some experience in the life of the patient which made a deep and shocking impression, so painful that it could not be endured for long in consciousness. The mechanism of repression helped to insulate the wounded psyche from the source of the pain so that it could continue functioning. Sometimes a loss of feeling occurred, for repression is a kind of psychological anaesthetic, but when there is great suffering an anaesthetic serves a purpose. It leaves the wound untouched, but the patient is able to tolerate it.

Jung's work on the Association Experiment led him to reread Freud's *Interpretation of Dreams*, a book which he had put aside a year or two before. Now it was suddenly a revelation to him, for he recognized that in his work on dreams the father of psychoanalysis had come upon the concept of repression from an entirely different direction, but that his understanding of the mechanism was almost identical with his own. Much of what was new to Jung and had derived from his work with schizophrenic patients at Burghölzli had already been formulated by the older man.

This discovery led Jung to follow Freud's work avidly, and to introduce the study of psychoanalysis to the clinic where he worked. Jung even started a study group on Freud among his professional colleagues. Bleuler followed this trend in Jung's work with interest, if with some reservations. In time a correspondence began between Jung and Freud, which culminated in an invitation for Jung to visit Freud, and eventually full participation by Jung in the Vienna circle of psychoanalysts. Even before the first personal meeting between the two men had occurred, Jung was writing articles supporting the new psychoanalytical findings.

In 1905, Jung was named to the position of lecturer in psychiatry at the University of Zurich; the same year he became senior physician at the psychiatry clinic. His published works on association and dementia praecox (as schizophrenia was then called) were beginning to advance his status at the University. At this time Freud was definitely *persona non grata* in academic circles, and any connection with Freud would have been damaging to Jung in scientific circles.

I find it ironic, in looking back from the perspective of all that followed, to realize that at the very beginning of their association Jung was an up-and-coming member of the psychiatric establishment, firmly based in respectable scientific research, while Freud was considered a man of highly speculative theories which were mentioned surreptitiously if at all by "important people." Jung could easily have published his own work without mention of Freud. But in 1906, at a congress in Munich where a lecturer discussed obsessional neurosis but carefully avoided mention of Freud's work in this area, Jung decided to take a stand. In connection with the incident he wrote a paper for the *Münchener Medizinische Wochenschrift* on Freud's theory of the neuroses, which had contributed greatly to the understanding of obsessional neurosis.[1] Two German professors wrote in response to the article that if Jung continued to defend Freud he would be endangering his academic career. The learned professors' threats did not deter Jung, once he had taken his stand.

A decade later, when the Freud-Jung friendship had reached its apogee, then deteriorated and finally disintegrated with Jung's withdrawal from the psychoanalytic movement, Freud was in his full maturity and recognized as a giant in the world of psychology. At this time Jung was routinely being dismissed as a speculative philosopher who was incapable of loyalty to the psychoanalytic establishment. He was roundly criticized from that time on for "lack of scientific objectivity," and the Freudians studiously ignored him.

But we anticipate. The early relations between Freud and Jung were extremely cordial. It is reported that on the day of their first meeting, in Vienna in 1907, the two men who had been following each other's work so closely held a conversation which lasted for thirteen hours!

One of the effects of this mutual conversation, as Jung reviewed in his writings many years later, was his realization that sexuality had for Freud an emotional commitment that made it a central principle with the quality nearly of a religion for him. With respect to this subject, Jung found that Freud's normal skepticism and critical manner were not applied. This was the keystone upon which his whole theory was balanced; it must be upheld at any cost. With respect to the elaborations on the various aspects of his theory, Freud was able to elucidate each point with great clarity and precision. His logical structure was highly credible, and especially for the neophyte in the field it was nearly impervious to challenge. Once certain basic premises were established, they could be extended indefinitely to cover almost all psychological phenomena. His conclusions were definite and technical; they led to a method of treatment with specific techniques through which it could be carried out.

Jung's approach, in contrast to Freud's, was relatively vague, yet this permitted him to be more comprehensive in his view of the nature of man. Perhaps Freud attributed this to the fact that Jung was still in the early stages of his psychological development, his ideas not anywhere near to being fully formed. The passage of time was to show that Jung's focus of interest would tend to be in the direction of symbolization and through the symbol toward the essence of meaning. He would not be nearly so bound by concrete data and material facts as was Freud, but would lean more heavily on intangible factors in his search for meaning. Furthermore, Jung was essentially a man of religion, although he had left far behind the rather narrow fundamentalistic approach of his parson father as he, the son, immersed himself in the discipline of scientific and medical education. His early childhood, lived under the shadow of the church steeple, with all its mysteries attending the transformative experiences of life—birth, confirmation, marriage and death—had not failed to establish certain patterns in his thinking. His world was full of unseen forces, which could only be known through their manifestations.

For Jung, questions of the spirit were of highest importance. By "spirit" he did not mean the supernatural, but rather those higher aspirations which are so much a part of man's striving, whether they are expressed in works of art, in service to one's fellow man, or in attempting to understand the workings of nature and her order. He expressed the feeling that Freud was resistant to some of these impulses in himself, as he heard Freud saying that expressions of spirituality were to be suspected as stemming from repressed sexuality. "Anything that could not be directly interpreted as sexuality, he referred to as 'psychosexuality,'" Jung said of Freud. And Jung had protested that such an attitude, if carried to its logical conclusion, would place a dubious value on the achievements of human culture—a statement to which Freud unhesitatingly assented. Jung asked, "Could culture be construed as the morbid consequence of repressed sexuality?" Freud had replied, "Yes, so it is, and that is just a curse of fate against which we are powerless to contend."[2] Jung was not altogether impressed with Freud's pansexualism but at the same time he did recognize the enormous importance of opening up the sexual area as a possible way of approaching the sources of the patient's neurosis.

In the main, Jung was fully in agreement with Freud's basic principles, despite his questions about Freud's emphasis. Jung's own strong feeling was that there existed a whole tremendous area of psychic functioning which Freud recognized but did not fully accommodate into his psychological theory. Both men affirmed that the unconscious was a hypothetical entity which could be inferred from material that came to consciousness in an incomplete form, leaving a trail of ideas and experiences which could not easily be explained or understood. This material could arise in the form of dreams or slips of speech, bungled actions, or in superstition or errors, as Freud had pointed out in *The Psychopathology of Everyday Life*. It could also be seen in disturbances of association and in complex behavior, as Jung had shown in his *Studies in Word Association*.

Freud's chief, though not exclusive, interest in the unconscious came from his observance of its manifestations in his analytical work with patients. His investigations into the unconscious were methodical. Starting from the symptoms of his neurotic patients in their daily life situations, and also from their dreams, he inferred the unconscious as an unknown and hidden area where reality was cleverly concealed by an elaborate system of defense mechanisms. Freud had conceptualized the unconscious as being composed of two basic kinds of contents. The first part of that unconscious reality, which Freud called the *id*, is associated with the instinctual drives which are innate or *in potentia* at birth. Freud's sexual theory gave primacy to those drives which stem from the infantile need for gratification—a need which, he thought, is essentially sexual in its nature.

Posed against the *id* is the second aspect of unconscious reality, and this Freud called the *superego*. This refers to that part of the unconscious which arises not from within the human organism itself, but derives rather from the environment.

It has its origin in the standards of behavior and attitudes of thought which are imposed from earliest infancy by the parents and later by the agents of the culture in which the child is raised—namely his friends and relatives, his church and school, and then the traditions of his community and the culture at large. Insofar as the assimilation of these directives is conscious they fall under the category of learning, and are dealt with in the process of ordinary rational thinking. But much of what the environment imposes upon the individual is subliminally perceived and assimilated to the unconscious, so that the individual finds himself possessed of a value system and of certain kinds of expectations, hopes, beliefs, and prejudices, with very little idea of how they were arrived at. Indeed, the unconscious value system with its consequent expectations form a structure which then appears to the individual as part of his very being—as stemming from within himself. This psychic structure is the *superego*. Its unspoken rules come into play to exercise a restricting and controlling effect on the instinctive side, the *id*, thus giving rise to conflicts which are carried on in the unconscious and become apparent only as they interfere with the natural, relaxed, and productive functioning of the individual.

These two elements of the unconscious come into active confrontation very early in the life of the infant, perhaps as early as the beginnings of the emergence of the *ego*, the sense of being a separate entity, something different and discrete from the mother, set adrift in an alien world when the warm arms and nourishing breast are taken away. The various cries of infancy demand that the child express its instinctive needs in one way or another. These instinctive needs are accepted in the beginning by the parents as natural, but there comes a time when the rules of the household and the expectations of the parents or parental surrogates begin to be felt as inhibitory controls of the instinctual component. These rules and expectations are transmitted much more through unconscious channels than through active directives. There is an unconscious learning process going on constantly, in which children learn much more by tone of voice, manner of touching or not touching, the subtle quality of the attention they receive, the general atmosphere among the people with whom they are in contact, than they ever do by what they are actually told.

The central problem of infancy, as Freud had identified it, stemmed from the attachment of the young child to the parent of the opposite sex, with all of the sexual overtones, since gratification was to Freud essentially sexual in nature. This attachment, countered as it was with the fear of reprisal from the parent of the child's own sex, placed the child in a bind where to feel close was to invite punishment, but not to feel close was to invite alienation, which was also something to be dreaded. This resulted, of course, in the well-known oedipal dilemma.

Jung did not disagree with any of this, in fact he wrote several articles discussing the theory of infantile sexuality as it related to Freud's theory of dream interpretation. He even decided to follow Freud's methods explicitly in his own practice, for it was his opinion that only another analyst could properly study and evaluate the hypotheses put forth by the founder of psychoanalysis.

When Jung began to concern himself with child development, he started from the Freudian point of view by examining the so-called "incest wish" which occupies so central a place in psychoanalysis. He wrote to Freud in 1912, "I started out expecting that I would be able to confirm the established concept of incest, and had to see that it is different from what I thought."[3] Far from being blind to the "superhuman struggles of the child to effect a compromise between the compelling force of the primitive instincts and the growing harshness of reality," Jung's background in archaeology and anthropology had led him to an awareness of those primitive forces, and to a recognition that they are not purely individual drives or isolated propensities, but are rather collective in nature, shared aspects of the general human condition. Thus he came to regard the neuroses and psychoses of childhood as universal phenomena, and he saw them in a different perspective from that of Freud.

In exploring how the hypothesis of the unconscious could be enlarged to include Freud's discoveries as well as phenomena that seemed to be outside of their scope, Jung began his own investigation of psychic images and ideas. He carefully observed his own dreams and those of his patients, paying particular attention to those features which did not appear to refer to actual experiences in the life of the dreamer. He also analyzed the fantasies and delusions of the insane, and he engrossed himself in the study of comparative religion and mythology. Noting that similar images and myth motifs could be found in widely separated places all over the earth, and at different periods throughout the history of mankind, he came to a decisive insight: that *the unconscious is at its basis collective in character*, that is, it is composed of contents that are universal in their nature. He wrote: "From the unconscious there emanate determining influences . . . which, independently of tradition, guarantee in every single individual a similarity and even a sameness of experience, and also of the way it is represented imaginatively. One of the main proofs of this is the almost universal parallelism between mythological motifs . . ."[4] The unconscious, therefore, contained a wealth of potentialities for image formation, and this could lead to the creation of new ideas and positive personality development.

Jung pointed out how Freud had shown in a little essay on Leonardo da Vinci[5] that Leonardo was influenced in later life by the fact that he had two mothers. This was real enough in Leonardo's life, but the idea of double descent has played an important role in the lives of other artists as well. But beyond this, double descent is a mythological motif, occurring over and over again in the lives of legendary heroes. Sometimes it is two mothers, sometimes two fathers, and sometimes two sets of parents. Otto Rank, a colleague of Jung and Freud in the Vienna circle, had developed this idea in his book *The Myth of the Birth of the Hero*[6] published in 1909. In brief: the hero is the son of parents of the highest station, his conception takes place under difficulties, and there is a portent in a dream or oracle connected with the child's birth. The child is

then sent away or exposed to extreme danger. He is rescued by
people of humble station, or by helpful animals, and reared by
them. When grown he rediscovers his noble parentage after
many adventures and, overcoming all obstacles in his path,
becomes at last recognized as the hero and attains fame and
greatness. The best known, as mentioned in this series, are
Sargon of Agade, Moses, Cyrus, and Romulus; and Rank has
enumerated many others to whom the same story applies either as a whole or in part: Oedipus, Karna, Paris, Telephos,
Perseus, Heracles and Gilgamesh. To the list we would surely
add Sri Krishna and Christ.

Freud had contended that the inner source of the myth
was the so-called "family romance" of the child, in which the
son reacts to the change in his inner relationship to his parents, and especially to his father. He theorized that the child's
first years are governed by a grandiose estimate of the father,
and that later on, under the influence of the disappointments
and rivalry within the family, the child becomes more critical
of his parents. He then concluded that the two families in the
myth, the noble one and the humble one, represent images of
the parents as they appear to the child at successive periods in
his development.[7]

Jung could not accept as complete this view of the unconscious sources of universal mythological motifs, or *mythologems*, as the core elements of myth are called. He had, after
all, subjected the hypothesis of the unconscious as put forth
by Freud, to exacting tests by using the psychoanalytic
method on his own patients. And, in the process, from many
separate investigations it became increasingly clear to Jung
that *the psychopathology of the neuroses and of many psychoses
could not dispense with the hypothesis of the collective unconscious*. It was the same with dreams. In dreams, in neurotic
fantasies, and in the hallucinations of psychoses, Jung saw
numerous linked ideas to which he could find parallels only in
mythological associations of ideas, that is, in mythologems. If
his thorough investigations had shown that in the majority of
such cases it was merely forgotten or repressed material, he

would not have gone to the trouble of making extensive researches into individual and collective parallels in legend and comparative religions. But, he wrote, "typical mythologems were observed among individuals to whom all knowledge of this kind absolutely was out of the question, and where indirect derivation from religious ideas that might have been known to them, or from popular figures of speech was impossible."[8] Jung asserted that such conclusions forced him to assume that he must be dealing with "myth-forming" structural elements in the unconscious psyche which produced out of themselves revivals of these mythologems, independent of all tradition. These products were "never (or at least very seldom) myths with a definite form, but rather mythological components which, because of their typical nature, we can call 'motifs,' 'primordial images,' types, or—as I have named them—*archetypes*."[9]

These archetypes represented certain regularities, consistently recurring types of *situations* and types of *figures*. Jung categorized them in such terms as "the hero's quest," "the battle for deliverance from the mother," "the night-sea journey," and called them archetypal situations. He suggested designations for archetypal figures also, for example, the divine child, the trickster, the double, the old wise man, the primordial mother. Of archetypal situations and figures Jung makes his meaning clear in a footnote to his discussion: "To the best of my knowledge, no other suggestions [for archetypes] have been made so far. Critics have contented themselves with asserting that no such archetypes exist. Certainly they do not exist, any more than a botanical system exists in nature! But will anyone deny the existence of natural plant-families on that account? Or will anyone deny the occurrence and continual repetition of certain morphological and functional similarities? It is much the same thing in principle with the typical figures of the unconscious. They are forms existing *a priori*, or biological norms of psychic activity."[10]

The great primordial images, as Jacob Burckhardt once aptly called them, give evidence of the inherited powers of human imagination as it was from time immemorial. Jung believed that this inheritance accounts for the phenomenon that certain motifs from myths and legends repeat themselves the world over in nearly identical forms. He also found in it an explanation of why his mental patients were able to reproduce the same images and associations that could be discovered in ancient texts. He has given innumerable examples of these textual parallels with the fantasy life of modern patients in *Symbols of Transformation*, and in other places.[11]

It was Jung's understanding that *the archetypes, as structural forming elements in the unconscious, gave rise both to the fantasy lives of individual children and to the mythologies of a people.* Unlike Freud, who had early asserted that the fantasies of children stemmed entirely from their personal experiences in confrontations with their own parents, and the conflicts between instinct and the controls imposed by the parents, Jung formulated the concept of the archetypes as preformed patterns of thinking into which the child's actual experiences fell, and through which the resulting childhood fantasies were given their shape. Freud had asserted that the myth forms were reflections of children's experiences somehow transferred to an entire people, along with their attending fantasies. But Jung, in what appears to be a more parsimonious explanation, saw the myth as a collective version of the emergence of the archetypal expression into a society, just as he saw fantasy as the emergence of the archetypal configuration in the individual.

The archetype, according to Jung, is a dominant of the collective unconscious. In order to comprehend the role of the archetype, therefore, it will be necessary to see how Jung conceived the collective unconscious. This is an extremely important issue, in which Jung has gone beyond Freud in viewing the scope of the unconscious—an issue which is crucial in its application in the therapeutic process.

We now need to consider briefly the difference in the views of Freud and Jung on the matter of the *structure* of the unconscious. I find these differences comparable in their therapeutic consequences to the divergence between the two men with respect to the role of the infantile trauma in the formation of neuroses; there Jung had accepted the Freudian concept of the *contents* of the unconscious, as far as it went, but he did not regard the early Freudian view of the contents as sufficiently inclusive.

As outlined by psychoanalyst Edward Glover, Freud had postulated an *unconscious system* of the mind on the basis of his having demonstrated that ideas and potential affects (an individual's subjective experience of his emotions) exist apart from consciousness and yet can be made conscious by the use of a technique which overcomes certain "resistances." These resistances indicated the existence of a barrier of repression, a kind of psychic frontier. *Consciousness* was henceforward regarded as another system of the mind, having the functions of perception to perform. Between these two systems was a borderline area, the content of which could be described as generally unconscious, although with appropriate stimulation it could be more or less recalled at will. He called this the *preconscious* system, thereby avoiding the term "subconscious" which would have confused the vital distinction between consciousness and the true (dynamic) unconscious. "This tripartite division constituted Freud's first outline of the *mental apparatus*, an organization whose function was to receive the incoming charges of (internal) instinct and stimulation coming from the external world, to master these charges and stimulations and to procure them satisfactory discharge (adaptation)."[12]

It is not to be questioned that Freud created the foundations of modern depth psychology through his epochal discovery of the unconscious as a dynamic entity which makes a profound impact upon human awareness or human consciousness. The unconscious realm, according to Freud, manifests itself in dreams and in everyday conscious life through neurotic symptoms as well as in faulty actions. Freud's concept of the unconscious has greatly enlarged and deepened the human potential for self-knowledge and for understanding of the other's needs and motivations. The basic concept as enunciated by Freud, which met with such a storm of indignant rejection when it was first published, is commonly accepted in depth psychology and in psychiatry today. The question is no longer whether the concept is false or true, but whether it does indeed encompass all that needs to be said about the unconscious and its structure.

Jung's formulation of the concept of the archetype led him to what he called "another step forward" in his understanding of the unconscious. This was his differentiation of two layers of the unconscious. These are, in Jungian terms, the *personal unconscious* and the *collective unconscious*. Jung's description of the personal unconscious follows:

> The personal unconscious contains lost memories, painful ideas that are repressed (i.e., forgotten on purpose), subliminal perceptions, by which are meant sense-perceptions that were not strong enough to reach consciousness, and finally, contents that are not yet ripe for consciousness.[13]

The collective unconscious may be thought of as an impersonal or transpersonal unconscious because, as Jung says, "It is detached from anything personal and is entirely universal, and because its contents can be found everywhere, which is naturally not the case with personal contents."[14]

The difficulty experienced by many people in grasping Jung's concept of the unconscious may be the result of taking him too literally. They assume that there must be a clear demarcation between the personal and the collective unconscious, and that the personal unconscious refers to everything that Freud said the unconscious was, while the collective unconscious is some peculiar construct of Jung's that no one else had ever thought of. As we read Jung's works we become gradually aware that in the psychological material brought up by individuals, the personal material shows the effects of its collective background and often is as a personal voice giving expression to an age-old liturgy. The personal unconscious is not

really an exact parallel of the Freudian concept of the unconscious (including the pre-conscious), because it does not include specifically those instinctual elements common to all
men, which were for Freud an important aspect of the unconscious. These Jung considers to be "transpersonal," i.e., universal. Also, Jung stresses that the personal unconscious contains contents that are "not yet ripe for consciousness," these
contents, evidently never having been in consciousness in the
first place, are thus not a result of repression. It is important
to note that the "not yet ripe" is part of the personal unconscious and it is suggestive of the thrust toward becoming
conscious of *new material*, which defines the individual's
potential.

The collective unconscious is better conceived as an extension of the personal unconscious to its wider and broader
base, encompassing contents which are held in common by
the family, by the social group, by tribe and nation, by race,
and eventually by all of humanity. Each succeeding level of
the unconscious may be thought of as going deeper and becoming more collective in its nature. The wonder of the collective unconscious is that it is all there, all the legend and history of the human race, with its unexorcised demons and its
gentle saints, its mysteries and its wisdom, all within each one
of us—a microcosm within the macrocosm. The exploration
of this world is more challenging than the exploration of outer
space, and the journey to inner space is not necessarily an
easy or a safe trip.

4

Are Archetypes Necessary?

. . .

ARE ARCHETYPES NECESSARY? Most academic psychologists, if they have addressed themselves to the question at all, have answered *no*. It is difficult for me to imagine that there can be those who have failed to recognize that human beings are often moved by strange, mostly inexplicable forces; yet those very people who profess expertise in dealing with the human psyche have hesitated to name the mysterious pattern-forming elements which play so fundamental a role in human experience. Consciousness consists primarily of what we know, and what we know we know. As far from conscious experience are the archetypes as the center of the earth is from its crust. That the archetype defies the scientific mind is clear enough when we read one of the leading interpreters of Jung's thought: "It is impossible to give an exact definition of the archetype, and the best we can hope to do is to suggest its general implications by 'talking around' it. For the archetype represents a profound riddle surpassing our rational comprehension. . . . [It] expresses itself first and foremost in metaphors; there is some part of its meaning that always remains unknown and defies formulation."[1] Since archetypes cannot fully be grasped by our minds—their being, in a sense, the very source of our thought processes and, consequently, of our attitudes and behavior—the concept of the archetype is bound to raise more questions than it can possibly answer.

It is understandable that most psychologists might consider speculation about the archetypes beyond the area of their competence. They work painstakingly to try to remove vagueness and mystery from mental functioning. I, for one, have no wish to plunge the infant science of psychology back into the realm of metaphysical conjecture from which it has only in this century emerged. But I do not believe we can avoid questions about the ultimate ground of human thought and behavior simply because answers do not present themselves with clarity and precision.

Nor can I, as a Jungian, be satisfied with reducing these primordial forming elements to a few well-known instincts such as hunger, self-preservation, sexuality, power drive. These are important, to be sure, but they do not account for the richness and productivity of the human mind when it is rooted in its ancient ground.

Are archetypes necessary? Are typical patterns of behavior-potential present in the young at birth? Perhaps the experimental psychologist will be the last to know. But the great playwrights and artists have always known, and the poet William Blake has asked the right questions:

> With what sense is it that the chicken shuns the rav'nous hawk?
> With what sense does the tame pigeon measure out the expanse?
> With what sense does the bee form cells? have not the mouse and frog
> Eyes and ears and sense of touch? yet are their habitations
> And their pursuits as different as their forms and as their joys.
> Ask the wild ass why he refuses burdens, and the meek camel
> Why he loves man: is it because of eye, ear, mouth or skin,

Or breathing nostrils? No, for these the wolf and tyger
    have.
Ask the blind worm the secrets of the grave, and why her
    spires
Love to curl round the bones of death; and ask the
    rav'nous snake
Where she gets poison, & the wing'd eagle why he loves
    the sun;
And then tell me the thoughts of man, that have been hid
    of old.[2]

Psychologists have turned away from the *whys* of behavior, even while they have attempted to manipulate the *hows* of behavior. Even the great pioneer of depth psychology has hesitated at the portals of the darkest level of the collective psyche. It may be that Freud's bent toward speculative abstraction was so powerful that he was afraid of being mastered by it, and so he felt it necessary to counter this tendency by studying concrete scientific data. Ernest Jones reports in the biography that he had once asked Freud how much philosophy he had read. The answer was, "Very little. As a young man I felt a strong attraction toward speculation and ruthlessly checked it."[3]

It was Jung's belief that Freud had repressed the archetype of *spirit* in his own nature, with his insistence on his sexual theory. David Bakan develops this idea more fully in his book *Sigmund Freud and the Jewish Mystical Tradition*, the thesis of which is that in the background of Freud's development the Kabbalistic mysteries which had occupied his rabbi-grandfather had been transmitted to him—not directly, but via the negativistic attitude toward those ideas on the part of his father, who told him in effect: "We don't any longer subscribe to these antiquated superstitions." Yet Jung knew that the two problems which most occupied Freud were sexuality and archaic vestiges in people today.

Jung said that he alone of all Freud's followers logically pursued these two problems which most interested Freud. He recognized the large part that sexuality plays as an essential—

though not the sole—expression of psychic wholeness. But Jung's main concern, he said, was to ". . . investigate over and above the personal significance and biological function [of sexuality] its spiritual aspect and its numinous meaning, and thus to explain what Freud was so fascinated by but unable to grasp."[4]

The record of Jung's divergence from Freud and the discovery of his unique position vis-à-vis the unconscious is to be found in the autobiography of his own soul's wanderings. There, in a chapter titled "Confrontation with the Unconscious," he tells how he observed the formation of various subpersonalities which appeared as personifications of aspects of the unconscious. Gradually over the years these images fell into categories, as though they were formed on specific patterns. Jung came to know the forming elements out of which these patterns emerged as *archetypes*. The dynamic symbols, based on the interaction between the archetype and a particular culture, he called *archetypal images*.

Are archetypes necessary? That Jung found the concept of the archetype fundamental to the understanding of the psyche would be merely a metaphysical assertion if the archetypal elements did not manifest themselves in human experience, and particularly in that experience of the deeper levels of the psyche that are exposed in psychological analysis. Jung's collected works are filled with examples of what he called archetypal phenomena. The archetype always seems to lie behind and beyond the personal experience. The poet perceives that the child is born out of the primordial past of humanity. A few lines from Tennyson's *De Profundis* express the human condition—consciousness emerging from the great mystery:

> Out of the deep, my child, out of the deep,
> Where all that was to be, in all that was,
> Whirl'd for a million aeons thro' the vast
> Waste dawn of multitudinous-eddying light—
> Out of the deep, my child, out of the deep,
> Thro' all this changing world of changeless law,

And every phase of ever-heightening life,
And nine long months of antenatal gloom
With this last moon, this crescent—her dark orb
Touch'd with earth's light—thou comest . . .

Out of the deep, my child, out of the deep,
From that true world within the world we see,
Whereof our world is but the bounding shore—[5]

The recognition of the two worlds which are really one, that of consciousness and the unconscious, is necessary if we are to make the concept of the archetype meaningful in our own lives. But were it only in theory or poetry that the archetype occurred, it would be of little significance. Therefore, I want to indicate, through the use of some examples from my own analytic practice, how the archetype takes on meaning for people in our own day, indeed, how the archetype concept may deliver the suffering individual from a sense of personal disaster.

Sara is a woman of about forty. She is a business executive, well respected by her peers and subordinates. To the public she looks like a successful career woman, and the fact that she is not married is accepted as probably a matter of her preference. But this is far from the truth. Sara has never been able to establish a close love relationship with a man. In college she had dated some, but whenever it came to the possibility of physical intimacy, she would find some pretext for breaking off. Sara had always been very close to her widowed mother, and though the mother now lived in another city, she would spend many weekends and most vacations with her mother. She was frequently on the phone with her mother. "We kept in touch and looked out for each other," as she put it. She felt responsible for her mother's happiness and sense of security. Gradually, in the course of her analysis, Sara was able to recognize the domineering element in the old woman's "protectiveness." She brought into consciousness her resentment for the mother's having kept her in a very restricted life-

style, making her remain close to home, criticizing all friends
of her own age until she gave up inviting them to her house.
There had been always the ominous, inexplicit warnings
about "keeping away from boys." As well as about modesty
and humility and going to church. And being good to maiden
aunts.

As the analysis progressed, Sara reviewed the events of her
childhood, adolescence and young womanhood, and she began to express the anger she felt against her mother. She arrived at the point where she could verbally release her hostility
to her mother, but still there was much bitterness. She relived
traumatic episodes. She cursed. Although she understood the
personal bases of her mother problem, it was by no means
resolved. She was as tense as ever in relationships, even while
she was trying to free herself from the sense of being watched
over, controlled. The hypothesis that repressed affect is at the
root of the neurotic development did not seem to be useful
here. Repressions had been lifted. There was insight into the
"cause" of the problem, but the insight did not bring relief.

Affect is the way in which feelings and emotions are experienced. In the psychologically healthy person the affects are
freely expressed; feelings surrounding pleasant or unpleasant
experiences are accompanied by appropriate facial expression
and body postures and movements. These same affects can be
noted when the person is merely talking about the experiences. The observation of affects is one of the most important
diagnostic tools of the therapist. When the affect is inappropriate, when the patient smiles while recounting a sad event or
becomes anxious totally out of any anxiety-producing context,
it may be assumed that the real affect has been repressed. This
then becomes a clue to investigate in attempting to uncover
the workings of the defenses—to try to discover what kind of
material is being covered up.

It was more difficult in the case of Sara to determine the
basis of her difficulty. If liberating the repressed affect was not
the key, then it might be possible that the root of the neurosis
did not stem from her personal experience entirely. I had, af-

ter all, dealt quite thoroughly with the personal history of the patient.

Then suddenly one day everything was different. Although in the past several sessions she had been vituperative in her anger against her mother, I had had the feeling that there was still more there, and that perhaps the still more did not really center on her mother at all. I did not intend to tell this to the patient because I thought she would have accepted it intellectually as she had accepted other ideas I had presented in the past, and she would have continued as before, confident that she had achieved another bit of insight. So I waited, expecting that what I knew and what I was attempting to stimulate by keeping her as close to her affects as possible, would erupt in its own time. I was not surprised therefore when one morning she came to our session deeply shaken. I could see she had not slept much that night, that whatever had occurred had been a deeply moving experience. I listened as she told me about it:

"A few days ago I awoke in the morning before daybreak in a sweat, aware of a 'presence' within me; so intensely aware that I can recall exactly how it had felt:

"In the middle of the marrow of the bone in me, as far in as you can go without coming out, there was a mist in me that condensed into this shadowy form. . . . I felt it in every portion of my being . . ."

Then she went on to talk about the maternal image which she recognized not *as her mother*, but as existing *in herself* and *in her mother* as well, and also in her grandmother, and through the maternal line throughout generations. Each generation had carried that possessive and devouring style of behavior from the generation before—as a wraith, permeating the body and the soul. The image was so impressive that Sara was able to confront it, to speak to it. She did this in her fantasy, and it was so vivid that she felt compelled to write down the words afterward:

"You have controlled me, stunted my growth, kept me from fulfilling mature sexual function. You frightened me with a story of men who have a big organ they stick into you—I thought it was a stick. You said not to disagree in public, you cut off my expression. You told me to 'come on in'—to see your friends—I wasn't ready to, I was angry, you forced me. You threw a murky shade over me, undermined my own expression, my own confidence. I was not me. You controlled my brothers—usurped their lives, shattered the identity of my father.

"Why have you done these things? Why do you live in me now? You *are* in me, Specter-form. My mother is not my enemy—*You* are. You hold her captive too. You are not even my mother's image in me—Separate Spirit—Thing that has lived in her to capture me—I should slay you!

"I refuse to keep the peace—which is on your terms. I will awaken, arouse you—confront you. You may wrap me in indifference but I shall needle you enough to engage you. You shall answer why—maybe, even, I can forgive you—but it may be dangerous to think thus."

What more striking example could there be of the emergence into consciousness of an archetypal image, the Great Mother? She is the terrible female whose awesome power looms over the child—boy or girl—she knows all there is to know and from her everything must be learned—she metes out punishment or affection according to her own unfathomable laws, she has control over life and death through giving nourishment or withholding it, through inflicting pain or offering comfort and healing. Each mother-child pair acts out the archetypal drama in the nursery—of power standing over weakness, wisdom looming over ignorance. And if, in the confrontation with the Great Mother—a symbol arising from unconscious depths—the enemy can be seen in its archetypal rather than its personal form, then there is a chance that the personal aspect of the problem can be separated from its archetypal core. Through such a separation, the profound effect of the archetype upon the individual can be markedly depotentiated.

The archetype of the Great Mother can also present itself in a positive way, unlocking the strength and power of the individual. The Mother image appeared under strange circumstances to my analysand Margaret in an hour of very great stress, providing her with an experience of heightened consciousness.

Margaret is a mature woman who had been recently widowed when she came to me. She was working with the problem of discovering inner resources within herself which would help her to compensate for the loss of a strong and competent life partner. She insisted that she had no religious faith, and that she did not believe that there could be any possible help outside of herself. And, since she felt quite inadequate to the demands of readjusting her life, she had come to me to help her find new ways of thinking about her problems. When I probed the question of whether she had ever been open to the possibility that some of the helpful character she associated with her husband or with her relationship with her husband might still be accessible to her, she brushed off my remark as unrealistic. However what I said must have struck a responsive chord below the level of her awareness, for shortly after that in the course of her analysis she revealed the following incident:

"Some years ago I was spending a few days with a friend of mine in a remote area of the country. Her husband had to be away on a business trip, and since she was well advanced in pregnancy she had been reluctant to stay alone. One night a tremendous storm came up and there was a power failure so that the lights went out and even the telephone service was interrupted. We both became anxious, though I tried to hide my feelings as much as possible and to reassure my friend. At this time it happened that she went into labor, and there was no hope of getting any help to deliver the child. I felt absolutely lost, not having the faintest idea of what to do, except that I busied myself making sure that there were candles around and heating on the gas stove the water we had thoughtfully drawn while the storm was approaching.

"I guess you might say it was the classic situation of being 'beside myself' with fear of what might happen and with no one to turn to. And at the same time the feeling grew within me that help would come. It arose at first, I think, as a wordless sureness, and then I felt myself relaxing, growing nearly numb, but no longer anxious. I sensed the formation of words in my head, something like, 'I will do it' or 'I know how to do it,' and then the words became distinctly audible and seemed to come from a certain direction. I turned my head from my friend who was breathing heavily between her pains, lying there sweating on her bed, and saw in the gloom in the far corner of the room up near the ceiling a faint glow of light. As I stared at it, the light took the form of a woman, my mother, who had been dead some fifteen years. In the same moment I knew that the voice I had heard was her voice. Then the scene shifted, and I could see my mother standing by the bed, next to my friend, and it was as though I was off in the corner of the room observing. And yet I was also with my mother. As her hands moved to soothe the woman in labor, to help her bear down, as her voice gently encouraged my friend, I felt a great relief that it was going all right. I saw, to my great wonder, the baby slowly emerge from between the thighs of his mother, saw as though I were right there that this was a strong active little boy, heard him cry, and yet the cry was heard still from the distance of the corner of the room. Soon my mother was holding him, wrapping him in a tiny blanket, placing him beside his mother.

"What occurred then is vague in my mind, but it seemed that I swam out of that dark corner and entered into the place of my mother, or I came there and she entered into me, and then departed. A shimmer of dim light in the far corner of the room was there for an instant, then disappeared, and I found myself fully present and fresh as though just awakened from a good night's sleep, sitting at my friend's bedside. There was blood on my hands and on my apron. Her child was cradled in her arms and sucking at her breast, and she smiled up at me and said, 'Margaret, I felt so calm, so secure—however did you manage?' I never told her, and in fact did not allow myself to think about it, and soon the memory of those uncanny moments faded. I have never spoken of them until this day."

Margaret is an upper-middle-class, well-educated woman who has always been well adapted to her life as a suburban matron with family and community responsibilities. She is not a person whom one would ever suspect of seeing spirits, nor has she ever shown an interest in the lore of the occult, quite the contrary. I have chosen her experience to indicate that she represents a very great number of people who have had one or more profound experiences with archetypal phenomena. In this case the mother-archetype was embodied in the familiar image of Margaret's own mother. The experience is not explainable by the rules of ordinary sense perception, the ways in which we come to know the external world. It rather belongs to those intuitive phenomena by which we apprehend directly the inner experience, without the intervention of rational thought or inference.

The experience of the archetype in the parent-child relationship requires an explanation that goes beyond the theory of infantile sexuality as propounded by Freud. This experience was the subject of research which occupied Jung's major attention during the period from 1911 to 1913 when he was most active in the Vienna circle. At this time he had become so valuable to the psychoanalytic movement that Freud had designated him as "crown prince" in the hope that he would some day assume its leadership. However, Jung's independent spirit demanded that he follow where it led, and at this time it was leading him far from orthodox psychoanalytic doctrine. He had for a long time struggled with Freud's theory of infantile sexuality as delimited with respect to the personal experience of the individual, and now he began to investigate the archetypal roots of the oedipal situation.

This was a difficult and painful period for Jung. As he was clarifying his own ideas he was drawing further and further away from Freud, for whom he had all the ambivalent feelings of an aspiring son for a brilliant father.

For one thing, Jung felt that he had been overpowered to some degree by his older colleague, who had advanced his sexual theories with all his usual vigor for which he was well known. In the main Jung was highly interested and agreed in principle, but he did hold certain doubts and hesitations. When he tried to advance these reservations he was met with Freud's suggestion that his questions were due to his lack of experience. Here the "patient father" figure exercised a gentle control over the ebullient Jung. And Jung, for his part, may have expected to be joined in a discussion as an equal, even though he recognized that he did not, indeed, have enough experience to support his objections.

In his autobiography Jung referred to his crucial essay "The Sacrifice," saying that while he was working on it he knew it was the statement which would cost him his friendship with Freud.[6] Here Jung presented his own conception of the meaning of incest, which had been the cornerstone of Freud's sexual theory. Jung felt that the incest problem was to be understood symbolically and not literally. Thus libido had become for him more than the force behind sexuality; it had become the divine creative force of nature. The problem of incest was seen no longer as a purely individual dilemma, but as a phase in the collective human experience as we develop toward a higher form of consciousness.

The problem of the sacrifice, the dissolution of the oedipal tie, had been treated by Freud as an individual problem. All children have to work it out with their own mothers or mother-surrogates in the process of moving toward maturity.

Jung saw the child's sacrifice of the paradise of the early and rewarding unity with the mother in a far wider context. He turned to a series of myths, which he regarded as the language of the collective unconscious, to Greek and Norse mythology, to Goethe's *Faust*, and to the Gilgamesh Epic of the Babylonians, finding everywhere the eternal and ubiquitous theme of sacrifice—of slaying the primal being in order that the world may be born. Perhaps this theme was most beautifully expressed in the Rig Veda:

Purusha (Man, Anthropos) was the primal being who

> Encompassed the world on all sides
> And ruled over the ten-finger place
> The highest point of heaven.

Jung wrote:

As the all-encompassing world-soul, Purusha had a maternal character, for he represented the original "dawn state" of the psyche: he was the encompasser and the encompassed, mother and unborn child, an undifferentiated, unconscious state of primal being. As such a condition must be terminated, and as it is at the same time an object of regressive longing, it must be sacrificed in order that discriminated entities—i.e., conscious contents—may come into being.[7]

Then came the sacrifice of this primal being by gods and men and it was said:

> The moon was born from his mind;
> From his eye was born the sun;
> From his mouth Indra and Agni;
> From his breath Vayu was born.
> From his navel grew the atmosphere;
> From his head the sky; from his feet the earth;
> From his ear the directions.
> Thus the worlds are made.[8]

Jung declares it is evident that "by this is meant not a physical, but a psychological cosmogony. The world comes into being when people discover it. But we only discover it when we sacrifice our containment in the primal mother, the original state of unconsciousness. What drives people toward this discovery is conceived by Freud as the 'incest barrier.' The incest prohibition blocks the infantile longing for the mother and forces the libido [Freud's term for sexual energy] along the path of life's biological aim. The libido, driven back from the mother by the incest prohibition, seeks a sexual object in place of the forbidden mother. Here the terms 'incest prohibition' and 'mother' etc. are used metaphorically, and it is in this sense that we would have to interpret Freud's paradoxical dictum: 'To begin with we knew none but sexual objects.' "9 Jung insisted that the fact that the infant takes pleasure from sucking does not prove that it is sexual pleasure, for pleasure can have many different sources. That the archetypal experience appears in the young child by no means implies that it is limited to the young child. Archaism is a dynamic factor in the psychic life of civilized adults as well, according to Jung, and the evidence is all about us if we will but notice it. One place where it may appear is in our dreams.

An example of an archetypal dream in a young adult will show how a Jungian analyst looks at a dream which contains material which the patient cannot connect with his early life or, indeed, with any personal experience. David, a patient of mine, began his university career studying physics. Behind this choice of a field of concentration, he told me, lay his desire to find out how the world works. But as he gathered more and more knowledge he found himself becoming increasingly dissatisfied. It seemed to him that there was more that he needed to know, or a different *kind* of knowledge, from what he was being taught. Seeking an understanding of the logical structures behind the processes observable in the material universe, he turned to philosophy. This, too, failed to provide him with answers; it only gave him neater ways to deal with the questions. Finally, he had taken up theology. Here he sought a wider meaning behind the apparent order of nature, one that would go beyond the logical processes which could be contained and controlled by his own intellect. But even theology disappointed him—"Who can say what God is, and how much less, what He wants?"

David came into therapy in despair; everything he had

tried to study had led him to *culs-de-sac* in the labyrinth that
was his world. He felt that life was pointless. He had learned
so much and he had discarded so much that he found it difficult to communicate with anyone who had not achieved a
similarly high level of education. Even many of his professors,
he found, espoused only one view. "You can't talk to them." He
felt isolated, and he derived little joy from anything except
possibly his compulsion to add more and more books to the
library that overflowed his shelves.

One night he had the following dream: *I am watching a
rocket take off. Suddenly it curves around and becomes a ship. I
am aboard—there is a tempest. The rocket-ship pitches me
about on a stormy sea until finally it overturns. I manage to
escape drowning by getting into a small lifeboat. Then a dragon
rises out of the water and swims rapidly toward me. I am terribly afraid. For a moment I try to hide in the bottom of the boat,
but I know it will be of no use. He has come up to the edge of my
boat. Nearly paralyzed with fright, I do the only thing I can do. I
reach my hand overboard and into the water and grab the fearsome dragon by its leg. In this moment he turns into a small
horse, a toy made of wax about ten inches tall.*

David commented on the dream: "In thinking about this
the morning after I awoke, I was amazed at how the dragon
became small and harmless after I reached out and grabbed
its leg. Also, I think of it in a positive way ever since. It seems
like a psychological victory for me. I felt in a festive, jovial
mood as I held up the small horse as if to say 'this is the great
giant that I feared; he is really small and harmless.'"

The etymology of the word "jovial" was not overlooked.
David had broken out of the boundaries of a constricted intellect by making an immediate and direct contact with the fantastic dragon, which symbolized the irrational element within
himself. Victorious in bridging the gap between his own limited powers and the mysterious power he ascribed to a totally
exterior supernatural force, he was able to assimilate to himself some of the energy that had been until then inaccessible
to him. The psychic energy that had previously been con-

tained in the unconscious, "bound up in the dragon," or in his fear of the non-rational, now became accessible to the conscious part of him, his ego. No wonder that he felt suddenly strong, like the immortal Jove, ruler of Olympus. No longer would the student have to live off the frothy scum of knowledge on the sea of the unknown and unknowable. Now he understood that he could reach into the depths, and bring up contents of the unconscious, rational or irrational—no matter how they might appear—and take hold of them and see what they might look like.

The archetype may be manifested in archaic form and so be terrifying when one faces it as a helpless individual. But when we know that our own experience of fear or disillusion or futility is more than a matter of personal dismay, that it is an experience that shares a common core with all of humanity, then we become aware that there must always have been ways of dealing with the archetypal problems. Mythology provides us with classic solutions—sometimes we can become aware of them through a diligent search, but more often we bump into them somehow, without ever having been told how to apply them.

Another patient of mine was introduced to his personal myth in a peculiar way. Murray was an artist who lived in a shabby apartment with his girlfriend. He loved her very much, but he was not entirely sure of her affections. She had told him that she wanted to go on a trip for a couple of weeks to visit her parents in another city. While she was gone he wanted to do something for her which would show her how deeply he loved her. He thought about what to do, and then he hit upon an idea. He found a few planks of wood around his studio and he built a bedstead of his own design, to surprise his girl when she returned. I asked him why, of all things, he had done *just that*. He told me that the idea just occurred to him one day as a very strong impulse; he knew it was the right thing to do to express his feelings, so he did just that.

I asked Murray if he had ever heard the story of Ulysses' return after the long years of wandering on his way home from the Trojan War. I told him how the traveler had returned incognito to the palace of his wife so that he could look over the situation without being recognized by the suitors who had taken control of his lands and were contending over who should have the hand of his beloved Penelope. A contest was suggested, in which it was agreed that the strongest among the suitors should win the lady. Ulysses, in rags, displayed his strength by stringing the great bow which he had left behind him, and which none of the suitors could even begin to bend. But Penelope, fearing some trick, or that some god was attempting to seduce her, demanded still further proof from her professed husband that he really was who he said he was. Thereupon he told her what no one knew but the two of them and the single maid who took care of the bedchamber, the guarded secret of how he had built with his own hands from a living olive tree the bed that they shared when their love was young. No one else could have known that he had constructed their bedchamber around a sturdy tree, that he had cut down the branches, and had used the stump for the centerpost of their bed.

My lovesick analysand may or may not have known the myth of the *Odyssey;* he did not recall it. Yet he had somehow known that the act of fashioning the bed had a symbolic meaning to him which he had not understood, but truly felt.

The mythologem reappears and reappears.

The archetype, as we have seen in the case of Sara, manifested itself by a sudden awareness in the course of the analytic process. In the case of David, it became apparent in a dream. Murray came to it through the work of his hands. Still another way in which the archetype emerges in psychic life is through language. As a matter of fact, only recently have scientists begun to recognize the "innate symbolic machinery, common to all men, [which] may have been used before the beginnings of formal language to communicate about such basic concerns as birth, life, death, love, combat and fear of the elements, which are common to both animals and men."[10]

According to a report headed "Language study indicates

collective unconscious exists," Joseph Jaffe, M.D., is willing to admit that "the existence of a collective unconscious common to all men is quite believable when translated into terms of recent studies on the foundation of language." He notes that babies all over the world begin to exhibit language behavior at the same time and in the same way. This behavior, he says, is not taught but is innate and preprogrammed and coincides with certain stages of brain maturation and the ability to form concepts. "The specific language being spoken in the environment serves only as a vehicle for selection of a set of rules and distinctions which are automatically abstracted by the child" as the powers of conceptualization grow. . . . "That which is innate and common to the world's babies in learning a language, then, is a schema or catalogue of concept categories [this is exactly what Jung has understood as the archetypes of the collective unconscious] that are related by the brain to the subject matter of the environmental language by means of transformations (i.e., sentence X fits into category Y in such and such a way)." Dr. Jaffe concludes, "The fact that there is no natural language which does not contain a comparable catalogue of directions, assertions, negations, etc., is evidence for the existence of a universal grammar and semantics in all races."[11]

The evidence produced by research like that referred to above is often supported in surprising ways by the unconscious itself, which produces its own proofs for its existence and its nature. A dream brought to me by Ben, a schoolteacher in his first year of teaching elementary-school children and only beginning to perceive the manifold ways in which learning takes place, is a case in point: *I am in some kind of underground laboratory, teaching animals to speak. I'm trying to teach them to say words with a long "e." A man comes in, some kindly caretaker, and asks me if I've lost my mind. He says that animals have their own language. They don't care about my goddam phonics.*

The kindly caretaker, the man who knows animals because he has watched them day after day, is intuitively aware of what the teacher often does not know, and the scientist strains to discover. What the caretaker has known for a long time, and what he has to teach the teacher, is not so very different from what linguistics scholar Noam Chomsky had to say on television recently. I cannot reproduce what he said verbatim, but based on the notes I took as I was listening, the sense of his remarks was that the major properties of language structure are inherent in the human mind. Children are born possessing these qualities, and they have only to learn the particularities of the specific language of their own culture. Chomsky cautioned: Do not underestimate the originality and initiative of the human mind to develop language.

How very different is this point of view from that of the behaviorists who look upon the human organism as born possessed of a more or less inert and vacant machine called the brain which is programmed by the effects of the environment (television, parents, teachers, etc.) as input. If the organism-machine has been inadvertently fed the wrong data and exposed to the wrong stimuli, well, then, let's get busy and delete the objectionable concepts, and then reprogram the person in our own way. In the dream, is not the unconscious (personified by the old caretaker) telling the dream ego (Ben's school-teacher aspect) that he is not to overlook the innate potential for development that expresses itself spontaneously in children as in all forms of life?

Two ways of thinking must be considered in connection with archetypal experience: *convergent* and *divergent* thinking.

Convergent thinking is reductive. It tries to reduce psychic experience down to its "causes"—which may be found in the early experiences which established behavioral patterns, and which in their turn set the stage upon which future episodes of life's drama would be enacted. The residues of the past must be examined, of course, for they contaminate the present with their content, and I cannot imagine that any depth psychologist would deny that. But we must not forget that the archetypal core, too, is present in all human experience. Its importance is that it not only helps to explain the past, but that it also provides a basis for anticipating possibilities in attitude and behavior for the future. Of course it is possible to change behavior without resorting to an understanding of archetypal processes. Men and women and children can be trained and retrained much as animals can be domesticated. People can become useful citizens, adapted to their world, willing to accept its glories and defeats, to fly the flag of their country, even to march off to senseless wars—for the glory of those who sit back and pull the strings or push the buttons and smile as they regard their profit-and-loss sheets. People can be changed, they can be made more productive, they can be pacified, they can learn to live in our world—all this without ever a reference to the concept that people carry within them the potentiality for initiative, for independent thinking, for becoming what they are meant to be.

Convergent thinking conceives of life processes as being susceptible to being broken down into "problems" which then have to be solved. For every problem there is only one answer, or there is a "best" answer, and the objective is to find that answer. Sometimes problem-solving takes the form of a search for the cause of the trouble, the single traumatic event. Sometimes problem-solving consists in attempting to resolve difficulties by shifting behavior from a less acceptable kind to a more acceptable kind. Invariably, convergent thinking is permeated by the idea that there is a right way, which has only to be found and instituted. In an era of "managed competition" in health care where the emphasis is toward "efficiency" and cost cutting, pressure mounts toward achieving the "quick fix." Surely there are times when a practical solution to a practical problem is all that is required. Or changing external circumstances can sometimes relieve psychological stress and allow the psyche to perform its natural self-healing tendency. Medications may help to facilitate the healing process by relieving the symptoms. But often it is absolutely necessary to penetrate into the depths and seek self-understanding in the very roots of the self, before any lasting change is to take place.

Problem-solving is not the primary aim or goal of an archetypally based psychology. If anything, the ability to handle problems may be a by-product. If we are ever to effect constructive and lasting changes in our own lives, we must strive for a *transformation* (note: I did not say a "cure") of the potentially disturbing or disrupting problems, by reaching toward their archetypal cores. Such a transformation cannot take place before one has gone beyond the personal to the universal dimension. In this process, as we become more and more conscious, we will not be satisfied by being told what our place in society is. Modern individuals need to rescue themselves from their cultural provincialism. No one can do it for us. To accomplish this, the convergent way of thinking is often just the wrong approach. The view that directs our thinking reductively, always and again backward toward childhood, infancy, and birth, soon reaches the limits of consciousness.

Divergent thinking is a more creative approach. It is an approach whereby many avenues fan out from the central core—which is the situation in which we find ourselves in a given moment. The roads may indeed lead backward, but they may just as well lead forward, and there are ways that lead in other directions: neither backward nor forward. Divergent thinkers regard their situations as being a "given" simply because they are there at the moment in which they contemplate them. It does not matter that they could have avoided them, nor that they should be somewhere else right now; the fact is that they are there, and that is what they must deal with. Recognizing this, it is not difficult to see that the situations in which they find themselves are similar in certain fundamental respects to experiences other people have had before. There are, they find, fundamental life experiences, which become apparent when they begin to observe the nature of human experience. They will see the importance of discerning in which ways people are alike or similar—and where their experiences are primarily collective in nature. For only by knowing what we have in common with others does it become possible to understand how we stand away from the mass, as free individuals. The study of mythology and fairy tales, and of literary forms and comparative religions, helps us to understand and recognize the power of the archetypal elements within all people, and then to put our personal experiences into the larger perspective. The archetypal idea, as Jung has said, "is essentially an unconscious content that is altered by becoming conscious and being perceived, and it takes its colour from the individual consciousness in which it happens to appear."[12]

At this point one might be tempted to ask how the world managed to get on so long without Jung's concept of the archetype. It did not. Jung did not lay claim to having discovered the concept—it is a very ancient one. In his essay, "Archetypes of the Collective Unconscious," Jung traces the history of the concept back to antiquity. He informs us:

> . . . the term archetype occurs as early as Philo Judaeus, with reference to the *Imago Dei* (God-image) in man. It can also be found in Irenaeus, who says: "The creator of the world did not fashion these things directly from himself but copied them from archetypes outside himself." In the *Corpus Hermeticum*, God is called . . . "archetypal light." The term occurs several times in Dionysius the Areopagite, as for instance . . . "immaterial Archetypes" and . . . "Archetypal stone."
>
> The term "archetype" is not found in St. Augustine, but the idea of it is. . . . He speaks of "*ideae principales*, which are themselves not formed, but are contained in the divine understanding." "Archetype" is an explanatory paraphrase of the Platonic *eidos*.[13]

And Jung concludes, "so far as the collective unconscious contents are concerned, we are dealing with archaic or—I would say—primordial types, that is, with universal images that have existed since the remotest times."[14] In the literature of the late nineteenth century, which Jung read during his student years, the concept of the archetype was implicit if not mentioned by name. In the field of comparative religion, scholars Hubert and Mauss referred to "categories of the imagination." The anthropologist Adolf Bastian, a hundred years ago, predicated "elementary" or "Primordial" thoughts *(Elementargedanken)*. And Immanuel Kant stated that all human cognition possesses a priori sources of cognition, which seem to transcend the limits of all experience. Jung wrote that from these references it should be clear that his idea of the archetypes, literally a pre-existent form—does not stand alone but is something that is recognized and named in other fields of knowledge.

Joseph Campbell tells us that students of animal behavior have coined the term "innate releasing mechanism" (IRM) to designate the inherited structure in the nervous system that enables an animal to respond in a predetermined way to a circumstance never experienced before. Chicks with their eggshells still adhering to their tails dart for cover when a hawk flies overhead, but not when the bird is a gull, duck, heron or pigeon. Furthermore, if the wooden model of a hawk is drawn over their coop on a wire they react as though it were alive— unless it is drawn backward, when there is no response.[15]

Tinbergen, who has given particular attention to the problem of animal learning, has shown that not only do differing species have different dispositions to learn, but that such innate dispositions come to maturity only in certain critical periods of the animal's growth. He writes about the Eskimo dogs of east Greenland who live in packs of five to ten. The members of a pack defend their group territory against all other dogs. All dogs of an Eskimo settlement have an exact knowledge of the limits of their territories and where attacks from other packs may be feared. Immature dogs, however, do not defend the territory. They often roam through the whole settlement, sometimes trespassing into other territories from which they are promptly chased away. In spite of frequent attacks during which they may be severely hurt, they do not learn their territorial boundaries, and in this respect they seem amazingly stupid to the observer. When the young dogs are growing sexually mature, however, they begin to learn the extent of the other territories and within a week their trespassing forays are over. In two male dogs the first copulation, the first defense of territory, and the first avoidance of strange territory, all occurred within one week.[16]

Nature films have shown the phenomenon of the laying and hatching of eggs of the sea turtle. The female comes out of the water, and finds a point on the beach safely above the tide lines. There she digs a hole and deposits hundreds of eggs, covers the nest, and returns to the sea. Eighteen days later a small army of tiny turtles comes flipping through the sand and unerringly makes for the waves as fast as possible before the gulls overhead can dip low enough to pick the little ones off. Campbell, in describing this scene, observes that no more vivid representation could be desired of the spontaneity of the quest for the not-yet-seen. There is no opportunity here for trial and error, nor is there a question of fear. The tiny turtles know that they must hurry, and they know how to do it. Evidently they know where they are going, too, and that when they get there they must swim; and they know how to do that immediately as they reach the water.[17]

What does it all mean, the awakening to the functioning of the archetype all about us, and especially in our own lives? How shall we utilize this recognition? Is it a way of synchronizing the beating of our own hearts in time with the cosmic rhythms? Is it a way of sensing that we are not only the products of our history, we are also the makers of history, and moreover that we are living history itself?

That which is now known as myth and legend was once the core of belief. Today, because another age has created another language, the ways in which the archetypes manifest themselves are strange to us. We may recognize the archetypal image in the cathedral, but it is not so easy to be aware of it when it beams upon us from the television tube. The contents of the archetypes have changed, as they change with every age. But the forms of the archetypes are the same—there is still the encompassing Great Mother, the awe-inspiring Father-God, the Divine Child, the Hero, the Trickster, the Old

Wise Man, the Mana-personality, and all the rest. Only they appear in new shapes. There is a new format. Dialogues have a new twist, but themes recur and recur.

Are archetypes necessary? It is not the task of the investigator, it seems to me, to determine whether what he discovers is necessary or not. (Is a space walk necessary?) The investigator's task is to make his observations and report on them, on "what is." Whether the investigator is an experimental psychologist studying animal behavior in the laboratory, or a clinical psychologist interpreting test results, or a psychotherapist analyzing a patient's dreams—certain conditions inherent in the subject become evident to him. He formulates them in concepts. These concepts, when traced back to their roots, lead eventually to the archetypes. It is not that the *archetypes are necessary*—that would be the kind of value judgment the scientist is often reluctant to make. It is simply that the *archetypes* exist as useful categories for thinking about the vast realms of the collective unconscious, and that they surface as images which help us to organize our life experiences in ways that point toward their ultimate meaning.

Part Two

. . .

THE INNER
PROCESS

. . .

5

Individuation: The Process of Becoming Whole

...

WE MOVE NOW from an exploration of some of Jung's most basic concepts: his ideas about the movement of psychic energy, the formation of complexes, and the archetypes as an organizing principle in the collective unconscious. Although we have illustrated these concepts with examples from the case histories of people in Jungian analysis, we have yet to regard the different aspects of the analytic process. As the unconscious reveals itself through the analysand's day-to-day experiences, through dreams, through reflection and meditation, through fantasy, through creative expression, and in countless other ways, the archetypes emerge. We have said that archetypes belong to the deeper layers of the psyche, the collective unconscious. Since they *are* unconscious, we cannot observe them directly, but we can see their manifestations everywhere about us in the form of archetypal images and symbols. These images and symbols lead us from the known to the unknown, as we seek to better understand ourselves. Analysis proceeds in the tradition of the mythical founder of Western esoteric thought, Hermes Trismegistus, whom Jung was fond of quoting: "Who knows himself, knows the All."

The *individuation process* is a path to self-knowledge. Since whatever we know or claim to know must pass through the portal of the psyche's perception, we utilize the process of analysis to help us develop the psyche's perceptual function through the introspective training that Jung calls the "individuation process." On this path, we will encounter some of the major archetypal images shared by people of every age and every place: the *persona*, or mask, which mediates between the person and society; the *shadow*, which holds those aspects in the unconscious that the persona shunts aside as it faces the world; the *anima* and the *animus*, those unconscious parts of ourselves that carry the mystery of the sex which is not ours; and the *self*, which is the archetype of wholeness, of the "All."

Human beings are to a very large extent conditioned in their attitudes, thoughts and behavior by the culture in which they are born and grow, and by the people with whom they come into contact. Yet this conditioning falls not upon a blank slate but rather upon a complex set of predispositions and characteristics that make up the individual nature of the child at birth and channels its subsequent development as a unique individual. The individuation process moves along two tracks. The first is designed to help people recognize and fulfill their own unique potentials. This involves differentiating the self from the constraints of the conditioning that are imposed by family and other external influences. The second track requires differentiation from one's environment: one asks, How am I a part of that which surrounds me, and how am I different? Put another way, it is the development of an ability to discriminate between the "I" and the "Not I."

The ideal of the individuation process, as Jung described it, is the conscious realization and integration of all the possibilities contained within the individual. Needless to say, few people achieve individuation. As with so many ideals, it is more valuable to engage in the process than to lust after the distant goal. Jung was opposed to conformity with the collective as a matter of principle. From his background as the son of a parson in a small town in Switzerland, he found his personal identity by taking a strong stand against the collective attitudes. He regarded those collective attitudes as prefabricated rules for an orderly society in which most people would like to live. For himself, he found them stifling, and offered instead the individuation process whereby people could find their own direction and live according to their own sense of purpose. Individuation can attach a sense of worth to the lives of those who suffer because they are unable or unwilling to measure up to collective norms and collective ideals. To those who are not recognized by the collective, who are rejected and even despised, this process offers a way toward restoring faith in themselves as they establish their own inner values. It may give them back their human dignity and assure them of their place in the world.

There are many people who are successful by the world's standards, and yet seek a better understanding of who they are and a deeper sense of what their lives are about. Even though they may be able to deal with the collective in its own terms, they are aware that there are untapped resources in the psyche as well as in the world, and they seek access to the riches of the unconscious. For they know that they are more than their image in the world, and want to discover this "more."

As we proceed to explore the individuation process we will turn from the concept of the archetypes to the images they assume as they enter into our personal lives and demand our attention.

In Chicago, which depends for its existence largely on mechanics and electronics, there is a section called New Town. It is the successor to Old Town, which used to be the center of counterculture activity until it started going downhill when the pushers of hard drugs moved in. People who had begun to fear for their lives in Old Town and who had outgrown their fascination with the psychedelic experience as an end-in-itself have been opening up small shops and businesses in New

Town, where they make, display and sell interesting and unusual products. You can walk down a busy street when suddenly the delicious odor of bread baking streams out from a little storefront bakery and wraps you in nostalgia. The "Clay People" make and sell ceramics and invite you to come in and learn their craft. Artists paint in shop-studios, and there is a shop where people sit around and do macramé and sell their ingenious belts and ties and wall hangings at a fair price.

These are children of the generation who grew up in the Great Depression, whose parents married during or just after World War II, settling down to work hard for the good life. Father was the Organization Man, with his home in the suburbs and his new car every two years. He had to pay a high price for his security—the loss of his individuality—and most of the time he never realized that it was gradually slipping away. But his children, unhampered by fear of hunger or the unavailability of education, have looked about them and have become disenchanted with the stereotypes of the affluent society. Many have withdrawn from an overorganized and overstandardized system, and are searching for alternatives that seem to offer a better opportunity to express their individual needs and talents.

While this expression seems related to a need which is especially congruent to the state of the world today, it is also in the spirit of what Jung was advocating as early as the First World War; in this as in other ways he was far ahead of his times. His advocacy of coming to selfhood through a distinctly individual and personal effort offered a way which is increasingly attracting the attention and then the commitment of those who have felt the necessity of breaking out of the bonds imposed by the collectivity that characterized our cities in the seventies and eighties. That effort, as Jung conceived it, is the way of *individuation*.

The individuation process, in the Jungian sense, means the conscious realization and integration of all the possibilities immanent in the individual. It is opposed to any kind of conformity with the collective and, as a therapeutic factor in analytical work, it also demands the rejection of those prefabricated psychic matrices—the conventional attitudes—with which most people would like to live.

What is this "individuation process" in which people become free to realize themselves in a way which does not depend on the approval of any outside agency? In "The Relations between the Ego and the Unconscious," an essay in which Jung set forth the fundamentals of the individuation process, we find that "Individuation means becoming a single, homogeneous being, and, in so far as 'individuality' embraces our innermost, last, and incomparable uniqueness, it also implies becoming one's own self. We could therefore translate individuation as . . . 'self-realization.' "[1] It is an easy thing to say "be yourself" but quite another thing to know who you truly are. How can you be yourself if you do not know that self? Therefore, the process of individuation becomes a seeking after self-knowledge.

The criticism is often made that searching for self-knowledge is a very introverted, self-centered thing to do. I have had analysands confess to me that they are abashed at admitting that they are spending so much time and energy on their own inner processes. They find that it is hard to justify, when, as they correctly observe, there are so many problems out in the world crying for solution.

Is it not true with respect to social problems of our day that the nature of the person who deals with these problems and issues will affect the nature of the solution? I see it in psychotherapy all the time—a person studying to become a psychotherapist will master the basic subject matter in the field of psychology and he will learn certain rules, techniques, or methods of this or that discipline. But in the end, the person of the therapist more than anything else determines the progress of the case. Likewise in social issues, the *values* set by individuals upon different kinds of changes or improvements in the environment determine the courses of action that are eventually taken. Values stem from the viewpoint of the individual; they are the result of the collision between his essential

nature and the impact upon that nature by the experiences of
living.

The essential nature of the individual includes not only
strength but weakness. Each of us has the potentiality for creativity and, equally present, the potentiality for destructive-
ness. The Hindu gods, Brahma, Vishnu, Shiva—Creator, Pre-
server, Destroyer—live in each of us; all must be reckoned
with. It is as though we exist in a psychic system where an
ecological balance must be maintained. One analysand of
mine put it this way: "I was reading about how the government took all that highly dangerous nerve gas and sealed it in
tons of concrete and took it out and dumped it in the Atlantic
to 'dispose of it.' I realized how wrong that statement was, for
we never really get rid of anything, there isn't any 'out there' to
consign it to. Even in the Atlantic it is still with us, and even in
the ocean the space is limited and what is there affects the
land. And so in the psyche, we cannot 'dispose' of dangerous
or destructive aspects of ourselves, we can only know of their
presence and how they tend to function. If we work at it we
may be able to transform these dark elements from something
virulent to something manageable. That is part of the greatness of Jung's concept of the self-regulating nature of the
psyche: he never supposed evil could be done away with, but
sought to expose and understand the potentiality for evil in
our own souls as well as that for good."

When my analysand understood that, she understood that
individuation requires the discovery of what is operating in us
and determining our determinations. What are our goals and
how do we come to them? Jung noted in his Introduction to
The Secret of the Golden Flower[2]: "An ancient adept has said: 'If
the wrong man uses the right means, the right means work in
the wrong way.'" This Chinese saying stands in sharp contrast
to our typically Western product-oriented or success-oriented
belief in the "right" *method* irrespective of who applies it. Jung
wrote, "In reality, in such matters everything depends on the
man and little or nothing on the method. For the method is
merely the path, the direction taken by a man. The way he acts

is the true expression of his nature. If it ceases to be this, then the method is nothing more than an affectation, something artificially added, rootless and sapless, serving only the illegitimate goal of self deception."[3] Perhaps the stress on method and the lack of stress on man's relatedness to his own deepest needs and commitments is one of the most serious problems in the practice of psychotherapy today.

Let me give you an example of how the right means fail in the hands of the wrong man, from a case of my own practice. Dale came to me in a state of utter despair. His latest marriage was falling apart and he was on the verge of quitting his tenth job in the past seven years. Dale was no fool, nor did he lack for charm or self-confidence. Or perseverance. He had been reared in a succession of foster homes where he learned to get what he wanted by manipulating and flattering people until they would fulfill his demands. Then he would enjoy his little luxuries so craftily won, and not be particularly concerned about exerting himself for the benefit of anyone else. The game came to be "see how much you can get and at the same time how little you can manage to give." He was marvelous about courting a woman until he got her to bed, and after the first successful conquest he would concentrate upon getting his own satisfaction whenever and however he pleased. Woman after woman would tell Dale, "As soon as I began to feel committed to you, you suddenly turned off." His marriages all started with the usual charming approach, but before the honeymoon was over, the wives, each of them in succession, would complain that Dale had completely changed. He didn't see it, he never could understand what went wrong.

This man had joined the Army, where he got into trouble in one relationship after another. He became involved in fist fights, was called down for insubordination, until at last it got so bad that he was given a psychiatric discharge. The Army recommended psychotherapy, and was willing to pay for it. In addition he was awarded disability benefits, so he did not have to go to work.

Therapy promised to be rather long-term and, having

nothing else to do, Dale decided that he might as well while away the time between the sessions by going back to school under the G.I. Bill. He happened to be intelligent enough so that he managed to get an advanced degree in engineering. He became engaged in research on waste and sewage treatment, and soon was an authority on the subject. At the time not much study had been done in the field, so that when Dale graduated he was very much in demand for employment. In fact he laughingly stated that he was one of the most sought-after garbage men in the nation. He felt powerful enough then, and whenever he took a new job he would make sure that his duties were clearly outlined so that he could do exactly what was expected of him, "not a bit more and not a bit less," he would say dogmatically. Taking any criticism was out of the question, or doing any bit of work that could possibly be done by a subordinate was not even a matter for discussion. He asserted that he wouldn't take any shit from anyone, but ironically the nature of his work was such that he was taking shit from everyone.

Despite his acknowledged expertise, he was continually either quitting or getting fired. Then he would get a new job for more money and the whole thing would start all over again.

His lack of stability made him anxious, and at length he sought analysis. I asked him about his work; he had little to say except that "it's a living." Or he would add that he wouldn't hang around past 4:45 in the afternoon. He would leave a boring job to go home to a boring wife, and be in a hurry to do it, but none of it meant anything to him. It was difficult to draw him out about the nature of the work he was doing, and only with a great deal of prodding did I learn that he had written several important papers and had given one or two at meetings on ecology; also that he had been invited to take positions in teaching or in research, but that in contemplating the material rewards he had turned them down—although not without some second thoughts.

It was only when we began to explore his unconscious feelings underlying the choice of his vocation that we began to understand what inner processes had brought him to this work. He had an unshakable feeling of rottenness about himself, through and through, as if to say, a child who has been rejected from the moment of his birth must be disgusting indeed. And ever after he had had to face a hostile environment, and somehow manage to make it endurable. The world, plainly speaking, was a pile of shit, and the best he could do was to clean it up a little. And so he learned to do this in a highly sophisticated way. The method was all right, yes, he was an expert in the method, but it didn't help much, either in the impact he was able to have on the world, or in his own feeling about himself.

Only in the analysis, when he began to confront the unconscious, could he learn that it was his own feeling of being garbage, worthless, that he was projecting upon the world. Then something began to happen. He first had to face the dark side of himself, to find out who the eminent scientist really was. And he was not a pleasant subject for self-knowledge. He could not clean up what he saw by getting an easy job that paid a lot of money; he could not redeem his self-image even if he fulfilled the explicit requirements of the job. He began to see that he had externalized his need to develop a thorough rebalancing of his psychic functioning by differentiating the positive and potentially constructive aspects of his individuality from the negative and potentially destructive aspects.

We talked a great deal about his "inner ecology," without much mentioning his work. Gradually he began to think of himself less as a discard from the human race, and more as a member of it, whose survival and productivity depended very much upon his making himself and his knowledge useful to the world, with its people and their needs. Gradually, he began to give a little, instead of only taking. And one day it dawned on him that the analytical work in which he was engaged could be understood as "psychological ecology." He had known it all along, in his *head*, but suddenly one day he accepted it fully as a fact of his total being. He knew that he was a microcosm of the whole world, and that in his inner life he could work to convert his own filth into clear life-giving waters and fertilizer, just as in his professional vocation he could act to convert filth and pollution in the environment into breathable air and drinkable water. A change of attitude appeared quite suddenly, but the potential for it had been in him all along. It had been the inner urge for redemption from his own filth that had arranged the neurotic behavior which got him out of the Army and into a place which could prepare him to fulfill his inner necessity.

As I worked with Dale I had to consider that the "garbage man" did not exist only in him, but that this character also lived in me. Isn't the analyst also a sort of garbage handler? Isn't it my job to pick out and sort the detritus of years in the lives of my analysands, and try to remove what is no longer needed? But, lest I become caught up in the image of the "do-gooder," I am sharply reminded that I have to deal with my own garbage as well. The training analysis that analysts go through is supposed to teach us how to clear out the trash and refuse of our lives so as to open up space for the new and the growing. But this does not end with the termination of the training analysis. I have not only to take out my own garbage, but to be very careful not to take in the garbage of other people. This is something to remember when I wake up in the night fretting over the injustice of what somebody did to someone else. I recall the advice given in the gnostic Gospel of Truth: "Make firm the foot of those who have stumbled and stretch out your hand to those who are ill." But this is followed with: "Be concerned with yourselves; do not be concerned with other things which you have rejected from yourselves. Do not return to what you have vomited to eat it. Do not be moths. Do not be worms, for you have already cast it off. Do not become a dwelling place for the devil, for you have already destroyed him."[4]

Once, at the start of our work together, Dale said that he had just drifted into this particular branch of engineering because it was a wide-open field—not many people were interested in spending their working days examining the decomposing wastes from the city sewers—and the pay was good. Some time later he admitted he had experienced the strong feeling of an inner voice that had guided him to choose the courses that he did, unpopular as these courses were in the university at the time. For some reason which he was unable to fathom, the field of work appealed to him, and so he followed his feelings there and applied himself to his studies. Recently Dale has come to see purpose in what he is doing, and I am guardedly hopeful that, if his potentialities now unfold, he will make an outstanding contribution to society. For analysis not only speaks to the individual, but must recognize the place of the individual in the social order. He is beginning to know who he is. Today there exists the possibility that the right man will begin to work in the right way.

The analysand who has gone through the current problems of his life and attempted with the analyst's help, to see what the meaning may be behind the symbolic forms of behavior, and who has been willing to trace back the current behavior to whatever earlier stages hold the key for unlocking the patterns that now operate, has come to a crucial point in the analysis. It may be that now that the crisis is passed, the urgency for psychotherapy is no longer present. It may be that some symptoms are no longer visible, or that if they are, the analysand begins to learn to live with them and to exert enough control on them so that they do not interfere overmuch with his functioning. He is better, the most obvious damage seems to have been repaired. It is at this point that a decision will be made, and that decision is whether to go on in the analysis, to take the dark journey which reveals what it is that has been hidden—not only that it was something unmentionable and unacceptable, but just what is its composition and how does it function.

The process of individuation, as it is experienced in analysis, requires a long and laborious process of pulling together all those fragmented and chaotic bits and pieces of unconscious personalities, into an integrated whole which is conscious of itself and the way in which it works. Referring back to one of our initial dreams, the question put was simply—is it sufficient that you have learned to drive the car, or shall we look and see what is under the hood? Most people go through life without ever knowing what is under the hood, and that is perhaps good enough on a city street where every few blocks there is a mechanic who can help you if you get into trouble. But, if you want to be self-sufficient on the longer journeys, and if you want to possess the freedom to take whatever road you will, then for you it is a necessity to see what is "under the hood."

How is the decision made whether to continue therapy past the point of the relief of symptoms, and toward the further end? There is no single answer for this, as one sees it in practice, and yet it is my belief that there is one answer under which all answers which are given by the analysand or by the analyst may be subsumed. Many people come into Jungian analysis after having been exposed to Jung through their reading, or through attending lectures, workshops, films, or other public programs, and have become deeply interested in the individuation process. They enter analysis knowing that no amount of reading will give them any more than a superficial description, and that they must embark on that journey—reading the guidebook is not an acceptable substitute. So the desire for individuation is expressed as an inclination from the very start. Even so, not all of the people who seek this way are able to do what they say they wish to do. An attempt at analysis simply may not yield up the symbolic material that evokes the archetypal substratum of the personality.

On the other hand, sometimes the analysis yields up too much. One woman had come into treatment after she had been having a great many impressive and moving dreams for several years. She had become interested in reading Jung and finding in Jung the symbolism which, she felt, could help her to interpret her own dreams. We began analysis. As time went on she found herself waking often in drenching sweats or panic, or feeling exhausted, as though she had been pursued all night. The more she read and tried to understand, the more she would get the bizarre and disturbing dreams. In analysis she brought several dreams each time she came to a session, and they were so fantastic in their plots and so luminous in their imagery that to my chagrin I sometimes found myself looking forward to her hour like an art student anticipating a day at the Uffizi. The following dream which she brought made clear that she was one of those people for whom the stirring-up of the unconscious could be more dangerous than helpful: *I was standing on a high balcony leaning out into the night. Out of the sky a star glowed brighter and brighter in the east, and came rolling toward me. As it approached it grew larger and glowed a deep sapphire blue. A silver halo surrounded it, and it came closer and closer, shining ever more brightly. I knew that all the air in the universe was bound up in it and that it would come close enough for me to step out onto it and be as light as air. It came as I expected, as huge as a moon and I could nearly reach out and touch it. I felt light enough to leap onto it, but then there in the distance I saw another star growing large and sailing toward me from the south. It was a huge glowing ruby, and as it neared I could see the fires raging within it. It came very close and hung in all its glory just a few yards beyond where I was standing, and I knew I could be warm forever if I let myself go out to it. Then out of the western sky a ball of purest white came flying in my direction, and I could see that it bub- bled and foamed as though a million whitecaps were tumbling over each other in brilliant sparkles. As I leaned forward it oc- curred to me to look back, and suddenly I saw that the balcony on which I stood had detached itself from the building, and that the whole earth was a brown ball receding from me in astonish- ing swiftness.*

Without going into the symbolism of the dream, it was clear enough to me that the analysand needed *not* to go for- ward into the mysteries of the collective unconscious, but rather that she should be protected from the fascination of the archetype. Standing on the brink of the abyss, the analysand needed more than anything the support which would help her regain her hold on the material world. The stress of the individuation process was surely contraindicated for her at this time.

But the following dream presents quite a different message. It was brought by a woman whose life situation was progressing adequately, and who was reasonably successful in her job, although it did not offer her opportunity commensurate with her ability. She felt that she could grow beyond that job were she able to loosen up and express her ideas in a more forceful way. But she lacked courage. She dreamed: *I was in a house that looked like the house in which I grew up, and I was standing before the door to my father's workshop. That was a room which I had been told not to enter; now I know that it was where father kept certain electrical tools which could have been dangerous. But, as a child, I had been warned that terrible things would happen to me if I went in there, and I imagined that it was full of monsters and bogeymen who would get me if I ever opened the door. As I stand before this door I see that it is of enormous size. In the center of it there is a square brass plate with a great brass handle on it, and underneath the handle a keyhole. I am standing there wondering what to do, and you (the analyst) come up behind me. You place a key in my hand and then I am alone again. I walk up to the door and place the key in the keyhole. It turns as of itself. I step back and the door slowly opens. I look inside, but all that I can see is blackness. I am trembling. I then hear a voice which says, "Why not go in?" I feel that it must be all right to do so, and I walk into the darkness. That black space stretches as far as I can see. Nevertheless I take a few steps inward. Soon in the uttermost distance I can distinguish the faintest shade of deep gray and I know that beyond my vision there must be light somewhere. I take another step and pause, and the darkness begins ever so gradually to pale.*

This woman was prepared to begin the exploration of the unknown depths, and we went ahead.

One more dream, this one from a young man who had difficulties relating to people in a feeling way. He tended to recognize only his own needs and to be unable to sense the more subtle responses of other people, especially those who were reticent in expressing themselves. He was afraid to be open with the people who were close to him. Therefore he felt unable to carry on any intense relationship. This is his dream:

I am in a new house. I find a bird stiff and dead. Maybe I make an effort to warm him. But he is dead.

Later I come back to move into this house. I am going to throw him out. Somehow I find that he is alive. Immediately I begin to try to revive him. It is very cold in the house. The coldness is what killed him. I begin trying to warm him. I bring him near a source of heat. The room is drafty. I cup my hands behind him so that the heat will be shielded in and the draft kept away. I do this for a long time.

Then he is awake. The windows in this room are open. I hold the little bird in my cupped hands so he won't get away and maybe fly out of doors by mistake. He would never live out there. Then I walk around the room closing the windows with my elbows.

Then I am standing near the source of heat again. I am cupping my hands behind him, trying to capture as much of the heat as I can for him. His feathers begin to soften. He fills out and softens. I think he is a white bird, with full soft feathers and a long tale (sic). [N.B. This is not a typographical error, but rather a slip which carries its specific meaning.]

Then he is nipping at my finger or hand. Why is he doing this? Is he trying to bite me? For a minute I am afraid. But that passes. He doesn't.

My parents come in or are there. I tell them about the bird, that he is alive. I am very moved in telling them. They don't seem to notice.

Then the bird climbs onto the source of heat, the radiator, and sits down. I am afraid that it might be too hot for him. I feel it and it seems fine. He gathers his legs under him, and sits up there looking out, collected and warm.

My mother and father open the window. I tell them not to do that. I go around and close the wide-open window and some

*others that were a little open. Now it will be really warm in here.
No chills.*

*Then I look to the radiator. There is the bird, sitting as be-
fore, looking out, collected, all there, himself.*

*Then I am worried about food. At one point I thought he
looked hungry. I look around and find a set of bird things on the
table there, with water, a place for him to go to the bathroom
and so on. I feel that he must know what he is doing around this
place. I decide to leave these things where they are. Then I look
and find a bag of bird seed.*

*The next thing I know, I look up and see the bird winding up
a toy doll on the mantel. I am absolutely amazed. I point this
out to my parents. They ask me if my brother didn't pick this
place out well with the fireplace and all.*

*Then the bird is skiing on little skis. He skis down the cur-
tain, then he skis down my shirt. He has little ski poles which I
saw first, and little silver skis.*

*I notice that somebody was skiing outside the window and
that the bird saw this and got the idea himself. I am amazed that
the bird is so intelligent. He is so amazing.*

Then I say:

"This is the spirit of a reincarnated holy man.

"This is the spirit of a human being of former times."

The young man's dream is rich with symbolism that could
be discussed and amplified to bring light upon his orientation
to his life, his difficulties and his potentialities. I have not re-
produced it in detail for that purpose, but rather to give the
reader the flavor of the dream as it was reported, the very slow
and gradual development of the relationship between the
dreamer and his bird. The bird, being a creature of earth yet
not entirely of earth, since he can fly, is a symbol for that
incomprehensible part of man that is sometimes called
"spirit." It evokes the feeling of relatedness on a plane which is
not strictly material—there is a non-corporeality about the
man-bird connection. In our discussion of the dream we understood the bird as the expression of that unconscious aspect
of the dreamer that is most responsive to the tender feelings of

being cherished and cared for. It is this quality in the dreamer that is portrayed as dormant, and all but dead. He nearly gives up on it, but then as he returns to make sure that there is no hope, he discovers that perhaps after all, there is still a breath of life there and it is worthwhile to try to revive him. Then comes the long and difficult period in which he bends all his efforts toward counteracting the coldness that killed or nearly killed the bird. The care and effort expended corresponds to the analytic process and the devotion manifested there; the close watch on the feelings and responses is what makes it possible to bring warmth and life to where there was before only coldness and immobility.

As the feelings became more active, the analysand was able to experience his emotional life more fully. The white bird with the long feathers and the white "tale" evoked the image and legend of the holy ghost. For the dreamer, this referred to a mystical aspect of relationship which required accepting another on faith—something that had always been difficult for him. The acceptance had first to take place as an inner experience, growing out of his receptivity to that threatened, hardly living, sensitive aspect of his own being. As if to test him, the bird nips at him; this suggests that his own openness makes him more vulnerable to being hurt, an idea which he resisted at first but then accepted as a necessary part of the process. It was even something to rejoice about—in the dream it was a sign of life and strength in the bird, in the psyche it referred to an increasing ability to deal with the possibility of rejection from others if he would reach out to them.

The appearance of the parents and their activity symbolized a regressive trend in the dreamer, for his parents in the dream, as in reality, tended to treat him as a child whose feelings were not worth noticing. He had wanted, even when very young, to express himself and to get back some reaction in depth, but he was usually merely brushed off—his parents were more concerned with other matters. The rejecting attitude, despised as it was, had been unconsciously adopted in childhood by the dreamer. In his efforts to win approval first from parents and then elsewhere, he had rejected his own sensitive spiritual side, his "white bird."

The dream showed him liberating the power of feelings inherent in the bird by not allowing the presumed death to take over. He considered the slightest sign of life as worthy of his full devotion. Gradually the dreamer was able to become mature enough to oppose his parents, who corresponded to his inner tendency to resist his feelings. Closing the windows meant that he needed to keep this newly revived capacity of his within bounds, and by all means avoid letting the parental "critical" attitude endanger the new development. When he decided to take a firm stand, to care for the bird regardless of what the parents might think, he found that everything he needed to carry through had already been provided for him— thus the bird's food and water and other things which appeared when the dreamer looked for him.

With the marvelous humor that dreams sometimes provide, the bird suddenly became an independent creature, and was winding up the little toy doll, much to the dreamer's amazement. How much like life: when we finally learn to do something in a new way, that knowledge takes over and begins to have an existence of its own, introducing us to possibilities of which we have never dreamed. The skiing is a case in point—it is sheer exuberance! The dreamer was utterly amazed that what he thought was a small creature who could at best be a pet, turned out to have imagination and flair. The dreamer associated the skis with the special meaning that mountains have for him—the pristine heights where spiritual values are the primary values. The dreamer had been interested in reading about mountain religions, and the symbolism from these religions often colored his dreams. In this particular dream, however, two opposing and disjointed aspects of the dreamer came together: one was the rarified intellectual interest in religion as a discipline acquired through reading and study, and the other was the capacity to extend the abstract concept of the unity of all things to a sense of relatedness with actual living things. That the bird was seen as the spirit of a reincarnated holy man, a human being of former times, seemed to convey a sense of the connection between "former times" and "this moment," a binding of the remote old wise man with the tenderly present fluttering creature in the hand of the dreamer.

I cannot say much more about this dream, except that in dealing with it both the dreamer and I were deeply touched. It was an important individuation dream in that it enabled him to move along in the process with a sense of having come through a period of being constrained and fearful, and in that he was entering upon another phase in which he would be careful and responsive, but no longer fearful in the same blindly anxious way. Concern would begin to replace anxiety. This dream, and others which came along, proved to be guide-posts which could provide orientation for a newly emerging personality as yet unsure of its direction.

The question was raised: how is the decision made as to whether to proceed from therapy into analysis on the way of individuation, or whether to conclude therapy when the symptoms which precipitated the call for help have been more or less satisfactorily resolved? Perhaps, in the course of reviewing these few dreams which clearly refer to the individuation process, the decisive factor has become apparent. That factor is, of course, the unconscious itself. The unconscious, through dreams and through its manifestations in everyday life, provides all the information we need to know. The unconscious, with its ingenious way of symbolizing, sets the picture before us: this is how it is, there are these and these obstacles, but there is a chance of breaking through to a new position with a wider perspective. Or the unconscious may place violent objections in the path, warning of disaster if the stirring up of archetypal material is encouraged to continue. Such a warning was clearly present in the balcony dream of the pre-psychotic woman. It is the responsibility of the analyst to "read" with utmost care the unconscious material that is brought up, and to allow himself to be guided by it.

This is not to say that the process is dependent entirely on

the unconscious and its manifestations. Jung laid great stress
on the decisive role played by consciousness and its capacity
for insight, though he rejected the "dictatorship of consciousness" and insisted that attention be paid to the contents which
emerge from the unconscious. It is a two-pronged effort in
which unconscious material is given the attention which is
due to it, while at the same time a continuing effort is made to
strengthen consciousness so that it may become equal to the
demands made on it in its encounter with the contents of the
unconscious.[5]

Each person will, in the process of his analysis, find his
own methods and ways of confronting the unconscious. The
possibilities are varied, and throughout the course of this
book I will continue to give examples. What is essential to all
of these ways is that the individual commit himself or herself
fully to the unconscious process, and, at the same time, determine to maintain a strong hold on the mundane realities and
responsibilities that his life imposes. I, for my part as analyst,
make it clear to the analysand that our work together will not
provide for him an easy out by which he can excuse himself
from difficult relationships with people, or demand extra time
off from his work because of emotional disturbances, or expect his wife to tolerate his bad temper or lack of attention. I
recognize, of course, that the analytic effort may at times put
the analysand under a great deal of emotional strain—and I let
him know this at the beginning. If it appears that he is not
able or willing to sustain the additional burdens of increasing
consciousness, he ought not to subject himself to the rigors of
the individuation process in analysis. That discipline is a personal discipline, and those who undertake it must do so on
their own responsibility, and not expect to be made whole at
the expense of their friends or wives or lovers.

Another question arises, perhaps more in my own mind
than in the analysand's. Should the analysand, entering on the
deeper levels of exploration, expect the analyst to carry him
along and to be an ever-present support and protector? Has he
a right, by virtue of the mutual commitment of analyst and

analysand, to expect the analyst to be available to him when-ever he gets into unusual difficulty? The answer is not easy—my first impulse is to say that he should be guided by the analyst not to proceed too rapidly, and to make sure that on each step along the way the new discoveries and insights can be thoroughly assimilated so that they become usable as the analysand prepares to move forward. Furthermore, it could be said that the analyst should encourage the analysand to utilize his own critical judgment in regarding his dream and fantasy material, by allowing him ample opportunity to participate in the interpreting of it during the analytical hour.

But the fact of the matter is, all this is purely theoretical; it simply does not work out this way in practice. The Jungian analysis, unlike most kinds of therapy that I know anything about, does not take place primarily in the consulting room. This is especially true at the more advanced stages of analysis. The consulting room is, in large measure, a sort of staging area, where the experiences and the insights stemming from them are assembled, and the analytic discussion takes place, a discussion which is aimed at finding meaning in what has been brought for consideration. Then the analysand is sent forth again into the battle with the world, armed with what-ever understanding has emerged as he and the analyst have together dealt with the material at hand. Often, after an illu-minating session, I have had to say to the analysand, "What is really important is what you do with all this now, now as you walk out of here, and between now and the time you return again. That is what will prove whether what we have done is valuable or not."

As it happens, there is nothing I can do to assure the anal-ysand or myself that he will be able to cope with unseen or unanticipated dangers. There is no guarantee that he will not get into a panic, or that he will not be seized with a depression that he cannot manage. If I sense this as a possibility, I may let him know that he is to deal with it as well as he can, and there are specific suggestions which I may make, depending on his needs as an individual. If, even so, he feels in urgent need of help, he may call me and I will try to be available to him. In my experience there have been very few people who have abused the knowledge that I could be accessible to them when necessary; there have been occasions when even talking together on the phone for a few minutes has brought about a calmer view, but more often the knowledge that I would be there, if it came to that urgency, was sufficient to tide the person over a difficult hour.

There is, too, the matter of the limitations of the analyst as a human being. I believe it is a mistake for an analyst to make himself unreachable by telephone except during certain brief and specified hours. On the other hand I believe it is an even greater mistake for an analyst to behave as though he were omnipresent and omnipotent. The analyst who does not reserve time for his own relaxation and recreation and reading and enjoyment will not sleep very well at night. The crown of thorns will become most uncomfortable.

In short, the tool with which an analyst works is himself. It is his responsibility to his patient to keep this tool, himself, in good physical and psychological condition, and he has to discover what is the best way for him to do this, so that he may keep functioning at the highest level he is capable of. There will be times when he will sit with a colleague and submit himself to the analytic process, to help restore his own objectivity and to re-engage with his unconscious life. Whatever else he does, he will need to set aside time each day to reflect on his work and evaluate it, to consider where he gained understanding, where he overlooked something important, and where he needs to reconsider what was done and find additional meaning in it. He must be aware of the feelings of his own that were stirred during the course of his day's work, and why. I usually review each session at the end of the day while it is still fresh, and note down any ideas that may come up in me as to how I may want to approach the next session. I need to do this in order to bring a degree of perspective to my work, but there is still another reason. I expect the analysand to reflect on the substance of the session and to integrate what he can of it into his awareness and possibly even into his behavior—have I the right to expect him to do more than I am willing to do myself?

The between-session work that is carried on by analysands is so varied that it might be said that each person's work is unique to himself. The one characteristic that binds all this work together is that all of it, in one way or another, is a confrontation of unconscious contents by the ego. Not all of it is verbal. The technique of the confrontation will be discussed in Chapter 10, "Dreaming the Dream Onward: Active Imagination," but here it may be helpful to offer a sample of that private and individual work which is done by the analysand alone, and which contributes so much in the long run to the transformation of the personality.

The example was brought to me in the form of a meditative poem. In the process of writing it a man was working his way through a depression. He had a boring job, and sometimes in his frustrations arising from work he tended to be unpleasant to his wife, who then reacted negatively. It became then just a matter of time until he began to feel that none of his efforts was appreciated, that he must be just a worthless person, and he sank into the morass of self-pity. In the past he had countered this tendency with a few drinks or an argument with his wife. He gradually learned in the course of his analysis not to try to escape his depressions, but to allow himself to go into them and experience them fully—to see what they were made of. To do this, he would retire to his room and write out his feelings just as they came to him. He gave the name "A Man's Individuation Hymn" to this example of his efforts to work his way through a depression. Here is the text as he gave it to me:

When I am low, when all my magic is scattered,
a little bit placed on each of my friends.
that's when my loving wife soothes my soul with
"For God's sake, the world doesn't revolve around you,
you Know."

That's when she becomes oh so panicky for it's rejection
that she feels,
and she is right as she can be.
i do reject her and all she stands for.

there are times when a man needs space,
when he craves to be alone
to let his mind wander and play with all sorts of notions
about himself and those with whom he has been in contact.
sometimes a good husband must entertain the idea of his
wife's death with joy.

but of course it is not she who is the problem
that is plain to me.
rather the demon who lives within and not without.
to remember that at the same time it is being projected
onto your wife is the key to a golden marital relationship.
that is no easy trick, you know;
it requires what i like to call
the delicate inversion of the butterfly.

i could explain this as i have been known to have done
so many philosophical times before,
but now let it stand as it is,
and let those who understand be quiet
lest this too be scattered in the wind.

i will go soon, again to try to cause to take place
all that is in my heart,
but in order to clear the air with my wife
and with myself, let me issue this final phrase,
"I reject myself, not my loving wife, and I will not run
away to some accepting image of the past. I will stay put
in my rejection of this sloppy, good-for-nothing
irresponsible, wormy day that is about to close, and already
I sense that by staying put
and keeping my wife out of my network
there is something like the dogged determination
being born within
that will be needed to get back on my path on the morrow."

There is no need to explain this, for he has said it well when he wrote "let those who understand be quiet." I only want to note one interesting detail of which the writer was not aware when he brought the piece into analysis. That was the capitalization of the word "I" at the very beginning, then the use of the lower case "i" all through until the very last lines, when again the capital letter is used. It is nearly as if the ego were in charge at the beginning, but then gave over the process to the unconscious throughout, until the end, when the ego returned with its big "I" to reassert itself as an individual who goes out to meet the world.

This movement is characteristic of the individuation process, especially as it proceeds during the first half of life.

I have often been asked whether it is necessary to undertake a formal Jungian analysis in order to achieve the benefits of the "individuation process." My response is that individuation is natural, and it occurs in most individuals as their consciousness increases in depth and complexity during the course of their lives. Many ways have been developed over the ages to enhance this process, with different practices and differing objectives. Jung's way is not suited to everyone's disposition or needs. For those who have a particular affinity to the methods evolved by Jung to deal with the human psyche, the individuation process can open up a relationship between consciousness, as mediated by the ego, and the unconscious, which is contained in "the All." It is a difficult and perilous path, as is every path which leads toward inner wisdom.

6

Persona and Shadow

. . .

A VERY PROPER YOUNG WOMAN from a respectable conservative family was in analysis with me. Early in our work together she brought the following dream: *I came to your office in a beautiful gown of black velvet with a high neck and long sleeves, but when I turned around there was no dress at all in back, just bare skin from top to bottom.*

In becoming civilized, we compromise between our natural inclinations and the patterns of society. We assume a certain character or stance through which we can relate. Jung calls this stance a mask or a *persona*, the name given to the masks worn by the actors of antiquity to signify the roles they played. The persona is oriented toward society or, more precisely, toward the expectation of society that an individual may have. Seeking to find his place in the particular milieu in which he must function, he assumes the accoutrements of the milieu. The side which fronts society is geared to meet it, and on its terms. Often the one who goes out dressed to the teeth for the party is the only one who does not realize that his backside is showing.

The persona is not altogether negative. It serves a useful function in that it mediates between ourselves and society. I often tell my analysands that a persona is necessary; it clothes the individual in a way that can help the casual observer come to an appropriate idea of what that person is like. I would say, if you are going to present a gift of a diamond ring, you would not package it in a paper bag, and if you were going to give someone a quart of milk you probably would not choose to give it in a crystal flask. The purpose of the persona is to indicate something of what the person is like, just as the mask suggests the role or emotions of the actor. It has its part in facilitating an adaptation to the requirements of society, and it also serves to help define the individual in a particular setting. We can present ourselves, depending on the situation, as teacher, parent, lover, business person, servant, guide.

Jung takes a somewhat harsh view of the persona:

> Only by reason of the fact that the persona is a more or less accidental or arbitrary segment of collective psyche can we make the mistake of accepting it *in toto* as something "individual." But, as its name shows, it is only a mask for the collective psyche, a mask that *feigns individuality*, and tries to make others and oneself believe that one is individual, whereas one is simply playing a part in which the collective psyche speaks.
>
> When we analyse the persona we strip off the mask, and discover that what seemed to be individual is at bottom collective; in other words, that the persona was only a mask for the collective psyche. Fundamentally the persona is nothing real: it is a compromise between the individual and society as to what a man should appear to be. He takes a name, earns a title, represents an office, he is this or that. In a certain sense all this is real, yet in relation to the essential individuality of the person concerned it is only a secondary reality, a product of compromise, in making which others often have a greater share than he. The persona is a semblance, a two-dimensional reality.[1]

The symbols for the persona are the cover-ups: they may appear in dreams as dress, hats, armor, veils, shields; or they may take on the characteristics of a profession or trade, as tools, equipment of various sorts, certain specific books; or they may be reflected in an automobile, or even in some instances a house or apartment. Or the persona may be expressed in awards, diplomas, or a variety of so-called "status symbols." Identification with the persona is common in all parts of society, for as people identify themselves as belonging to a certain category they begin to adopt behavior appropriate to that category and to discard what does not fit. They soon begin to believe "I am that. I am a successful doctor, or an intellectual, or a pop musician, or a great humorist," and they will let you know this almost before you have a chance to exchange a word with them. This may work well enough until something happens to change or damage the mask that has been interposed between the reality of the person and the desired image. Then the person begins to wonder, "Who am I?" The lack of a personal sense of identity—of knowing who you are—may lead to a serious crisis. And yet such a crisis is almost always necessary sooner or later in the individuation process, because until the false self is recognized the true self cannot be known.

This was the case with my patient, a priest in a large suburban church. He came to one analytic session carrying a letter in his hand, and evidently quite upset about it. The letter had come from a parishioner, an elderly lawyer who had recently retired and did not have very much to keep him busy. Church activities were the mainstay of his life, and he was a substantial contributor to the building fund. This man had attended church the previous Sunday, and had gone home and written a letter in a half-apologetic manner, stating that he had been greatly disturbed to find that the priest had allowed a woman to serve communion at the mass. This did not seem right to him. He also complained that Father Leo had overlooked the customary rubric of reading a certain prayer himself and instead had asked the congregation to join with him. The lawyer was adamant about maintaining the traditional practices of the church. The letter ended, "I am sure that you are glad there aren't too many lawyers in the church to pressure you about these kinds of problems!"

Father Leo was furious. He felt himself under attack. "There's no possibility of pleasing everybody! If I listened to the conservatives like this attorney, I would lose all the young people in the congregation. If I make all the changes these young people want in their cries for 'relevance' I'll lose the ones who have been members for years and who are the financial support of the church. I always have to compromise, but no matter what I do there is always somebody who gets unhappy about it."

We talked about his being what he thought he had to be, that he *was* the priest, that role was or seemed to him to be his entire existence. He was able to recognize that everyone, in the course of pursuing a career, assumes a role, whether it be that of clergyman or butcher, schoolteacher or analyst. We learn as we grow into our "position" that certain practices are acceptable and that other practices are not acceptable. Sometimes these are subtle matters; the preacher's tone of voice, the analyst's pause, are like the mask held before the face: when you see the mask raised you know what to expect from the actor. We talked about how dress indicates to people even before they meet us what they may expect. People dress for success or dress to show that they don't belong to a particular collective with its specific viewpoint.

Father Leo, who sat in front of me, customarily wears a black suit with a clerical collar. His persona makes it clear to people that they shouldn't swear in front of him, that he is to be treated with proper respect. Even the policeman who stops him for speeding waves him on with a smile, when he sees the garb, or lets him off, suggesting, "I'm sure you're hurrying to see a sick parishioner." But when Father Leo comes to see his analyst, he typically wears a sport shirt and a pair of slacks. He gets across that he doesn't expect to be treated with the deference here that he gets when he is wearing his preacher-persona; he wants a more direct confrontation, so that is how he presents himself.

The persona problem that Father Leo has is that he identifies too much with his persona. He doesn't quite know where the priest leaves off and the man begins.

The lawyer was not criticizing Leo the *man*, he was criticizing *his priest*, the one who appears in a black suit on Sundays in the pulpit and who does not quite correspond to his, the lawyer's, idea of how a priest customarily conducts a service. When Leo assumes that he is criticizing Leo, the person, he has identified with his persona. Ego and persona have become indistinguishable.

Leo had to discover that his reality is that of an individual who assumes a certain role for professional purposes. This is not to say that he doffs his beliefs or his concern with matters of the spirit when he takes off his collar, not by any means. But that aspect of his profession which is required by society must come to mean to him simply that "I have to do this in order to convey to people that I am their spiritual leader, but I remain my own person, with my own beliefs. I recognize that I cannot be all things to all men, and I make my peace with that."

But how to deal with the lawyer? Once Leo began to understand how the persona was functioning with him, he was then prepared to take the next step, which was to put into the life experience itself the insights that emerged in analysis. It would have been an easy thing to pass off the letter from the lawyer by telling him, "I'm sorry you were upset about that, but we have to make changes in the church from time to time," and then jolly him over a cup of coffee. But what if the lawyer was also identified with *his* persona? Could he be using his persona in an unconscious way as a means for getting attention from Father Leo? Here was an elderly man, retired, who had held positions of importance in the past, who now wanted some emotional support from his pastor, and who knew no other way to get it but to retreat into his traditional way of doing things, that is, into his own persona, that of a lawyer. So he made legalistic, nit-picking remarks about the church service.

When a person is in analysis with me, it is understood between us that he has the responsibility in his interpersonal relations to be conscious of what is going on below the level of appearances. If one does not gain the capacity to deepen his level of awareness, then of what need is analysis? So Leo was expected to be able to understand that the attorney was identified with his own persona, with his attorney role, and that he related to Leo's persona, which he mistook for Leo himself. It is with the persona that he took issue. Leo then had to understand that he was not personally being attacked but that it was his persona which got attacked. Once he recognized this he could step back and discuss the whole matter with his attorney-congregant without feeling personally threatened. It put a wholly different light on the confrontation. Instead of having to defend himself in an apologetic or self-deprecating way, he could meet it head-on. Leo could explain to his friend that, yes, he had considered the matter and he saw the validity of the other's viewpoint. However, a new generation and changing times necessitated his taking into account not only the very valuable contributions of the older people, but that he also had to maintain rapport with the younger people who wanted services in a language which they recognized as their own.

Father Leo could not expect his elderly parishioner to meet him halfway. It was his responsibility as an analyzed person to carry the burden of greater consciousness. That required him to meet his friend where he was, on his own ground, and to lead him along by presenting to him the dilemma in which he found himself; that was, the dilemma of maintaining the cohesiveness of the church by recognizing the needs of all the factions within it in such a way that no one would need to feel too far away from the central function of the church as a place of worship. But in order to do this, Leo could not allow himself to feel personally endangered every time his method of performing a service was attacked. He had to recognize that only the technique was being attacked, and not the individual who was acting in accordance with his own sense of what was valuable.

Ego functioning is always, to some extent, overlaid with a certain amount of persona. The ego is in a constant process of receiving stimuli from the environment and is also receiving impressions from the unconscious—which sometimes support the event that is going on and in which ego is participating, and sometimes in conflict with it. The ego needs always to mediate stimulus and response; what this means practically is that we are constantly having to make split-second decisions in the process of adapting or not adapting to the demands that are made upon us. Every decision means choosing one of the many possible attitudes and rejecting all the others. As we have seen, the individual's typology plays an important part in determining the nature of the ego and consequently the choices the ego will make. These decisions, supported by the underlying typology, act to build up a persona, a way of responding to a demand from some collective that is characteristic for its role. It would be wrong, according to Jung, "to leave the matter as it stands without at the same time recognizing that there is, after all, something individual in the peculiar choice and delineation of the persona, and that despite the exclusive identity of the ego-consciousness with the persona, the unconscious self, one's real individuality, is always present and makes itself felt indirectly if not directly. Although the ego-consciousness is at first identical with the persona—that compromise role in which we parade before the community— yet the unconscious self can never be repressed to the point of extinction. Its influence is chiefly manifest in the special nature of the contrasting and compensating contents of the unconscious."[2]

Besides the persona there is another, darker side to our personality which we do not consciously display in public: the *shadow*. It is what is inferior in our personality, that part of us which we will not allow ourselves to express. The stronger and more rigid the persona, and the more we identify with it, the more we must deny the other important aspects of our personality. These aspects are repressed to the unconscious, and they contribute to the formation of a more or less autonomous splinter-personality, the shadow. The shadow finds its own means of expression, though, particularly in projections. What we cannot admit in ourselves we often find in others. If, when an individual speaks of another person whom he hates with a vehemence that seems nearly irrational, he can be brought to describe that person's characteristics which he most dislikes, you will frequently have a picture of his own repressed aspects, which are unrecognized by him though obvious to others. The shadow is a dominant of the personal unconscious and consists of all those uncivilized desires and emotions that are incompatible with social standards and with the persona; it is all that we are ashamed of. It also has its collective aspects which are expressed mythologically, for example, as the devil or a witch. But the shadow also has a positive value, at least in its potential. There is no shadow without consciousness, no darkness without light. The shadow is a necessary aspect of man; he would be incomplete, utterly shallow without it. Jung writes:

> The shadow is a moral problem that challenges the whole ego-personality, for no one can become conscious of the shadow without considerable moral effort. To become conscious of it involves recognizing the dark aspect of the personality as present and real. This act is the essential condition for self-knowledge, and it therefore, as a rule, meets with considerable resistance. Indeed, self-knowledge as a psychotherapeutic measure frequently requires much painstaking work extending over a long period.[3]

An extreme example of what happens when the shadow goes completely unrecognized came out in the case of an elementary-school principal, whom we will call Brian B. On casual acquaintance he was the last person one would have expected would be in analysis, and indeed, he was careful not to let the fact be known. Obviously, it did not belong to his persona. Brian B. was a man in his late forties, handsome, clean-cut, a typical red-blooded American boy grown up. He described himself to me as "very lucky." "Things always go for me," he said. He let me know that he had a marvelous sense of timing, that he knew just when to promote a new program, when to hold off. He handled his faculty well, was popular with the students, put in long hours at his work, and frequently received commendation from the school board.

He came to me, he explained carefully, not because of himself but because of marital difficulties. (I have long ago learned to beware of the patient who comes into therapy to learn to live with somebody else's problems!) His wife, he said, was grouchy and irritable, and she constantly belittled him in public. She had a mania for neatness which he could not abide, and she was quite independent and controlling. He said that he would like to get out of his marriage, except that it would probably cost him too much and might jeopardize his position. Often in the evenings he attended the sports events at school or meetings of various sorts, and many weekends were consumed with outings and camping trips with students. Hardly much to criticize here, especially from the community's point of view!

Brian B. came from a farm background and a family with rigid conventional moral standards. He was brought up to respect women and to believe that the place for all sexual activity was within the structure of marriage, and that the purpose of sex begins and ends with *procreation*. He was initiated into sex by a prostitute when he was eighteen, and shortly thereafter he began to date a young woman whom he described as having "been around." He quickly became infatuated with her, and it was not long before she was pregnant. He married her, feeling that he had no other option. As he put it, "I felt trapped." But there had been little sex in the marriage—he did not especially want it. His bored wife had had a brief extramarital affair. He scolded her as he would a naughty student, then promptly forgave her. The impression he gave me was, he just can't be that good! If he were, I asked myself, why would his wife have been so obviously unhappy with him? Why had she become pregnant by him in the first place? Surely she was not that naïve? What did she find out later that was not apparent when she decided to marry him?

Brian B. told me about a recurrent dream he had. It was a dream of being in a fight: *I meet someone I don't like. In fact I hate him and I'm furious with him. In the fight you throw the hardest punch you can but in the end it is like slow motion, it droops over and you can't do anything.* These were Brian's exact words. I could not help noticing that when he came to the implication of impotence he could not associate it with himself, and so he switched from narration in the first person to the second person. The obvious reductive interpretation is that he was unable to make it sexually with his wife, and that sexuality was for him an aggression which he had wanted and needed to express, but had denied to himself, until it had become completely incapable of expression. But there was more to it than that; it went beyond the explicitly sexual. As he moved through life repressing his hostilities whenever they arose—and who in a position of constant contact with students and their parents and a faculty and an administrative body would not be at times frustrated and angry?—so the hostility continued to gather energy in the unconscious. There was a need to discharge this energy in his waking life, to relieve the tension it produced. However he was afraid to do so, because it did not fit the role, the persona. The dream offered the fight, by way of compensation for his conscious attitude. The proper nice guy became the aggressive bad guy. Then came the fear that he would not be able to bring it off; it showed up in the impotence, he could not follow through. This unconscious fear crossed the aggressive drive, creating an insoluble conflict in the unconscious. The ego was identified with the persona, the side facing the world confidently, amiably, agreeably. He allowed himself to be overworked because if he didn't "they" might have found out that he was really inadequate. The shadow, the mean one carrying all the aggressive needs, would not deal with the hostility he felt.

As his analyst I listened to his recital of a series of superficial symptomatic problems. All the while I was wondering where the shadow might be finding its way to expression, and I thought that it must have been in some deeply unconscious aspect of his life. I had a sense of foreboding. I have seen apparently well-put-together people stumble into analysis just before the personality begins to blow up, as though they knew the catastrophe was about to happen and they wanted to be in a safe place when the moment came! I had this kind of feeling about Brian B.

All the same, for several sessions all I got from him was the-power-of-positive-thinking approach. "I can do anything I really want to do, all I have to do is try hard enough." I felt like replying, "Whom are you trying to convince, yourself or me?" Then one day he told me about a crisis that had arisen at school concerning some racial tensions among the students. His handling of the matter had not prevented a bloody confrontation on the playground, and he was called to account by the school board. He was deeply shaken. I felt he was a different man. He appeared utterly frustrated, deeply depressed, relatively uncommunicative. His easy, pleasant manner had vanished. His persona had failed to prove invincible.

A few days after he had recounted this incident he came to his analytic session with some scratches on his face. He told me about a drinking episode. It occurred following a fight with his wife, after which he had stormed out of his house and gone to a bar on the other side of town, there consuming quite a lot of whiskey. He had then phoned an old army buddy who lived in that neighborhood, and, though it was past midnight, the friend had invited him over for "a few drinks." He went to his friend's house, and drank a good deal, he had not the slightest idea how much. The friend, he recalled, invited him to stay the night, but he remembered he had to get to work the next morning. The next thing he remembered was a flash of awareness that he was speeding down the expressway at about ninety miles an hour. Things went blank again. Then he was in a parking lot opening the doors of unlocked cars, looking into glove compartments to see what he would find. He fell on his face, and didn't know any more until he woke up, and dawn was beginning to gray. He looked around, had no idea where he was, but somehow managed to find his car and get back onto the road. He found the street intersection where he was on the road map, and from there traced his way home. But for the scratches on his face, there was nothing to show that any of it had happened; but he was all changed. This time he was ready to face his shadow. In fact, he had no choice.

It came out in subsequent sessions that he had had periodic episodes of drinking combined with stealing. The stealing only occurred when the drinking had released him from certain inhibitions. He never stole anything he especially wanted, and his stealing always had a certain dramatic flair about it. There was the time he walked out of the bus station with someone else's briefcase. When he got home and sobered up and realized what he had done, he took it back to the station and surreptitiously placed it near where he had picked it up. Another time he had taken a picnic table and two benches from a public park, and carried them off in his station wagon. Whatever he did was risky and defiant. When I asked him if he ever took money, he replied, "No, that would make me a thief!" He regarded his "episodes" more as adventures, to show "them" that he didn't have to follow their silly standards "unless I damn well want to."

When one attempts to live out only one side of his personality, the conscious, adapted attitude, the opposite side remains in the unconscious, waiting for some situation which allows it to break through. The turn-of-the-century French psychologists called this state an *abaissement du niveau mental*, a lowering of the level of consciousness, a state which allows the contents of the unconscious to break through into awareness. The state of sleep is such a condition, and that is why we have dreams which show us sides of ourselves we

would never have access to otherwise. When the ego identifies
with the persona, when the major concern of the ego is to
appear as the public image demands, then the repressed
shadow will sooner or later find a way to collapse the out-of-
balance persona.

Early in analysis it may be expected that there will be a
considerable struggle in which the ego tries to maintain its
position against rapidly emerging unconscious contents
which seem so destructive as they tear away at the person's
image of himself. The ego may clutch at the persona ever
more frantically, as the persona begins to disintegrate in the
face of pressure on it coming from the unconscious. Such a
situation was dramatically portrayed in the dream of a man in
this stage of analysis, and frightened at the prospect of having
to revise his entire view of himself. This was the dream: *I spent
the night building an electric netting around the house to protect
it from tanks and infantry. We also had anti-tank guns. Someone in the group kept trying to tear down the netting. He lived in
a house nearby, and when we saw him undoing our work and
saw him going over to his house we blew it up with an anti-tank
gun. Then the scene changes. I'm on the second floor looking out
the window in the morning and I see two or three elephants
busily tearing up the electric wiring and the camouflage. They
are under the direction of several men. For some unknown reason there is no glass in the windows where there should be. I
rush over and pull the switch. The elephants bellow and charge.
Wire sticks to their trunks. They have quite a time, but finally
they get the wire from their trunks with the help of their feet. One
of the men tells the elephants to find the switch. Apparently their
feet insulate them against the shock, or the current isn't strong
enough to stop them. One elephant comes to the window where
I am and pokes his trunk in and around to find a switch. I felt
sure he would see me, but he didn't. As soon as he leaves that
window I run down the stairs.*

The dream shows the ego forces trying to protect the
psyche from the onslaught of the unconscious factors that

were long repressed and had an untold amount of strength bound up in them. Electricity is the image provided by the dream to evoke the concept of the life energy which is, in this patient, all directed to protecting his house (his psychic structure) from destruction. There are also the anti-tank guns, instruments of attack which seek to destroy that shadow element of his personality, the one who is trying to undo the work of the defense. And even though the initial battle is won, it is of no avail, for in the moment he is asleep (unconscious) the electric-wiring-defense is again attacked, but this time by vast, inhuman forces. The elephants seem to belong more to the collective unconscious than to the personal unconscious, as they had no specific meaning for the life experience of the patient.

Jung addresses the psychological meaning of such a dream:

> Once the personal repressions are lifted, the individuality and the collective psyche begin to emerge in a coalescent state, thus releasing hitherto repressed personal fantasies. The fantasies and dreams which now appear assume a somewhat different aspect. An infallible sign of collective images seems to be the appearance of the "cosmic" element, i.e., the images in the dream or fantasy are connected with cosmic qualities, such as temporal and spatial infinity, enormous speed and extension of movement, "astrological" associations, telluric, lunar and solar analogies, changes in the proportion of the body, etc. The obvious application of mythological and religious motifs in a dream also points to the activity of the collective unconscious . . .
>
> The wealth of possibilities in the collective psyche has a confusing and blinding effect. With the disintegration of the persona there is a release of involuntary fantasy, which is apparently nothing else than the specific activity of the collective psyche. This activity brings up contents whose existence one had never dreamed of before. But as the influence of the collective unconscious increases, so the conscious

mind loses its power of leadership. Imperceptibly it becomes
led, while an unconscious and impersonal process gradually
takes control.[4]

Now we can understand the overwhelming significance of
the elephants. Huge, lumbering creatures of inestimable age,
they represent powerful forces in the unconscious which,
when they are stimulated, may overrun the conscious position. The very stimulation of these forces may be an effect of
the overzealous attempts to keep them at bay. A hopeful element in the dream, though, is the selection of this particular
image. For elephants can, with the proper treatment, become
friends to man exerting their greater strength to help him accomplish what he cannot do by his frail powers alone. The
question might logically be asked, Why stir up these dangerous forces? Might it not be better to leave them alone, and
encourage the conscious attitude to strengthen its defenses
against them? In this case that is exactly what the patient was
trying to do, more or less consciously, but his deeper problems
were of such magnitude that there was no way in which the
confrontations could be avoided. Jung teaches that to plunge
into this process may be unavoidable "whenever the necessity
arises of overcoming an apparently insuperable difficulty." He
tells us, "It goes without saying that this necessity does not
occur in every case of neurosis, since perhaps in the majority
the prime consideration is only the removal of temporary difficulties of adaptation. Certainly severe cases cannot be cured
without a far-reaching change of character and attitude. In by
far the greater number, adaptation to external reality demands so much work that inner adaptation to the collective
unconscious cannot occur for a very long time. But where this
inner adaptation becomes a problem, a strange, irresistible
attraction proceeds from the unconscious and exerts a powerful influence on the conscious direction of life. The predomi-
nance of unconscious influences, together with the associated
disintegration of the persona and the deposition of the conscious mind from power, constitute a state of psychic disequi-

librium which, in analytic treatment, is artificially induced for the therapeutic purpose of resolving a difficulty that might block further development."⁵

Anyone who has experienced it knows that the collapse of the conscious attitude is no small matter. Previously ordered systems become chaotic, burdens become intolerable, the life situation seems to be completely out of control and there is absolutely nothing one can do about it. It is an anguish beyond comprehension. What has happened is that the ego has given way to the collective unconscious, which has now taken over leadership. There are times when, in such a crisis, a " 'saving' thought, a vision, an 'inner voice,' came with an irresistible power of conviction and gave life a new direction."⁶ But just as often, the collapse brings about a catastrophe which destroys the former life and fails to offer a new way in its place. How will the individual react to this? That is the crucial question.

Jung proposes that there are several possibilities. One is that the individual will be overpowered by the unconscious and will take flight into psychosis where he no longer has to deal realistically with the morbid ideas, or into a suicidal depression. When this tendency appears it takes all the energy of the therapist to assume the role of the conscious ego, utilizing the power of the transference attachment, until the damaged psyche regains the strength to assume again the responsibility for its own independent functioning.

A second possibility is that the individual may "accept credulously" the contents of the collective unconscious. Then he may become obsessed with certain strange or eccentric ideas, probably ideas of apparently cosmic significance: he comes to feel that he is miraculously the possessor of a marvelous truth that no one has ever realized before. He may become an eccentric with prophetic leanings, but nothing ever comes of it because it all seems as real to him as it seems phony to those who listen to him. As his friends turn cool toward him, he may then revert to a rather childish petulance and gradually cut himself off from contact with others, becoming a social isolate, a sad man with a mission in which nobody is interested.

A third way is what Jung terms "regressive restoration of the persona." This tendency appears following some destructive turn of fate which destroys all that an individual has built up in terms of career, love relationships, hopes and plans for the future. Such a person, deeply wounded as he may be, laboriously tries to patch up his life with as much strength as he can muster in face of the fact that he is frightened that it will all go to pieces again. So he looks for a new position which will not be so demanding, or a new relationship in which the challenge is not so great. He restores his functioning but on a level which is far below his natural ability. As Jung says: "He will as a result of his fright have slipped back to an earlier phase of his personality; he will have demeaned himself, pretending that he is as he was *before* the crucial experience, though utterly unable ever to think of repeating such a risk. Formerly perhaps he wanted more than he would accomplish; now he does not even dare to attempt what he has it in him to do."[7]

Such a man will utilize most effectively the defensive measure of *projecting the shadow*. This means that he will not see his own weaknesses, but will find causes everywhere else for his inability to accomplish more of what he sets out to do. Always there will be an unfortunate combination of events which works against him, or there will be somebody who is out to get him. That somebody will inevitably be described with great vehemence as having just those despicable qualities which he fails to see in himself, but which dog his every step.

An Indian guru once told his disciple, "You have to gather your own manure and put it on your own plants. Some very foolish people carefully gather up their own manure and throw it away and then they go out and buy somebody else's manure to put on their plants."

The way which is sought for dealing with the shadow is a difficult one. It requires a continuing search for evidence of this dark force, and when it is found it must be brought to consciousness: this is what I am, this is what I am capable of doing. The dreams must be scrutinized for every occasion when the shadow asserts itself, in whatever disguise, and it is necessary to face the meaning of that image as it relates to the life-style of the dreamer. Every situation in life which carries for an individual a charge of strong affect, which makes him excessively angry or anxious or even delighted, must be considered in terms of the possibility that the extra investment of energy may be coming from the unconscious in the form of a shadow projection. This is, moreover, not something one undertakes for a limited period in the course of the analysis, and then, when the shadow is laid to rest, can assume that he is able to go on to the finer and more glorious aspects of the analysis. The shadow is, in truth, a devilish form, and just when you think you know who he is, he changes his disguise and appears from another direction. So it is, in the Jungian analysis, that the analysand is initiated into a lifelong process, that of looking within, and being willing to reflect long and hard on what he sees there, in order to avoid being taken over by it.

Nor, I must add, is the analyst immune from the onslaught of the shadow. It is a quest which the analyst must continue as long as he is an analyst, and probably as long as he lives. In his work he must be able to differentiate his responses to the analysand so that he will know what actually is coming from the analysand to him, and what is a reflection of his own unconscious contents that he is projecting onto the analysand. Furthermore, he must know that the matter of shadow projection is a double-edged sword, for even while he looks out for what he may tend to project onto the analysand, he must also be noticing what the analysand may be projecting onto *him*, else he may fall into the trap of accepting the analysand's judgment of him, when at bottom the analysand is judging those hidden aspects of himself which he dare not face, or envying those potentialities which he fails to recognize in himself. Unless the analyst is able to sort out all of this, and utilize it in the analytic process to enlarge the area of awareness, first in himself and then in the analysand, he stands in danger of himself being unknowingly entrapped by the influence of the unconscious. Again, I must point to the importance of a long and thorough training analysis which is required to prepare the therapist to deal in depth with complexities of unconscious processes.

The shadow problem occurs not only within the individual as a conflict between the conscious mode of adaptation and the negative or repressed autonomous aspects of the unconscious. The social or societal aspect of the shadow problem is analogous to what is experienced in a personal way. We have seen how certain qualities which have been unknown to an individual are recognized as hostile and evil when they are brought to consciousness. Because the ego is not prepared to assimilate them as its own, they are projected onto other people and onto destructive events, which are sometimes termed "accidents." Most people feel no particular need to make these projections conscious, although by refusing to do so they place themselves in an extremely precarious state. If this is true for the individual as microcosm, it is surely true for the nation as macrocosm. "The psychology of war has clearly brought this condition to light: everything which our own nation does is good, everything which the other nations do is wicked. The centre of all that is mean and vile is always to be found several miles behind the enemy's lines."[8] This statement written by Jung in 1928 is as applicable today as it was when it was written. How tragically we watch as the inhumanities of war perpetrated by our own side are justified as being in the long run for the common good, while those of the enemy become a justification for the continuations of our own immorality. It is only when our own youth return from the war zones, wounded and drug-ridden and sick in their souls that those who stay at home and watch the war from a lounge chair propped up before a television set begin to get the message. Those who have been there have had the projections stripped from before their eyes; they have had to confront reality in the faces of the enemy, and also in the faces of this nation's friends.

We, as a nation, need to discover our own shadows. We can find them in the images we project, if we can only remember that they are *our* images. Such recognition can only begin with the *individual's* willingness to recognize his *own* shadow. Before he does this he is ill-equipped to assign praise or blame to other individuals, much less to nations. This is not to suggest that social concerns are incompatible with an analytical approach. Quite the contrary. The person who will be most effective in his strivings toward social justice is the one who is most critical of himself, who takes care to differentiate his own flaws and to take responsibility for them before he goes out to correct his neighbor's. He will make his impact more effective by setting an example, than by bludgeoning his opponent into submission. The person who commits himself to a life of continuing confrontation with the unconscious within himself, will also confront the unknown in the world at large with an open mind, and what is more, with a heart of wisdom. I am reminded of a phrase quoted to me by a friend which was supposed to have been a remark of Jung's, although my friend confessed he never could find the source of the quotation and may even have dreamed it. In any case, I pass it on to you—the old man is reputed to have said, *"Meine Herren, vergessen Sie nicht das Unbewusste ist auch draussen* [Gentlemen, do not forget that the unconscious is also on the outside]!"

7

Anima and Animus: The Opposites Within

...

ONE OF THE AREAS in which our cultural perspectives have changed most radically over the past half century has been in our concepts around sex and gender, and the relations between the sexes. As these were, and still are, perennial issues involving the psyche, Jung devoted much of his thought and writing to the subject. His major essays on this were published between the 1920s *(Two Essays in Analytical Psychology*[1]*)* and the 1950s ("Concerning the Archetypes With Special Reference to the Anima Concept"[2]), so it is not surprising that today we find that some of his ideas on the subject are bounded by the cultural context in which he lived and worked, while others have a timeless quality. I have always struggled with the question of what in his formulation of *anima* and *animus* is fundamental to our understanding of gender differences, and what can only be read as historical relics of a time gone by.

When I was still at the Jung Institute in Zurich training to become an analyst, I once asked my supervising analyst, Dr. Heinrich Fierz, the tantalizing question, "What are the innate differences between the masculine and the feminine, and what differences are culturally based?" He paused for a while, reflecting on this question, and then replied, "For many generations people have been pondering this question, and there has been much talk about it in terms of nature versus nurture, or heredity versus environment. After all the talk and all the research, the only thing that everybody seems to agree on is that *there is a difference!*"

For Jung, whatever is true in our conscious attitude, an attitude representing the opposite view resides in the unconscious. Jung developed the concepts of anima and animus as the unconscious correlates of our conscious attitudes. He posited the idea that, while members of each sex, from the standpoint of ego consciousness, identify with their biological sex (with rare exceptions), the unconscious carries the complementary contrasexual "personality." So, for a man, the anima represents his unconscious feminine "other" while for a woman the unconscious masculine "other" is represented by the animus.

Let us begin by trying to understand what Jung meant by the words *anima* and *animus*. These he expressed as twin archetypes of the contrasexual: the anima standing for the "eternal feminine" aspect in a man, and the animus representing the "eternal masculine" aspect in a woman. As our conscious attitudes about what is feminine and what is masculine vary in every society, what is unacceptable in the framework of that society also varies. So certain ideas and qualities that men associate with the "feminine" in themselves are repressed and live in the unconscious as aspects of the anima, while for the woman the repressed "masculine" lives a hidden existence as the animus. Because of their archetypal connections, anima and animus have been represented in many collective forms and figures: the man's anima may appear as Aphrodite, Marilyn Monroe, Mary Magdalene, Sophia the embodiment of wisdom, or Kali the embodiment of destruction; while the woman's animus may appear as Hermes, Apollo, Hitler or Bill Clinton. The possibilities are endless—but these figures are all in some way "bigger than life" and evoke something powerful in us as they appear in dreams or imagination.

Anima and animus, for Jung, were the image-making functions in the psyche par excellence. The images are infinite in number, and are usually related to something prevalent in the culture at a given time; but the capacity for creating the images and for being affected by them is timeless and universal. The contrasexual elements in the psyche, anima and animus, function as archetypes in their tendency to produce psychic images. The images themselves are usually culture bound. If we understand this, we can apply the archetypal meaning of the opposite sex as we explore the differences in sex and gender, no matter what the cultural setting, while realizing that every culture introduces the appropriate images for its own time and condition. The important thing to remember is what my mentor said to me: "there is a difference."

An important kingpin of Jung's formulation of the structure of the psyche depends upon the interaction between the sexes in people's conscious and unconscious lives. Let us say at the beginning that when Jung talks about "the Feminine" he is not referring to something that belongs only to women, nor is "the Masculine" something that belongs exclusively to men. In almost all human beings it is clear enough to which sex one belongs. If only the matter of gender were so clear! It is not, because gender is mostly the result of language—of all the words and concepts built with words that we attach to one sex or the other whether or not they rightfully belong there. Gender is psychological, not genital.

I said above that the contrasexual opposites are a "kingpin" of Jung's structure of the psyche. "Kingpin," that is a gendered word. I shocked myself as I saw what I had written. Why not "queenpin"? Or simply "cornerstone"? Because we have built into our natures, or we have acquired, a way of thinking in gendered terms that is almost wholly unconscious and, in fact, was unconscious until the feminists of the late twentieth century called our attention to it. Now, most publishers ask writers not to assume that male-gendered designations refer to females as well. Women no longer are willing to be relegated to the realm of "it goes without saying." Thanks to the efforts of feminist writers, women today are claiming voices of their own and taking the responsibility for making their voices heard.

And so we must recognize, when we begin to think of the anima and the animus, that we are living in different times from those in which Jung offered his original formulations. When people criticize the cultural limitations of Jung's descriptions of what is feminine and what is masculine and what is conscious and unconscious, they are correct in calling into question much of what seemed true to Jung but no longer seems true to us today. The old patriarchal tradition was evident in such statements of Jung's as the following:

> But no one can evade the fact, that in taking up a masculine calling, studying and working in a man's way, woman is doing something not wholly in agreement with, if not directly injurious to, her feminine nature. . . . Female psychology is founded on the principle of Eros, the great binder and deliverer; while age-old wisdom has ascribed Logos to man as his ruling principle.[3]

One wonders what Jung would have said if he had known that before the end of his century at least two women would sit on the bench of the United States Supreme Court, that women would hold such important and intellectually demanding positions as Attorney General and Surgeon General and that an increasing number of women would serve in the Congress of the United States. Many of the positive changes in contemporary attitudes toward sex and gender can be attributed to the psychologists, anthropologists and others, including Jung, who have called our attention to the degree to which every society defines what is acceptable behavior for one sex or the other. Societies establish stereotypes of how women and men are supposed to act and reward people for conforming to those stereotypes. But the archetypal reality, according to Jung, is that fulfillment of the human potential does not rest only with what is acceptable to the collective consciousness.

Our human potential also contains all that we are, or that we could be, if we were to recognize and develop those aspects of our nature which may be unconscious, out of fashion, unconventional, or considered inappropriate to members of our sex. The psyche strives toward wholeness. But on the path we stumble upon what we have come to believe that society expects of us, and these beliefs have a strong effect on the way we behave as men and as women.

Even if, in top leadership positions today, the differences between men and women are beginning to be de-emphasized, both men and women seek to express their personal preferences around sex and gender in their private lives. It seems that whenever society begins to minimize the differences between the sexes, the freedom to express the contrasexual aspect of one's nature increases. This freedom does not appear to damage either the "femininity" of the woman or the "masculinity" of the man. The differences between the sexes are ever present; it is the way we identify these differences that keeps changing—and today the changes are occurring with such rapidity that a great deal of confusion exists around this issue. Jung's descriptions of the specific characteristics of the Feminine and of the Masculine as cultural forms may seem out of date to us, but people's awareness of differences between men and women continues to provide a never-ceasing source of exploration, discussion, consternation and delight!

There have always been certain nearly universal ideas about what is masculine and what is feminine. We call these gender concepts "archetypal ideas." We can recognize that their universality is based primarily upon the differences between the sexes in their physiological structures and functions. Add to these the differences in gender concepts between cultures and within cultures, and it becomes practically impossible to sort out which gender experiences are innate (archetypal) and which are imposed by the society in which we live. I am inclined to believe that in the long run it really doesn't matter. There is so much that is subject to development and change in the inner relationships between the Masculine and the Feminine, and so much that can be changed and is changing between people and in the larger society, that there is little point in troubling ourselves about what is immutable.

When I first read Jung's work on the anima and animus, I was put off by the qualities he ascribed to the Feminine and to the Masculine, but mostly to the former. I had not sufficiently realized that the *archetypal* aspects of anima and animus were extremely significant, but that many of the specific qualities associated with the anima and animus belong more to the realm of cultural distinctions than to essence. The essence, the archetypal foundation, lies in the recognition that, in every age and across all cultures, there not only exists the sexual difference between male and female, but the culture to a great extent establishes appropriate gender roles which have their profound effects upon the psyche. So we have differences in both sex and gender between males and females, and consequently neither sex seems to be able fully to understand the other—although it is a wonderfully enlightening experience to try.

For Jung, the man's anima is a "soul-figure." Anima, the word for soul in Latin, is in the feminine gender. Why must the soul be feminine? She must appear to be feminine for a man because she represents that which is "other," which is different, which he can never fully fathom because she is subject to certain experiences which he can never know. I am speaking here not only of the mysteries of birth-giving, of menstruation, of nursing and other biological functions, but also of the roles and functions that woman assumes as a member of the society in which she lives, simply because she is female—and further, by the images of the Feminine that prevail in the society and the times. These images, so visible in the media, play on the sense of difference that exists and has always existed between men and women. The differences are sometimes celebrated, sometimes disdained and sometimes revolted against, but do with it what you will—there is a difference! So the anima-soul in a man, being essentially hidden or unconscious, stands in opposition to his ego, which is the center of his consciousness.

Jung also posits the animus, an inner figure for the woman that carries that masculine aspect of which her conscious femininity is unaware or has not fully lived out. Jung formulated his concept of the animus in the context of the culture in which he himself grew up, with its late nineteenth-century patriarchal values. The role of woman was to provide emotional support to her man while he went about this business out in the world. *"Kinder, Kirche, Kueche* [Children, church, kitchen]" was woman's place, and most women did not venture far from it. That the unconscious animus figure represented the masculine aspect of the woman must have made sense to Jung, since in the society in which he moved most women were likely to repress their energetic, creative, outspoken selves, the part that longed for acceptance. When pushed away, out of consciousness, the animus often erupted in ways that caused a stir in the well-ordered Swiss society; hence most women thought of this part of themselves as being "unseemly" or "mannish." A great deal of resentment built up in women as a result of feeling that they were required to conform to the conventional attitudes. Jung, who observed such women in his practice and elsewhere, assessed the state of their unconscious feeling in such statements as, "We must . . . expect the unconscious of woman to show aspects essentially different from those found in man . . . as the anima produces moods, so the animus produces opinions."[4] For Jung, opinions, when expressed by women, were "opinionated" statements. Many women today become incensed when they read his words: "Animus opinions often have the character of solid convictions whose validity is seemingly unassailable. If we analyze these opinions, we immediately come upon the unconscious assumptions. . . . In reality the opinions are not thought out at all. . . ."[5] Today most people recognize that unfounded opinions vehemently expressed are not the exclusive property of women's repressed masculine function, for example, if they watch the televised deliberations of the predominantly male U. S. Congress. Jung suggested that the anima or animus is the part of the unconscious that is most difficult to come to know, to begin to acknowledge, and to integrate in the individuation process. I believe that this was true for Jung and for his time and place. But judging by the number of books on the best-seller lists dealing with the topic of explaining one sex to the other, more than half a century after Jung wrote on the subject, much light is being cast on this mystery today and the old stereotypes are visibly crumbling. Still, as the old gender images give way to newer expressions of what is masculine and what is feminine, the important fact remains that there is a difference.

As I see it today, while major efforts during the first stages of the women's movement were directed toward minimizing the differences between the sexes, there has been a gradual shift until now, as we approach the end of the century, we have come to respect and value the very real differences that do exist between the sexes. Yet whatever we make more conscious, we may rest assured that the opposite of that becomes less conscious. So, while the socially acceptable images of the Feminine and the Masculine may change, their repressed opposites also undergo complementary changes.

In fairness to Jung it must be said that he recognized that the animus, when integrated into the conscious awareness of the woman—which is to say, when she lives out the full breadth of her potential—truly acts as the "soul-figure" for her. The animus helps her to become a whole person by turning the energy that was formerly repressed into active and creative endeavors. That Jung recognized the intellectual as well as the emotional gifts of women is evident. In his early circle the majority of the people whom he trained as analysts were women (unlike Freud and his early circle, composed almost entirely of men). Among the distinguished women who worked closely with Jung and who were instrumental in interpreting analytical psychology to the public and in establishing the first Jungian training program in Zurich were my own analyst, Liliane Frey-Rohm, and Jolande Jacobi, Linda Fierz-

David, Barbara Hannah, Marie-Louise von Franz, and Aniela
Jaffé. These women were articulate and talented individuals,
who were largely responsible for initiating the spread of
Jung's psychology during his lifetime and after his death in
1961. Even today in the Jungian community, women exercise
their full creativity with little inhibition. One female Jungian
analyst, it is reputed, was recently asked if she would desire
for women full equality with men in the Jungian community.
She thought awhile, and then replied, "I'm not quite sure. It
would require stepping down a bit, wouldn't it?"

Jung attributed the formation of the anima and animus to
three major factors: the *archetypal,* the *developmental* and the
social. The *archetypal factor* includes the universal biological
differences between the sexes, which give rise to a psychological tendency to form images and concepts based on these differences. Jung reasoned that we are whole and complete individuals with all aspects of ourselves functioning in an
interrelated and interdependent way; therefore, what is true of
the physical structure of the individual is echoed in the psychological structure. Today, as we know more about hormones and their relation to sexuality, we see that Jung's intuition here was correct. The psyche is strongly influenced from
the unconscious side not only through the physical structure
of the body but also by body chemistry and particularly
through the presence of male and female hormones.

It should be borne in mind that body chemistry changes
over the years, and for women the production of estrogens
during the childbearing years diminishes with menopause,
while the production of androgens increases. The changes in
men at midlife are somewhat more subtle, but men also tend
to respond to biological changes that signal to them the end of
youth and the necessity to reassess the direction of their lives.
It is at this time that the anima and animus become more
active. Regardless of which sex we belong to, individuals respond to this change in different ways, but essentially the
ways can be grouped into two categories. Some people expend
their energies in denying the changes that are occurring in the

mind/body, and seek to prolong youth, often desperately. Large industries are based on this effort: cosmetics, cosmetic surgery, hormone replacement therapy, products promising to restore sexual desire or potency, radical weight control measures, and so on. The other category accepts the reality that youth cannot be indefinitely prolonged, and recognizes that they are in another life stage which offers its own pleasures and opportunities for personal fulfillment. Instead of chasing the sweet bird of youth, these others use their acquired wisdom to teach, help and serve as mentor for others. They may direct their energies toward quieter pursuits than they once did. They follow their interests by furthering their own education, traveling and serving in their communities. They attend to their health by following sensible regimes of diet, adequate exercise and rest. They see growing older as an opportunity to live ever more fully, now that they are freed from the responsibilities of rearing and providing for a family, and establishing themselves in their line of work. They recognize that they have more choices now, and they are glad for it. They have become conscious of the anima or the animus as the case may be, and as a consequence they see themselves as being far more liberated from constricting sex roles than they were in the past.

The *developmental factor* in the anima or animus is rooted in the parental *imagos*, the images of the parents or parental surrogates that have been imprinted on the child's consciousness from birth on and that exerted a crucial early influence on them as children. The child's relationship with siblings is also significant here. Jung does not deal with this specifically, possibly because he was himself an only child and had a lonely childhood. According to Jung, as children grow older the influence of the parental imago is split off from consciousness, while the restrictive effect it sometimes continues to exert may acquire a negative tone.

Our early experiences with our parents and the family constellation determine to a very large extent the psychological image we carry of the opposite sex. The young child not only experiences the parents and significant others as they are, but derives subjective impressions of them. These impressions are highly charged with the child's responses to hurt and jealousy and also to love and dependency needs. The recognition of the subjective experiences of children by Jung, Freud, and other prominent figures in the early study of the psyche, pointed the way toward a fuller understanding of the child's emotional world. It has remained for their followers to take us further on this path. Today we acknowledge that early experiences, especially those most painful or terrifying, may endure and exert a strong influence from the side of the unconscious even though they may have been repressed from consciousness. In my work, I discover in almost every analysand the presence of forgotten memories which have only to be invited, to return within the safe sanctuary of the analytic session. These memories reveal how the child's treatment by parents and others in the first formative years has yielded impressions of the opposite sex that form the background for all subsequent experiences.

A man dreams: *I am in Africa on a safari with my brother. A dangerous elephant approaches us in a threatening manner. My brother says, "Help me, we must shoot it." I turn away, panic-stricken. I can't do it. I don't want to see the blood.*

He associates elephants with hugeness and with unreasoning power and says that elephants have a prodigious memory. If you hurt them, they will never forget it and someday they will take it out on you. Questions reveal that the man had a powerful, domineering mother who restricted his development in many ways. He still sees her as an insuperable obstacle to anything he might dream of accomplishing. His brother had broken away from the family and followed his ambition to raise venture capital for new businesses, a career his mother had criticized as foolhardy. The dreamer had pleased his parents by becoming an attorney and later a judge. The brother in the dream represents the aspect of the dreamer that is adventurous and creative and doesn't flinch from taking risks. That quality is an unrecognized latent part of the dreamer. For the part of him that his "brother" represents, the elephant is a challenge, a creature on whom he can test his strength. But all this remains in the dreamer's unconscious, repressed by the fear of the powerful and terrible mother. The dreamer, in waking life, would never go on a safari with his brother. The idea of attempting something so unstructured, so unpredictable, would be too reminiscent of the mother's criticism (or rather, of the mother's animus) that placed all sorts of demands upon him to succeed in the world in ways that she would have liked to do but did not have the opportunity. The dream offered a window into the dreamer's shadow, represented by the brother, which had an opportunity to get rid of the parental imago if only he could muster the courage to do so.

I see also images of the "terrible father" in women who have been sexually or emotionally abused in childhood by a man, a father or someone in a father role. Often these women dream of powerful monsters, or dark suspicious persons, out to chase them or torture them or kill them. Sometimes, on probing, memories of actual physical abuse emerge; at other times such abuse serves as a metaphor for emotional abuse: the father who is never satisfied with what the child does, who is suspicious of her motives, or who unjustly accuses her of wrongdoing. These experiences can inflict pain that the psyche translates into images of memory which, like dreams, stand metaphorically and not literally for what actually did happen. Sometimes even a seemingly harmless remark from a parent can be the cause of a lifetime of suffering. One woman wept bitterly as she told me her mother had once said to her, "I never wanted more than two children." The woman was the fourth child in a family of five. She felt that she never should have been born. Her whole life was colored by an insatiable desire to prove her worth. There are many ways in which parental imagos form the basis for our concept of our worth as females or as males.

On the other hand, in well-functioning households, parents can serve as models: the same-sex parent as guide for what the child may become, and the opposite-sex parent as a guide for what to look for in a future partner. Naturally, this is the sort of image most of us want to provide. We can do so only to the degree that such images exist in our own lives. To come to this point requires a great deal of self-understanding.

Today, owing to the lengthening of the life span, people can expect to spend more years after "midlife" than ever before. A far greater proportion of people today than formerly live active and healthy lives well into their seventies and eighties. So there comes another phase of life after the traditional retirement age of sixty-five that is just as important in reshaping gender roles as that of early adulthood. Whereas in early adulthood human biology aimed at the differentiation of the sexes and the separation of the primary gender roles into nurturing family life for the women and career achievement for the men, now in late adulthood the roles tend to reverse. As Jung so aptly said, "We cannot live the afternoon of life according to the programme of life's morning; for what was great in the morning will be little at evening, and what in the morning was true will at evening have become a lie."[6]

Women who are now free of most family and household responsibilities can and often do choose to become active in their own careers or in community service, and to exercise the assertiveness and creativity this requires. No longer need these efforts be subordinated to the needs of others. The animus, so often repressed in early adulthood, now can move freely into the world. It is a new and exciting adventure and it keeps these women vital and strong. This is the positive side of late adulthood for women. The negative side comes when there is an unwillingness to come to terms with age and to pretend to a youth which no longer exists. Such women suffer from the "empty nest syndrome" and from the discomforts of menopause, which more active women scarcely notice.

Men, on the other hand, usually retire around sixty-five. Sometimes they do this through choice when they find themselves weary of the stresses of the working life and of having had to put so much of the softer part of their natures aside in order to compete in the business world. More often, they stop working because they are forced to or because they realize it is expected of them. If they are flexible enough then to turn their attention to activities in which the anima has an opportunity to be expressed, they will find other types of endeavors that will continue to stimulate them and enable them to give of their long experience to guide others in some way—but perhaps on a less demanding schedule. They may take a great interest in their grandchildren, in a way compensating for the attention they could not pay to their own children while they were busy making their way upward in the world of work. In general the late adulthood transition is more difficult for men, because they no longer receive the same rewards and camaraderie that they enjoyed in their former positions. Unless they, too, can make the inner changes that will allow them to integrate the aspects of their lives that were formerly delegated to the female partner, they may feel that they have lost something vital. What they stand to gain then may offer welcome recompense for what they have given up.

The individuation process does not end with maturity; it can continue into old age as long as we carry on our inner work of examining our own lives and our world and finding meaning in both. When we have learned to disidentify from the persona, to recognize the shadow, and to admit into consciousness the values of the contrasexual opposites, anima and animus, we will have found that, almost without knowing it, we have been close to the archetype of wholeness, the Self.

The *social factor* is the third important determining factor in the formation of the anima or animus. Here I include all interpersonal relations from the family through the intermediate structures from community to the world at large. Today, most children do not grow up in a household of the sort with which Jung was familiar: two parents, a father who was the wage earner and went to work in the morning and returned in the evening, and a mother who remained at home and cared for her children. Among the variations on "the family" in which children grow up today, there are many "parental imagos" that influence the development of young children:

blended families, single-parent families, the new "matriarchy" —especially prevalent among African Americans although not limited to this group—when the single mother works outside the home and the grandmother cares for the children, children who are in day care centers from six months of age and younger, and extended families. For better or for worse, the "parental imago" has been diluted almost beyond recognition, and also the edges of what is masculine and what is feminine have been blurred in an infinite number of ways. Consequently, what does not belong to the masculine or feminine ideal, what we repress if we are male or if we are female, is not nearly so clear as it was when Jung wrote about it. What is remotest in the psyche takes on the image of the opposite sex, and this is not limited to the parental imago.

The modes and mores of society, today as in the past, play an enormous role in determining what shall be considered acceptable behavior and acceptable thoughts for men and for women. In Switzerland, where women had not even been allowed to vote during Jung's lifetime, woman's role was narrowly circumscribed. I remember, when I was a student at the Jung Institute in Zurich in the early sixties, that we students would go out to a restaurant to have a sandwich and a glass of beer in the evening and there we would see many Swiss men, but rarely any Swiss women. We concluded that the women were either at home with the children or that it was no place for a young unmarried Swiss woman. In the mornings, however, the Swiss housewives were very much in evidence. You could see them shaking out their feather beds from the window, or standing out in the backyard with a wire beater in hand, swinging at their carpets hanging over the clothesline. Perhaps that was how they dealt with their frustrations.

From my somewhat limited vantage point, the only place I saw intellectual women pursuing interesting careers was at the Jung Institute. Jung always had students around him who, in the process of self-examination, were discovering the unconscious aspects of themselves and learning how to make these more conscious and to express them. People of both sexes came from all over the world to the Institute, where the opposites within were a legitimate subject for study.

Aside from experiencing the Jungian openness to the possibility of women dealing with the complex factors of the psyche and becoming analysts, I had another experience which led me to see that we were on the verge of some incredible changes. It was 1962. My gynecologist told me about a breakthrough in contraception, the oral contraceptive pill, available in Switzerland but not yet in the United States. Throughout history the most frequently used method of birth control had been abortion, and women mostly used various herbs to achieve this. More recently, mechanical means of contraception (such as diaphragms, intrauterine devices and condoms) had become popular among the middle classes in the Western world. But The Pill was something new and different. I saw the tremendous implications: now, for the first time, masses of women could have at their disposal reliable means of preventing conception, and its use would not require the male partner's knowledge, agreement or cooperation. I could foresee that sexually active women would no longer be at the mercy of fate as to whether or not they would have children, or pursue an education, or follow a career. Women would be able to choose family, economic independence or higher education, and they could determine their own priorities and timetables. I could see that women would have opportunities to discover and use their own abilities and power in ways that had not been possible previously. When I returned to the United States in the mid-sixties, the women's movement had not yet gotten under way, but the wheels were already turning in the heads of some forward-looking women.

The concept of the anima and animus has been helpful to both women and men in bringing to awareness the unrealized potential that has been repressed for so long, simply because of the restrictions that history, myth, biology and society have imposed. The animus of the woman is not so much the repressed Masculine as it is the repressed Other, the unconscious Other that she has been prevented from living out. The anima of the man may function in a similar way. There is a mystery about the unknown, and the unknown is often the unconscious Other within. When we see another person carrying the qualities or potentialities that we do not see in ourselves, we envy the other one. Penis envy and womb envy are opposite sides of the coin. We do not have the one or the other, we see it in another person, and we envy it. Now I am not speaking literally but metaphorically—penis and womb represent that mysterious Other which seems most desirable and yet most unattainable.

The potential of man's anima and woman's animus is that they can be guides to the depths of the unconscious; yet they will so function only if men and women can learn to relate to them in an open and constructive way and let go of the restrictive influences they have carried over from the past. Men will need to understand the inner experience of the Feminine better, as women will need to understand that of the Masculine. But this is not an easy matter, for animus and anima are not to be experienced directly, since they represent a point of view that is opposed to the dominant attitude of consciousness.

As long as the anima or animus is unconscious in us, we can find ourselves powerfully attracted to another person, usually of the opposite sex, who bears some resemblance to the inner figure. We unconsciously project the inner image onto the other person, who immediately assumes the form of someone infinitely desirable, the person whom we had always hoped to meet, the "soul mate." Whatever qualities in ourselves we believe to be lacking appear in the form of the beloved. He, or she, is everything we need to feel complete, and we expect this person to fulfill the empty spaces in our heart and home. Of course the individual with whom we become infatuated must appear to be close to the "ideal" we have in mind, and we take the surface appearance to be deeper than it really is.

Ian fell deeply in love with Diane. She was about his age, but he saw her as much younger. His impulse was to protect her from all harm and insecurity. He wanted desperately to marry her, but hesitated because he had behind him two failed marriages that had cost him a great deal both financially and emotionally. Still, he was lonely in his big house and longed for companionship. Diane was soft-spoken, gentle, and Ian liked her easy way of living, her ability to take things as they came along, something he had never been able to do. His own nature was quite compulsive—everything had to be done on time and according to strict standards. Diane, a widow, had reared her children by herself. She had worked hard for many years, becoming efficient not because it was natural for her but because it was an absolute necessity if she wanted to provide for her family's needs. She saw in Ian a strong competent person who would take care of her and her children.

They married, and at first all went well, but it was not long before the mutual projections that each had placed on the other began to dissolve. Diane, relaxing in her new security, began to take less and less interest in the home to which Ian had brought her. Things became somewhat disordered. She lost her job and did not show any interest in finding another one. She said she would have more time for him now, which pleased him. Her financial demands for herself, her children and the house increased considerably, and this did not please him. There was college for her children, a new car, changes to the home. Ian paid without complaint because he was afraid of losing her. He stopped looking at expenses, and soon began to spend as freely as his wife did. Eventually they had to face the fact that they were deeply in debt. Each blamed the other. They also blamed each other for the many ways in which each had failed to fulfill the partner's expectations. Nothing would help until they came into therapy where, under the eye of an impartial therapist, they had to confront the reality of the other person. Each one had to withdraw the projections and recognize that they could only retrieve the marriage if each would take responsibility for the parts of themselves that they had expected the other to provide for them. Each had to come to know the opposite within, and to let that part, anima or

animus, develop and grow. Only then could each of them begin to feel more whole and function more independently, and still be willing to support the other to the degree that this was truly needed. This meant that they would respect each other for who the other was, and not for how the other could serve them.

When Jung talked about "woman," he spoke from a man's perspective, and it is easy to see how he had been affected by his own familial relations as they occurred within the rural Swiss culture of a century ago. His own projections onto women are not difficult for us to discern. He wrote:

> In place of the parents, woman now takes up her position as the most immediate environmental influence in the life of the adult man. She becomes his companion, she belongs to him in so far as she shares his life and is more or less of the same age. She is not of a superior order, either by virtue of age, authority, or physical strength. . . . She produces an imago of a relatively autonomous nature—not an imago to be split off like that of the parents, but one that has to be kept associated with consciousness. Woman, with her very dissimilar psychology, is and always has been a source of information about things for which a man has no eyes.[7]

I would amend this statement of Jung's. Men did have eyes for what a woman knows, but those eyes were tightly closed! But there have been some changes, especially in the working world, since Jung wrote those words during the Second World War. That war had inadvertently provided the seed for the women's liberation movement that emerged in the mid- or late sixties, though almost no one recognized it at the time. Before the war most people lived in nuclear family units, and unless you were very rich or very adventurous you didn't go far from your place of residence. Many lived and died within a few miles of the hometown. People were bound by a narrow set of mores. I remember that when I was a teenager I firmly believed that if an unmarried girl became pregnant there were only two options: a shameful marriage or suicide. And I was typical of the people I knew. When the war came, people began to move to distant places when they were called to serve in the armed forces. The men went off to fight and the factories and shops needed employees to replace them, so women rushed into the "man's world" and did quite well performing "man's work." Rosie the Riveter enjoyed her short career, which was cut off as soon as the men returned to their jobs, their homes and their women. The women who had put off marriage did marry now and started producing babies in great numbers because the impetus to give life follows the impetus to kill and destroy as surely as day follows night. In any case, women embarked upon an intensity of housewifery and motherhood with a vengeance, and soon they were up to their eyeballs in dishwater and diapers. But there was a difference. Motherhood in the past had been taken for granted. These women had tasted something else. Money in their pockets for which they did not have to account. Independence. Success based on their own accomplishments, not related to their marital role. Time out with "the girls," when they could talk about their feelings without having to rush home to put dinner on the table at six o'clock. Yes, we missed our men, but not as much as later we would let them think.

My generation, the women who were newly married or soon to be married at the end of the Second World War, soon found ourselves caught in the endless round of feminine responsibilities and expectations much as they had been before the war, but we had a different consciousness about it. The animus had reared his head, and then gone under again. A few of us white middle-class women, when our children were sufficiently grown to be in school most of the time, had the temerity to go back to school to complete our education, and even to get a job. If it was financially necessary for the family that the woman work (and keeping house and caring for four or five children was not, in those days, considered to be work), she was pitied and praised. But, if she were married to a man with a good position and an adequate income, and she then went back to school and later to work, people would think that there could be only two reasons: either her husband couldn't support her, or he couldn't keep her happy in other ways. That a woman could *want* to do such a thing was rarely acknowledged. Men objected to their wives' seeking a career because they felt it cast a poor reflection upon them; women criticized their working sisters, I suspect, because they were either jealous of them, or because they lacked the nerve to do the same thing, or both.

It was Betty Friedan, foremost author early in the women's movement, who, with her book, *The Feminine Mystique* (1963), gave expression to women's frustration. She shocked her readers by printing that "information for which a man has no eyes." She wrote of the progressive dehumanization that "has carried the American mind for the last fifteen years from youth worship to that 'sick love affair' with our own children; from preoccupation with the physical details of sex, divorced from a human framework, to a love affair between man and animal. Where will it end?"[8] she asked. And in a prophetic statement which could have been a manifesto for the women's movement that ensued, she stated:

> I think it will not end, as long as the feminine mystique masks the emptiness of the housewife role, encouraging girls to evade their own growth by vicarious living, by non-commitment. We have gone on too long blaming or pitying the mothers who devour their children, who sow the seeds of progressive dehumanization, because they have never grown to full humanity themselves. If the mother is at fault, why isn't it time to break the pattern by urging all these Sleeping Beauties to grow up and live their own lives? It is society's job, and finally that of each woman alone. For it is not the strength of the mothers that is at fault but their weakness, their passive childlike dependence and immaturity that is mistaken for "femininity." Our society forces boys, in so far as it can, to grow up, to endure the pains of growth, to educate themselves to work, to move on. Why aren't girls forced to grow up—to achieve somehow the core of self that will

end the unnecessary dilemma, the mistaken choice between femaleness and humanness that is implied in the feminine mystique?[9]

This book, the arrival and widespread availability of The Pill in the United States, new technology that released more time for women to think about themselves, read, meet with other women and talk about their common frustrations—all these fueled the women's movement. So did a whole spate of books by women who had found their voices and dared to use them to arouse, support and inspire other women. . . . And, as more and more of Jung's *Collected Works* were translated into English, the women who read them discovered the name of their repressed but vigorous and powerful side—the animus.

I had returned from Zurich after completing my analytic training at the Jung Institute in the mid-sixties. Among my first analysands were a number of students from the University of Chicago. Many of them had read some of Jung's writings, and many were involved in the student uprisings on campus and in the city of Chicago during the Democratic Convention of 1968. Some had used or were using psychedelic substances. Old images of consciousness were being shattered and people were looking for something to replace them. There was a new camaraderie in these groups between men and women and more spontaneous expression of feeling, both publicly and privately, than had been seen in many years. But still, political and economic power remained in the hands of the white male establishment. Women who were trying to move into the mainstream of the work world were having a very difficult time of it. Everywhere, doors were slammed in their faces. Women were discouraged from entering graduate schools, particularly professional schools. A few token women were accepted, but their lives were not easy. A woman physician told me that when she was in medical school her male colleagues taunted her to "toughen up," as they gave her the messiest and most gruesome assignments. Then, when she fi-

nally learned to do what she had to do without wincing and to
speak the same language as the men and to insist upon being
treated with respect as an equal, they criticized her for being
"too mannish."

Women began to talk with one another. A woman I'll call
Sara told me how it started for her. She was attending a professional meeting where the membership was about two
thirds male and one third female. There was a panel discussion on stage in which only men participated. The floor was
open to questions and discussion, but the questions came almost entirely from men. If, occasionally, a woman summoned
up her courage and raised a question, she would barely be
acknowledged by a "thank you" and then the panel would
move on to the next question. Sara noticed that, if a woman
did speak, no other woman would rise in her support. After
the meeting, Sara cornered a few of the women who were
present and asked them what they thought about the meeting.
Opinions were shared. Most had felt squeezed out, outraged
that no woman had been asked to participate on the panel,
angry that they were made to feel invisible. So the women
agreed to meet for breakfast the next morning without any
men present. At breakfast, the fury at the indignity the women
had experienced on this and many other occasions began to
surface. Animus, recognized, was finding its expression. But it
was not "masculine" although it might have seemed so in that
it had a domineering, and demanding tone. It had a peculiar
quality of a woman whose feminine side had been put aside in
order to experience and express the emotions that had been
masked for so long. The women decided to meet on a regular
basis as a group, and they did so. There wasn't any agenda.
They wanted a place where they could reflect on their experiences as women and share those experiences with the others.
Perhaps they could learn from one another.

This is how, in many different places, the consciousness-
raising groups began to take shape. Many books came out on
the women's movement, accounts of how women had suffered
from the excesses of the power drive in a society controlled by

an ethic that resembled a football game: power to the strongest and the toughest, brutal competition, winning is all that matters, and you don't mind jumping on top of other people to get to the goal line. The general tone of these books by and for women, however, stressed the victimization of women. Truly, this is how most women felt in those days. When you have been passed over for advancement and a person with a penis but with less experience and less competence than you gets the better job, how do you feel? Women commiserated with women about how they felt victimized in their families, how they received less attention than boys in school, and how they were discriminated against at work. Supported by their "sisters," they began to be more assertive, while looking carefully at their husbands' or bosses' faces to see if they were going too far. Despite their resolution when women sat together, it was terribly difficult to claim that forthright aspect of themselves when they were in the company of men. These women understood, intellectually, that they had a right to speak up. Feeling it, feeling it with real conviction, was something else. They could not quite accept the animus in its positive aspects. At this time I became aware that several women in my practice would have what I call a classic animus dream. The gist of it is: *I discover that I have a penis!* They reacted with anything from dismay to horror.

Meanwhile, men were closing ranks against the first encroachment of women into what they considered their domain. When a woman would make a demand, or seem a bit more assertive than she had been in the past, men would become uneasy, to say the least. Research has shown that those in leading positions tend to exaggerate the numbers and strength of the underlings who first show power. The old boys' networks strengthened their ties. I have it on good authority that many men actually believed that the women were plotting to take over! They thought that this was what was being discussed in the women's consciousness-raising groups. They would have been quite surprised to find out that there was more talk of victimization and feelings and self-pity than there was of revolution in those early days. The anger of women was directed against those men and those institutions that they characterized as "oppressors." As long as women concentrated on their weakness and vulnerability and how they were taken advantage of, men had little reason to fear a social upheaval.

Men continued on the same path they had been pursuing, except that they now felt it necessary to throw some bones to quiet the barking dogs. These came in the form of token advancements for women in business, admission of a few more women to faculty positions in universities, and electing an occasional woman to fill a public office vacated by the death of her husband. Still, the feminine aspect of the man was not yet recognized by him. Men continued to project the anima, or soul image, that was buried deep in the psyche upon a woman out in the world. Many men, too proud for the most part to admit it, were also feeling oppressed by the social order and victimized by those who had more power than they had. They had much to cry about, except that Real Men don't cry. Men who kept their wives at home with the children had to work hard as the only breadwinners to supply the family's needs. Often they had to work for bosses who made unreasonable demands, and in conditions that were less than pleasant. Many had to cope daily with fierce competition. Often they had to put aside their dreams of following a longed-for life path because they were responsible to fulfill their commitments to the women and children in their lives. Often, when they would have loved to sit at home and be with their children, they had, instead, to do the man's chores around the house, or to work an extra job, or do business out of town. To complain would have been unmanly. At the same time, the negative aspects of the man's anima envied the woman her righteous anger.

This phase, too, began to pass. In some segments of society, consciousness went through another stage of metamorphosis, again led mostly by women but affecting men as well. This was a stage we could characterize as "androgyny." Androgyny was the word for the recognition of the psychological capacity within each individual to function freely, utilizing all his or her qualities, including those that had been assigned to the feminine or the masculine gender. It implied acceptance by men of their own feminine side, the anima, and by women of their own masculine side, the animus. I was a very strong supporter of the idea of androgyny in the mid-seventies, and I carried out some research on mythologies from many lands and cultures which described how the world had come into being through the combined efforts of the Masculine and Feminine, embodied in gods and goddesses. This work pointed to an archetypal basis for the equality and cooperation between the Masculine and the Feminine. One could view it either objectively, as referring to events in the world, or subjectively, as referring to the inner contrasexual figures, anima and animus. My book on this subject, *Androgyny: The Opposites Within,* was an effort to legitimize the presence and positive value of what had formerly been rejected or repressed. Other books in a similar vein also appeared, signifying a new freedom for men to bring the anima out into the open, and for women to give expression to the animus. This "androgyny" movement characterized a second stage in the development of the anima/animus concept after Jung. A visible result of this was a minimizing of the differences between the sexes, while the similarities between the two sexes in capacity and potential were maximized. When women took on more responsibility for their own liberation from the prison of gender stereotypes, men began to respect them more. As women talked more openly and freely to men about their feelings and their needs, men found the voice to do the same. Each discovered more commonality with the other than they had experienced in the past. Specific gender roles began to break down. As women became more involved in work outside the home, men began to be more active participants in various aspects of family life. Nurturing and providing for the family came to be shared to a greater extent than before. Again, the classic animus dream would be reported by some of my women analysands. *I awaken, or look in the mirror, to find that*

I have a penis. But now the reaction is different. It's more like, "Oh, well, that's all right. It must mean that I have some masculine qualities, and they could be useful."

However, not all were ready to think of themselves as psychologically androgynous. Women, particularly, now began to fear for their lost femininity. I recall lecturing in the late seventies to a group of women students at an Ivy League university which had just begun to accept women students. These women were pioneers, testing their mettle in a first-rank university that had been open only to male students in the past. To be sure, these women were the daughters of highly successful women, many of whom had been in the avant garde for women's rights. Their daughters came to my seminar in jeans and cowboy boots, mostly without make-up and rather grungy-looking. After a while I asked them what they wanted or needed to be happy. Several wistfully replied that they were missing their lost femininity. From today's hindsight, it appears to me that these young women were in a place where androgyny was "politically correct" although the phrase had not yet been coined. As androgyny became another gender stereotype, the freedom to be themselves, irrespective of "correctness," had slipped away.

Another trend now emerged. This was the redemption of the distinctive gifts of the Feminine. Not all women who had ascribed their suffering to oppression by the "male establishment" had found release in the movement toward androgyny. Instead of a redress of the inequality between the sexes, they sought to validate the special experience of women, and to elevate it. The image of patriarchal authority in societies was to be superseded by images of woman-centered societies or goddess cultures. Historians and anthropologists had to go back to a time before the period of recorded history to discover evidence of preliterate societies in which women were honored. Uncovered in the ruins of Anatolia and Crete and elsewhere were sculptures of female forms believed to be goddesses. The existence of goddess-cultures was said to be an important feature of a Golden Age some four thousand years

B.C.E. A book with the title *When God Was a Woman* became a best seller.

All this was important for women in the process of re-evaluating their feminine side. It was necessary to establish a firm connection with the archetype of the Feminine before the animus could be embraced with less fear, anger or resentment. We must first know who we are and where we have come from before we can risk embracing the lesser-known aspects of our beings. More recently, I have noted that, when women have the classic penis dream, they seem to be quite pleased with the addition to their anatomy!

The adventure of being fully woman has had much appeal. All kinds of women's groups have come into existence. They have taken forms that are different from the traditional male group structures. Organically, out of the evolution of mutual trust among women have come women's networks in which women strongly support other women. This has only become possible as women have learned to trust the Feminine principle in themselves and in their sisters. As the Feminine becomes more firmly established in women, the animus becomes more friend than foe.

This development in women's consciousness has not gone unnoticed by men. A men's movement started quietly enough, with small groups and seminars led by such men as Sam Keen and Robert Bly. Bly's popular book, *Iron John,* was an exhortation addressed to men who had been traumatized into submissiveness by women or by the women's movement to assert themselves more effectively. Keen moved beyond dealing with men in virtual late adolescence and encouraged men to recognize the worth of the anima as well as of the feminine principle in the world. Jungian analysts Robert L. Moore and Douglas Gillette followed, with *King, Warrior, Magician, Lover,* to validate and describe variations on the character of the male psyche and to show both its ideal and its shadowy expressions. Psychiatrist Alan Chinen, in *Beyond the Hero,* has spoken to the need for the development of the *mature* Masculine. So, while women were venerating the Great Goddess, men were carrying out rituals that enabled them to experience their manhood in greater depth. While this trend is far from universal even in the United States, members of both sexes are becoming more grounded in the consciousness of their essential beings. And, in the process, men have dared to discover their vulnerability and their feeling sides, while women— more confident now of their strengths—are beginning to take risks which would have frightened them before.

Another outcome of the deepening of relationships between members of one's own sex has been the growing openness in our culture toward homosexuality. As members of each sex have come together to share their intimate thoughts and cares and frustrations as well, it was inevitable that close same-sex relationships would develop, and that those which had already existed would come out of the shadows. What had in the past been condemned by the mainstream culture as unnatural affection now is coming to be better understood. Our natures are complex, our inner lives are not limited by our biological sex, for men can relate to both the masculine and the feminine in themselves and in the world. The same is true for women. If we are truly open to the many facets, both conscious and unconscious, in our own natures, we have before us the possibility of many kinds of relationships. The more comfortable people are with themselves and their own natures, it seems, the more willing they are to accept and appreciate those who are in some way different and who make different choices. Even though our culture has a very long way yet to go in this respect, the direction is clear. With every new discovery in the field of consciousness, we are moving toward wholeness.

All of this is not to deny that there remains in our society a very strong group of conservatives who resist change and insist upon retaining some old traditions that seem to others to be anachronistic in today's world. These people have extensive vested interests in the old ways that have proven comfortable or profitable in the past. Whether their hold can be loosened, or whether it will remain for a younger generation with more flexibility and creativity to outlast and supersede them, is yet to be seen.

There are some other dark aspects to the struggle for freedom from the old stereotypes. No longer bound by the rigid conventions that were formerly imposed by society, marriages and other relationships that would have survived in the past now come under great strain when one or the other partner begins to develop and grow toward the fullness of being that he or she sees as possible, while the other wishes to remain in the old restrictive situation. Many women who would have stayed on in unhealthy marriages in the past have gone to work and sufficiently freed themselves economically so that they could manage alone. Men who have been stuck in unhappy relationships no longer feel so responsible to maintain the situation. They can and often do help the partner to find herself and to make her own way, and the marriages break up. And many people, although they are emotionally bonded, do not feel the necessity to commit themselves to a permanent relationship. Even the arrival of children does not necessarily signal a lasting commitment. The wreckage of the old-fashioned family lies all around us. Much revisioning and repair is necessary here.

But this situation does not need to signal the end of lasting relationships. The pendulum swings, and it swings back again. We learn from our mistakes and our pain, often far more than we learn from our successes. Experience is the price of consciousness. As individuals become more and more aware of who they are and what they believe in, they will communicate this to partners and potential partners. When we realize early on that it may be projection that first attracts people to one another, it follows that the projection must be recognized and withdrawn before a real relationship can develop. As individuals feel more free—socially, economically and spiritually—it is likely that they will be more honest with each other and will let themselves be seen. They will not be afraid to say aloud what their values are and what is important to them.

Another generation has passed since Betty Friedan wrote

her pioneering work. We are beginning to find answers to the question she posed at the end of her book: "Who knows of the possibilities of love when men and women share not only children, home and garden, not only the fulfillment of their biological roles, but the responsibilities and passions of the work that creates the full human future and the full human knowledge of what they are?"[10]

The task is under way. The time is at hand when both men and women must listen to the voices within themselves that drive them on to become complete.

8

Circumambulating the Self

...

INFUSED WITH ENERGY that is liberated from the conflict of the ego with the animus or anima, and quickened by the assimilation of shadow contents once alienated by too much identification with the persona, the process of individuation now takes another twist in the spiral. The same problems which occupied us in the past may come into view again, but now they are regarded from a new level; they take on a different importance. The emphasis in analysis at this stage no longer needs to be placed on the development of patterns that led us to just that situation in which we find ourselves today. Irritation and pique and even loneliness and grief associated with personal problems are transcended, although the problems themselves remain in awareness and may not be avoided in the course of the wider quest. Events begin to be seen in terms of their intentionality. It is as though all events are manifestations of some purposive force, a force which has been appropriately termed "the goal-directedness of psychic energy."[1] It is this energy which provides the thrust for the individuation process. I cannot describe what it is, for I do not know, but I can tell how it feels. It feels as if one were being drawn inward toward a center of great luminosity, yet to fly straight into it would be like a moth darting into a flame or the earth hurtling itself into the center of the sun. So one moves around the center instead, close enough to see the brightness, to feel the warmth, but maintaining the orbital tension, a dynamic relationship of a small finite being to a source of light and energy that has no limits.

The small finite being is, of course, the "ego," the "I" of which each one of us is aware. The mysterious "non-ego" or, as M. Esther Harding has called it, the "not-I,"[2] is termed by Jung the "self." Jung's use of the word "self" is different from that of common usage, in which the self is synonymous with ego. "Self" as Jung uses it has a special meaning; it is that center of being which the ego circumambulates; at the same time it is the superordinate factor in a system in which the ego is subordinate. Self, as we use the term here, will refer to Jung's meaning, and the ego is defined as being subsumed under the broader concept of the self.

I have not wanted to get involved in abstruse philosophical constructs in this work, because my intention has been to write about the *experience* of analysis and not the philosophical justification for it. That something is justified and can be "proved" is no indication that it works. Jung arrived at his own rationales by observing and confronting the actual experiences of his patients, and then attempting to place them in the context of the experiences of mankind throughout the ages, namely, the mythologems. Likewise, we too, may talk about individual experience and draw parallels, as we regard the way in which individual experience recapitulates archetypal experience.

We come to know the self as it appears to the perceiving ego; we come to approach the mystery of it through the clues that become apparent to the searching eye. In religious terms one could say something analogous, that we come to know God as God manifests in and through human beings. When the ego is barred from achieving the task it has set for itself, through the intervention of passion, impotence, pain or death, it must realize that it is not the supreme directing force in the human personality; it finds out that it is confronting a more powerful entity. When individuals bow before the awesome order of nature and realize that they cannot subdue it, that the best they can hope for is to discover ways of learning its laws and functioning in accordance with them, then they know that they are facing a greater entity.

One way to confront the self is through analysis. One way to approach God is through prayerful contemplation. I am not so sure that in their essentials these two ways are so fundamentally different. At the beginning of analysis the patient brings symptoms and places them in the lap of the analyst, very much like the child who brings small problems before a picture of Jesus, making bargains with the Lord. As time passes, each relationship, the analytic and the religious, goes through several transformations. Gradually, in either case, one grows out of the egocentric position and into an awareness of the true nature of the relationship between that which is finite and temporal, and that which is infinite and eternal. In my own experience, and in that of certain of my analysands, as analysis progressed beyond the elementary stages, the common thread of the two apparently different kinds of goal-directed movement gradually became visible. The variation comes mostly in the language of metaphor, which is demanded when we speak of the unknowable.

In the beginnings of human experience on this planet earth, all was primordial chaos. This was the undifferentiated self. Its primary characteristic was wholeness: everything was in it and nothing was separate from it. The discerning human eye began to make separations—were they really separations or did they only seem so to us? As our consciousness developed we began to be aware of a tension of opposites: wholeness and separateness, the one and the many, totality and otherness. The problem can be stated in an endless number of ways; it has fascinated people from their earliest beginnings. It was a problem which preoccupied the medieval alchemists who projected it onto "matter" and then went on to project "spiritual content" onto the material with which they were dealing. In those days science had not yet been differentiated from religion, for people did not see any need to isolate the study of the ways of God from the study of the ways in which nature functions. So their researches were at once "chemical" and "religious."

Jung believed that while the boundaries between science and religion have been drawn ever since the Enlightenment and to some degree even before, that nevertheless in the deeper layers of the collective unconscious the analogies are merged into something like the identity that was apparent in the writings of the strange and mystical alchemists. For this reason he was interested in studying the old alchemical texts. Here he could see how the alchemist and the soror (female partner) projected their own psyches into their work. The alchemical "opus" was at once an attempt to transform base matter into something of great value and an attempt to transform the animalistic aspect of a person into the spiritual aspect. Needless to say, neither opus was then, nor has yet been, entirely successful. The point to be made here is that the opus corresponds to the work of the individuation process, and both may be best expressed in symbolic terms. The symbol is the best way to speak of that which is in large part unknown, since it evokes the feelings and associations which make it possible for us to be in a relationship with a mystery which cannot be touched.

The self, then, is most aptly expressed through the language of the symbol. Jung looks at the study of alchemy as a symbol system. He begins with the *prima materia*, the original matter, referred to as "primordial chaos." It is the same as the undifferentiated self. Of it Jung has written,

> It was of course impossible to specify such a substance, because the projection emanates from the individual and is consequently different in each case. For this reason it is incorrect to maintain that the alchemists never said what the *prima materia* was; on the contrary, they gave all too many

indications and so were everlastingly contradicting themselves. For one alchemist the *prima materia* was quicksilver, for others it was ore, iron, gold, lead, salt, sulphur, vinegar, water, air, fire, earth, blood, water of life, *lapis* [stone], poison, spirit, cloud, sky, dew, shadow, sea, mother, moon, dragon, Venus, chaos, or microcosm . . . Besides these half-chemical, half-mythological definitions there are also some "philosophical" ones which have a deeper meaning. . . . "Hades" . . . "the animal of the earth and sea," or "man," or a "part of man."[3]

The self embraces all there is, whether known or unknown. Where is the end of it? In asking the question the expansive human mind soon finds its limits, for the self is "greater than great." Then the thoughts turn inward, seeking the essence of the self, and there it is found to be "smaller than small." How this paradox can be is addressed by Aldous Huxley in a story which he takes from the Chandogya Upanishad, in which a father is educating his son in these matters:

When Svetaketu was twelve years old he was sent to a teacher, with whom he studied until he was twenty-four. After learning all the Vedas, he returned home full of conceit in the belief that he was consummately well educated, and very censorious.

His father said to him, "Svetaketu, my child, you who are so full of your learning and so censorious, have you asked for that knowledge by which we hear the unhearable, by which we perceive what cannot be perceived and know what cannot be known?"

"What is that knowledge, sir?" asked Svetaketu.

His father replied, "As by knowing one lump of clay all that is made of clay is known, the difference being only in name, but the truth being that all is clay—so, my child, is that knowledge, knowing which we know all."

"But surely these venerable teachers of mine are ignorant of this knowledge; for if they possessed it they would have imparted it to me. Do you, sir, therefore give me that knowledge."

"So be it," said the father. . . . And he said, "Bring me a fruit of the nyagrodha tree."

"Here is one, sir."

"Break it."

"It is broken, sir."

"What do you see there?"

"Some seeds, sir, exceedingly small."

"Break open one of these."

"It is broken, sir."

"What do you see there?"

"Nothing at all."

The father said, "My son, that subtle essence which you do not perceive there—in that very essence stands the being of the huge nyagrodha tree. In that which is the subtle essence all that exists has its self. That is the True, that is the Self, and thou, Svetaketu, art That."

"Pray, sir," said the son, "tell me more."

"Be it so, my child," the father replied; and he said, "Place this salt in water, and come to me tomorrow morning."

The son did as he was told.

Next morning the father said, "Bring me the salt which you put in the water."

The son looked for it, but could not find it; for the salt, of course, had dissolved.

The father said, "Taste some of the water from the surface of the vessel. How is it?"

"Salty."

"Taste some from the middle. How is it?"

"Salty."

"Taste some from the bottom. How is it?"

"Salty."

The father said, "Throw the water away and then come back to me again."

The son did so; but the salt was not lost, for salt exists forever.

Then the father said, "Here likewise in this body of yours, my son, you do not perceive the True; but there in fact it is. In that which is the subtle essence, all that exists has its self. That is the True, that is the Self, and thou, Svetaketu, art That."[4]

The primary, all-encompassing archetype is the archetype of the self. The archetype in this sense is the element in the human psyche which makes it possible to conceive of such an entity as the self. And immediately as the self is conceived of there has to be that which conceives of it, the organ of awareness, which has been named the ego. Does this mean that the ego, which is somehow related to the self, is outside the self? I do not think so, any more than the brain, which is capable of conceiving of the body of which it is a part, is separate from that body. Nor are the hands separate from the body, although they are agents of the authority which resides in the body and directs their movements. The separation of the ego from the self is a separation that is made conceptually, for the purpose of thinking about ego/non-ego relations. When we say that the development of the ego is a process of becoming aware of one's own being as a separate unit of humanity, at first someone other than one's mother and later separate from all the elements in one's environment, we are speaking "as if." We strive to attain our individuality, yet at the same time we struggle to establish our unity with the whole. As I sit across from my analysand I raise the question: "This space that is between you and me—is it a space which separates us one from the other, or is it a space that unites us one to the other?" The answer, clearly, is that it is both or either, depending upon the way we choose to look at it. A child fights for independence as a human being. At the same time the child wants to be accepted as a member of the family.

Looking inward we see that the process of relating the ego to the environment is not unlike the intrapsychic process of relating the ego to the unconscious, and to its dominant archetype, the self. In analysis one aim is to differentiate the ego, which should direct the conscious modes of functioning, from all the unconscious aspects of the psyche which affect the conscious ego and guide it in ways not subject to the dominance of the will alone. The task in the early stages of analysis is to recognize the non-ego forces operating in us. These include, as we have seen, the persona and shadow, and the anima and animus, in all their many forms and guises. Other archetypes emerge in the analytic process, and some of them will be seen as we explore more dreams and other approaches to the unconscious. The ego's confrontation with figures of the unconscious is a counterpart in the inner experience of the ego's confrontation with people and situations in the environment.

The first half of life is spent mainly in finding out who we are, through seeing ourselves in our interaction with others. We establish our own position vis-à-vis these others; we develop an attitude toward them; there are struggles for dominance in which our strength is tested and also that of our adversaries. If it works well, we find our place in the world—our own level, so to speak. In the visible world, one hallmark of maturation is the realization of what we can do by ourselves, what we can do with the help of others, and what we cannot do at all. Mature people have discovered themselves as differentiated personalities spending their days and nights doing what they are fitted for by their unique natures, without frittering away their energies in pointless strivings or useless regrets.

If the aims of the first half of life or the early stages of analysis are reasonably well fulfilled, different aims will emerge during the second half or the later stages. While the first part is directed toward achievement, the second part is directed toward integration. Where the first part is directed toward emergence as an individual, earning a living, rearing a family, establishing a home, the second part is directed toward achieving harmony with the totality of being. In the beginning, the ego arises out of the depths of the unconscious. In the end, the ego surrenders to those depths. That is why the ancient Hebrews were told to rejoice when death comes to a friend, and to mourn at a birth—for it is a fearsome thing to send a ship forth on a voyage to an unknown destination, but a glad welcome is due when the ship returns at last to its home port.

Long before the ultimate union with the self can be

achieved, the goal is shown to us, if we will but see it. The initial glimpse of what it would be like to achieve a seemingly impossible goal is often sufficient inspiration to carry the seeker through the laborious process of self-discovery. That glimpse may come through the image of the anima or animus, the guide to the depths of the unconscious. It may occur during the analysis itself. Or, it may occur outside of analysis as a mystical experience or a striking insight that may become the foundation stone for a lifetime of endeavor. Or, it may simply become the stone that the builders rejected.

Such a glimpse came to Vincent during his undergraduate years. Reared in a home that was strictly religious by conventional standards, he had been indoctrinated with a strong belief in a personal God who meted out rewards and punishment in accord with his moral laws. As Vincent studied science and philosophy and was exposed to iconoclastic students and teachers, he lost his traditional faith and the support it provided him. After a time of struggle, he consciously put all religious ideas out of his mind and concentrated instead on all the usual things that undergraduates concentrate upon. During this period he was struck by a dream so vivid that he was unable to forget it, indeed, he found himself strangely preoccupied with it. Eventually, circumstances brought Vincent to analysis. In his initial session he related the dream: *I am walking with a woman slightly older than myself along a mountain path. It is a glacial idyllic scene by moonlight. I am also somehow watching myself. We come to some huge gray boulders. They are blocking our path. We stop, and she turns to me and looks at me. We are engaged in pleasant conversation. Suddenly she turns extremely ugly. Her face takes on a greenish color and she turns suddenly very old. I realize there is only one way to help the situation and that is to have intercourse with her. My penis enters her vagina then goes through her body and into the rock behind her. Then she disappears and I am alone, having intercourse with the rock.*

Sometime later, with the dream still on his mind, Vincent was sitting on a bench in front of the university library. These words began going through his mind insistently. "By this rock I will heal you, through this rock I will save you." Over and over again. He told me what he had then thought about all this. "I thought the woman was part of myself—I thought something was wrong inside myself—that the unconscious was extremely ugly. I started reading psychology and I stumbled upon Jung's small book *Modern Man in Search of a Soul.* After that I began reading more and more of Jung. He had taken on a deep religious significance for me." Then Vincent told me about how he had quit his church during his junior year at college, and had started reading Mahayana Buddhism, yoga and Zen. He had lost his sense of communication with his own past and he was not at home in the Eastern religions altogether, although he sensed that something existed there that might have meaning for him.

This young man, who had not known anything about Jung at the time of the dream, had experienced an archetypal configuration. Then some event in his life had led him to discover what the experience was all about, if not to understand it. Through his analysis Vincent was able to accept that the woman in his dream was a representation of the anima, who can lead a man to his unconscious depths if he will but dare to approach her in all her beauty and sometimes terror. The rock symbolized the basis, the solid, unchangeable impenetrable reality which in some mysterious way a man must penetrate with his creative potential. The self challenges us to this task, and when it does there is no turning away from the challenge without serious consequences.

The self is the instigator of the process of individuation. This is true whether the process is undertaken consciously, as in analysis or in the dedication of oneself to a life of contemplative searching, or unconsciously, as in a commitment to any goal which goes beyond the merely personal. The self embraces the whole of psychic totality, incorporating both consciousness and the unconscious; it is also the center of this totality. The ego belongs to it and is part of it, the ego being the whole of consciousness at any given moment and also the organ that is capable of becoming conscious.

From the point of view of the ego, growth and development depend on integrating into the sphere of the ego as much as possible of that which was formerly unknown. This unconscious content comprises two categories. The first is *knowledge* of the world and the way it works; basically this is a function of education of both the formal kind (schooling) and the informal kind (empirical experience). The second category is *wisdom;* this is essentially the understanding of human nature including one's own nature as an individual. Thus the goal of the individuation process as seen from the standpoint of the ego, is the expansion of awareness.

From the point of view of the self, however, the goal of individuation is quite different. *Where the ego was oriented toward its own emergence from the unconscious, the self is oriented toward union of consciousness with the unconscious.* It may be said that life begins with the ego striving for ascendancy, as the infant begins to wrest knowledge from the vast realms of the unknown and thus to increase its competence in coping with the ways of the world. Our whole lives are more or less engaged in the confrontations between the ego and the unconscious, whether consciously undertaken or not. Each day we begin with conscious intentions, and all day long we are involved in interacting with forces within and forces without, whose aims seem different from those we recognize as our own. So follow the days and the years; and the ego, if one is fortunate, acquires more and more of those skills which enable it to fulfill its needs and desires in the face of whatever opposition it incurs. But ultimately each life ends with the defeat of the ego, however many victories it may have won during its time. No matter how long or short the individual life may be, the "identity" so bravely achieved by the ego gives way to the anonymity of the unconscious. The victor of the final battle is the self.

What then, it may be asked, is the point of all the struggle for awareness? The truth is that not many people want to do this. It is too difficult, so they say that they are not interested. They live as in a trance, mesmerized by the television talk shows, news of the world that comes in byte-sized pieces, films with so much violence and music so ear-splitting that their sensibilities are blunted. They seek pleasure and excitement without asking, Why am I doing this? But others ask in true sincerity, Why undertake the wearying and often fearsome journey? Why strain and strive and seek to know more, when knowing more is only to open the gates to deeper mysteries? I have often pondered this question myself, and especially in my writing, as I ask myself what possesses me to sit with my computer on a beautiful summer's day when the sky is a singing blue and the sailboats are bright in the harbor. And you, the reader, may also be asking why you engage yourself in your own search for understanding, rather than satisfying yourself only with pleasures of the senses. I remember watching the landing of the Apollo 15 mission on the moon, and hearing Astronaut Dave Scott proclaim as he set foot on the lunar surface: "As I stand out here on the wonders of the unknown at Hadley, I sort of realize there is a fundamental truth to our nature. Man must explore. And this is exploration at its greatest." I do not think it is fame, or fortune, or the need to sublimate a neurosis, that leads people to undertake perilous journeys either outward into space or inward into the depths of the psyche. That "man must explore" is reason enough for the archetypal journey. The hero's quest is an archetypal journey. Though all who undertake it are not heroes, there is a touch of the heroic in all of us, else we could not live in this dangerous and desperate world.

In the archetypal journey the ego winds its way between the snares of the persona and the traps of the shadow. The persona has developed as a compromise between the ego's intentions and the entire personality structure that supports it, on the one hand, and the demands of society on the other. The result is that we take on the mask which is "a segment of the collective psyche." Often, the ego becomes identified with this persona. We believe that we are the image we attempt to portray to the world. As in every compromise something is sacrificed; certain natural and spontaneous qualities of personality fall into the unconscious, where they become part of the shadow aspect. One of the first tasks of analysis is to strip off the mask of persona. Next, is to learn how to recognize the shadow in its many and varied aspects so that the genuine person can emerge into the light. As the process continues, deeper realms of the unconscious become more and more accessible to the ego. Each insight leads to the capacity for further insight. Anima and animus begin to appear in dreams and in projections onto other people. These prophetic visions of the night lead the seeker closer to the center.

I do not mean to suggest that the awakening of consciousness is all a methodical process that advances step by step. Jungian analysis does not follow a set format that supposedly exists in the mind of the analyst. The unconscious material determines the character of the process, and it is the analyst's task to follow where it leads, along with the analysand who produces it. Because the persona is on the surface, it is the logical place to begin. Whatever the presenting problem which the analysand brings into the initial session, the persona usually is a factor in it. Most of the time it can be readily recognized by analysands. They will generally admit quite easily that while it is a part of them which they freely display, it is not entirely what they envision as the personality in its totality. As soon as the persona is tampered with, defenses arise to protect what lies behind it. As the defenses are dealt with in analysis, more and more unconscious aspects of the personality begin to emerge.

These unconscious aspects may appear as dream figures who resemble people we know in our everyday lives, or dream figures who are strangers to us; they may be characters in fantasies or they may be the fantasies which we apply to real people. They may come to us out of forgotten myths and legends, or they may strike a responsive note when we meet them for the first time in literature or on the stage or screen. Or they may be brought up from our own depths through specific techniques which are used in analysis to gently probe the unconscious. While the figures appear to be individual, they reflect the archetypal background of the unconscious which gives rise to their formation. In this sense they may be thought of as archetypal figures often projected onto real people.

These archetypal figures came to be conceptualized by Jung as a result of his empirical observations of the vast amounts of unconscious material presented to him by his patients. They were augmented by his own inner search, a search which led him from his own dreams and fantasies to research into their parallels in myth, folklore and a variety of religious doctrines and practices. The images seemed to him to coalesce around certain themes. Jung used symbolic terms to express the themes of persona, ego, shadow, animus, anima and so on, because the symbolic approach was the most effective way he knew to address the area of the unknown. Anything else would have tied down and concretized something which is not to be concretized. By being too explicit we run the risk of constricting the flow of thought and imagination. When we feel that we have the answer to a problem there is little reason for further exploration.

The struggle with the anima and the animus, sometimes leads us deeper into the unconscious and sometimes blocks the path for a time. If we persist, the anima or animus brings us into contact with other archetypal figures along the way. Each one plays its role in the archetypal drama which has as its theme the fall from the original state of oneness with a primordial unity, to separation, loss of integrity, and despair —and at last to regeneration within a new unity that is marked by an awareness of all the component parts of the psyche, and by a harmonious relationship among them. The drama of transformation is played on many stages. The characters appear in all varieties of make-up and costume, but they are cast into certain definable types, who act in somewhat predictable ways.

The archetype of the *divine child*, for example, tends to

appear in advance of a transformation in the psyche. His appearance recalls the marking of aeons in the history of the world which were heralded by the appearance of an infant who overthrows an old order and, with passion and inspiration, begins a new one. The power of this archetype is nowhere better expressed than in William Blake's poem, *A Song of Liberty*. The Eternal Female, the anima, gives birth to the divine child, a sun god with flaming hair. This evokes the jealous rage of the old king, the "starry king" of night and darkness and all the decadence that has come upon the world. Though the king flings the divine child into the western sea, the child will not be drowned. A night sea journey will take place and when it is finished the son of morning will rise in the east to bring his light to the world:

The Eternal Female groan'd! it was heard all over the Earth!
. . . In her trembling hands she took the new born terror, howling:
On those infinite mountains of light, now barr'd out by the atlantic
   sea, the new born fire stood before the starry king!
Flag'd with grey brow'd snows and thunderous visages, the jealous
   wings wav'd over the deep.
The speary hand burned aloft, unbuckled was the shield; forth
   went the hand of jealousy among the flaming hair, and hurl'd
   the new born wonder thro' the starry night.
The fire, the fire is falling! . . .

The fiery limbs, the flaming hair, shot like the sinking sun into the
   western sea. . . .
With thunder and fire, leading his starry hosts thro' the waste
   wilderness, [the gloomy king] promulgates his ten commands,
   glancing his beamy eyelids over the deep in dark dismay,
Where the son of fire in his eastern cloud, while the morning
   plumes her golden breast,
Spurning the clouds written with curses, stamps the stony law to
   dust, loosing the eternal horses from the dens of night, crying:
Empire is no more! And now the Lion & Wolf shall cease.[5]

The divine child, most often a boy, is unusual from the very circumstances of his birth, or even of his conception. Perhaps he is taken from his mother in order to prevent some dire fate to the family or the community. Moses, Oedipus and Krishna were taken from their mothers and reared by strangers; Romulus and Remus were abandoned to the wilderness; all of these children were saved for a special mission. Some miraculous design kept them safe until the time was ripe for their task to be fulfilled. In the intervening years the child would overcome many difficulties, and develop his own sense of meaning and a style of living which expresses that meaning. At the appropriate time he manifests himself and brings into reality that dynamic change for which he was appointed. Shortly thereafter he dies, having accomplished that for which he came.[6]

In analysis, the motif of the divine child frequently appears in the course of the individuation process. At first analysands tend to identify this with their own infantilism, and this may be appropriate to a degree. Wherever the appearance of the child in dreams or other kinds of imagery bears a resemblance to the dreamer, or to a form of the dreamer's behavior, the image may be helpful in understanding the personal aspects of the material itself. It may be helpful in tracing back neurotic elements to an earlier stage of development in the individual. However, just as fantasy material may, in part, be identifiable with the history of the one who produces it, the image of the divine child may in part also be new, bearing no resemblance whatever to the previous experience of the individual. It is this latter element that encourages the imagination to dwell on the futurity of the archetype—that is, to ask what this image may suggest about developments which are still embryonic in the psyche but which may have the potentiality for growth and change.

As our own children are, to a certain extent, extensions of our own egos, so the "divine child" may be thought of as an extension of the collective consciousness. As we pin our hopes and dreams on our children, wishing for them the fulfillment of our unfinished tasks, the realization of what we were never able to realize—so the "divine child" represents the ideals of a culture which it is not able, in reality, to fulfill. Often the "savior" becomes the scapegoat for the sins of his society, and by reason of his suffering and his sacrifice the society is enabled to continue, to have another chance.

In our own dreams the appearance of the special child often carries with it a profound meaning. In my practice I have found that it is common to dream of a child who is maimed or ill or dying. This may have no correspondence to the life of the dreamer, and so I find myself wondering—in what way is the dreamer's innate potential being distorted or cut off? The analysis of the specific details in the unconscious material, and some comparison with similar details as they appear in the archetypal situations in the literature of myth and comparative religion may enable individuals to get beyond their immediate concerns and to see where they are going in terms of their life tasks. As Viktor Frankl pointed out in *Man's Search for Meaning,* his report on his concentration camp experiences, those who regarded their lives in the camp as "provisional" and lived only from day to day quickly lost their strength. The few who were able to find through their suffering in a place where their physical bodies were imprisoned, the challenge to free their spirits, these few tended to survive against nearly impossible odds. The divine child within us gives meaning to our immature strivings; he shows us the unconscious side of the limitations which we experience, and that is a vision of potentiality coming into flower.

Another archetype that we are likely to meet on the way of individuation is the eternal youth or *puer aeternus,* as Ovid called him in *Metamorphosis.* He also appears as a divine youth who is born into the mother-cult mysteries at Eleusis[7] and elsewhere. He is a god of vegetation and of resurrection, for it is his fate to die and to be reborn, or to be dismembered and then reassembled. Thus he embodies some of the qualities of the redeemer. The man who is identified with the archetype of the puer aeternus, with eternal youth, is one who has remained too long in adolescent psychology. In him, characteristics which are normal in a youth in his teens are continued into later life.[8] Perhaps the expression "high living" best describes this archetype: the young man indulges his high-flying fantasies, living out experiences for their sheer excitement, picking up friends when he wants amusement and dropping them when they become in any sense a responsibility. Some of the heroes of the youth culture fall into this category, and again, for some "getting high" is the objective in and of itself. The aimless traveling, moving in and out of various groups, is characteristic of the puer. Compulsive sexual activity is often an expression of this archetype. The puer indulges in casual and promiscuous relationships, forming one liaison after another, only to drop each one at the first suggestion that some commitment may be required of him.

Von Franz, in her study of the puer aeternus archetype,[9] suggests that the man who is identified with this archetype often seeks a career in flying, but that he is usually rejected on application for the reason that psychological tests show up his instability and the neurotic reasons for his interest in this profession.

The dreams of an individual who is established in his life in a secure position, who may be already middle-aged, may disclose the operation of the puer aeternus archetype. The motifs of flying (sometimes without any plane, just by flapping the arms), high-speed driving, deep-sea diving, climbing precarious mountain cliffs, are all typical of one whose unconscious is dominated by this archetype. They may be taken as a warning signal to be aware of the ways in which the unconscious may be preparing to intrude its autonomous will in the way of consciously determined functioning.

There is, of course, a feminine counterpart to the puer and that is the *puella aeterna*, the woman who is afraid to grow old, although she will never admit it. Still, the fear dominates much of her existence. She is the one who never tells her age, who falls for every diet fad and for every new make-up with the fantastic promise of rejuvenation written into the advertisements. She is a "pal" to her children, and an everlasting coquette where men are concerned. In her dreams she is often on a pedestal, inspiring the adoration of men, or she is a siren or a whore or a nymphet. In life she generally is reckless and impulsive. When it comes to making an important decision, however, she vacillates a good deal and asks many people for advice. She then acts with surprising suddenness, and she regrets her actions almost before they are completed.

Living the archetype of "eternal youth" has its creative potential, also, as we may infer from the ways we see it manifest itself. Some aspects of the puer aeternus or the puella aeterna are youthful enthusiasm and the boundless energy to carry it along, spontaneity of thinking, production of new ideas and new ways to solve problems, willingness to strike out in a different direction without being held in by a desire to conserve the past and its values.

The puer and puella as unconscious factors provide the needed impetus to start out on new paths. They do not necessarily offer the wisdom to discern whether the endeavor is worth the struggle, and they often do not provide the steadying and staying power to carry it through if, indeed, it is worth while. When this archetype is active great dreams and schemes will be hatched. If they are to succeed, even in the smallest part, a compensatory archetype must come into play. This is the "senex" archetype.[10]

Senex means old or aged and, as an archetype, it stands behind the forces that would preserve the traditional values, that hold out for keeping things the way they are, for applying sober judgment and consideration to the schemes of the eternal youth. At best this factor in the unconscious is expressed in mature wisdom born of experience and, at worst, it represents a hidebound orthodoxy that tolerates no interference from those who would break with established patterns.

A variant of the figure of the puer aeternus, sometimes even incorporating aspects of the senex, is the enchanting archetypal figure who is known as *the trickster*. Of him, Jung says:

Anyone who belongs to a sphere of culture that seeks the perfect state somewhere in the past must feel very queerly indeed when confronted by the figure of the trickster. He is a forerunner of the saviour, and, like him, God, man, and animal at once. He is both subhuman and superhuman, a bestial and divine being, whose chief and most alarming characteristic is his unconsciousness. Because of it he is deserted by his (evidently human) companions, which seems to indicate that he has fallen below their level of consciousness. He is so unconscious of himself that his body is not a unity, and his two hands fight each other. He takes his anus off and entrusts it with a special task. Even his sex is optional despite its phallic qualities: he can turn himself into a woman and bear children. From his penis he makes all kinds of useful plants. This is in reference to his original nature as a Creator, for the world is made from the body of a god.[11]

The contradictory figure of the trickster has been associated with the carnival in the medieval Church, and today is present at such affairs as the Mardi Gras and the celebration of Fastnacht in Switzerland—festivals which precede the somber holy days and which are marked with merriment and partying and jokes of all kinds—when the natural, simple nature of people can be given full expression. He fits the medieval description of the devil as "the ape of God," and in folklore as the simpleton of whom everyone takes advantage.

We experience tricksters in our individual lives just when we are most unsuspecting. We meet them when we find ourselves at the mercy of the most annoying "accidents." A woman recently received an award for unusual distinction. She did not feel she had properly earned it, indeed, it was something of a fluke and all the more embarrassing because there was newspaper publicity about it. She received many letters of congratulation which she felt obliged to answer personally. However she had no more than just begun to write when she got up for a glass of water, stumbled over her own doorstep, and broke her right arm.

In dreams tricksters are the ones who set obstacles in our

path for their own reasons; they are the ones who keep changing shape and appearing and disappearing at the oddest moments. They symbolize that aspect of our own nature which is always nearby, ready to bring us down when we get inflated, or to humanize us when we become pompous. They are satirists par excellence, their trenchant wit points out the flaws in our haughty ambitions, and makes us laugh though we feel like crying. In society we find them as critics or gadflies, and they even pop up in the highest offices of our land.

The major psychological function of the trickster figures is to make it possible for us to gain a sense of proportion about ourselves. This they do by testing and trying us, so that we discover what we are made of. Their motto might well be, "If the fool would persist in his folly, he would become wise."[12]

The figures of the divine child who becomes a hero or savior, the puer aeternus and his feminine counterpart, the senex and the trickster, are only some of the aspects under which the archetypal forming-elements of the psyche may appear. There is no need to go into all the possibilities here, except to say that in principle they are unlimited, and that individuals encounter those archetypes which are relevant to their personal myths. Incorporating these various unconscious aspects into the sphere of consciousness divests them of their uncanny power to influence the individual unaware. They can be seen instead in both their positive and negative aspects, and the individual is then free to make a choice from the various possibilities they offer. It is not an easy matter to integrate these contents of the unconscious. It is a long, hard task that is never completed because the unconscious is too vast to be brought into the domain of the ego. It is possible, however, to become well enough acquainted with the forces at work in us below the level of consciousness so that we become familiar with their tricks and devices, and are able to recognize them through illusion and disguise.

The anima and the animus are probably the most difficult to integrate of all the unconscious contents. This may be because anima and animus are tied up with our sexual drives on one hand, and the utter mystery of their otherness on the other. We are both desirous and frightened of these mighty figures, yet the anima or animus, as the case may be, must become a part of our conscious experience if we are ever to approximate the ultimate goal of wholeness.

An aim of analysis is to reach a state where enough of the unconscious contents become conscious so that they no longer need to express themselves as those anima and animus functions which interfere with relationships, inhibit productivity and undermine the possibility of inner peace. This means that the animus and anima are capable of being rescued from their roles as autonomous complexes. When this occurs, they lose their negative charge and become partners with the ego in what has been described as the inner marriage. The man is no longer anima-possessed, nor the woman animus-possessed. Each sees the function of the contrasexual part as a guide to those further mysteries of the unconscious which will arise out of the necessity of human curiosity.

The conquest of the anima or the animus and its integration into our own lives as a consciously experienced guide to the unconscious releases us from the kinds of conflicts brought about by the projections of these inner figures onto women and men whom we know. As the projections are withdrawn, the complex of energy that was bound up in the projection is also withdrawn. What this means practically is that a woman stops blaming her "lack of opportunity" on the construction of her genitalia, or on the prejudices of society. No longer identifying herself as a victim, she begins to consider her own self-image as a possible basis for the inadequacy she feels. Instead of trying to be what she thinks will "succeed" in the world, or "what the world wants," she resolves to turn her attention to becoming more fully what her authentic nature longs to express. Jung describes the comparable situation as it applies to the man who has reached this stage of development with respect to "the conquest of the anima as an autonomous complex, and her transformation into a function of relationship between the conscious and the unconscious." He says:

"With the attainment of this goal it becomes possible to disengage the ego from all its entanglements with the collectivity and the collective unconscious. Through this process the anima forfeits the daemonic power of an autonomous complex; she can no longer exercise the power of possession, since she is depotentiated."[13]

The process of individuation can then move on in its spiraling path, circumambulating the center, which is the self. As, one by one, the complexes that arose from the archetypal configurations lose their power over the individual, we would expect the ego to experience a new freedom, a relatively complex-free state. It is true that much energy is released and the individual feels expanded, uninhibited, open to the storms of the world and able to withstand them. The new sense of power that we experience will very often endow us with a sense of our own very great importance. We are now "enlightened," no longer subject to the moods and tensions or the neurotic defenses that had previously been a load on the personality. Now we feel that we can do just about whatever we set out to accomplish, and, most particularly, that we are well qualified to advise anyone who comes to us with any problem. We are at once a "person of action" and a "sage."

The feeling of being able to subjugate nature through the use of this special power is, of course, not always what it seems to be to the person who experiences it. If we are able to resolve a conflict that had been absorbing our attention and consequently our energy, we may claim the mana—the power —that formerly was caught in the conflict, as our own. We may hold the conviction that we are able to exert our unusual power upon others. At the same time we may appear ridiculous to others who recognize the limitations to which we, as individuals, are momentarily blinded. The truth is that the individual does not possess the mana, but rather is possessed by it, in the sense of demonic possession.

Mana is a Polynesian word having to do with power. The meaning can best be expressed by the concept of the "virtue" that resides in a person, or the "grace" that descends upon that person. Whoever holds it is someone particularly blessed. In the beliefs of many primitive tribes (the Malays, the Malagasy, various African people, and some American Indians) disembodied souls (ghosts) and spirits (which were incorporeal) possess mana. Psychologically speaking, mana appears as a sense of unusual psychic energy. It may be experienced as a result of dealing successfully with archetypal phenomena. Or, after an experience in which a difficult problem is solved, mana may be felt as a tremendous sense of vigor.

The danger comes with identification with the mana-personality. Folk heroes from television dramas, Hell's Angels, Indiana Jones, and the like, provide plenty of models of "mana" for young people today just at the age when they are breaking away from parental controls. Following the promise of mana, the young are willing to take unbelievable risks, in everything from drag racing, to hitchhiking in distant countries, to ingesting dangerous drugs without any notion of their source, strength or potential effect. The attitude may be something like this: I can do it, I can make it doing the forbidden thing, for the power to control myself is in me. I know that to gain knowledge demands experience, and that involves risk. But I have the power to overcome the dangers involved.

The situation is classical. It goes back at least as far as Phaëthon, the Greek teen-ager who had boasted to his friends that his father was Helios, the sun god, and had to prove it. Old Helios had warned him that he would never make it, for though his father was a god, he was a mortal on his mother's side. Disregarding the well-meant advice, Phaëthon waited around until the gates of morning were opened, sprang into the sun-chariot and dashed off on a mad, ecstatic ride through the heavens that ended with hero, chariot and horses falling headlong into the sea.

Reference was made to this myth at the time of the assassination of John Kennedy, who, people said, behaved as if he had a feeling of invincibility. The many risks he had taken throughout his life were climaxed by the last risk, that of refusing to accept the bulletproof covering for his limousine on that fateful day in Dallas. He and others appear to have been acting on the premise that they were endowed with the magic power—mana—which would save them from harm.

So, too, with Icarus, son of the architect of Crete who was imprisoned with his father in the labyrinth he had designed, with all exits barred. Daedalus carefully collected feathers of birds, and with these and the wax from candles, he fashioned wings. Then he and Icarus took flight. Daedalus warned his son to fly low over the sea but Icarus, possessed by this new and wonderful sense of power, soared delightedly up and up, paying no heed to his father's anguished commands. The heat of the sun melted the wax, and the youth fell to his death.

There are those who feel that the power is their own, and who believe it to be entirely under the control of the ego. Forgetting to reckon with the unconscious dimension of their natures, with the important forces within them which they are able to understand to a degree, but not to control completely, they are overcome by the real power. The problem is that they really do not know where the mana lies.

An analysand of mine had reached an important turning point in his analysis. Ever since Walter could remember, he had been repressing his emotions in any situation where expressing them might have involved taking the risk of being rejected. He ascribed his tense, inhibited manner of functioning to the pattern established in childhood of pleasing his mother, whose rigid rules and requirements allowed no room for the spontaneity of youth. "If I ever said anything wrong, she would let me know how worthless I was, so I hardly ever said anything to her." Whatever emotions he felt, he invested in religious fervor, since the family belonged to a church which preached man's complete submission to the will of an authoritarian God who would look out for his own, provided that they adhered closely to his requirements. There was no mercy anywhere. A torturous process was required in order to uncover complexes that had built up over the years and had blocked off normal feelings and responses to people and situations. It seemed for a long time that it would be impossible for

Walter to ever gain a sense of personal value. Every time he
would make a step in that direction, he would set up a situation in which he would be rejected, and rejected he was, in
nearly every area except in his analysis. It was difficult for me
to withstand his constant criticism and attacks without becoming personally aroused, and the only thing that saved me
was the awareness that it was not the man himself who was
deliberately trying to wreck the analysis but the demonic element in him, from which he suffered far more than I did.

The anima problem was foremost, since the face which
the anima had shown him in the past was that of the all-
powerful Great Mother in her terrible aspect. Walter kept projecting that image onto me in every way the unconscious
could devise. I continued to behave in a manner contrary to
his image until, little by little he had to expand the concept of
the feminine so as to include his experience with me. I had to
walk the fine line between putting him under the same kind of
pressure he had felt coming from his mother, and encouraging him in any way. The difficulties extended into the most
minute matters. An example of the first instance occurred
when one day he brought a raincoat and placed it in my closet.
As he was leaving I noticed that he was forgetting to take it on
his way out. I immediately knew that if I reminded him of it, I
would be for him the mother who scolded him for his forget-
fulness, and that if I did not remind him he would have to
come back for it, and in doing so would run the risk of interrupting my next session and incurring my "maternal anger."
There was no way to win; the only possibility was to openly
discuss the problem that presented itself so that he, too, could
participate in the process of dealing with it. In a second instance, when he had one day come to some important insights, I was caught between deemphasizing them by an attitude of neutrality, in which case he would feel himself again
as undervalued, or commending him. I did the latter, and he
seemed pleased and relieved at the end of the session. Later on
that night he got into a panic, having concluded that I would
be expecting similar insights from him every time he came for

analysis, and that he would be incapable of gaining them, so that inevitably his sham would be out in the open. Again, I had to confront him directly with the problem.

After dealing with innumerable problems arising from consideration of the autonomous elements of the psyche, Walter began to get better. He loosened up, became able to speak more freely and openly. His relationships with his coworkers improved considerably. His marriage was the only area that failed to improve. Among other problems, he was impotent with his wife, which was not surprising. He had married a younger edition of his mother, a woman who took no interest in his development and who took every opportunity to depreciate his analytic work. The only weapon he had against her (and of course this was at first totally unconscious) was to deprive her of sexual satisfaction. On the rare occasions that he felt sexually aroused, he would numb the feeling with alcohol or sedatives.

After many a battle, the slaying of the dragon finally took place when he had become free enough in his emotional life to establish a warm relationship with another woman. Also in his professional contacts with women he became more relaxed. He rejoiced, feeling that at last he had overcome the negative anima. He was a changed man, enjoying life as never before, pouring new energy into his work and into his relationship with women. He even managed to be more engaging and pleasant to his family at home than he had been in years.

At this point Walter had a short but extremely important dream. It was characterized, as such dreams often are, by the recollection of every nuance of the strong emotion that accompanied it. Here is the dream: *I dreamed that I was Christ and was doing the things he did for people. When I awoke I found the dream made me quite uncomfortable, so I kind of tended to change it into seeing colored slides of Christ in different situations.*

For a man who has formerly thought of himself as worthless, to dream of himself as Christ is evidence that he has identified himself with the mana of the Christ figure. In light

of the circumstances of the man's life, the evidence was confirmed. The unconscious had presented the problem in symbolic terms, and with its uncanny wisdom had also offered the
possibility of correcting the abnormal condition of possession
by the archetype of the mana-personality.

To be Christ means, according to the dream, not just holding the power to accomplish whatever the person wants to do.
It requires that the one who has the mana be the one who
actually does the things that the Christ figure was able to do,
and to do them "for people." This does not mean saving one's
own soul, for this was the least of Christ's concerns, and the
dreamer readily admitted that. The dream had pointed out
that it was necessary to bring matters down to size, for the
dreamer to disentangle himself from the archetype and to see
himself with his own human limitations, while at the same
time holding before himself the image of a savior whose
power derives from that "otherness" which is beyond the capacity of the ego to assume.

The mana-personality appears in many forms, but what
they all have in common is a superior ability to subjugate
nature which is not available to ordinary people. The mana-
personality is a godlike person. Sometimes the priest assumes
this role and sometimes it is associated with him. But the
mana-personality is also the wizard, the witch, the siren, the
sorcerer, or the medicine man. In our time the archetype is
projected onto the magnetic men and women who capture the
imagination and the loyalty of their admirers and all the more
if they can die a violent death or commit suicide. Frequently,
the mana is associated with the heads of state, the doctor, the
analyst, or the great spiritual leader.

One of my analysands dreamed: *I come home from work
early because my boss had sent me away due to some misunderstanding. I am in my apartment and I know that Dr. Jung is
down the hall. I get up the courage and knock on his door. It is
still early evening, but he is getting ready for bed, in pajamas. I
ask him over for a drink. He comes over. I can find nothing to*

say. He finally says, why did you ask me over? I still say nothing. Then I tell him I am in analysis. He gets up to go, but motions for me to come over to his room. When we get there he takes two small liqueur glasses and pours a black liqueur into them. Handing me one, he says, "You must drink this cup with me."

The dream suggests that the power comes through the agency of the revered teacher figure, but it must be sought, accepted, and assimilated by the dreamer. He is a man who has been in analysis long enough to recognize most of his shadow aspects. He has struggled through difficulties in his relationship with his wife, and learned to separate her being from his anima, and he no longer holds out expectations that she provide what he needs to make his emotional life complete. He is able to relate both to his wife and to his anima, and no longer confuses one with the other. In the process of his analysis, as he struggled with the shadow, the anima, and many of the other autonomous figures that had been split off from consciousness, he was able to release much of the energy that had formerly been bound up in those psychic contents.

Now, with every new insight, he was experiencing a subtle increase in his sense of personal power. The source of this power he ascribed to Dr. Jung. For him, Jung's teachings held the ultimate mana, for the work he had done led him to believe that Jung possessed a certain magic—though he would not have put it that way—that could redeem him from the Hades of his unconscious. He would call upon Jung much as some people call upon a particular saint in a time of trouble. The dream shows that he closely identifies with Jung. He realizes there is something irrational about this—it takes courage to knock on Jung's door. When Jung asks why he has invited him, he cannot find words to describe his condition. He says that he is in analysis. He tries to show Jung that he is "all right" because he has accepted Jung's precepts. But Jung, apparently, is not impressed. It is not what you have learned but what you actually can take in, absorb, integrate, assimilate that is important. So Jung provides, not words of wisdom, but a black liqueur. It is a sort of dark communion, during which what has come from Jung must now become a part of the dreamer.

When in the course of analysis we begin to feel that we have understood the unconscious and that we have the power to deal with it effectively, we may acquire the tendency to assume the mantle of the mana-personality. We begin to believe that the powers of the unconscious belong to us, that is, that they have come under the aegis of the ego. But this is far from the case. Even though we see our ego personality in a new light, expanded through the assimilation of certain unconscious contents, we remain within the structure of our own limitations, bound by time and space, life and death, in a world with limits.

The next step toward the realization of the self requires liberation from identification with the mana-personality. We come to recognize that this identification, too, works to aggrandize the ego. The power that we seek is not a possession that we can either wrest from another or keep for ourselves. The power comes from somewhere else, but we can open ourselves and allow that power to flow into us—indeed, we can be a conduit for it. But only when we have come to terms with our own limitations and have seen that there is a greater Other.

As we discover the limitations of our individual consciousness we begin to realize that this consciousness, whose center is the ego, is subject to that greater consciousness whose center is the self. The ego is to the self as the earth is to the sun. From the standpoint of the ego, all we know is consciousness and that which we are able to draw into consciousness from the unknown. The self embraces the ego within a larger system, which includes everything that is conscious and unconscious from the ego's point of view. As the sun warms and energizes the earth, so the self is the source toward which the ego yearns as it circles around it, drawing from it the sustenance for its life.

The self is "half immanent and half transcendent."[14] That

which is immanent in it is the aspect through which the self is related to human understanding, even within the limitations of its finitude. That which is transcendent in it is the aspect through which the self is related to the unconscious, to the impenetrable, to the infinite and the unreachable. This is why Jung has said of the self, "The self . . . is a God image, or at least cannot be distinguished from one. Of this the early Christian spirit was not ignorant, otherwise Clement of Alexandria could never have said that he who knows himself knows God."[15]

The major work of the analytic process is the uncovering of unconscious contents and their assimilation into the ego. Jung makes this clear when he says that "the more numerous and the more significant the unconscious contents which are assimilated to the ego, the closer the approximation of the ego to the self, even though this approximation must be a never-ending process."[16] We have seen how this tends to produce an inflation of the ego, an unwarranted sense of its own capacity and potentiality. The only help for this is the clear differentiation of the ego from the unconscious contents: "I am not that, although that represents an element in my total nature. The better I know it, the less it will exert control over me." Jung warns against the attempt to psychologize the unconscious components of the personality out of existence. By our very nature we are in part conscious and in part unconscious, and we rest on the threshold between the two. As well try to escape this as to escape the necessity for sleep at the end of each day. The more we try to escape, the more it overcomes us, but the more willingly we accept it, the fresher and stronger we will be for it.

In our discussions of the shadow, the anima and animus, and other figures of the unconscious, we have seen that the images and symbols which infuse these archetypal forms are limitless. We draw from the residue of human experience those palpable symbols which for us best evoke the images of the invisible and mysterious archetypal elements which are, in themselves, forming tendencies without specific content.

The self is also expressed symbolically, in images of many kinds. Jung has made the exploration of these symbols the subject of several of his major works.[17] Of all the symbolic expressions of the self, the circle or sphere seems best to give shape to the ideas of the self's centrality, its extensity and its encompassing character. The circle as center and circumference is a symbol that is, of course, not exclusively Jung's, but one which has appeared as a motif in every realm of human endeavor, and in every corner of the world we know. It is a motif in art and design, and, since the invention of the wheel, is an important element of technology. The circle is a synonym for a social group; a model for a city, a wedding ring or a royal diadem. Its path may be traced over and over again for it has no beginning and no end. As such it carries the meaning of everlasting life, for it is birth and life, death and resurrection, in an unceasing chain. Likewise, it is the journey of the sun hero crossing the sky in an arc from east to west by day and, from dusk's descent, returning under the night sea to dawn's arising. As such the circular path is the analogue for the way of individuation.

Mandala is the Sanskrit word for circle; it means more especially a magic circle. The circular design with the virtue of power attached to it is found in the East, where it is frequently seen in a *yantra*, an object used to focus the attention in meditative practice. It is also prominent in our own culture; the rose-window of the medieval Church structure provides an excellent example of the mandala. So, also, do certain of the sand paintings of the Navajo Indians. Jerusalem, the City of God, as described in the Book of Revelation is a mandala city. The gates on every side lead into the center, and in the center is the image of God in the human mind.[18]

Suffering human beings come into analysis. They have lost the sense of primordial wholeness that represents the paradise of innocence. They are troubled, feeling separated from the world or from the mystery which they intuitively know as their real selves. Their equilibrium is shaken. They need to be made whole again. They need to be reunited with that from which they have departed. I must tell you that in my experience I have seen many who have approached this task, but only a few who have fulfilled its arduous demands. Most people give up somewhere along the way, often very much helped by their participation in the process even though they have not seen it through as far as it can go. For many, the disappearance of nagging, annoying or blocking symptoms is sufficient, and when this is accomplished they can return to their everyday concerns. For some, and this refers especially to younger people, some psychological problem interferes with their ongoing lives, and it has only to be removed or overcome for the individual to terminate in therapy and get on with the business of living. Others go further and take into themselves as much of unconscious contents as they can comfortably deal with, and let the rest go awhile, perhaps forever, perhaps until another situation arises which demands returning to the confrontation with the unconscious. Any of these people may be changed to a greater or lesser degree through their experience of analysis, limited though it may be.

The journey into self takes as long as it takes, and when it has been long enough, both the analyst and the analysand know it. I cannot tell you how we know it, but it is clear. Not that the questing is ever truly over, for it lasts as long as life itself; but there comes a time when the individual is able to carry on the search independent of the analyst and this became evident to Mark through changes in his life and was confirmed by his dreams.

For a long time Mark and I knew that his analysis was drawing to a close. It had gone through many phases and his whole personality had greatly shifted in the process. He had developed from a frightened, inadequate young man to one who was moving toward recognized goals, with sureness and confidence and absolute humility. Toward the end we had spaced the sessions more widely apart as he developed the independence successfully to interpret his own unconscious material. There was an affectionate tie between us, for we had joined hands in a complicated and trying mutual endeavor.

Still, the analysis was not ended, although we were both aware that soon it must end.

To the last session he brought two dreams, which had come to him just a week apart. These are the dreams.

The first: *I am in an airplane which is flying over the mountains. It is a stormy day, and the passengers are upset as the plane rises and falls upon hitting air pockets. I go about the cabin reassuring people, calming them, making sure that everyone is securely fastened in his seat. I look to see where the exits are and I plan in my head how I will handle an evacuation if we should make a forced landing. I am not afraid, and I am prepared for whatever might happen. But we do not have to land there in the mountains after all.*

The second dream: *Again I am in an airplane, but this is a small one, a two-seater. I am beside the pilot. We find ourselves in difficulty. This time we are over a deep forest. We are not far from the treetops, and the pilot is trying very hard to handle the controls. I say, I think I can manage it, I'd like to try. I take over the controls as the pilot exchanges places with me. The wheel is very hard to handle. It takes all my strength, but I am determined to hold through. I look around and notice that the pilot is perfectly relaxed. The wheel now becomes more responsive to my direction. It is still difficult, but now I know that I am going to make it.*

There was not much to say after this. Both Mark and I knew that he was ready to take charge of his own life. He had learned as much as I could help him with, and now it was time for him to go away. At the door, we embraced as he was leaving. He looked back at me and smiled as he went down the hall. I smiled back at him. Only after the door had closed did I realize that my eyes were wet. In good times as well as in bad, it is a hard thing to be an analyst.

9

Understanding Our Dreams

. . .

I BELIEVE THAT the experience of dreaming is the clearest proof we have that the unconscious exists. The inner life of an individual unfolds through dreams, and those who carefully observe their dreams may gain access to dimensions of their natures that would otherwise remain impenetrable. The way we approach our dreams depends very much upon our own attitude toward the unconscious.

Long before they met, both Freud and Jung were committed to the importance of interpreting dreams as a means of gaining access to unconscious processes. Freud's monumental study, *The Interpretation of Dreams,* provided a basis for experimentation by the members of the Vienna psychoanalytic circle. This group collected a great deal of dream material from their patients to provide the basis for their scientific research. They discussed methods of treating mental disorders and advanced new theories about the way hidden processes of the mind affected attitudes and behavior. A controversial aspect of psychoanalysis was its insistence that dreams not only contained important clues to the unknown, but that they also offered guidance on healing the troubled psyche. Freud showed that the conscious mind resists the pressure of uncomfortable ideas. Non-psychoanalytically oriented doctors and psychologists objected that the psychoanalysts were exposing aspects of the human personality that they would have preferred to ignore. No one likes to have secret wishes revealed, or to be told that beneath apparently respectable adult behavior there lurk unresolved sexual conflicts, or even infantile, incestuous aspirations. Under the most virulent kind of criticism, Freud steadfastly maintained his theoretical position.

During their early years together, beginning in 1907, Jung supported this position publicly, against the advice of his elder professional colleagues in Zurich, and knowing that by doing so he was risking his promising career in academic medicine. In 1909 Jung published a paper entitled "The Analysis of Dreams,"[1] which is a straight explication of Freud's theory of dream interpretation. At that time he agreed fully with Freud's contention that dreaming, like everything else we do, has a meaning that does not arise out of bodily sensations felt during sleep, or even out of the events of the day. These merely furnish the elements upon which the psychological processes do their work. He explained how Freud saw the manifest content of the dream as a cover story for the real situation of the dreamer, which had to be a state of conflict between a repressed wish seeking expression and the need to keep the wish unconscious. In this essay, Jung made a passing reference to the possibility of getting to the latent content of the dream— the story hidden behind the dream events—through the use of the association experiment. Then he went on to explain how Freud would use the entirely different method of "free association" to lead back to the real basis of the dream. In free association the analyst asks about a specific dream element and invites the analysand to say anything that comes to mind about it, and to allow the associations to follow one another without interruption until they provide the clues which enable the analyst to follow the traces from the manifest content of the dream to the latent content which is behind it and which has been repressed.

Emerging differences in approach to dream material became explicit in 1909, during a lecture trip to the United States which Jung and Freud made together. They saw each other daily on board ship and spent a good deal of time analyzing one another's dreams. In that very uncomfortable process, each must have withdrawn from the other in terms of revealing his own inner life. Jung described the whole affair in his autobiography. From his point of view this encounter foreshadowed the dissolution of the relationship. Freud had presented a dream of his own, and Jung had indicated that he could do much better in interpreting it if he knew some more details about Freud's private life. Freud regarded him in that moment with a look of "utmost suspicion" and replied, "But I cannot risk my authority!" For Jung, in that moment he had already lost it.[2]

Jung also related a dream of his own to Freud at that time, a dream which Jung regarded as extremely important. It showed him descending through several levels of a house, each level representing an earlier period of history, until at last he was in a low cave cut into a rock, with thick dust on the floor and in the dust scattered bones and broken pottery and a couple of human skulls, all like remains of a primitive culture. For Jung the dream was a gripping experience; it seemed to him like a ritual of passage from the personal unconscious into the collective unconscious, where the remnants of his archaic heritage rested.

Freud had paid relatively little attention as Jung related the succession of downward transitions which brought the dreamer from a cheerful room such as might have been inhabited by his grandparents, to older and more ancient dwelling places, the deepest of which contained only the two skulls as evidence that it had ever been a human habitation. Out of all this wealth of dream material, Freud had focused primarily on the two skulls. He hinted that these must be some manifestations of a death wish, for were not all dreams instigated by an unfulfilled wish in the unconscious? He demanded that Jung say whose the skulls were.

Jung knew perfectly well what Freud was driving at, but he could not see the dream in purely personal terms. Yet he was still somewhat sensitive about challenging the older man, or at least about doing so openly. Jung found his own way to the significance of the dream after he rejected Freud's interpretation. He was unable to agree with Freud that a dream is a façade behind which the meaning lies hidden—"a meaning already known but maliciously, so to speak, withheld from consciousness."[3] Jung saw the dream as an image of the dreamer's unconscious psychic situation, expressed in symbolic terms that could be unravelled to reveal an underlying meaning.

In this particular dream, Jung saw the house as representing an image of his own psychological space, with the room on the upper story referring to the conscious level with its experiences of everyday life. Below were the strata of the unconscious, retreating into successively greater depths, each one being farther removed from personal experience and embodying more and more of the collective nature of humanity in which all individuals participate. The deepest layer to which the dream allowed him to penetrate displayed the most primitive aspect of his own psyche. The skulls were decaying images of the primitive aspects of his own nature, far removed from conscious functioning, but still contributing their substance to the fundamentals of his individual personality. Jung thought that those skulls were as much a part of his psychological heritage as remainders of the genetic patterns of our ancestors are a part of our biological heritage. The latter is apparent in our physical structures, while the former is manifested in dreams, images and visions and, paradoxically, in "new" ideas.

The dream proved an important factor in bringing Jung's growing awareness of the collective aspect of the psyche into conflict with Freud's more personalistic approach to the dream. Many years later Freud was able to integrate into his own theory, his realization of the role of the "archaic heritage" in the life of the individual. At this time, however, the disparity between the approaches of the two men to the dream acted as a source of crucial conflicts. These served to stimulate Jung's own unconscious processes. He questioned: "On what premises is Freudian psychology founded? To what category of human thought does it belong? What is the relationship of its almost exclusive personalism to general historical assumptions?"[4]

By 1914, several of Freud's closest collaborators, including Jung, had broken away from the Vienna circle in order to work in settings where they could treat their own patients without being bound by what seemed to them a rigid orthodoxy. None of the dissenters challenged Freud's assumption that dreams were meaningful phenomena, but all of them disputed to some extent the specific kinds of meaning he ascribed to dreams and the techniques he employed to interpret them. Jung was dissatisfied with the emphasis Freud placed on wish fulfillment, and also with what seemed to him to be Freud's overvaluation of the sexual aspect of the unconscious.

Not that Jung denied the importance of the unconscious wish in the formation of dreams. He recognized the role of this factor, and saw how exploring the element of the unfulfilled wish could often lead the investigator back to the antecedent factors behind the formation of a particular dream. He had some skepticism about the use of this approach as a standard technique, however, for he felt that the analyst and analysand need not engage in a long and distracting search for the origin of the dream at times when the immediate situation in which the dream took place could provide all the information necessary to proceed with diagnosis and treatment.

An example from my own practice will show how a dream which was brought to the second analytic session enabled me to move in on the problem of the analysand without first recovering irrelevant sexual details of the patient's childhood. Alex, twenty-nine, had drifted from job to job over the past several years. In discussing his jobs, there was always something wrong with the employer or with "conditions." His objective seemed to be to make as much money as possible while expending as little effort as possible. His sex life followed much the same pattern. He joined every singles group in his neighborhood and went to as many parties as he could with an eye for a good-looking woman he could get into his bed as quickly as possible. He had come into analysis with the statement that life was empty and meaningless for him, that he was bored, and that he was afraid to get married because he had never stayed with anything he had started. He asked for help saying, "I hope you can do something for me."

I did not accept Alex unequivocally in the initial session. I told him that we would give it a three-month trial to see if he was able to make the kind of commitment that an analytical relationship requires. He returned the following week for the second session, and brought this dream: *I am fooling around with a bolt that is about three inches long and a quarter of an inch in diameter. I have a nut but can't seem to find the way to get the nut and bolt together and I ask you to help. You place your hands on mine and show me how, by patient and careful movements, I can get them to fit together perfectly.*

Alex fastened on the sexual symbolism of the nut and bolt as "obvious." He was sure that the root of his difficulties was his inability to find the right way to get along with women. This was, in his eyes, the result of a long history of failure with women; it probably stemmed from his early problems with his mother, he said. This was in fact why he had decided to come to a woman analyst. He felt that if he could somehow re-enact his early history with an analyst who would substitute for his mother, that he might be able to get to the bottom of his inability to find sexual fulfillment on a stable basis. He had pinned his hopes on me; I was the one who would help him. He saw the dream as expressing his "unconscious" wish, that my help, my laying on of hands, would solve his problems.

I realized what Alex was up to. He wanted to take control of the process, and to lead it back to the events of childhood where we could spend many sessions reviewing his early history including all his childhood frustrations. I suspected that when this did not produce quick results he might follow his characteristic pattern, saying, "I tried analysis, but it just didn't work out. I know why I can't get along with women, but that doesn't really help to change things." Alex was like so many people who seek psychotherapy in order to absolve themselves of the responsibility for their failure to come to grips with their own reality. The act of sitting with an analyst is supposed to work a miracle. You come and talk about yourself, you reveal your secrets, you pay your bills, and you wait for something to happen. There is little or no change, and heaven knows you have tried, so it must be the analyst's fault.

I followed the practice described by Jung of looking into the context of the dream itself, instead of moving back in time to try to find the supposed "cause" of Alex's difficulties.[5] This is based on Jung's principle that the dream really means what it says. The unconscious presents a point of view which enlarges, completes, or compensates the conscious attitude. Through the dream it supplies the missing elements of which the ego is unaware, thus exercising its function of striving toward wholeness.

To discover what is missing from the conscious viewpoint, it is helpful to *amplify the associations* to specific elements of the dream itself. This means to widen the associations by bringing to them analogous material from myth and fantasy which has the power to illuminate the dream symbolism. Even in Alex's very brief dream there were numerous such elements. I was interested, first of all, in the associations that he would bring to the material of the dream.

I asked him what he thought "fooling around" meant. He supposed it meant playing with something, not taking it very seriously. I asked him whether he thought fooling around was purposeful activity. No, he felt it was idle or aimless. We explored some other meanings. To fool is to speak in jest, to joke, to tamper with something carelessly or ignorantly. It can also mean to deceive another person, or to take advantage of him. As these meanings came out, I could see that Alex was growing distinctly uncomfortable considering the role in which the dream portrayed him.

The next elements of dream material were the nut and the bolt. Alex was sure that the bolt was a penis and the nut was a vagina. And clearly the root of his problem was that he couldn't get the two together properly. Or was it?

Jung's research had led him to say: "The sexual language of dreams is not always to be interpreted in a concretistic way . . . it is, in fact, an archaic language which naturally uses all the analogies readiest to hand without their necessarily coinciding with a real sexual content . . . As soon as you take the sexual metaphors as symbols for something unknown, your conception of the nature of dreams at once deepens . . . So long as the sexual language of dreams is understood concretistically, there can be only a direct, outward and concrete solution . . . There is no real conception of, and attitude to, the problem. But that immediately becomes possible when the concretistic misconception is dropped."[6]

I asked Alex to try to free himself of the stereotyped interpretation and to consider what a bolt really was. He knew, of course, that a bolt was a metal pin used to fasten things together, and usually secured by a nut.

I asked him, "Is this all you can think of in connection with a bolt?"

He thought awhile, and then mentioned a thunderbolt, or a bolt of lightning.

"What do these images mean to you?" I asked him.

"They mean great power, something I can't manage, it's out of my control. Energy is all bound up in that."

"Anything else?"

"You can bolt a door. The bolt is what fastens it, keeps it closed, keeps out intruders."

We then moved on to look at the associations occurring to Alex around "nut." The nut in the dream was the kind of nut which has internal screw threads and fits on a bolt.

I asked him what the purpose of a nut was.

"To connect something to something else, or to tighten a connection."

"Is there anything else that the word 'nut' means to you?"

This brought a wealth of associations from Alex. "A nut is a kind of fruit or seed, its kernel is a seed. Also, a nut is something hard—when you have a real problem you say that you have a hard nut to crack. Or, in business, the nut is how much you have to make before you can begin to show a profit."

"Anything else?" I asked him.

"Well, nuts are testicles. That certainly fits in with the sexual theory."

"Maybe so," I replied, "but notice also that nuts as testicles have something in common with nuts as fruit-bearing seeds, they both carry the potentiality for germination into something new. That's not exactly unrelated to sex."

This was clearly something he had not thought of, he said. I wondered aloud why it had not occurred to him, and he quickly realized that his ideas about the sex act had very little to do with procreation, in fact it held very little meaning for him beyond immediate pleasure. Little by little the dream was beginning to yield up clues to the source of Alex's difficulties. These sources were not in the past, but were ongoing, giving rise each morning to problems he would experience before the evening.

I did not permit him to get off the track by letting him free-associate to the associations. Since the dream is a self-portrait of the unconscious at a given moment, I find that the best way to understand it is to fix my total attention upon it, and to establish the context. I bear in mind that Jung wrote: "Free association will get me nowhere, any more than it would help me to decipher a Hittite inscription. It will of course help me to uncover all my own complexes, but for this purpose I have no need of a dream—I could just as well take a public notice or a sentence in a newspaper. Free association will bring out all my complexes, but hardly ever the meaning of a dream. To understand the dream's meaning, I must stick as close as possible to the dream images."[7] I have found that this course makes for immediacy in the relationship of analyst, analysand and dream material.

The next part of Alex's dream consisted of the words *you*

showed me how. . . . A typical mode of operation in the dreamer was demonstrated here. He was always expecting the other person to perform the magic. No exception would be made for the analyst. Everything would work out if the analyst would just take the dreamer's hands in hers and show him how to do what had to be done. Alex was prepared to play a passive role again, as usual.

The dream says that the way to resolve the problem is by "patient and careful movements with my hands." He has to learn a different way of functioning from the way in which he has been approaching problems in the past. The old way is "fooling around." The alternative that is presented is "by patient and careful movements." By its versatility, the hand distinguishes humans from lower animals and makes possible all sorts of specifically human accomplishments.

The dream brings into awareness the message from the unconscious, that in his habitual conscious approach to his problems Alex is only half serious. He is not as interested in the meaning of what he does as he is concerned with deceiving someone, or taking advantage. Sexuality is a part of his problem, but not the whole of it, and it would be a mistake to overemphasize this. More important than a concretistic approach is the joining of the disparate elements of the dream into a chain. We cannot do this carelessly; no amount of struggling or forcing will do it; but if we approach the task with care and delicacy, we can accomplish it quite easily. We need to be open to the implications of the associations. The natural power of the psyche to restore its own balance is locked into the components of the dream. Our task in interpretation is to free that power.

We moved through the entire dream and related it to the associations to Alex's life situation. In this way the dream served as a diagnostic tool. It opened up to exploration several possible avenues for therapy.

An important aspect of this sort of approach to dreams is that the major portion of responsibility for bringing up material that would lead to interpretation rests with the analysand

and his unconscious. When the analyst offers interpretations, these always have a tentative quality. "Understanding a dream" requires agreement between the analyst and the analysand. It must grow out of the dialogue between the two, and it must be *felt* as valid by the analysand, it must "click" with him. Otherwise the analyst's pronouncements are mere intellectualizations. The analysand may follow what the analyst is saying, but the words will have little effect.

There is the further danger, if interpretation is a unilateral function of the analyst, that the analyst's own projection onto the patient may be mistaken as the message of the dream. Unless the analyst can say, "*I* think it may be like this; what is *your* reaction?" there is no way to check as to whether the analyst is really on the right track. If the analyst's interpretations are allowed to go unchallenged, if the analysand is led to believe that any objection that may be offered will be treated as a mechanism of defense against a truth he is expected to recognize, the analysis stands in grave danger of being controlled by the preconceived notions or theoretical scheme of the analyst. The questionable "results" which stem from the impositions of the analyst's interpretations depend largely on suggestion. The analyst in the dialogue imposes ideas on the analysand, a process which can easily lead to dependence of the analysand upon the analyst. This is a condition which I usually try to avoid, and, certainly, in the case of a man like Alex, whose problems were complicated by his need to get as much help as he could from external sources while making the minimal contribution from his own inner resources.

Jung stated the case very clearly, "The analyst who wishes to rule out conscious suggestions must therefore consider every dream interpretation invalid until such time as a formula is found which wins the patient's assent."[8] The whole point of dream analysis is to teach people eventually to become independent of their therapists, by acquiring the ability to carry on the dialogue with their inner aspect which has a therapeutic quality, that is, with "the therapist within."

The dream images themselves point to the causes of the

dream, to the immediate events that preceded the dream and provided material for its formation. By tracing the causal material backward we can bring about the recollections of an earlier time. Through systematic inquiry concerning antecedent events it is sometimes possible to return the patient to a childhood trauma and to recapture with him the intensity of feeling which accompanied the incident. When repressed feelings which have been contained for a very long time break through into consciousness a tremendous emotional release may occur. Pent-up feelings of anger and hostility burst forth with unimagined fury. It is like a copious bowel movement after a long period of constipation; hence Freud's term, "catharsis." This does a great deal for the individual at the moment, and helps to deal with the emotion of the past, but it does not necessarily imply any promise for the future.

Understanding the cause of a neurosis is not enough to explain its nature, nor is it effective in transforming the neurosis into a productive and rewarding aspect of the psyche. Nor is belated railing against the evildoing parents very useful. The *causalistic* point of view is insufficient; a second viewpoint must be brought into play. This second view is called by Jung the *finalistic* standpoint. By *finalistic* he means to suggest that the neurosis can be seen as striving for a purpose, an end or goal.

"All psychological phenomena," Jung says, "have some such sense of purpose inherent in them, even merely reactive phenomena like emotional reactions. Anger over an insult has its purpose in revenge; the purpose of ostentation over mourning is to arouse the sympathy of others, and so on."[9] In a wider sense, the neurosis and the dream which carries its message have, as their purpose, the drive toward individuation. This involves correction of some conscious attitudes that prevent people from more fully realizing their total capacities. When normal productive means of achieving one's purpose are blocked off, neurosis develops as an effort to find a way over or around the obstruction. Neurotic symptoms often direct people's attention to their inner development through the medium of dreams.

Steven brought a nightmare to his analytic session which was so full of horror that he was deeply shaken for several days after it occurred. He could hardly bear to read it to me, and broke into tears as he did so, more than once. He could have looked at the dream from the causalistic point of view without coming close to the meaning of it. But in the end he was able to take a finalistic view of it, and the effect was transformative. I present the dream in its entirety, not because the details need to be discussed here, but because anything less than the total presentation of the dream would diminish its impact.

The scene seems to be in an open area. There is a brick structure with two openings on one side and on the opposite side there are two more openings. In each of these openings is fitted a long, heavy iron box that slides on rollers into the hole in the brick wall. In the opening scene my aunt has crawled into one box and is pushed into the wall. On the inside of the brick walls is a hot fire. My aunt had been told that she had cancer of the lungs and that she was going to die anyway and this would be an easier death than by cancer. I found this very horrifying, but didn't question it.

Then I am told the same thing about myself and am again horrified because now I'm supposed to follow my aunt. However, I want to check with another doctor because I just had a chest x-ray and no one reported cancer then. Before this, however, I was standing at the furnace thinking I had incurable cancer of the lungs and I thought I must take the furnace as the way out. After I thought about it, I decided to get some x-rays somewhere else, or to ignore the whole thing. As I am hurrying to get x-rays somewhere else, my Dad runs up from behind and hands me the keys to his car and the papers in his pockets. I am glad to see him. He too has cancer of the lungs, he says, and is preparing to go to the furnace. It is as though this is what one has to do. I tell him there is not much point in his handing over his things to me because I've been told I have the same thing. He insists, though, and I accept. I go to get an x-ray done elsewhere and my father goes toward the furnace. The brick walls to the furnaces are only one layer thick of non-firebrick, with a rather thin layer of concrete on the top. The fire in such a construction would be hot enough to kill one, but not hot enough to cremate one, which would appear to be what the furnaces are for.

We need to know that the patient had been suffering for a long time from a depressive neurosis. He had feelings of great personal inadequacy, which restricted him from attempting new relationships or from accepting challenging opportunities in his work. He had grown up as the third and youngest child in an unloving household. His mother had been a strict disciplinarian, using the authority of religious doctrine as the basis for her unloving, moralistic rigidity. The best that young Steven could hope for was to be saved from hellfire if he would behave as his mother required him to do. There was never any commendation or appreciation of his efforts that he could remember, but he stood in constant terror of his mother's anger and rejection should he displease her. His father was cool and distant. While he did not necessarily support his wife in her zealous attitudes, he did not take Steven's part either. Steven's brother and sister were older than he, and did not show much interest in him. He thought that they were the favored ones, that he had been born late and was probably unwanted. He tried in vain to justify his existence before his parents, but he never felt that he had been able to do so. The pain in Steven was evident in the lines on his face, the expression in his eyes and in his carriage. When he first came into analysis he had been taking large amounts of antidepressant medication for a long time and had become something like a zombie—a certain vacancy of expression was superimposed over his suffering face.

During the course of analysis, Steven began to face his buried angers and to give voice to them. Each confronting experience was accompanied by a burst of relief; then a reactive depression would set in, in which he was filled with guilt and shame. The analytic relationship, specifically the transference aspect of it, carried him. Here his expectations that he would be punished or rejected for expressing his feelings were not met; instead, his expressions were seen as indications that attitudes can change and that change is acceptable. During this time Steven gradually stopped taking the antidepressants, and concurrently his dream life increased in activity and in the powerful way it affected him. The above dream was the climax of a series.

Reading the dream, Steven could hardly manage to get his words out. At the point of relating where his father appears and tells him that he has cancer and is preparing to go to the furnace, Steven broke into uncontrollable tears. "You don't know the worst of it," he cried, "you don't know where this led me." He managed to pull himself together enough to read the rest of the dream, then quietly wept until it was all out. Then he told me what he understood of the dream: "I interpreted it to mean, I am going to have to think for myself. I cannot accept what people have told me, that my life is hopeless, that I am dying inside and that it may as well be all over. I will have to find out what is in me, or it will be a wasted life—I must, else I will die and burn in hell. But you don't know where the dream leads—the meeting with my father . . ." Here he could hardly go on. But he soon continued, "*He* didn't make it, but he thought *I* could. The last time I saw him, a few weeks before he died, I realized for the first time that under his cool, critical attitude—there was love there. It came too late." Steven recalled the last days of his parents. His father had, indeed, softened in his attitude toward him. And later, when his mother was terminally ill she had called Steven to her bedside. She had given him two goblets from her wedding crystal, and six silver iced-tea spoons. Similar cherished items were given to his brother and sister. But for Steven there was a special gift, the small hand-carved table that his mother's parents had brought with them from Austria when they had come to settle in America, the only remainder from the life in the old country. Steven realized from this that he, the youngest child, had been selected to carry on; that in her way, his mother had indeed loved him, although she was unable to let him know until the end of her life.

We could have reviewed the dream from the causalistic point of view, but it is doubtful whether anything particularly new or helpful would have been revealed. To retrace the agonies of his childhood, to reiterate his anger and helplessness, would have been counterproductive. It would have distracted him to look at the dream from the finalistic point of view. Toward what purpose did the dream guide him, and what was its meaning for the future? His "sickness" was associated with the "sickness" in his family; he had apparently fallen heir to the orientation toward life and its problems that was characteristic for his family. But, stop, the dream seems to say, notice that just because someone has told you that you are doomed to go the way of the others in your family, you need not accept your fate without questioning it. The dream dramatizes the unconscious revulsion against the passive conscious attitude that Steven had held up until this time—the attitude that he had been irreparably damaged in his youth and would never get over it.

The dream tells him that his father, though dead in reality, still exists as a psychic factor in him. The father *in him* once exerted control and dominated him and likewise did the mother, in a different way. That father element was weak and dependent; it stemmed from the example of a man who was not able to take responsibility for his own life, much less for the rearing of his son, Steven. But now it was time for the father to go, to be deposed from his position, and the son was to take over. The keys to his car were handed over—the dream was saying that Steven was to gain the instrument from the father which would enable him to take control of his own life. He had to let the hated father go into the furnace and be burned, not destroyed, but transformed into spirit. The confidence of the father spirit in Steven had been unconscious until this time. It now passed into consciousness via the dream. The purpose of the dream, then, was to let the father go, in one sense, and in another sense to allow Steven to assume the power of the father as his own. The keys and the papers point to this.

Discussion of this dream helped Steven to make its contents his own, to assimilate them into consciousness with an active resolve to carry forward the meaning and purpose that were seen in it, first by him, and secondly in the dialogue of analysis. I had very little to say after Steven gave his own interpretation. More important than anything that was said in the exchange, were the feelings that passed between us in those intense moments. Steven, who had always been reserved, could not be reserved with me any longer. The dream broke through all that. We were able to be in it together, for I, too, was profoundly moved by the horror of the dream and I shared the intensity of his reaction. What was unsaid between us seared more deeply than the actual verbal communication. The dream was full of the inescapable fact of death as the end of life, the tenuousness of life, and the importance of embracing the time that is left—each of us—and loving that time and being committed to use it well. There is no room for self-pity in this brief span, we both knew that, nor for regrets about the unlived past. The future is too swiftly upon us; but today we know what our task is and, therefore, today we must address ourselves to it.

There are moments in analysis when feelings overflow the brink of tears. Sharing this with the analyst is very different from experiencing it alone. Many people ask, why can I not interpret my own dreams? If, after all, the information that is needed is all embedded in my own psyche, why should it be necessary to come to someone else for help in interpreting my dreams? It is true that the work of analysis is directed toward helping people not only with interpretations of specific dreams, but also with gaining an understanding of the dream process so that they can discover the essential meaning in their own dreams. The difficulty is that the dream comes from outside one's conscious orientation, and one often cannot assess the value of the interpretation solely on the basis of one's own work on it. It takes a long time of diligent work in relating to the unconscious before one is able to step aside from his conscious standpoint. Exploring a dream with a person skilled in interpretation, who is able to participate in the dream with one aspect of his being and at the same time remain outside of it with another, may bring the necessary objectivity. Analysts are trained to exclude their own projections from the interpretation of a dream, and to leave out their own wishes and moral judgments.

Frequently, analysands want to discuss their dreams with their husbands or wives or close friends. Much as I dislike some esoteric aspects of analysis, there are occasions when it is absolutely necessary to maintain silence, and my feeling is that this is especially true of the "virginal dream" (the dream as it freshly appears, without having been exposed to anyone). Jung believed that to tell it prematurely to another person was to break the special relationship between the ego and the unconscious, a relationship that is carried by a slender bridge that can only be walked alone. I am reminded of the tradition of the earliest Jewish mysticism, having to do with the vision of God's appearance on the throne, as described by Ezekiel. The Jewish mystic, in contemplating the "throne world" as the center which embodies and exemplifies all forms of creation, is interdicted from speaking about these most sacred matters.[10] There are some things, he is told, that may be discussed in groups of ten, some things in groups of five, and some may not be told to more than three; some things are to be told only to one other, and there are some which may not be uttered at all.

For the tension to be kept between consciousness and the unconscious, Jung insisted that it was vitally important that the material be held in and contemplated, that the full feelings associated with it be experienced in all their strength and not dissipated in idle conversation. The very fact that the dream is not told to the analyst immediately as it occurs, but that analysands have an interval of time to reflect on it and to extract from it all that they possibly can, means that they bring their dreams to the analytic hour in all their purity, and even intensified by contemplation. In my experience I have found that analysands who allow their dreams to work on them in solitude are likely to be the ones who find their analyses most productive. As they learn to maintain the tensions of their dreams, they also learn to live with the tensions of their lives. They learn to express their feelings in the right time and in the right way, after filtering them through the discrimination and differentiation that powers a sensitive ego which has developed a partnership with the unconscious. However, there are some exceptions to this rule. Some people have tried working with their dreams in a group setting, and they have had a quite different experience. Dream groups were not something that Jung would have approved, since he distrusted what he called "the collective," associating it with mass or mob psychology. In his time, and especially during the First and Second World Wars, he learned to eschew groups of all kinds, and to prefer to trust the individual or dyad as the freest and most productive kind of association. But since his death, we have learned much about the value of working with groups, and dream work in groups has been shown to be valuable in ways Jung could not have dreamed of.

Occasionally, I have the experience that an analysand may not wish to discuss a dream with me. Recently an analysand brought a dream which, he said, had very deep meaning to him, not fully understood, but so strong that he did not feel he could deal with it. He wanted me to know about it, but he said that he would show it to me only on the condition that I would promise not to say anything about it. I respected his wish, and he handed me the dream to read after the session was over. I did so, and I hold the dream and all my thoughts about it in confidence. It is important to him that I know what it was about, and that I give him the right to live with it, while I do the same. Perhaps there will come a time when he will wish to discuss it. That will be his decision.

So far, in speaking about dreams, we have dealt mainly with single dreams. The reason for this was that the dreams were used to illustrate particular points. However, dreams do not occur generally as isolated psychological events, even when they appear to. They may be regarded rather as emerging evidence of the ongoing unconscious processes. Certain themes may be followed through series of dreams. Each dream may have its own meaning, yet take on far more significance in the light of its position with respect to other dreams. So it is necessary for the analyst to keep the "dream history" of the analysand in mind just as much as it is necessary to keep the ongoing life history before him.

The dream series that follows will show not only how dreams may be related to one another, but also how they may, in turn, direct the process of psychotherapy itself. This is possible because so much of emotional disturbance is due to a lack of correspondence between the conscious orientation and the purposes of the unconscious. It is necessary that the unconscious make known its own direction and we must allow it an equal voice with that of the ego, if each side is to be able to adapt to the other. As the ego listens, and the unconscious is encouraged to participate in the dialogue, the unconscious position is transformed from that of an adversary to that of a friend with a somewhat differing but complementary point of view.

There will follow, greatly abbreviated, a series of four dreams, which belong in turn to four important aspects of the analytic process. The dreams took place over a long period of time, with many other dreams between, but these nevertheless show a cohesiveness of theme. The first dream is *diagnostic*, describing the situation that needs to be corrected, the "neurosis," if you will. The second dream has to do with *prognosis;* it suggests what can happen as a result of treatment. The third dream deals with the *method of treatment.* The fourth has to do with the *resolution of the transference relationship*, a necessary element in the conclusion of analysis. This fourth dream is not my analysand's; it is my own. I think it is admissible here, because I strongly feel that the analyst is part of the process, rather than either an observer or the one who makes it happen. This is why the analyst's unconscious material cannot be excluded from the process.

Nicholas came into analysis shortly after he had accepted an important position which required him to pull together his life work, including all his education and his previous experience. He was to be in charge of a large project which involved a number of people. A high degree of talent and creativity would be demanded from him as director. He had been encouraged by friends and associates to seek the position, and he had applied for it despite a strong personal feeling that he was insufficiently qualified. When he obtained the position he reacted with a depression that had within it elements of panic. He came to his first analytic session appearing calm and well possessed, well covered by his persona. Here is his initial dream: *I am climbing a rocky cliff made of shale and loose rocks. I have to put my foot into rough depressions and holes, and grab onto protuberances of rock. Sometimes rocks break loose and go hurtling down into the valley. I am afraid of losing my balance, or of starting a huge landslide.*

This dream offers a diagnosis of the situation. He is aiming much too high, and he is not comfortable with the task or with his own ability to master it. He feels vulnerable, and is fearful of falling from the place to which he has come through so much effort. He may lose his balance and come crashing down at any moment. Or, even if he hangs on, the people in the valley below him are in danger—he can destroy them in a moment by an accident, a miscalculation. But, judging from the way in which he was climbing, he was not concerned for anything but achieving his goal. As we discussed the dream it became apparent that his only concerns were ego concerns.

The dream shows that Nicholas' conscious attitude—to go ahead and do his job to the best of his ability and not to trouble himself about who might get hurt as a result—was an unproductive attitude. His efforts might come to a disastrous end if he continued on in the direction he had chosen.

All of this would appear to be an external interpretation. Jungians hold that the external situation (in the world) generally reflects the inner situation of the individual. When we are feeling calm and secure and smoothly functioning on the inside, it is nearly certain that things will go well for us or, if they take a bad turn, that we will be able to cope with that and even to extricate something of value from an apparently unfavorable circumstance. On the other hand, if we are "at odds with ourselves," with the conscious and unconscious parts running at cross purposes, we tend to make a mess of even the most favorable of circumstances. The external situation in which we find ourselves is merely our way of looking at the "box" which we call experience, from the outside. We could also look at the box from the inside and call it subjective experience. But the box, "experience," is neither inner nor outer, it is that which joins together the outside and the inside. For the purpose of indicating something about the dream series, we will for the present look at these dreams from the external or objective side.

Nicholas' second dream in the series: *I am standing alone at the foot of a huge mountain. It is of unimaginable size and I am so small. A footpath winds its way up on the lower slopes and disappears behind a rise in the distance. I do not know if I will live long enough to climb that mountain, but at least I will begin.*

This is a prognostic dream. Nicholas has come down from his precarious position of the first dream and his feet are on solid ground. The dream reflects the coming change in his attitude. He is beginning to realize that he will have to reorganize his work, and even before that, his attitude to the work. He must not be in too big a hurry, as he has been in the past. He must not try to salvage the mistakes of the past, but must go back and begin again on a sounder basis. The task is enormous, it is the fulfillment of his whole life, but it is not important that he concern himself too much about the end result. He has to be prepared for a long and arduous time ahead—no man would start out on the kind of journey the dream presents without making sure that he is in good health. This means total good health, physically and psychologically. The dream suggests that the only way to go is upward, and that the process will require more attention than the goal.

It may well be asked here whether dreams predict the future. Jung has answered this question by saying that dreams are no more prophetic than a meteorologist who predicts the weather. What the dream does is to present a reading of the unconscious, so to speak, and if we can discern its message we have a basis for expecting that, on the basis of certain conditions present, there is a good chance that certain occurrences will take place in the natural course of events. The dream then, while not actually predicting the future, can help us to realize what forces are in motion and in what direction they are headed.

The third dream: *I have reached a plateau high in the mountains. Before me stretches a calm, smooth mountain lake. Seated crosslegged with his back toward me is a man whom I do not know. He is facing the lake, immovable.*

The dream left Nicholas with a peaceful feeling. Upon awakening he felt like taking the time to make a small drawing of the scene. He did, and he taped it to his bedroom mirror where he could see it often, so that he would remember the dream and the feeling it engendered. The dream seemed to have two functions. The first was to compensate the one-sided attitude of consciousness, which from time to time became obsessed with the responsibilities of work and with other problems, and made it difficult for Nicholas to concentrate his energies. The dream showed a thoughtful figure, representing perhaps an unconscious demand, perhaps a repressed wish, for distancing himself from pressing problems and finding perspective and restfulness. The second function of this dream was to suggest a method of treatment. It clearly indicated that meditation of some sort would be helpful for Nicholas. He could find the necessary balance for his life if he would set aside time from his busy schedule for quiet reflection. He should not hesitate to turn his back on the upward struggle from time to time, and gaze instead over the smooth waters, in which he himself could be revealed.

Other dreams reiterated this message in varying ways. Nicholas began to recognize the importance of taking time for those practices which would provide for him a temporary separation from the demands of his external life, and then allow him to return with new energy and vigor. He followed the attitude prescribed by the dream, and though there were better times and worse times came along, he gradually gained the capacity to return at will to the high mountain plateau when it was necessary to view his situation from another perspective.

The fourth dream was my own. It occurred near the termination of the analysis, and let me know that my role in Nicholas' development was nearly finished. My dream: *I have climbed to the top of a snowy mountain with Nicholas. We look down and see some men and machines cutting a hole in the ice, maybe for fishing. It is noisy. But atop the mountain the sun is warm. I lie back in the snow and enjoy the sun. Nicholas remains standing.*

I have said that this fourth dream had to do with termination, which requires the dissolution of the transference relationship. The dream points to the unconscious relationship between analyst and analysand, from the point of view of the analyst. This is more properly called "countertransference." Countertransference in orthodox psychoanalysis was thought of as a dangerous, unconscious condition which the analyst should by all means try to avoid. Analysts were advised to remain remote and objective and not to allow their personal feelings to enter into the analytic relationship. In contrast to this view, it is accepted as a matter of course by Jungians that in an analysis extending over a long period, with intense emotional involvement, the analyst will participate in depth and not purely out of the conscious position. This is confirmed when the analyst dreams of a patient and may be helpful in letting the analyst know what is going on between himself and the patient, far better than if the judgment were based on thinking alone. Analysts must, therefore, consistently pay attention to their own dreams. And, when they are unable to understand dreams that seem important to them, they may be obliged to discuss them with colleagues who will help them achieve the necessary objectivity.

As I regarded the foregoing dream, I had to recognize that Nicholas and I had gone as far as we could together. We had reached a stage of development which had seemed impossible when we first began our work together. I say "we" because I, too, grew in the process of this difficult analysis. The problems and difficulties which were brought to the analysis were by no means entirely solved, but the means for dealing with them were at hand. Nicholas' panic had disappeared and a relaxed but ready attitude took its place. It was time for me to withdraw from the relationship. I thought of how far Nicholas had come. Some words of Jung's on the goals of analysis came to mind. They seemed relevant to the image of Nicholas standing there in the sunshine:

> The greatest and most important problems of life are all in a certain sense insoluble. They must be so because they express the necessary polarity inherent in every self-regulating system. They can never be solved, but only outgrown. . . . This "out-growing" . . . on further experience was seen to consist in a new level of consciousness. Some higher or wider interest arose on the person's horizon, and through this widening of his view the insoluble problem lost its urgency. It was not solved logically in its own terms, but faded out when confronted with a new and stronger life-tendency. It was not repressed and made unconscious, but merely appeared in a different light, and so, did indeed become different. What, on a lower level, had led to the wildest conflicts and to panicky outbursts of emotion, viewed from the higher level of the personality, now seemed like a storm in the valley seen from a high mountain-top. This does not mean that the thunderstorm is robbed of its reality, but instead of being in it one is now above it.[11]

Jung has suggested three ways of approaching a dream, and they are not necessarily mutually exclusive. One is to analyze the dream on the *objective level*. Every character in the dream may be taken as the person in real life, and the events and relationships in the dream may be seen as referring to real life events and relationships. The dream is seen as the reaction of the unconscious to what is happening in the conscious life of the dreamer. Or, the dream may either be confirming or objecting to some action in which the dreamer is involved. If it is a prognostic dream, it may represent the attempt of the unconscious to work out the solution of some problem in the dreamer's life situation.

Another way to take the dream is on the *subjective level*. Here we can interpret dream figures as personified aspects of the dreamer's own personality.[12] A person whom the dreamer knows in daily life may appear in a dream as the embodiment of an archetypal element of the unconscious. In this case the dream figure is to be taken as referring to some aspect of the dreamer himself. Subjective-level interpretations are indicated in dreams where the dream figures evoke more emotion than one would expect from their role in the waking life of the dreamer. Steven's cremation dream is a case in point. When Steven meets his father, who is about to go to the ovens for a quicker death than that from cancer, we may be sure that the subjective interpretation—father as an internalized aspect of Steven—comes closest to the meaning of the dream.

Sometimes there are no recognizable or familiar characters in a dream. Then it is nearly impossible to interpret the dream objectively, and we turn to a subjective interpretation. If the dream figures, however, can be associated to actual events in the life situation, it is simpler and usually more helpful to interpret the dream objectively. A subjective level interpretation is necessary in cases where the objective level interpretation does not strike the dreamer as relevant or meaningful.

This strange Kafkaesque dream of Edith, a middle-aged woman, illustrates this point further: *I am being chased by those who would exterminate my race. I have friends among my enemies—who would protect me by beating me lightly, in order to avoid the more destructive beating. Also, I have enemies*

among my friends, who would betray me. Alas. I awaken feeling
that something in my life has changed.

In exploring this dream with her on the objective level I
found it necessary to raise first the question of "race." Edith is
Jewish, so I asked if perhaps she felt in some way discriminated against by anti-Semites. She did not respond to this
probe with any particular feeling, for she was not aware of
ever having suffered for this reason. She could think of no
event in recent days that would have provided any basis for
the content of the dream. As to friends among her enemies,
she thought of some men in her business firm who were immediately above her. They would often help her in various
ways, so that she had gained a reputation for excellence which
she thought was better than she deserved. Enemies among her
friends might refer, she conjectured, to other women on her
same level who may have been jealous of her accomplishments. But somehow this objective level interpretation of the
dream did not seem significant to the dreamer—it did not correspond to the strong feelings she experienced when she
awakened from the dream.

Reading the dream from a subjective point of view
brought quite different results. "Race" was seen to refer to the
dreamer's character: Edith was an energetic and ambitious
woman with high aspirations. There were inner obstacles
which she felt were working against her: personal feelings of
insecurity, intuitive insight into the sensitivities of others
which sometimes inhibited her action, and a tendency to become distracted from something on which she was trying to
concentrate. These qualities of personality were "enemies" in
her eyes, yet the puzzling dream urged her to examine them
and to see whether each in its way might serve as an impetus
to growth. Accepting these aspects of her nature might be the
"lighter beating." In the individuation process the "more destructive beating," that is, failure due to unconsciousness of
her weaknesses, would be avoided. Feeling insecure would
lead her to seek out and work on the less developed talents;
intuitive insight could help her in establishing better relation-

ships; and the tendency to become distracted, if not repressed, might allow her to enjoy a wider range of interests and aspirations. So these were "friends among my enemies."

Edith had then to consider the "enemies among my friends, who would betray me." These seemed to refer to characteristics of her own which appeared to be productive in nature, but which she had a tendency to carry to excess. They were such qualities as energy, which could become compulsivity; ambition, which could become greed; singleness of purpose, which could become ruthlessness. All these inner qualities displayed her characteristic way of being which, as it happened, were also reflected in her current life situation. Naturally Edith had been totally unaware of these forces underlying her behavior. In working through the dream with the analysand, I had the distinct feeling that it was not the objective life situation which precipitated the dream, but the contrary: the condition of the unconscious which is portrayed so graphically in the dream is the same condition which, quite unknown to the dreamer, created the life situation which she was currently experiencing. The confirmation that the subjective interpretation was valid in this case came as the dreamer recalled that her ongoing life problem was not an isolated one but bore a resemblance to other situations which had come up before—all in response to the ongoing character problems which the dream indicated.

There is still another possible level on which we could interpret such a dream: *the archetypal level.* Race is a constant, a universal idea about belonging to a group, finding identity and security within that group, and feeling threatened by those outside the group. Yet it is, again, a universal experience that we cannot always be sure on whom we can depend, and those whom we most fear often turn out to be quite decent and caring people. It is the very ambiguity of "friend" and "enemy" that this dream brings to Edith. If, within herself, she discovers that she cannot depend on the "good" aspects of herself, and that the "evil" or less desirable aspects may help her at times, she has to make a significant change in her outlook.

She must realize the relative nature of good and evil in the world, and let go of her easy characterizations of what is sinister and what is right. The problem is her own, certainly, but it also has a universal aspect, an archetypal dimension. There is some comfort, and surely some sustenance, in knowing that our problems are not ours alone, but part of the human condition.

Much more could be said about the process of dreaming. We could discuss how dreams are classified, or how they may be systematically approached.[13] But all this would be theorizing. What we do in the analytic process is to carry on a dialogue with the dream, instead of trying to make it conform to a theory. The few general principles that have been illustrated above may suggest avenues of approach to the dream. The important thing is to record the dream, to pay attention to it, and to allow the dream to speak for itself. It is not even absolutely necessary that the dream be understood. As in the most intimate of human relationships where much can transpire which is not fully understood, so with dreams. This or that element reveals something that was not known before, or one is reminded of some quality or capacity that has been all but forgotten. And there is always the possibility that more of a dream's meaning will be revealed as time passes.

The dream has been called everything from a "temporary psychosis" to the "gateway to the treasure-house of the unconscious." Much of what we see when we close our eyes at night depends upon the attitude with which we go to sleep. And much of what we do by day may be affected by the attitude we bring to our dreams.

10

Dreaming the Dream Onward: Active Imagination

...

DREAMS MAY BE a source of potential strength and wisdom, but unfortunately they present their difficulties and problems too. For one thing, I do not find that it is always possible to understand dreams. Often they are unclear and it seems that no amount of reflection and examination will produce the feeling of having come to the essence of the dream. Dreams may have to be put aside until some future time when they may become clearer—meanwhile we can keep them in view and turn them over in our thoughts, now and again.

Since dreaming is a spontaneous function of the unconscious, we cannot, by any conscious efforts, "cause" dreams to appear—much less can we command dream content that will serve our needs at any given moment in time. The unconscious is like the vault of a great bank in which is stored all the wealth inherited from our ancestors and in which we, as individuals, also have deposited our own coin. All of this treasure belongs to us, and we like to think that it is at our disposal, but the trouble is that we cannot withdraw it on demand. We have to wait until the guard at the door is ready to open up, and we must be present at that moment and ready to receive what is offered to us. We cannot withdraw more than what the guard may decide to give us. This may be more than we need at this particular moment, or it may not be enough. Or we may wait in vain, and nothing comes. The ego-aspect of the human personality is weak and powerless against the guard-aspect who bars the door to the vault of dreams.

It is not only dreams that have their vagaries. Other secrets of the unconscious may be equally inaccessible to the ego and to its capacity to deal with them. In the course of analysis we may need to seek out other approaches to that chaotic underworld which intrudes into our lives when we least desire it and often eludes us just when we try to penetrate its depths.

Looking at this problem from the standpoint of the ego, we can see two kinds of situations that demand some different modes of relating to the unconscious other than the straightforward analysis of dreams. The first situation occurs when the individual's ego is barricaded against the unconscious, when there is little sense of flow, of fresh ideas, of genuine expression or even perception of feelings. In this situation, dreams may be completely absent, or they may be so fragmentary and superficial that they are practically valueless. The second situation is the opposite: here the ego actively attacks the unconscious, stimulating it to produce more contents—dreams and fantasies and a tendency to act out in bizarre behavior—than the ego can deal with in any creative or productive way.

A different way of working with the unconscious may be suggested by the unconscious itself, instead of coming from the ego standpoint. The unconscious may spontaneously flood the ego with contents—such as anxieties, fears, obsessive ideas, visions—that threaten the very survival of the ego position. Or—and in a sense this is a less apparent but more excruciatingly painful situation—the unconscious becomes isolated from the conscious ego, and leaves the individual feeling disconnected from anything which might possibly have meaning or importance.

These are, of course, gross categories of possibilities. They are meaningless in themselves, but they provide a framework for the discussion of certain human experiences in analysis which give rise to a third element, less transitory and rambunctious than the dream, which may be utilized in the therapeutic process. This third element, called *the transcendent function,* belongs neither to the ego sphere nor to the unconscious, and yet possesses access to each. It stands above them, participating in both. It is as though ego and unconscious were points at either end of the baseline of a triangle. The third element, at the apex of the triangle, transcends both the point of the ego and the point of the unconscious but is related to each of them. The transcendent function's emergence grants autonomy to the ego and also to the unconscious by relating to both of them independently, and in doing so, unites them.

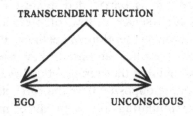

How this works in the several situations involving strained or disharmonious relations between the ego and the unconscious can best be seen by considering what happened in several cases in which the transcendent function came into play. Maureen's analysis required facing a central problem in which the ego was barricading itself against the onslaught of the unconscious.

Maureen came into therapy with me after she had been

discharged from a mental hospital. She had been admitted there six months previously, after she had slashed her wrists with a razor, and now the psychiatrist who had been treating her in the hospital had refused to continue seeing her on an outpatient basis. When she first came to see me she looked and behaved like a frightened little girl of about twelve, although her chronological age was nineteen. She would curl up in the corner of a large chair in my office, as if she would have liked to disappear. Yet she answered every question I put to her in the beginning with clarity, although without any show of feeling. She said that her former doctor had told her not to call him any more, and that she felt that he had rejected her, "just like everybody else." It came out that her father, a successful businessman, had interests which kept him away from home most of the time while Maureen was growing up; he was always either working, or sailing his boat, or flying his plane. Her mother had been at home, but Maureen remembers little about her until the birth of a brother, when Maureen was about three-and-a-half years old. Following this, her mother had become severely depressed and had to be hospitalized. Mother and the new baby had disappeared from the home at the same time. Actually, the baby was taken by an aunt, but Maureen thought that her mother had chosen to go off with the baby and left her behind. Maureen's grandmother came to take care of her, and her father was rarely home during the three-month period until her mother returned. Maureen remembered her mother from that time on as cold and unfeeling. She expressed only hatred for this mother who had left her when she was little. It was not surprising to learn that her mother had told her, "You were born without trust," and Maureen, in telling me this, said she knew it was true.

It was nearly impossible for Maureen to communicate with me in any depth. I had to pull the facts of her life from her bit by bit. She had few recollections of her past, and these few could only be brought to the surface through much energetic questioning on my part. Not that she was unwilling, but she seemed to be blocked off from any relationship with her life up to this point. So, for the most part she would sit in the chair with eyes averted, picking at her fingernails and answering my questions and observations with brief, often monosyllabic responses, if she spoke at all.

But she did try to communicate. Once, just before she left my office, she gave me a poem she said she had found somewhere. I read it as the most beautiful diagnosis of a dissociative disorder I had ever seen:

> the other
> one laughs
> is worried
> under the sky exposes my face and my hair
> makes words roll out of my mouth
> one who has money and fears and a passport
> one who quarrels and loves
> one moves
> one struggles
>
> but not i
> i am the other
> who does not laugh
> who has no face to expose to the sky
> and no words in his mouth
> who is unacquainted with me with himself
> not i: the other: always the other
> who neither wins nor loses
> who is not worried
> who does not move
>
> the other
> indifferent to himself
> of whom i know nothing
> of whom nobody knows who he is
> who does not move me
> that is i

I knew that she was trying to explain to me how she felt, and that the poem she had come across said what she would have liked to have been able to say. It was clear that there were two figures in conflict within her, the ego, which was represented by a very small girl who could not make herself heard, and a bigger, older, wiser person who could express herself without being self-conscious. We began to talk about these two, and although Maureen was not too responsive, I had the feeling that I was beginning to reach her.

Often, however, she would sit through the hour hardly saying anything. Then at the end of the hour she would become clinging and begin to bring out what had obviously been on her mind all along. She would attempt to extend the hour this way, and to get control of me—she must have sensed that I would not want to play the part of the rejecting mother by sending her off just when she wanted to talk to me, which was of course true. Furthermore, she must have known that I did not want to miss these bits of communication at last so tantalizingly dropped. It is always amazing to me how certain patients are able unerringly to zero in on the therapist's own weaknesses and sensitive points! I could see Maureen was making it nearly impossible for me to act as a mediator between herself and her unconscious material, and it was clear to me why her former therapist had been eager to refer the case. Maureen was doing whatever she could to make her therapy hours with me ineffective.

One day she was even more withdrawn than usual. She admitted that she was afraid to speak out. At the end of the hour she cried a little, and just as she was getting ready to leave she pulled a note out of her pocketbook and handed it to me. In her neat schoolgirl handwriting, she had written:

> Telephone booths are such blissful places to hide in. I guess the problem with the little girl is that she doesn't want to be mothered by the big girl—the big girl has no feelings or emotions—she is cold and hard and efficient and maybe brave—but the little girl doesn't want to grow up without feelings and is afraid of what the big girl could do to her— little girls are a nuisance—they reduce efficiency and get in

the way—they have feelings and needs that big girls want no part of—and when they're neglected they scream—but sometimes after something screams loud enough and long enough, it just gives up and withdraws into a corner too hurt to react—that is what this little girl has done—and she is sitting in the corner refusing to grow—the big girl likes it this way except for the nuisance involved, because as long as she sits in the corner no one will ever know her or love her—little withdrawn girls are much less of a nuisance than growing girls—growing girls need mothers and the big girl doesn't want to be a mother—she scarcely knows what one is—and growing girls scream continually, they never stop—so the little girl out of necessity will stay little and reasonably quiet—and the big girl will maintain her coldness to protect herself.

Here was the whole story of herself and "the other." Maureen had clearly shown what her feelings were, growing up as she did, which meant not really growing up emotionally. She told me how, in the hospital, she had been allowed to regress to the age of six or seven and how she had loved being free and uninhibited, and being able to crayon all over the bathroom walls. Now, she said, she still wants and needs to be a little child, to withdraw from responsibility. But there is also the "big girl." The original model for this figure may have been Maureen's mother, but the big girl is also an aspect of Maureen, the person she is expected to become and in one sense has already become, although she is not yet able to assume the responsibility and the mature attitude that would be appropriate.

What she had written was more than idle fantasy, it was a conscious attempt to bridge the gap between the conscious "little girl" sense of herself and the frightening image of the "big girl" with all of her big demands and requirements. Maureen, who had not gotten any help from her dreams, had stumbled upon the rudiments of the transcendent function as a way to gain a position outside of the inadequate ego position, and also outside of the power of the unconscious. It was that aspect which could stand over the big girl and the little girl and view them both, as well as the relationship between them. As we talked about the telephone booth paper, Maureen began for the first time to be able to acknowledge her fears openly, but she was obviously still terrified by much more than she was saying. It seemed to me a good time to help her embark on the kind of interaction between ego and unconscious that makes use of imagination to perform the work of the transcendent function.

Imagination, employed in this way, is not the same as fantasy. Jung has called this use of imagination by the term *active imagination*, to distinguish it from the ordinary passive imagination which is nothing else than a self-propelling fantasy. Active imagination is entered into consciously, in an effort to engage the unconscious in dialogue with the ego. And, since the unconscious is not limited in its expression to verbal intercourse, the varieties of approach to it are many. Words presented great difficulty for Maureen, therefore her active imagination needed a medium that would permit uninhibited flow of thoughts and feelings in both directions, from the unconscious to consciousness, and from the ego to the unconscious. I thought of the crayons she had enjoyed so much at the hospital. They had given her freedom to express her passive fantasies, without any attempt to direct them in any way. Now perhaps we could move to the next step, active imagination, in which she might give the unconscious a chance to speak for itself, and provide some material for the ego to work on. I suggested that instead of our usual session, perhaps Maureen would like to sit at the table with me and do some drawing. She agreed to do this, and was even somewhat eager. I suggested to her that she draw a picture which would represent the way she felt about herself at that very moment.

While she was drawing I reflected on what had happened to her during the past two months since she had started to work with me. She had secured a clerical position and was doing routine office work, fitting into the office very much like a part of a machine. She was efficient, bland, and compulsive about getting her work done. Her employer was well satisfied with her work. She had made no friends, and she always came straight home from work to her small apartment where she spent her time alone until she returned to the office the next day.

Soon Maureen's picture was done. It showed a large stick figure in a running position, with a round head, and a crowd of smaller similar figures off to the right apparently running also, with one of their number out in front. I asked her about the drawing. Her response was, "I'm running away. Everyone is chasing me. If I stop running they will trample me. The only way for someone to communicate with me is if they can run faster than I." Maureen's self-portrait was pitiful, with her painted smile, her face devoid of personality, her sexless body without weight or substance, just something to support the head, and something that can run away. The crowd of people represented to her just "they," everyone outside herself. In other words, "they" referred to the terror of the unconscious. It is a nameless terror, but it has the shape of other human beings. In a new way Maureen was able to see both herself and what she was afraid of.

It did not seem important to try to analyze the meaning of the feelings that came up. It was more important that we looked at the picture together and felt that something in her was capable of expressing itself, and it might not have to be in words. We agreed that pictures could help us to find out more about herself, and especially about that part which was so hard to reach. To seal the compact I gave her the box of crayons to take home "in case you feel like letting the other side of yourself say something more to you."

To the next session Maureen brought two pictures. The second picture was almost like the first one that she had made in my office, but there were significant differences. For one thing, the large figure which represented her idea of herself (the ego figure) was now carrying a box of crayons. Maureen had titled the picture "Running with Crayons." I sensed that the crayons were the visual representation of the transcendent function, that they were incorporated into the picture as the thing that would enable the unconscious contents to flow over into consciousness. In another way, the crayons represented my own role as mediator in the process. It is the analyst who carries the transcendent function for the patient in the beginning, as a rule, showing the analysand the way to make use of the new movements that develop once the process is set in motion. Facing the unconscious is facing all the agonies of the past that have been conveniently forgotten, and for some people it is just to avoid this that neurotic symptoms have been invented. So, in order to ward off the dangers that have long been feared, the analysand needs someone to go through it with him, namely the analyst. In Maureen's picture, all this is represented by the crayons. Moreover, perhaps the crayons were a magical protecting amulet for her.

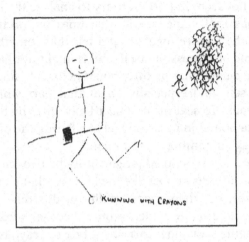

KUNNING WITH CRAYONS

Another difference between this picture and the first one was that in the first picture the ego figure had been drawn with hesitating, sketchy lines. In this one, the lines were clear and definite. And, interestingly enough, the crowd in the second picture was smaller than it had been in the first.

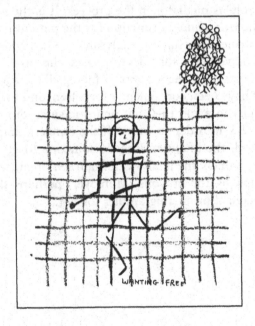

WANTING FREE

The third picture showed her running head-on into a fence or grill. "They" were still following after, but the crowd was a little smaller still than the one in the previous drawing, and no single figure was out in front. The title of this picture was "Wanting Free." I had asked her how long the little girl could keep on running away. She had put this question to the unconscious when she had started to draw. Here was the answer that came: "One day you will come up against something that will stop you from running. Wanting free means wanting to be able to stop running. That is what you want, and you may as well recognize it." I saw this picture as hopeful. It was the first expression of the idea that things could possibly change, that there might be any point in "wanting."

In the analytic session, I suggested that perhaps Maureen would like to try something even freer than crayons, to give the unconscious the freedom it seemed to be asking for. We took out finger paints and she selected a rich golden yellow which she overlaid with brilliant red. Then with her fingernails she made circle after circle in a spiraling movement over and over, spiraling around a center. When she was finished she had a primitive form of a mandala, a spontaneous representation of the motif of centrality. I had the feeling that this picture pre-formed the pulling together of the conscious and unconscious elements of her personality into a cohesive whole. It seemed as though the unconscious was offering an image, a glimpse of the self in sun colors nearly blinding in their brilliance. It was particularly striking as an expression coming from this quiet, inconspicuous girl who liked to hide in telephone booths or sink into the corners of chairs. The picture was exciting, it was an experience, and it was not necessary to say much about it. Without interpretation it had a strong effect on Maureen, and I felt it with her.

After this, things went along fairly well for a while. The fears were less than they had been, and Maureen began to become a little more verbal. She talked about her work and her day-by-day experiences. She began to take an interest in decorating her apartment. Still I knew the fears were present even though she did not speak of them very much, and I did not prod her to do so. I tried to remain as close as possible to the level of her feelings, and to let her know that I was reacting *with* her as well as reacting *to* her. During this time she brought out many details of her life and they began to assume a pattern which corresponded to the pictures that were coming from those quiet hours when she would sit down at home with her crayons and trace out the images that would come to her. She brought the drawings to her sessions. Gradually "they" began to diminish in size and at last they lost their legs and arms. The running was less frantic in a picture called "Running to her friend, Gray Mouse."

At this time she told me that her bedroom was filled with stuffed animals that she had been collecting for years, and that she often talked to them. To the next session she brought an armful of them to show them to me. It was apparent that they, too, had been helping her to cope with the unconscious contents which frightened her so much. And her telling me this, revealing this secret, showed the degree to which I was carrying the transcendent function for her. I felt that her dependence upon me was growing far too great, even though this dependence had made it possible for Maureen to establish a relationship that allowed her to express her feelings. There was always much reserve in her way of being with me, almost as though the more she could speak about herself the more she became afraid that she would overcome her neuroses, that she would be "cured," and that she would have to go out into the world to face the unknown all alone, without the support of the therapist. She wanted me as the mother she would have wanted to have, and she tried to force me into the role of mother by constantly asking me for advice and for special little favors in a childish way.

There came a time when she told me that she was thinking of moving to share an apartment with a girl with whom she had gotten acquainted at work. This took me somewhat by surprise and I responded that it appeared that she was getting ready to interact with someone on an ongoing basis. I knew the moment I said it that it was the wrong thing to have said. At the end of the session she just sat in the chair and would not leave. The next several sessions were especially difficult. She seemed to lose ground. At last she attacked me furiously:

Maureen: "You're trying to bust it all up."

Therapist: "Bust what up?"

It came out that she was in the position of trying to defend her fortress. I realized that it was being defended against the old mother image which she feared, the one who also represented a hostile world which regarded her presence in it as an intruder. I was trying to break her fortress down, by encouraging her, by expressing my confidence that she was getting better and might not need it. The deeper fear, underlying all the other fears, now emerged. That was the horrible, empty feeling that there might be nothing in the fortress after all her trouble—this was what she was so desperately trying to defend against. That is what she was feeling when she said, "I cannot put my gun down when you are also holding your gun."

When she next came she was tense and distant, really quite out of touch. She said, "I don't want to talk, I feel too flipped-out." When I suggested that she might prefer to paint what she was feeling, she readily agreed. She made one finger painting after another, always the stereotype of the stick-figure girl-ego, always running. Finally I encouraged her to show me what the girl was running from. She painted furiously, a painting in which the figure in front is about to be overtaken by the one approaching from the rear. She stared at the picture and said coldly, "One of them will have to be killed!"

This marked the beginning of the most crucial period in the therapy. Maureen was testing me and she even went so far as to make a gesture in the direction of another suicide attempt, which was obviously not genuine. She thought I would hospitalize her and thereby reject her as her mother had done. I did not. I asked her whether I could trust her to continue working on her problems and not give up. She said yes, and I did trust her. Gradually she began to trust me again, and this time it seemed that she was involved in therapy in a different way than she had been previously. The pictures had helped her to feel that she had some way of reaching the unconscious and looking into it. She did not have to close herself off from it any longer.

One day she brought a drawing which she titled "Sometimes the mind runs faster." She said that she had taken out her crayons and then had put a question to the unconscious, "Why do I become afraid?" Then she had let her imagination find an image. What now appeared before her was the same figure, but this time the head was separated from the body and was running ahead of it. "They" had retreated far into the background. I asked her what was happening in the picture, and she laughed. "My fantasy life runs ahead of me, it disconnects from me as a person, and I am always struggling to keep up with it. It looks as though what I am running from is not those others, whoever 'they' are, but I am running to keep up with what is in my head."

Then she wanted to fingerpaint again. The painting she made was the last of this series. The figure was seated. She saw what she had painted and knew that she was able at last to stop running. She would allow to happen whatever would happen. She had become aware that—just as her pictures had in a sense created themselves—there were forces in her which needed expression and that would follow her relentlessly like her own shadow no matter how she might try to avoid them. One cannot avoid what is part of one. The pictures provided a point of view that was able to transcend her ordinary aware-

ness and also to avoid capitulating to the unconscious. She
had objectified the struggle, and so could deal with it in a new
way.

From this point in the analysis, Maureen began to have
dreams, and the spiral of individuation took another turn.

Active imagination is, more than anything else, an attitude
toward the unconscious. It cannot be said to be a *technique* or
even a *method* of coming to terms with the unconscious, because it is a different experience for each person who is able to
use it. The common feature of all varieties of active imagination is its dependence upon a view of the unconscious that
recognizes its contents as containing innate structures (archetypes) which inevitably define the potentialities and the limitations of the personality. Through the use of active imagination, analytical psychology works in specific ways that differ
from the approaches to the unconscious employed by other
psychotherapeutic methods. It helps to heal the split between
the ego and the unconscious by using the resources of the
unconscious itself to help bring the dissociated material back
gradually into a relationship with the conscious ego. As the
therapist allows the dialogue to proceed without intervention,
the material returns precisely in the amount and within the
kind of time frame that makes it possible for the individual to

deal with it. Once it is out in the open, in verbal or some other form, it can be looked at with more objectivity—either alone or in the presence of the therapist.

Gerhard Adler, a Jungian analyst who wrote extensively on active imagination, summarized the difference between this and other methods of working with unconscious material.

> The root conception which gives the approach of Analytical Psychology its specific character, and which indeed forms the foundation on which its whole technique is built, is the absolute directedness and seriousness with which it accepts the reality of the unconscious and its contents as an essential part of the whole personality. For the unconscious is, as Jung has so often pointed out, not merely . . . nothing but repressed sexuality or repressed will to power; but, as the matrix of the conscious mind, it is the really potent and creative layer of our psyche. The unconscious contains all the factors which are necessary for the integration of the personality. It possesses, as it were, a superior knowledge of our real needs in regard to their integration and the ways to achieve them. Only when the unconscious is understood in this way as the "objective psyche," containing all the regulating and compensating factors which work for the wholeness of the personality, does it make sense to advise a patient to face his unconscious in such a direct and forceful manner.[1]

Active imagination is not without its dangers. Unlike dreams, which are self-limiting, since we eventually wake up, active imagination may become extremely fascinating and may even pull the individual so strongly toward the unconscious that the ego position may be endangered. In a well-defended ego the danger is not so great, for the individual constantly brings into consciousness what he discovers, and relates it to his own thoughts or circumstances. This was the case with Maureen at the start, yet even with Maureen there was a period of grave risk when she felt that one of the two figures of her painting would have to be killed.

Charles was a graduate student in psychology, interning as

an occupational therapist at a mental hospital. He was at the opposite extreme from Maureen when it came to approaching his own unconscious processes, as well as those of everybody else. If Maureen barricaded herself against the unconscious, Charles wanted to dive in head first. He had taken LSD on two or three occasions and he smoked marijuana from time to time, but, of late, more rarely, as he realized that he had at hand more unconscious material than he could begin to understand and that it was more important to derive some meaning from it than simply to pile ecstasy on top of ecstasy. His dreaming was full of collective unconscious material. There was clearly too much to deal with already and when he broached the subject of his wanting to try active imagination, I hesitated. Yet it seemed clear that Charles for all his interest in fantasy, was nevertheless a person with a clearly defined view of himself as one who was solid and well balanced. In a way he regarded himself almost as *too* well balanced, and this suggested to me that he had been trying to fit his dreams and fantasies into a plan dictated wholly from the conscious point of view. He was interested in finding out just how the psychological mechanisms he was studying worked out, and every aspect of behavior had to be accounted for both in theory and in practice.

He enjoyed long personal discussions with his friends in which he would gain their confidence and then use his facile reasoning to "explain" the intimate details of their lives that they had disclosed. Charles had found it necessary to explore the emotional life history of every companion, no matter how brief the relationship had been. He did not become deeply involved personally, and he failed to feel any ongoing sense of obligation to those whose feelings he had exposed when they had been with him. In fact, he seemed to be less than aware that the encounters had left any residue as far as other people were concerned—they certainly did not leave any with him. His attitude in personal relationships was, one might say, "pseudo-clinical," a combination of clinical curiosity without an accompanying sense of responsibility.

In his studies, Charles was careful to master the subject matter which was assigned. His papers and research projects were carried out in a highly professional manner. He conformed to the standards of style and content that were required, and he also managed to anticipate his professors and give them the content they wanted, even when they were not aware that this was what they were looking for. In short, it looked as though Charles was sailing through graduate school without a worry.

Underneath appearances, things were not so smooth. Charles felt under constant pressure to produce, to find out, to relate to women. He was always figuring out how, he was always manipulating in his head; and after any experience he had a compulsive need to fit it into place in the mental picture of his own psychological structure. It may be asked, wasn't Charles attempting to do what we have been talking about all along, to gain a greater degree of self-knowledge? Superficially, it did appear that way. But he was not guided by the aims of the self in the sense of moving toward a sense of the fitting place of the ego in the total psyche, much less in the sense of his place as a human being within a field among other human beings. Rather, it seemed that his goal lay in the direction of ego mastery over the self on one hand, and toward his own domination of other people's psychological space, on the other. Charles's preoccupation with unconscious material seemed to be an effort to escape from a dry, superior, intellectual approach, and yet his very way of viewing this material was from the stance of a superior controlling ego. It was out of this truly paradoxical situation that he broached the subject of attempting some active imagination.

I suggested that painting would be a good medium for him, since he had studied painting in the past and he had enough technical skill so that he would not be discouraged by the obsessive character of his perfectionist needs in other areas. I suggested that he take a good long look at himself in the mirror, and then without any notion of what he would paint, to simply address the canvas and let it reply to the touch of his brushes. The canvas might become the ground upon which a representation would appear; I could not say more than that for I did not know any more than he what might come out of it, if, indeed, anything would come at all.

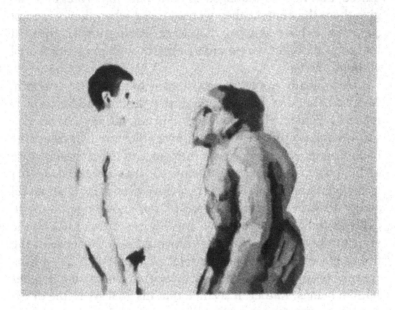

To the next analytical session Charles brought a large painting. I was struck at once by the color of the background, a vibrant yellow, shimmering as though one were looking directly into the sun. It was a picture of two men. One was a pale, sunken-chested, potbellied, slightly slumped man with pinkish-white skin. He resembled Charles, but was a weaker and older-looking version. The other had the appearance of a Neanderthal man, a little shorter than the first man, with shaggy hair, earth-toned skin, and heavy muscular structure. The two men, both naked, stood facing one another, looking each other in the eye. Charles told me: "The painting was spontaneous, and so it was very mysterious when that ape-man appeared. I started painting a hunched-up oval-like image, and out he came."

Here was a clear expression of a situation in which the conscious side with its self-image had become separated and dissociated from that aspect of the unconscious that touches the most primordial part, the archetypal layer of the psyche. The man of the well-developed intellect had seen for the first time a primitive side which could not and did not interpose the process of rationalization when instinctive behavior was indicated. The dark man was non-rational, at least according to the preconceived notions of the white man as to what rationality is. Consequently, the dark-man-aspect had been rejected as having nothing of value to offer to this sophisticated student. It was seen by him as "illness," and not any illness he could discover in himself. It was, rather, the illness of the world, which was concentrated in the mentally disturbed—those who were not as "balanced" as he regarded himself to be.

It had made good sense for him to work as occupational therapist with these unfortunate people whom he saw as so underdeveloped in comparison with himself. But when the most primitive of all men appeared on his own canvas, face to face with an older and sadder image of himself, there was no possibility of avoiding the evidence that these were two elements of a single psyche, his own. The glowing yellow light pervaded the picture with a feeling of clarity. No escaping the implications of this picture!

Then Charles did a lot of painting on his own, without any suggestions from me. He would just sit aimlessly before his table, letting images come up and then transcribing them to paper. One was a painting he called "Africa." It was a large design something like a map of the continent of Africa, broken into many pieces of all different shapes and colors. Of this he said, "I made layer upon layer of overlapping colors. All I can remember of that evening was the feeling that what I needed to do was build and change, I needed constant change."

This marked the beginning of a long series of experiments with painting which were allowed to "paint themselves" in a way which seemed nearly automatic. During this period,

Charles felt a growing dissatisfaction with his work as occupational therapist. He faced the hopelessness of ever accomplishing anything with the patients. He was not able to see them through day by day, but could only work with them for an hour or two a week when they came to the O.T. room. It irked him that the psychiatrists regarded what he was doing as "busy work," and did not pay the slightest attention to it.

Around this time Charles had quite a few dreams dealing with conflicts between men—between brothers, or between himself and an enemy soldier or someone criminal or uncontrollably impulsive or in some other way socially unacceptable. He learned to recognize these figures as aspects of the ape-man, and gradually was able to see that although this character was not compatible with his conscious image of himself, he nevertheless had some valuable qualities. First, there was great strength and endurance in the ape-man. He would not easily be dissuaded when he had determined to do something. There was an absence of indecision. There was a strong capacity to sniff out a situation instinctively, to sense the total environment and to be able to react to it directly and spontaneously. Charles, as he saw himself, in contrast, was flabby and rather weak physically. He had to rely on his will and his reasoning to assure his supremacy. His skill was all learned, and the only way he could stay ahead of other people, he had felt, was to learn more and to develop more skills in exploiting his learning to his own advantage. It became apparent that he was missing in his life much of the vitality that the ape-man stood for, and that this vitality was encapsulated in the unconscious waiting to be experienced if only he could accept it in an unprejudiced way. He began by getting into closer touch with his own body by allowing himself to experience his physiological sensations in a more conscious way, to face his own sensations with an open curiosity, and to allow himself to reflect on his experiences and to give some expression to them. The mode of expression could be of any sort, but it would be necessary to go beyond pure reflection and carry his psychic experience either into artistic form, verbal form, or into physical activity.

Throughout this period the image of the ape-man appeared from time to time in dreams. One day Charles decided that it was time to have a direct confrontation with this shadow figure in active imagination. But, as he later reported, he did not know how to go about it. A verbal encounter would be impossible, for the ape-man would be able to utter only guttural sounds. He thought of dancing with the ape-man—dancing is also a form of communication. But when he came to it, it did not happen that way at all. He sat alone in a room with a pencil and paper on the table before him. The ape-man appeared and sat on his left, beside him at the table.

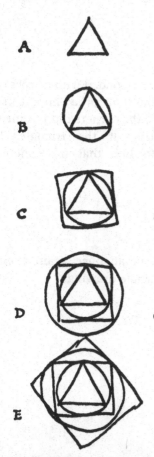

A

Charles picked up the pencil and drew a triangle on the blank sheet of paper. Then he put the pencil down.

B

The ape-man reached over and picked it up. He then drew a circle around Charles's triangle, and replaced the pencil on the paper.

C

Charles drew a square around the ape-man's circle.

D

The ape-man once more encircled the square.

E

Now Charles drew a larger square, this one at a forty-five-degree angle to the one he had drawn the last time.

Now the ape-man made a cross.

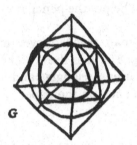

Charles responded with a cross of his own, but it disturbed him; it was not "neat"; the corners did not meet the corners of the triangle. It seemed to him that they should have.

The ape-man once again encircled the whole drawing.

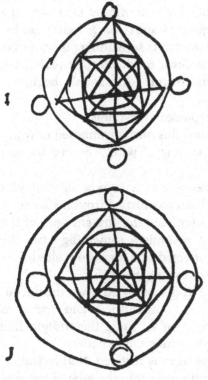

Now Charles made four small circles.

Charles was left with a sense of well-being.

The ape-man encircled the whole once more, then disappeared.

The drawing finally created by the two was a mandala circle, corresponding to many symbols for wholeness which are often used for focusing the attention in meditation. His mandala called for some meditation from us, and we turned to the composition of the parts. Charles brought forth his own associations, and I suggested some amplifications, beginning with the initial triangle.

[A] "It is a form which we do not find anywhere in nature. It is like an arrowhead, moving, dynamic. Three is a masculine number, the triangle is like the arrangement of the male genitals. Three is the holy trinity. Again all male."

[B] The ape-man encircles the triangle. The circle is a natural form, we see it in the sun, moon, in flower forms, many places throughout the natural world. The ape-man belongs to nature.

[C] This is squaring the circle. It means enclosing the mystery of nature. The square stands for a fourth added to the masculine trinity. The fourth is something other, it may stand for earth, perhaps the devil, or shadow, or perhaps it brings the feminine into the picture. A mandala begins to emerge.

[D] Again, nature encompasses everything.

[E] A new square now, and this one is composed of triangles like the one that Charles started with. The one has become four.

[F] The one that has become four is now divided into quarters. This time the ape-man has turned from his game of always encircling, and has attempted the straight lines of the civilized man. He begins to assimilate something from the other. The unconscious is affected and somehow altered by the interaction between these two figures.

[G] Charles, as ego figure, is disconcerted when the unconscious aspect comes closer to consciousness and begins to function in a conscious way, that is, using the straight line which is not of nature but of human construction.

[H] The primordial circle form is restated. Nature will remain constant, even though it enters into the area of the ego. Charles does not need to feel threatened by the nearness of his instinctual side.

[I] As if to confirm this, Charles ventures into the ape-man's scheme. He makes four circles at the point where his own square touches the ape-man's circle.

[J] The whole is encircled by the ape-man and the mandala is complete. There is a new sense of relatedness between Charles's conscious ego and the rough primordial figure. The conscious position has not been relinquished, nor has the other been repressed. Charles experienced a sense of well-being as the symbol acted to help him find a connection with his own unknown depths. He did not forget this image; at times he could reflect upon it and regain the feeling of inner harmony that came to him when he first meditated upon it."

A couple of months later Charles experienced still another

encounter with the primitive man. This one came in the form of a dream.

I saw the ape-man carrying me with the greatest of ease high up on his hands, very gently. I felt very secure. Then he put me down and we stood face to face and embraced each other. He drew a picture of the dream.

I asked Charles, "What could be the meaning of the erection that both of them experienced in the dream?"

"There is an exhilarated feeling on the part of the ego figure. He has gained his manliness through his relationship with the other one, the primordial man who is for him the representation of a potency he did not know he possessed. Not alone sexual potency, though that was part of it, but potency in the sense of the vigor and drive to carry through what he intended with energy and delight."

We looked closely at the picture, and I noted, "The primordial man is stocky, built close to the ground."

Charles: "He gains power from his knowledge of the earth and the ways of nature. He takes her as she is, he does not have to try to subdue her, he accepts her and he finds it easy to be in harmony with her. He gets power from her, this is his carrying power, and this is what can carry the man of today if he allows himself to trust it and rest easy with it."

"Then the ego side is able to assimilate some of the energy of the unconscious?"

"Yes," replied Charles, "and the ego side also gives something. He gives to the primordial energy a delicacy of expression which he has acquired through his long experience with the culture and the arts, through his education, his training, his personal discipline. So, through the union of the pale man and the cave man the possibility of a newly created point of view comes into being. It is a great and exciting challenge for both of them, nearly an ecstasy, and their readiness to experience this union of opposites is symbolized by their erections."

It was clear that the sexual element of the dream, and in fact of the whole encounter between the two, was to be understood as a metaphor for the creative act of synthesizing conscious attitudes and unconscious contents. Here symbolism that appeared in sexual images did not refer to a problem that was primarily sexual, nor did it suggest homosexuality. Intimate relationship had to occur between these two male figures who represented ego and shadow, the opposing aspects of the masculine nature within a single human being.

Through these encounters Charles learned the nature of the potential which he had previously kept locked up in the unconscious. Gradually he was able to establish a two-way transactional relationship between his critical, evaluating, and controlling ego, and the energetic spontaneous, and irrepressible archaic man within him. Where in the beginning I had served as the primary mediator for the transcendent function, Charles now took over that role.

I can imagine that the reader who has never participated in this kind of experience may be asking himself, why in the world when there is so much trouble everywhere that needs attention should a grown man be spending his time having imaginary conversations with some prehistoric character, and engaging in paper and pencil games with him? What practical purpose does it serve?

I would not want to suggest that any practical purpose is served directly, nor is that the intention behind active imagination, dream analysis or any other analytic procedure we may decide to use. Through the process, if seriously undertaken, transformations of personality do occur. Narrow attitudes become broadened, one-sidedness gives way to the capacity to view a situation from several positions, aggression is replaced by productive activity, and passivity becomes receptivity. The changes are often subtle, but they go deep, and people who experience them know that they are living in a different way than they did before. This difference may not be readily evident to people who know them, for often they have hidden their self-doubts and insecurities well enough from public view; but *they* know, and this is what is important.

In the case of Charles the analytic work and specifically the active imagination led him to withdraw the projections he had made on the patients with whom he was working in the mental hospital. He no longer looked upon them as sub-humans any more than he saw himself as a superior being. Of course he would never have admitted, early in his analysis, that this is what he had been doing; but his very attitude of hopelessness toward what he was trying to do and the patronizing way he spoke about the patients gave away his real view of them. His manner of distancing himself from his patients by standing over them and observing them and waiting for the psychiatrists who never came, was evidence enough that he was acting out in his work the split in himself between the natural intuitive energetic side and the cool professional side. One side was projected onto the patients, who were "hopeless," and the other side was projected onto the psychotherapists, who stood for an idealized version of his own ego.

As the alien sides within himself became friends, he began to deal with his O.T. patients in a new way, as though seeking out their potential for change, regardless of how deeply buried that potential might be. He no longer had to wait for the psychotherapists who would never come; *he* was the person who was there, and he began to be fully there in a way that was different from before.

The case of Charles illustrates an important point, not only with respect to active imagination, but also to the whole of analytical psychology. The source of change, of transformation, in the individual comes from within the individual, rather than from any outside agent. There is no dictum in analytical psychology that the environment must or should shape the individual, nor is there the implication that the behavior of the individual ought to be modified to conform with the environment or its demands. Analytical psychology does not seek to achieve a race of happy, productive sheep. People are troubled in a troubled world; they do not cry " 'Peace,' when there is no peace." Nor does this psychological view suggest that individuals submit to any external authority which is given the power to determine what kind of activity or behavior is acceptable and what is not. Analytical psychology casts its lot with the champions of individual freedom and offers another source of guidance than that of the political or psychological despot, however "benevolent" that person may be. That other source is the inner mystery, the unconscious, which has its own individual way of manifesting itself to every man and woman who is open to see it. Active imagination is one of many ways in the analytic process which teach an individual to develop the capacity for relating to the interlocking worlds of soul and society.

Active imagination is not always a long and involved process. Sometimes it comes as a flash, a momentary experience for an individual who draws the meaning out of it, and is changed by it.

Such a moment came to Clara at a crucial time in her analysis. Clara was a woman in her early thirties who had never married, although she was charming and intelligent and attractive. Certain attitudes instilled in her early childhood, as well as events in adolescence, left her with a pathological fear of intimacy, so that her sexual drives were thoroughly inhibited. While she was in analysis she began to lessen the strength of these inhibitions, and in time the possibility of a close relationship with a certain man appeared on the horizon. She had one or two erotic dreams, and then the dreams stopped, or she stopped remembering them. She put off taking any active steps toward encouraging the relationship with the man. I had written in my notes after her last analytic session: "An arid session. She is in a rut. Can't move out into life enough. Inertia. Finds it hard to get up in the morning."

When Clara came to the next session she was obviously eager to tell me something. It was about a waking fantasy that she had experienced the day before: "I was standing over the sink, peeling something. All of a sudden the water started coming up in the drain in a kind of rush. It was spouting out. I had a feeling of panic, of loss of control. I was afraid of getting inundated. Then I thought, what's the use of getting excited, all it can do is overflow. The word 'unconscious' floated through my mind."

What seemed to be the difficulty underlying the "aridity" of our last sessions was Clara's fear that she would be overwhelmed by the unconscious, that is, by her own deeply buried sexuality. She had attempted to stop the flow, but in discussing the matter with me in her previous analytic session the unconscious had evidently been stimulated to the point that it released some of its contents. This was experienced as the gushing waters. What was especially interesting was that it appeared in such a humdrum place, so near at hand, and furthermore, that the unconscious provided its own balance. It seemed to say, "Let it happen, at least something in your life will be moving, and it may not be as dangerous as you believe." The interaction with the symbolic presentation came as Clara found a way to accept the message in the flow of water upward from the deeper levels of her being. She saw it as permission to avoid imposing controls upon any spontaneous responses she might have. She could anticipate that now some blockage between herself and the unconscious had been dissolved, and she could also expect that this greater freedom would reflect in her dealing in interpersonal situations as well.

Active imagination may provide access to a person who is deeply depressed, when no amount of "rational conversation" can have an effect. Fortunately today it is possible to intervene in a severe depression with medications that can often stop the downward pull of despair that seemed bottomless. Psychoactive drugs, properly prescribed and followed, may sufficiently alter the moods of individuals so that some who otherwise might not have been accessible to psychotherapy or analysis are now able to be reached. While the drug may provide symptomatic relief, psychotherapy can help the person to gain an understanding of the process that led to the depressive attitude, to work with it, and eventually to transcend it.

There is a very common kind of depression in which people feel despondent, alone and helpless to face their tasks and responsibilities. Such a person was the middle-aged professional woman whom we will call Dolores. Her isolation appeared to her to be a separation from the world of people but, as I saw it, underneath her feeling of isolation was the real problem. The unconscious had drawn away from consciousness and had ceased to stimulate and nurture the ego. Therefore, Dolores projected everything outside; she had problems with her aged father, she suffered from stomach ulcers, she had "financial problems" which were completely unrealistic in view of her more than adequate income, but mostly she complained that she felt no zest for life, she was always weary; she regarded herself as being without love and without purpose.

Dolores had suffered for many years from periodic depressions. Several years ago she had gone to Zurich for a summer and there she was able to undergo a few months of Jungian analysis. She had improved considerably at the time. Now the depression had returned full force, and she was not able to return to her former analyst. She came to me for help, and circumstances were such that it was vitally important to bring her out of the depression as rapidly as possible. Four sessions were arranged on four successive days. I counted on her previous experience in Jungian analysis to provide us with a common frame of reference so that we would be able to move into the problems without having to spend much time communicating our basic premises to one another.

In the first session she talked about her history of depressive episodes. She told me that it seemed to her as if some of the most dramatic changes in her life had come out of her attempts to handle depression and boredom. In this way she went to college, went into the Peace Corps, and went to graduate school. In a way, she said, her trip to Zurich had a similar motivation. One reason she felt so depressed and desperate now, was that she could see no place to run, just an endless procession of days leading eventually to retirement which she both anticipated and dreaded. She asked, "What will I do when I am left entirely upon my own resources? I can hardly tolerate being alone for a day now—how will I ever face a lifetime of being alone?"

I tried to help her to get down into her feelings and to let me know how it was. I did not allow her to put up her knowledge and experience in Jungian therapy as a barrier between us; in fact, I dismissed her theoretical framework completely. In this first session her feeling of having no place to escape was intensified. When she left, I suggested that between now and the next day she should examine her feelings and express them in some way, either by writing or drawing.

In the interim she did both. She wrote, "Perhaps I was expecting instant relief from all the tension I have been under, but I was disappointed to continue feeling badly today, especially nauseated and as if I would throw up any minute. This is disconcerting and makes it hard to concentrate."

She had also drawn a picture, and brought it to me. I

asked her to describe what she saw there. She said, "It's me, it's how I feel. I'm sitting alone, in my cage and that is all there is, nothing inside the cage but me, and nothing outside it. That's all there is."

I looked at the picture carefully. The figure was seated, her head bent over and resting on her knees, her arms forward, hands clasped about her ankles. The color she had chosen was a flat, monotonous blue. There was a horizontal black bar at the top and bottom, and vertical lines between. I wanted to know better how Dolores felt, so I sat myself down on the floor and took the position of the figure in the painting. As my head dropped forward onto my knees, I automatically closed my eyes. It was a position of complete passivity. Even if I had been seated in the midst of the most beautiful garden, I would not have known it. The position made it impossible for me to experience anything outside of my sense of being by myself.

When I had let the feeling work on me and had some sense of it, I then asked Dolores how she could be sure that she was, in fact, in a cage. Had she examined it carefully? It had no back, after all, and no sides. Perhaps it was only the front of a cage, that she had mistaken for an entire cage. Perhaps there were ways to get out that she had not seen because she had not looked for them.

It all seems so obvious when looking back to it. But at that moment Dolores was amazed to discover that she was not in a cage at all. She could get up and walk around the edge and be free of it. She felt as though she had experienced a revelation! Anyone could, of course, have told her that her problems were not real, that they were "all in her head," but this was quite different. The information came from herself, from her own drawing and from the implications of the drawing which she was able to discover. There is a great difference here. When the insight comes from a friend, an adviser, or a therapist, it comes from "just another person who doesn't understand." The patient has a right to respond, "Yes, I know that I ought to change my ways, but if I could change them I would. That's just the trouble, I can't change, that's why I am coming to you." The analyst does not take the viewpoint which opposes that of the patient's ego in order to impose the new view. The new view can and will come from the unconscious itself, given the enabling situation in which it can happen. The analyst's role is to follow the emerging contents of the unconscious and, only when it is necessary, to help the analysand recognize what is happening.

When Dolores appeared for her third session she announced that she was feeling a great deal better. "The last session," she said, "was like a cold shower—it woke me up to a few things." She had made two pictures and now wanted to explain them to me. The first showed a vast horizontal blue plane resembling the curvature of the earth. Upon it stood a tiny black female figure very much alone, with arms outstretched. Above were huge black-gray clouds.

Dolores had broken out of her self-imposed prison. She seemed very small, facing the immensity of her problems, which were symbolized in the great foreboding clouds. But she was free—at least for the time being—frightened, perhaps, but free.

The second picture, also done in blue and black, was devoid of any human life. The black curvature of the earth was seen, this time more like a gentle hilltop. From it rose a straight tree, a scraggly pine with only two branches and, on top, a crown that could have been of leaves except that they were not differentiated, so that all one could see was the tree's blackness silhouetted against the sky. The sky was infused with a blue light, in the midst of which gleamed one star. At the bottom of the picture Dolores had lettered in these words:

> A lonely God—enthroned in lonely space
> Created us as we are—
> As single as a tree—
> As separate as a star.

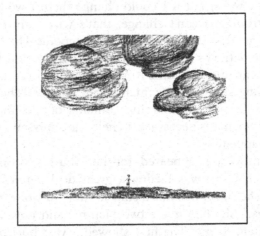

The second picture had come as an interaction between Dolores's conscious attitude and the first picture, which had represented her unconscious fears and hopes. She stood before immensity and enjoyed the freedom of being there, even though it terrified her.

The third picture showed her the wonder which she was capable of contemplating once she could accept her loneliness as an aspect of the human condition, even as an aspect fashioned in the image of God. From this point of view, "lonely" loses some of its agonizing texture and becomes "single," that is, individual, and also "separate," differentiated from all others and, therefore, unique. To accept this is to take another step on the way to individuation.

She told me, "I felt much more at ease today, both inwardly and outwardly. Through these pictures some contact must have been made with the unconscious. I have not suffered from tension and nausea as I did the first days."

I asked her if she knew what had happened.

"I am not at all sure," she replied. "Perhaps it was your direct confrontation of my own responsibility for my mental state—the cold shower I mentioned. Whatever it was, it has enabled me to look more favorably on my total life situation."

We then went on to discuss the specific problems with which she was faced, and her attitude was indeed much more open to new possibilities than it had been before.

Little needs to be said about the last session with Dolores. Her final picture told it all, unmistakably. The elements of the previous picture were all there, but this picture was entirely different. The ground had become a grassy meadow reflecting the blue of the sky and the yellow sunshine. The tree was there, but it was not the same tree. It was now a strong tree with many branches, an old tree, solid and substantial. Sunlight and shadow played on the trunk, which was rounded and dimensional, not flat as before. Most exciting was the crown of the tree, full of many-colored leaves in great joyous clusters, interspersed with pink blossoms. The sky was light blue with gentle, white clouds floating across, and in this sky four birds were flying—separate, alone, yet belonging where they were and sharing their condition with each other.

Dolores's mood had changed to match the picture. She was ready to move back into life and to become active again. I do not mean to suggest that any problems had actually been solved, only that she was able to view her problems in a different way. This was a first step toward dealing with the objective situation, the next step would have to be taken by her, and in her own setting of everyday living. This is where the transformations of analysis are tested anyway. Statistics be damned, the only validation that I know for the analytic process is the validation which is stamped on the life of the individual who has experienced it.

The unconscious has many ways of communicating with the ego besides through visual imagery such as we have seen in these examples of active imagination. Some people are able to personify the figures of the unconscious and engage them in conversation. These figures may have appeared in a dream without yielding up the meaning of the dream in a way in which the dreamer is able to understand it. The dream figure may then be called upon while one is in the waking state, and actively confronted. In this form of active imagination a true dialogue between the ego and the unconscious may take place. The conscious side states its position vis-à-vis the dream, or asks the question that the dream has evoked. It then suspends all critical judgment and allows the unconscious an equal opportunity to express itself. Often words will come, or ideas, which have meaning, and to which the ego may respond. And so it is possible to carry on a conversation with a dream figure or some other unconscious aspect such as the anima or some representation of her.

It may seem to some that this is a way of manipulating the

unconscious, that the power of suggestion is a strong element here. Those who have been able to enter successfully into the kind of dialogue that is true active imagination know that it is something different from suggestion or "seeding the unconscious." The material that comes forth when the controlling tendencies of the ego are suspended is often what is least expected or wanted. The impact with which these "new" ideas come forth indicates that they have their own autonomy and are not at all a reflection or distortion of the conscious position.

What is important is that the dialogue between the ego and the dream figure be transcribed onto paper or put into some other form so that it can later be analyzed, very much as a dream or a picture from the unconscious is analyzed. Only then can the greatest value be derived from the assimilation of the unconscious contents.

There are many other ways of getting into active relationship with the unconscious. In *Memories, Dreams, Reflections*, Jung described some of the methods he discovered which were for him doorways into the unconscious. In every case there was some tangible product into which his emotions could flow freely, and which could later be regarded not only from the side of the emotions that produced it, but also from his rational side. He described how, as a child, he used to spend many hours "playing passionately with building blocks." He recalled how he built little houses and castles with bottles to form the sides of gates and vaults. When he was a man, he built a retreat house for himself at Bollingen far down the Lake of Zurich from the house in which he lived with his family. The shape and form of the house were dictated by his inner needs, and with the passage of years new parts had to be added as he himself grew.

Jung also carved in stone; the ring of the chisel against the rock gave shape to his emotions during some of his most difficult times. He wrote of the help he found through stone carving after the death of his wife and how this work helped him to shape the contents which poured forth from the unconscious so that he could later express them in words in a series of important writings. There followed a period of introspection and objectification through the successive phases from idea to stone to the word. Nor was this all. There were periods when he inscribed and painted manuscripts, and at other times he wrote out his inner experiences by hand in beautifully illuminated books. He painted murals on the walls at Bollingen. His imagination was not a matter of the head—his whole person was involved in it; every skill and craft he could master was enlisted in its service.

If we take our inspiration from Jung, we will find many avenues through which we may pass in the quest of the mysteries of our own inner natures. Jung was an innovator and much of what he did was to venture into new areas which had never been related specifically to the task of psychological healing. It would not be in the spirit of Jung to slavishly copy Jung, to attempt to do what he did in the way that he described. The spirit of Jung, it seems to me, demands that we utilize the means and skills, the techniques and devices that are natural for us as individuals to use in our encounters with the unconscious. Writing and the graphic arts are available to everyone, but we need not be limited to these. Any of the creative arts—when practiced as a form of self-expression rather than for the purpose of producing an acceptable product—will do: sculpture, instrumental music, singing, dance. Technology provides a whole new set of possibilities, if one can avoid getting caught in the net of the technics but can use them to free the soul to express itself. For example, one of my analysands writes poetry on his computer and says that he likes it ever so much better than writing it by hand because while he works at the computer he can see the words as they will appear on the printed page and arrange them as one would a painting or a mosaic, so that they speak to the eye as well as to the ear. Young people, who grow up using computers and other newer media as their parents used the typewriter and their grandparents the pen, will find a whole host of novel ways to follow the dictum we find in the ancient gnostic Gospel of Thomas:

That which you have within you will save you
If you bring it forth from yourself.

An analysand of mine had heard about active imagination and asked me if I would tell her a little about it. What I told her, briefly, was this: Active imagination is not a confrontation of the ego and the unconscious directly. It entails getting *outside* of the ego position and yet not letting the unconscious take over the control either. The task is to assume the role of the transcendent function, which means being able to give equal credit and equal opportunity for free expression to both the ego and the unconscious. If the ego takes control and forces, it doesn't work; it is a fabrication. If you have to ask yourself whether it is really the unconscious that is speaking, then it is not. On the other hand, if the ego gives way to the unconscious completely, then there is the danger of getting lost in it. I see no virtue in encouraging yelling, screaming, crying, panic—I see no particular virtue in inducing a psychotic episode, however temporary. The potentiality for it is present in everyone, and a skillful therapist can bring it to the surface quite easily. (Often an unskillful therapist does so even more easily, and also unwittingly.)

I believe in keeping functioning people functioning. Therefore I do not remove the support of the orientation to the real world. I am often reminded of a passage in William Blake's *The Marriage of Heaven and Hell*, in which Blake and his infernal companion look into the "infinite Abyss" (hell, the unconscious), "till a void boundless as a nether sky appear'd beneath us, & we held by the roots of trees . . . hung over this immensity." I, too, feel strongly that in our katabases we must be held by the roots of trees, that is, by our connection with the real world. That is just the danger of uncontrolled use of psychotomimetic drugs—that they may cut off the connection with the objective world, especially in cases where the ego is not sufficiently solidly based to begin with. I believe that active imagination is to be employed with utmost care and respect for the volatile nature of the unconscious.

I conclude this chapter on active imagination with a sort of postscript. I continued to hear from "Charles" from time to time after the analysis had terminated. We had kept "in touch." He had continued his inner work on his own, and was happily engaged in what the Buddhists call "right livelihood." On the occasion of a special birthday, this came in my mail from Charles:

When I was a boy I would occasionally
be visited at night by a large white
ball. It would come closer and closer
to me!
When it came so close I thought I
could touch it, I would reach out —
and wake up.

Part Three

. . .

THE PERSON
IN THE WORLD

. . .

11

Psychological Types:
Key to
Communication

...

THE SUBJECT of the television talk show was "Actors in Politics."
The interviewer, after commenting on the number of actors or
former actors who had won elective offices, asked the well-
known screen star this question: "Do you think actors should
enter politics?"

The actor thought about it for a moment, and then replied, "I think that an actor, like anyone else, should take an
interest in government. But as far as running for office, I don't
think that is a good idea, because actors are essentially introverts, while politicians are essentially extraverts."

The interviewer asked how he could consider a man who
continually faces an audience to be an introvert. To this he
answered, "For actors, the greatest concern is placing ourselves into the role of the character; that means we have to let
the feeling of that character affect us, we have to live it in a
very personal way from our own insides. This requires knowing yourself, for unless you know yourself you cannot really
know another person. Actually the audience is a relatively un-

important consideration to actors as they master their roles. But with politicians it is all different. There the game is to conquer the crowd. Playing the part is incidental."

The words "introvert" and "extravert" were used as household words that were understood by everyone, though perhaps few in the audience were aware that Jung had coined these words many years ago. He had identified two basically different attitudes which characterize people, and called these attitude types extraversion and introversion.

Today the idea is widely accepted that there are many different ways of approaching "reality" and that these ways depend to a large degree on differences in personality type. The psychology of typology has made its way into clinical practice and business and industry. To understand the width and depth of typology, it is necessary to look into its origin and development. In his essay, "The Psychology of the Unconscious," the first of his *Two Essays in Analytical Psychology*, Jung described the thinking that led him to his theory of psychological types. His book *Psychological Types* was published in 1920. Jung stated that it was the fruit of twenty years of consideration of the problem of individual differences. This consideration had been brought into sharp focus between 1907 and 1913 when he was working closely with Freud and the members of Freud's early circle. Among these was the brilliant analyst Alfred Adler, who was one of the first to leave Freud after a series of violent disagreements with the master. Adler founded his own psychological school, which he called Individual Psychology. This proceeded from quite different premises than did Freudian psychoanalysis, despite the fact that both Freud and Adler had been working with the same kinds of cases, the same general body of data.

Jung had observed the dissension and bitterness, and also the great variance of position between the two men in their understanding of the root causes of neuroses. He saw that Freud's basic assumption was that the growth of culture consists in a progressive subjugation of the animal in man. Culture is "a process of domestication which cannot be accomplished without rebellion on the part of the animal nature that thirsts for freedom."[1] Jung traced the Freudian point of view back historically, all the way to the Dionysian orgies that surged into the Greek world from the East and became a characteristic ingredient of classical culture. He described how the spirit of those orgies had contributed toward the development of the stoic ideal of asceticism in the innumerable sects and philosophical schools of the last century before Christ, and had produced from the polytheistic chaos of that period the ascetic religion of Christianity. Later, during the Renaissance, and afterward, successive waves of Dionysian licentiousness swept over the West, each bringing in its wake another variety of repressiveness, as in the puritanism at the time of Freud. The Freudian reformation was based mainly on the sexual question, which had come up as a major issue in European society during the last half of the nineteenth century.

Freud confronted directly the fundamental fact that the human instinctual nature is always coming up against the checks imposed by civilization. He recognized that neurotic individuals participate in the dominant currents of their times and reflect them in their own conflicts. For Freud the major areas in which repressions were imposed were those which created the "erotic conflict." As Jung capsulized it in discussing the Freudian system of dream interpretation: "The Freudian mode of investigation sought to prove that an overwhelming importance attaches to the erotic or sexual factor as regards the origin of the pathogenic conflict. According to this theory there is a collision between the trend of the conscious mind and the unmoral, incompatible, unconscious wish."[2] He went on to say, "The Freudian school is so convinced of the fundamental, indeed exclusive, importance of sexuality in neurosis that it has drawn the logical conclusion and valiantly attacked the sexual morality of our day . . ."[3] Jung objected to the narrow view which he read into Freud's concept of "the Eros principle" and, for himself, insisted that Eros belongs on one side to man's animal nature and on the other is related to the highest forms of the spirit. "But he only thrives when spirit and instinct are in right harmony."[4] We see that already here Jung had identified the harmony of the opposites as a key to wholeness and a healing principle.

Leaving his concerns about the Freudian approach, crediting it fully for its breakthrough on the side of freeing sexuality from the repressiveness that had held it crippled, while at the same time noting the limitations of the "Eros theory," Jung moved on to consideration of another point of view. This was Adler's "Individual Psychology," which Jung characterized by the descriptive phrase, "the will to power." The phrase is Nietzsche's, and refers to the philosopher who taught a "yea-saying" to instinct which, carried to its extreme, resulted in his establishing for himself his own morality, which he characterized as "beyond good and evil." Nietzsche believed and wrote that he lived his instinctual life in the highest sense. But Jung saw this as an impossible contradiction. For living the instinctual life suggests a simple naïveté, expressing directly and without a lot of intellectualization the feeling and desires that arise in one. Nietzsche was a philosopher, and as such he did more philosophizing than he did living out his instincts. Jung asks the pertinent question, "How is it possible . . . for man's instinctual nature to drive him into separation from his kind, into absolute isolation from humanity, into an aloofness from the herd upheld by loathing? We think of instinct as uniting man, causing him to mate, to beget, to seek pleasure and good living, the satisfaction of all sensuous desires."[5]

He then comes to the issue where Nietzsche's attitude struck a respondent note in Alfred Adler. He noted that sexuality and, more broadly speaking, the desire for a harmonious human relationship, is only one of the possible directions of instinct. "There exists not only the instinct for preservation of the species, but also the instinct for *self*-preservation."[6] According to Jung, Adler saw the instinct for self-preservation as being expressed in a power instinct which wants the ego to be in a controlling position under all circumstances and by whatever means. The "integrity of the personality" must be preserved at all costs. Adler stressed the great need of the individual to meet every attempt or apparent attempt of the environment to obtain dominancy over him.

Adler formulated his view of neurosis based as exclusively on the power principle, as Freud's was based on the sexual question. Their views contrasted in a whole series of principles. As Jung explained: "With Freud everything follows from antecedent circumstances according to a rigorous causality, with Adler everything is a teleological 'arrangement.' . . . The Freudian method at once begins burrowing into the inner causality of the sickness and its symptoms . . . If, however, we look at the same clinical picture from the point of view of the 'other' instinct, the will to power, it assumes quite a different aspect."[7] Then it becomes a situation in the environment which affords the patient an excellent opportunity to exert a childish urge to power.

Jung imagined the dilemma of a judge called upon to decide between two views and he says: "One simply cannot lay the two explanations side by side, for they contradict each other absolutely. In one, the chief and decisive factor is Eros and its destiny; in the other, it is the power of the ego. In the first case, the ego is merely a sort of appendage to Eros; in the second, love is just a means to the end, which is ascendancy. Those who have the power of the ego most at heart will revolt against the first conception, but those who care most for love will never be reconciled to the second."[8]

Jung advanced the theory that the greatly varying views espoused by Freud and Adler, and the tenacity with which each insisted on his own position, corroborates the differences in the attitudinal sets of the two men. Regarding these incompatible views, Jung felt the need of a position superordinate to both in which it would be possible for the opposing views to come together in unison. In examining both theories without prejudice it became apparent to him that both views were attractively simple, both possessed significant truths, and that though these were contradictory they should not be regarded as mutually exclusive. From this Jung concluded that these two theories of neurosis must represent opposite aspects of the phenomena being observed, and that each theorist had grasped only one aspect. "But how comes it that each investigator sees only one side, and why does each maintain that he has the only valid view? It must come from the fact that, owing to his psychological peculiarity, each investigator most readily sees that factor in the neurosis which corresponds to his peculiarity."[9]

This realization had far-flung implications for Jung's entire point of view, but most of all for his still gestating theory of Psychological Types. He carefully compared all aspects of Freud's and Adler's theories. I do not wish to go into the theoretical aspects here[10] because my interest is in indicating how these concepts actually work, both in psychotherapy and in their wider implications. For one thing, differences in attitude type seem to be deeply rooted in the personality formation of the individual. It does not seem to me to be particularly important whether these differences are inherent and present at birth or are derived from relationships and experiences at a very early age.

Jung seemed to believe that these differences may be present at birth as a part of the "psychological constitution" of the infant, at least in the sense of predispositions toward certain types of attitudes and consequently of behaviors stemming from those attitudes. My own experience has given me a basis for supporting his argument, at least with reference to some cases. I recall my work with a couple who were receiving psychotherapy for help in dealing with a pair of difficult four-year-old girl twins. The father told me that just after the twins were born he had spent many hours watching them from the outside of the glass window-wall of the hospital nursery. From the first moment he saw Colette, she was wriggling about in her crib, flailing her little arms and legs. Often she would be squalling, until a nurse would come and attend to her. Meanwhile Colleen lay peacefully in her crib; if she moved, she moved rather slowly and tentatively. Colette usually seemed to be red-faced; Colleen was pale. When the girls were taken home it was clear from the first day that Colette was the one who drew the most attention, and as time went on she became clearly more responsive to other people than Colleen. By the time they were two or three, Colette was generally pushing her sister around, taking away her sister's toys, and not infrequently bashing them over her sister's head. Colleen was relatively placid and indifferent, only the greatest indignities would cause her to cry, and then it was a soft, mournful sobbing. In nursery school Colette was the one who would pick a fight with the other children, and when the fray was heaviest, Colleen would be found shrinking away in a corner.

It was thought that Colleen's tendency to withdraw was a reaction to Colette's way of coming on so energetically, so the teachers decided to place them in separate rooms, with different teachers. Here the same kind of personality development went on, with the exception that Colette developed into a manager and an arranger in the classroom, and unless she were interfered with she would soon have the class pretty well organized to carry out whatever she wanted to do. Colleen, freed from her necessity to come to terms with Colette, became closely attached to her teacher, and became a little "do-gooder" in order to win the teacher's approval and affection. And who could not warm up to Colleen, with her shy, winsome ways, Colleen who, if you didn't take care to bring her into the group, would become lost in her own daydreams?

At home there was a constant struggle between the twins. Whatever Colette wanted to do was opposed by Colleen. Colette would scream and demand, and Colleen would cry and cajole. Colette used the power approach and Colleen appealed to love. Neither could make her peace with the other, and the parents were at a loss to understand what was happening in their household. The whole matter was complicated by the fact that the parents, because of their own differences in attitude types, did not see eye to eye on any aspect of how the children should be handled. The necessity of recognizing broad typological categories which account for striking individual differences had to be made clear to this family before there would be any hope of a successful outcome to the psychotherapeutic efforts.

Theories of types are not new with Jung, but he was possibly the first to utilize typology as a therapeutic tool. Differences in typology can be traced back to antiquity, as Heinrich Heine has done when he wrote in *Deutschland:*

> Plato and Aristotle! These are not merely two systems; they are also types of two distinct natures, which from immemorial time, under every sort of cloak, stand more or less inimically opposed. But pre-eminently the whole medieval period was riven by this conflict, persisting even to the present day; moreover, this battle is the most essential content of the history of the Christian Church. Though under different names, always and essentially it is of Plato and Aristotle that we speak. Enthusiastic, mystical, Platonic natures reveal Christian ideas and their corresponding symbols from the bottomless depths of their souls. Practical, ordering, Aristotelian natures build up from these ideas and symbols a solid system, a .dogma and a cult. The Church eventually embraces both natures—one of them sheltering among the clergy, while the other finds refuge in monasticism.[11]

The introverted nature is Platonic in that it is mystical, spiritualized, and perceives in symbolic forms, while the extraverted nature is Aristotelian in that it is practical, a builder of a solid system from the Platonic ideal. Introverts are directed primarily toward an understanding of what they perceive, while extraverts naturally seek means of expression and communication. In introverts, the subjects themselves are at the center of every interest and the importance of the object lies in the way in which it affects the subject. In extraverts the object, the other in and of itself, to a large degree determines the focus of interest. Introverts' interest in self-knowledge prevents them from being overpowered by the influence of their objective surroundings. Extraverts have a tendency to abandon concern for themselves to their interest in others. Hence the concern of introverts is in the direction of development of their individual potential while that of extraverts is more socially oriented. Introverts tend to set themselves and subjective psychic processes above achievement in the public domain, while extraverts seek the recognition of others as a predominant value. If we look at this from an evolutionary perspective we can see the relations between subject and object as a matter of adaptation. Extraverts, seeking fertility, spend and propagate themselves in every way; while introverts, seeking security, defend themselves against external claims and consolidate their positions.

Jung held the opinion that the innate disposition is the determining factor in the type the child will assume, under normal conditions. In an abnormal situation, for example when there is an extreme valuation of one attitude on the part of the mother, the child may be coerced into the opposite type. A neurosis will almost always occur in such a case. Then a cure can only result when what is sought is the development of the attitude that corresponds with the individual's natural way.

It must be made clear from the start that no one is altogether an extravert or altogether an introvert. Each of us utilizes both tendencies, but in different proportions. Those of us who call ourselves sane find ourselves somewhere on the continuum between the two extremes, perhaps closer to one or the other of the poles, perhaps closer to the center. A few are far more introverted, a few far more extraverted, but most of us are somewhere in the middle. We are reasonably balanced and able to function in an introverted way when the situation calls for it and in an extraverted way when the situation calls for that.

Still, almost everyone has a preference. That preference is natural; only when it is extreme and we are totally in the grip of one side or the other do we get into real difficulty. A person who is unable to be flexible enough to move between the two would have trouble coping with the ever-changing demands of life in the world, and would probably end up being seriously disabled psychologically. When people are introverted to the

328

absolute extreme, they may be diagnosed as autistic or schizophrenic, and would live lives that in many respects were detached from everyday reality. People who are extraverted in the extreme may behave in a manic or hysterical manner, or they may suffer from psychosomatic illnesses, all in a pathological effort to control the environment and the people in it. The comment has been made that many of the troubles of Western culture stem from the fact that we in the Western world are, as a whole, far too extraverted. The culture of the East is said to be more introverted, and hence has developed in different ways. However, if one looks closely at current trends in the development of consciousness, one may observe that these stereotypes are beginning to fall apart, if indeed they ever were accurate representations of differences in human consciousness. With the changes in Asia and the third world, it seems clear enough that extraversion is gaining more of a foothold there, while we in the West, who have always trusted external values, are beginning to look more and more within ourselves for the meaning and significance of what we do.

It is still true in some circles, however, that introversion is thought to be rather odd. Children who would rather curl up with a good book or spend long hours at the computer than go out and play ball with their friends are often looked upon as a little disturbed, and their parents urge them to get out and join the other children. Introverted children invariably find themselves at a disadvantage in our educational system also, for their way is to take hold of things slowly, reflect upon them, and to be hesitant to display their knowledge or their understanding, since they are acutely aware of their limitations.

Extraverts, on the other hand, have a relatively easy time of it. They are naturally able to see what the situation demands. Their desire for approval from others leads them to behave in ways that will secure this approval, whether it comes from helping people, or earning more money, or placing themselves in a position where they will win favorable publicity. Indeed, there are plenty of rewards for extraversion as anyone can plainly see. Consider which professions are most highly paid: many are those which please the public. The comic entertainer, for instance, is richly rewarded in contrast to the character actor, who is more interested in portraying his own understanding of a role than he is in what others may think of him. Then there are those who function with an eye toward public acceptance: the advertising account executive, the politician, the businessman, the manufacturer of what the public wants, and the manufacturer's representative who sells it. How much less our society rewards the members of the more introverted professions: writing, teaching, scientific research, and the composition of serious music!

It is to Jung's credit that he pointed out that these two types exist and that he accorded them *equal value.* He recognized that, although individuals tend to live out their conscious lives either on the side of introversion or of extraversion, there is a tendency in the unconscious to express the opposing side. The unconscious, as we have seen in our discussion of dreams, operates in a compensatory fashion toward consciousness; this is also true in terms of the attitudes. A person who is in a group, and consciously concentrating on the needs and experiences of other members of the group, is nonetheless experiencing individual emotional reactions to what is happening—even though these reactions may be unconscious. The unconscious carries the opposing attitude, in this case introversion, which often makes itself heard by coming out with a thoughtless or inappropriate remark, or by interrupting another person in order to put out an idea which has suddenly burst forth with unreasonable urgency.

The attitudes, introversion and extraversion, are broad general categories. Jung further differentiated the typological system into four functions, or *functional types.* The functional types are: *thinking, feeling, sensation,* and *intuition.*These four functions represent ways in which we perceive and process the information that we receive, whether it comes from the external environment or from within ourselves. Altogether, then, Jung distinguished eight *cognitive modes:*[12] *introverted thinking, extraverted thinking, introverted feeling, extraverted feeling, introverted intuition, extraverted intuition, introverted sensation and extraverted sensation.* Before looking at these combinations, it is important to have some idea of the nature of each of the four functions.

Intuition and *sensation* are the pair that perceive information, so they are called the *perceiving functions.* They are sometimes called the "non-rational" functions, because they simply gather information in a non-critical way, that is, without processing it. Intuition and sensation perceive reality quite differently. Intuition is the perceiving function that sees things whole, or in the broad context. It grasps the big picture and also sees the implications. When it looks at something, it imagines where it came from and how it arrived at this place. It looks for antecedents, for history, for broad general trends. It also speculates about the future, asking, where is this going? And perhaps, what is most important, intuition asks, what are the possibilities of what I am seeing?

Sensation is the perceiving function that notices details. It is interested in the precise nature of things. It asks, what does it look like? How is it constructed? How does it function? Sensation likes to take apart things, data, ideas, to see what makes them tick. It will pursue its search for information until it finds every piece and fits it into a picture. Only then, when it is all complete, is it able to see the whole picture, but it has shown infinite patience in the process of gathering. Sensation depends very much upon the senses, which are its primary source of information. This is why it is called "sensation."

Thinking and *feeling* are the functions that process information. To do so, certain judgments must be made, therefore these two are called the *judging functions.* However, they process information in different ways. Having received information through either intuition or sensation, and most likely from both in varying degrees, it is now the role of thinking or feeling to determine a course of action. Thinking proceeds with some deliberation, evaluating the situation and looking at the pros and cons. It applies certain values or standards to determine the general direction in which to move, and sets forth goals or objectives. Thinking then begins to formulate plans that will lead step by step from the data to the desired result. I am not speaking of business here, necessarily, although it may sound as if I am, but the thinking process can apply to any situation, to anyone, at any age. It is a reasoning process, and it aims to carry through from beginning to end.

Feeling is also a judging process, but it operates quite differently from thinking to achieve its ends. Feeling depends upon a personal or subjective value system—there is something conscious or unconscious, against which objective reality is measured. Feeling operates with spontaneity, responding directly to a situation before analyzing its many aspects to determine its worth or usefulness. Feeling says, I like that, or, that will never do. Feeling has a way of sizing up a person or a place without stopping to figure out why it comes to the conclusions it does. It can easily decide whether something is acceptable or not. Feeling is associated with empathy; the person with a strong feeling function can look into the face of another and realize what the other is experiencing—pain or pleasure, hurt or anger. This is different from intuition, which sees things whole and does not have strong subjective responses. People with strong feeling functions base their responses to situations on their sense of what is right or wrong, appropriate or inappropriate, urgent or not urgent, or any other criteria by which something may be judged.

None of these four functions operates by itself. They operate in tandem with the two attitudes, introversion and extraversion. Intuition, sensation, thinking and feeling act differently depending upon whether they are introverted or extraverted. Combining each function with its attitude gives us the eight cognitive modes. Let us look briefly at each one, to get some idea of what they are like.

We return to Plato and Aristotle, whom we have already mentioned. We said that Plato represented the introvert and Aristotle the extravert. Plato's first concern was with his own inner world, the world of ideas, the world of abstractions. His primary way of dealing with the inner world, however, was through intuition. He observed human nature in its totality and dealt with whole concepts in his philosophy. He would make broad general statements first, and only later would he become somewhat more specific. Of course he was not limited to *introverted intuition;* he employed both thinking and feeling to process the information that came from his intuitive perceptions of the inner world. Sensation was the function to which he paid the least attention.

This was exactly the opposite of what we are led to believe was the style of Aristotle. As we have said, it was the external world that captured Aristotle's interest. He became intensely involved in what he could observe with his own eyes and with his other senses. If one reads the descriptions of his researches on animals, for example, on their appearance, their structure, their gait, one is struck by the close attention he paid to every small detail. He was a master at perceiving and collecting information. He tended to report on his information so collected with objectivity, which suggests that he was interested more in what a thing was than in why it was so. It seems clear enough that Aristotle's leading cognitive mode could have been *extraverted sensation*. But again, his repertoire of responses to reality was not limited to this one cognitive mode.

Now let us survey the other six cognitive modes:

Introverted feeling: When feeling is introverted, individuals use their own internal standards to judge people and things. These values may have originated with their parents or with society, but now they are solidly entrenched in the person. Introverted feeling people are not likely to change their beliefs to conform to current trends. They do not readily submit to peer pressure, unless their peers' actions are in accordance with their own beliefs and values. Introverted feeling people generally believe that they understand others very well, yet they often experience themselves as being misunderstood. However, their loyalty and devotion are known and appreciated by those who share their perspectives. The adage "Still waters run deep" applies to many introverted feeling people. Mother Teresa would exemplify this cognitive mode.

Extraverted feeling: When feeling is extraverted, people usually adhere to values that are compatible with those of the society in which they move, or are consonant with traditional standards. Even if their "society" is that of a subculture or anti-social group, they know very well the values of that group. They know the appropriate behavior for a given situation, and if they violate it they do so with a conscious intent. They know exactly what they like and dislike. They are able to express their feelings freely in public. They are seldom tactless. Their extraversion allows them to be amiable and responsive to others, often putting others' needs above their own. They value friends and professional and business relationships. Their empathic understanding of the feelings of others and their ability to make others feel valued and important tend to create harmonious interactions with other people. Often they become public figures. Martin Luther King could be an example.

Introverted thinking: Introverted thinking people tend to begin their problem-solving from a subjective position, starting out with some sort of inner conviction. This cognitive mode is used by people in poetry, philosophy, mathematics, statistics and computer programming, for example. Introverted thinkers prefer to work independently. The home office is just right for them. They prefer communicating by modem, fax or telephone to face-to-face contact. They can be stubborn in pursuit of their own novel views and they are good at making conceptual connections between seemingly disparate ideas. Introverted thinking can be a creative process, as these people are good at revealing similarities between ideas or bringing new ideas into realization. It is difficult to find well-known examples of this type, because they usually manage to keep out of public view, but Emily Dickinson or Annie Dillard would surely qualify.

Extraverted thinking: These people are most concerned with finding meaning in their lives in the world around them.

They believe that they are governed primarily by reason and not by emotions. They strive for perfection, and want to live in accordance with some sort of universal idea or law. They measure good and evil. They judge their own behavior and that of others on the basis of "shoulds" and "oughts" that are connected with their preconceived notions. They regard as moral and right those who share their ideals, and they make great efforts to persuade others to see things as they see them. As they direct their attention to the world around them, they organize facts into meaningful units. Charles Darwin, in his *Origin of Species*, exemplified a creative extraverted thinker in the way he classified and organized natural forms. Bill Clinton could be an example of this cognitive mode as it appears in public life.

Introverted sensation: These people are very much in touch with their own bodily sensations, and they use these for their perceptions, more than their observations of the external world. Introverted sensation, like all introverted functions, connects with an inner world. People who are strong in this cognitive mode are attracted to mythological images and stories, timeless images of the world and of their personal relationships. If an introverted sensing person happens to be an artist, the work tends to be inspired by some archetypal figure, as for example Henry Moore and his impressive sculptures depicting the Great Mother. Or the individual who identifies with the crippled craftsman, Hephaestus, may view life's events from the perspective of a person who is always at a disadvantage as compared to others. When introverted sensation people are not creative or artistic, they may experience some frustration in trying to communicate their eternal images to the temporal world. Some technical skills need to be developed if they are to bring their inward perceptions into concrete reality. Vincent Van Gogh is an example of an introverted sensation type who accomplished this.

Extraverted intuition: People with strong extraverted intuition may have the inclination to envision the future. They are rarely at a loss for speculative or imaginative solutions to problems. As they contemplate what is possible, they see the final state, but not necessarily every step needed to complete their grand design. An individual with strong extraverted intuition is often the idea person who leaves to others the details of bringing the task to fruition. Sometimes these people are entrepreneurs, gaining and losing several fortunes within one lifetime. They are likely to follow their hunches and speculations without necessarily questioning the origins of their intuitions. To extraverted intuitives, routines can be deadly, and existing situations can become prisons once the novelty wears off. They thrive in situations that provide variety and allow for spontaneity. The name that comes to mind is Hillary Rodham Clinton.

In actual practice I have found that very few people fall into the distinct categories that I have outlined. Most rely primarily upon a preferred cognitive mode, and to a lesser extent on a secondary cognitive mode, but the two work well together; thus, an extraverted intuitive-thinking type would be an extravert whose intuition is primary, and is modified by the thinking function. The truest thing that can be said about psychological types is that there are many of them and anyone who concerns himself with typology must ask the question, "Will one type ever truly understand another?"

The question is extremely pertinent in psychotherapy when one is dealing with couples who are experiencing marital difficulties. So often I see couples who seem, potentially, to have everything going for them, and yet they are so cruel and disagreeable with one another that I despair of getting them even to listen to each other, much less take each other's views into consideration. Or, at the opposite pole, there is a degree of indifference that exists which leaves no doubt of the fact that the two individuals may be living in the same world but, from the way they view it, it might as well be two worlds. It becomes necessary, in therapy, to give both people an opportunity to express their feelings and thoughts, their sense perceptions and intuitions, in their own characteristic ways. When both can present their views in all clarity with respect to a certain issue, and it becomes clear that the views are radically different, the introduction of the theory of types may be extremely helpful. No longer can each party make the assumption that there are two ways to look at the problem, "my way and the wrong way." They are forced to recognize that different views are frequently the only possible outcome of different typologies. They may be led to see that if each one can recognize the validity of the views of the other, and see the other's views as necessary to round out a more whole approach to a set of circumstances, the two may begin to consult each other before making a decision rather than fighting about it afterward. Each may learn from the other and so increase his or her own ability to respond in a variety of ways. And, where individuals cannot alter their own make-up, they can at least recognize the right of their partners to have free expression for their own intrinsic natures.

Recently I held premarital counseling interviews with a young couple who had contemplated marriage but couldn't come to a decision. They had been close friends and lovers for a very long time, and were accustomed to spending a good deal of time in one another's apartments without actually living together. Because of frequent disagreements and heated arguments they were hesitant about committing themselves to a permanent arrangement. In the previous session I had remarked that possibly some of the difficulty and uncertainty between them might be due to a difference in typology. At this interview I asked them how they had reacted to the last interview. Had they discussed it? Did they have any questions? The young woman said, "Yes, during the last interview you said something about our being of different types, and I wondered what you meant by this." I gave the couple a very brief overview of the problem of typology, how people basically can be classified into certain psychological types. I did not go into the details of each type specifically, except that I did mention the terms I knew they were familiar with, introversion and extraversion, and I reviewed the distinguishing characteristics of each type.

Then I described the young man. I said, "You are a person, I believe, who is interested in the shape of things, the feel of things, the look of things."

He replied, "Yes, that's very true. I'm a sculptor."

I said, "So what is important to you has a very concrete form, you're interested in touching it; as you touch it, it becomes reality, and that is what has meaning for you. The important thing is not so much how the world views it, but how you view it yourself, what it does for you when you construct your own reality, and perceive it as you are constructing it." I didn't use the term "introverted sensation" but I described the characteristics of this type, and he recognized himself without any hesitancy whatever. He agreed with my estimation of him.

Then I turned to the young woman. "Are you happy in your work?" I asked her.

She replied, "Oh, yes, it's really very satisfying and I enjoy it very much, and I'm good at it, I'm the best one in my office."

I asked her to describe what she did. "My job is writing responses to the letters that come into the office of a well-known politician. He has a whole staff of us who answer these many, many letters that come in with all sorts of questions."

I suggested, "Evidently you like to deal with problem situations, you like to take a letter from people you have never seen, and imagine what they are like, what their issues are, what their difficulties are, what kind of background they have, what kind of help they need, what their self-interest demands, what kind of language will win their support. You are able to project what you write into the future and somehow to realize how what you say will affect that person, how it will determine his or her vote." I described her speculating about this unknown quantity and being able to respond to it from within herself. She is not a trained psychologist, but she has a way of putting together material for which she has only the barest clues and coming out with some kind of statement, and directing this statement to that object, a person whom she has never seen. She is, of course, very clearly the extraverted intuitive type.

When the extraverted intuitive type gets together with the introverted sensation type, there are bound to be some disagreements. I told these two that when people are of opposite types, they are foreordained to see the world differently. I illustrated it with the following example: "Supposing you two were looking at a house." I said to the young woman, "You are at the front of the house, and you're looking into the living-room window." And to the young man, "You're at the side of the house, and you are looking into the same room. Now you're both looking in at the house, which is our symbol for objective reality. Supposing you, young man, described what you see. You might say, 'I see a beautiful room with plush furniture, wood-paneled walls, and all done in blues and green with an expensive oriental rug on the floor.' And you, the young woman, you say, 'No, it's not like that at all! There's a fireplace, and a hearth, a perfect place for parties, and the mood of the place is friendly. It's a really wonderful place, but not at all as you described it.'

"Well," I told the couple, "the two of you could very easily have a big argument about this—'you say it's like this and I say it's like that, and we'll never agree; I must be right and you must be wrong, and there's no reasonable conclusion.' On the other hand, you might say, 'I see this, and this is as much of the room as I can see, but you, with your different viewpoint, with your different orientation, see something completely different. I'll tell you what I see, and you tell me what you see, and we'll try to visualize what each other sees, and between the two of us we'll both have a much richer and deeper concept of this house that symbolizes reality than either one of us could have alone. But in order to have this, we have to trust each other, we have to respect each other, we have to give to each other the recognition that your point of view is every bit as valid as my point of view, that neither one of us has a corner on reality, and that we two can very well live together respecting and affirming each other, even when we disagree.' "

This couple was able to see that there are two possible ways to deal with the problem of typology. One is to allow it to become an insurmountable barrier and to become resigned to the feeling that one type can never understand the other. The second way is to recognize that each type provides the other with insights into the world which that person would never have without that particular partner. Rather than standing up for one's own point of view and tearing down or depreciating the other's, it makes more sense to try to understand the other's point of view, to learn from the other, and in doing so to fill in the gaps in one's own personality. In the case of this particular couple, the sculptor really could not verbalize; he could not see a problem in his mind but had to work it out through his fingers, and he did not concern himself with the implications for the future of what he was doing. The writer, on the other hand, was always busy thinking about what could be and what might be. Very frequently she would get into anxiety states and she would be unable to deal with a present situation because she was paralyzed at the thought of what might come of it. The two could very well learn from each other, and become much more whole as human beings, and, gradually, through their relationship, enlarge their own capacities for functioning.

In my work as a psychotherapist, I rarely have the experience of seeing people who have worked out typological differences naturally, without understanding Jung's typology. When I was teaching a course on Jung, I was particularly pleased with a short paper written by a student of mine. The paper had been touched off by my lecture on Jung's typology, which had been followed by a lively class discussion on whether a person should marry someone of a similar or dissimilar type. I am indebted to this student, who in the remarks below offers insight into the way a relationship of husband and wife of differing types can work out in a life situation. The student wrote:

"My mother and father are very dissimilar, but appear to have a happy and fulfilling marriage relationship. Mother and father have been married forty years, have had hard times and better times financially and healthwise, and have worked hard

all their lives so that their children could all have college edu-
cations—a 'necessity' which was impossible for either of them.
I have never doubted that they loved each other deeply and
they created a home and family atmosphere for their four children which was basically happy and free.

"Mother seems to be typed easily: she's the extraverted-
thinking-sensation type. When she was sixteen years old she
graduated from high school and left her extremely poor farm
home to begin nurse's training. She lived those three years on
the few dollars a month that students were paid to work on
the floors in the hospital. She was then, and is now, a 'doer.'
She's always doing something for someone else, even when
she's dead tired. She has lots of friends, loves her work, reads
little, and is thought by other people to be a 'rock' of common
sense. She's concerned with facts and reality. No matter what
the catastrophe, others can always count on her to be calm
and collected, showing little emotion, and able to grasp the
concrete situation from several perspectives. Though she
seems to have some creative ability, the general trend is towards conventional ways of thinking and acting. She 'needs' to
be liked and accepted by others—and she is, among other reasons because she is *over*-considerate of others. She finds it
extremely difficult to say 'no,' to anyone for anything that they
might ask of her. Mother loves a good time, beautiful things,
and cultural entertainment, though she has no talent herself,
at least no developed talent for any of the finer arts.

"Father, on the other hand, is more difficult to 'typologize,'
but he seems to be more the introverted-feeling-sensation
type. He graduated from eighth grade first in his class; but he
immediately had to find work to help support his family of ten
children. He became a plumber's apprentice by day and would
read books or sing in light opera by night. The first big thing
he ever bought for himself was a piano. Father is shy, so shy
that he panics if he is forced to talk on the phone more than a
minute or two before handing the phone to Mother. He still
loves to read, and he enjoys sharing quiet evenings with his
few but intimate friends. Though he lacks confidence in him-

self, he has been a successful business man operating a conservative but active printing company with his brother. While he shows little emotion on the outside, he's very sensitive and full of feelings on the inside. He's dangerously scrupulous about matters of religion and morality and carefully avoids any critical statements or negative judgments about anybody. He appears to be very accepting of others, but in reality I think is afraid to criticize or judge negatively, rather than positively accepting. Father likes quiet sessions at home with his family and is the beloved 'Grandpapa' of his eleven grandchildren.

"What seems to make this marriage so 'right' for both Mother and Father is that they admire, respect and cultivate the qualities dominant in the other. While Father thinks Mother's constant 'doing' for others is a quality of value and beauty and always tries to be helpful, Mother plans with an eye to making the situation pleasant for him. She encourages him to read and to be with his friends."

It is extremely heartening to see how the human personality and all its relationships may be enhanced with an understanding and respect for variety in typology. Unfortunately the opposite is also true, a great deal of misery can result from a failure to recognize one's own basic typology and to live in accordance with it. The result can be a great deal of neurotic suffering, which can only be set aright by uncovering the natural typology of the individual. Sometimes a dream, stemming from the deeper levels of the psyche, can lead the unhappy individual to an understanding of his real nature, and to the possibilities for realizing it in his life and work, as in the following example.

A young man in his second year of medical school suffered from periodic depressions. Often he would feel that he was exhausting himself in his studies and that it was all pointless; too much energy had to be expended and too little reward was forthcoming. In all, general feelings of apathy characterized the depressions. A little background will set the stage for relating the crucial dream which clarified the central problem for the student. James had wanted to become an architect when he was in high school and during his undergraduate years. He had enjoyed envisioning interesting structures in which form would follow function, and function would be the outcome of a philosophical approach to life. What stopped him in his plan to go into this field was the necessity of learning to handle the graphics—the extreme precision and attention to detail required in drawing went against something in him.

He shifted into a pre-med program, then went to medical school. Here was another way, he thought, of serving people's needs. At first he was delighted with the change, but his original enthusiasm soon began to wear thin as he found himself confronted with difficult course work—physiology and anatomy and much rote memorization. He was required to participate in discussions in seminars demonstrating his knowledge of great masses of detailed subject matter. Studying became more and more difficult for him; it was often boring. Concentration became hard to maintain. He would fall asleep over his books. All of this caused him much anxiety. He came into analysis and, as his life history unraveled and his feelings about what he was doing became clearer, I began to wonder if James might be a *turntype*, that is, someone who by force of circumstances was attempting to function in a type that was not his natural superior function, but rather the inferior function. His current dreams did not throw any light on the question, but he told me that he had had a dream just before he gave up architecture for medicine, and that the dream had haunted him ever since. It remained so vivid that at the retelling he could recapture the feeling tone with all the intensity that there had been when the dream occurred. It was altogether an auditory dream. There was no visual image whatsoever. This is the dream: *I was asleep. I heard vague music off in the background. It sounded like something that could only have been composed by Wagner. There were the deep sonorous tones, with really beautiful crescendos. The music grew louder and louder. At first I was fascinated, then I began to be afraid because the music was uncontrollable. It continued to increase in volume and depth, louder and louder. I got the shiv-*

ers and the shakes and I had to force myself to wake, and I woke
up in a sweat, in a real panic. As I became fully awake the music
stopped, and I gradually began to calm down. As I started to
drift back to sleep the music began again. It was more quiet
now, but slowly swelling and becoming more imposing. As it
grew I felt the great, spacious quality of the Wagnerian opera, the
wild Teutonic strains, at once primitive and utterly refined. As it
grew louder, the anxiety returned, and then the panic, and I
forced myself awake again.

After relating the dream, James commented, "I wish I had
been a musician, for then I could have written down this music."

The dream expressed the fundamental personality type of
the dreamer; he is an introverted intuitive-feeling type. The
dream, coming as it did at a period in his life which offered an
opportunity to change his vocation, sounded a clear call for
the dreamer to pay attention to the "music" which would
evoke his own personal harmony and life-style. In a sense he
had paid attention to the chords from the unconscious; he had
recognized that he needed to work in a profession that would
allow him to use his intuitive ability to grasp the whole of a
situation, along with his capacity for feeling with and responding to another person. He then told me that what he
most wanted to do was to become a psychiatrist. Medicine
was a means to that end, rather than an end in itself. Furthermore, the study of psychiatry, he now felt, would give him
more insight into his own nature—that was the introverted
aspect of his career choice. His remembering this dream at the
particular time that he did was not without its significance. In
order to become a psychiatrist he had first to complete the
general medical training program, which involved mastery
over an infinite amount of detail, and particularly at the
preclinical stage of study. This meant that he had to face his
inferior side and make use of his inferior function constantly
Sensation was his inferior function, and he was forced to con
centrate on it. It involved learning to note carefully anythin
that might possibly have reference to diagnosis or treatmen

He would be helped in this through his next most developed function, thinking, through finding meaning and order in the relations of the details. And lastly, he would have to utilize forced extraversion in making oral reports and in participating in class discussions to establish the level of his knowledge. All this time, then, he had to suppress his introversion, his intuition and his feeling—qualities which would serve him well in the practice of psychiatry, but were not exactly the most helpful assets in medical school.

The kind of music that the dream suggested, the kind of music that beat upon his ear with such strength and fury that it had to be listened to before it overwhelmed, this was music on a grand scale, rooted in myth and mystery. It was music of a transpersonal nature, dealing with the elemental dramas of mankind. If the dreamer could sink into the meaning of the myth which is given voice in the music, he would find a way of experiencing his life as more than a mass of petty details. He would begin to envision the larger plan, the archetypal model of man, into which every detail may be seen to fit, like single notes in the score of a great opera.

The theme of the dream was amplified by exploring the symbolism of the mythology which the dreamer connected with the music, so that it became an ongoing experience for the dreamer. That music was to have its place, always, in the background of his life as an expression of his own myth. Its sonorous tones would provide a welcome accompaniment while he would be living in conscious awareness of the necessity of keeping in touch with his natural typology, even while exercising perforce the less differentiated functions. But the music would become loud and insistent and demanding, nearly deafening, when he would become too one-sided, and not let his real nature have the space it needed to stay alive. The dream of music became for him a sort of inner gyroscope; it would help him to measure his inclinations and it would serve as a guide for him on the path toward individuation.

The concept of the psyche as a self-regulating system is seen more clearly as we come to understand that the least developed cognitive mode, like the dream, can lead the way to the unconscious and, with the cooperation of ego consciousness, can help to bring about a continuously growing synthesis between the conscious mind and the unconscious.

When Jung first wrote about typology, it was long before anyone had heard of psychological tests. Jung's major work in this area was done around 1920, and psychological testing only began in the 1940s with World War II, when it was first developed by the armed forces in order to classify personnel in various ways. While personality testing has become very sophisticated over the years since then and is now a large industry, it is important to remember that in Jung's time the statistical measures that were later used to develop psychological tests or inventories were not available. Whether he would have used them or not if they had been available is another question. Jung was, of course, still writing in the 1940s and 1950s, but by that time his interests had gone far afield from his early work on typology and he did not return to it in his later years. Although the concept of typology as developed by Jung is extremely useful, some of the assumptions he made about typology were the result of pure intuition, and were not called into question or tested empirically for many years.

One of these concepts that I have found reason to question was Jung's bipolar assumption. It is based upon the idea, so frequently alluded to by Jung, that the psyche is composed of pairs of opposites. This notion finds expression in the dualities which fill Jung's writings, such as consciousness/the unconscious, good/evil, light/dark, masculine/feminine, anima/animus, persona/shadow, ego/self, Christ/Antichrist, eternal/temporal, and others. The two elements in the dualities are always posed against each other as opposites and are considered basically to be mutually exclusive. It is not surprising, therefore, that this tendency inherited by Jung from nineteenth-century philosophy would have been applied to his theory of typology.

Indeed, Jung tended to set extraversion against introversion; you favored either one or the other. Thinking and feeling, although both judging functions, were regarded as mutually exclusive. If, as a thinking type, you dealt with issues slowly, methodically and deliberately, you clearly could not be a feeling type, coming to quick spontaneous decisions based upon your feeling values. Similarly with intuition and sensation. If, as an intuitive type, you tended to see things whole and to favor making generalizations, you could not pay great attention to particulars and talk in specific terms rather than in generalities, as a sensation type would. The theory, graphically portrayed, would look like this:

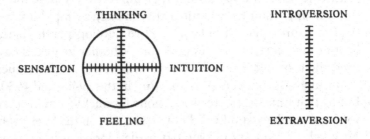

Jung made the further assumption that, if your leading attitude was introverted, your extraversion would, of necessity, be "inferior." And, if your thinking function was "superior," then your feeling function must be "inferior." If your intuition was superior your sensation function must then, *ipso facto*, be inferior. He suggested that efforts should be made to bring the psyche into balance, but of course these efforts would be of little avail because the superior functions were supposed to be conscious and therefore could be utilized easily, but the inferior functions were in the unconscious, and difficult if not impossible to reach. None of this was questioned or put to statistical testing until fairly recently.

In my own training analysis, my analyst thought my leading cognitive mode was introverted thinking. She based this on what she knew about me from her observations in the analytic setting, the only place she ever saw me. If thinking was my superior function, she had to assume that my feeling function was poorly developed. I suffered from this assumption, because it did not seem to me that I lacked capacities for empathy or for spontaneous and valid judgment. I just didn't do much quick judging in her presence, partly out of respect for her wisdom and authority, and partly because I was going through personal difficulties that I managed to cope with by using my intellectual capacities. My own assessment was that I was strong in both feeling and thinking, and it was hard to say which function was stronger. On the other hand, I was not so confident of either my intuition or my sensation function. So there was no place in the schema for me, and I decided that this mutually exclusive bipolar system of identifying typology was not something I would want to use. I put it out of my mind and so it remained until many years later, when personality theorists began to devise and statistically validate objective measures for assessing psychological type.

The first personality inventory based on Jung's theory of typology that I heard about was devised by Joseph Wheelwright, one of those rare Jungian analysts who was an extraverted feeling type. Interested in what was going on in the outer world as well as the inner world, he decided to develop an inventory to determine a person's psychological type without having to depend upon the intuition of the therapist or analyst. He joined forces with a psychologist, Horace Gray, who was well versed in statistical methods, and together they produced the Gray-Wheelwright *Jungian Type Survey (JTS)*. It was arranged according to the schema above, but it gave a score for each of the attitudes and all four of the functions so you could see which were the stronger and which were the weaker attitudes and functions, and what was the difference between them. The *JTS* was composed of a series of questions with two choices for answers, and the person had to select one of the two in every case. My score came out introverted, which I would have expected, but the surprise was that I had scored 11 points on thinking and 10 points on feeling. Statistically speaking, there was no significant difference between them!

In subsequent years, the *Myers-Briggs Type Indicator*

(MBTI), also based on Jung's theory of typology, came into wide usage. It, like the *JTS*, is based on a bipolar design. The *MBTI* is the product of extensive research and has been statistically validated over and over again. It uses the dimensions of Jung's typology to place people into sixteen different categories, each with its specific characteristics. This has proved extremely effective in classifying groups of people according to their typological preferences, as the popularity of the instrument attests. It is used in business and industry throughout the United States and internationally. People who take the inventory are encouraged to identify with the group of people whose test results are similar to their own. At the same time, they learn to respect and value individual differences.

I have long felt that it was necessary to call into question the assumption underlying the bipolar structure of inventories designed to measure the personality characteristics defined by Jung. If two of the "opposites," such as thinking and feeling, were so close in score that the preference would be unclear, was it correct to classify a person as thinking type and to disregard the presence of the feeling function? Or could there be another way of measuring typology that would show that there was little or no real difference between two functions when this was indeed the case? Would it not be useful to measure each cognitive mode separately, instead of forcing the person to choose between one and its opposite? A colleague, Jungian analyst Dr. Mary Loomis, and I tested out the hypothesis that, if the bipolar assumption were correct, it would make no difference whether the inventory measured the cognitive modes in a forced choice context or independently. Our research showed that there is a significant difference in the personality profile depending on whether the cognitive modes are measured on a bipolar scale or independently. Furthermore, when the cognitive modes are measured independently of each other, once the leading cognitive mode is determined by the highest score, any of the other seven can be next highest and any one can score lowest.

Loomis and I developed the *Singer-Loomis Inventory of*

Personality (SLIP), which was based on a scale that measured each cognitive mode separately. This inventory provides an individual profile for each person, with separate scores for each of the eight cognitive modes. It enables people to rank their cognitive modes in the order of preference, from the highest to the lowest. It is also able to measure changes over time in each of the cognitive modes. This is especially useful in evaluating growth and development.

Why should we be interested in objective tests like these in connection with psychotherapy or analysis? Isn't it enough that therapists make evaluations on the basis of their experience and training? There has long been a debate over the relative merits of clinical judgment versus objective tests and statistical measurements. As a therapist and an analyst I believe that I should have the clinical judgment to determine a person's typology. However, my judgment is not infallible. Furthermore, if I disagree with the patient's self-assessment, it becomes a struggle over who is right and who is wrong. An objective test responds to the patient's own answers to the standardized questions. It is not a matter of personal opinion. The results can be put on the table for both analyst and analysand to look at and discuss. Another virtue of objective tests is that they provide a check on the clinical judgment. If a test accords with the therapist's judgment, the person will be more likely to accept it. If not, then the therapist has to ask herself if there might not be something in the person's typology that she had missed seeing. There is no reason to have to choose between clinical judgment and an objective test. Both are useful, and they are complementary methods of assessment.

Most people, as they learn about the various cognitive modes, will identify more than one as being an aspect of their personality. This is not surprising, since all of us have at our disposal all eight of the cognitive modes. I like to think of them as eight colors on an artist's palette. If every artist would begin with the same eight colors and paint according to his or her own particular style, some would use more of one color, some of another. They would mix them differently. Some

would use many of the colors and some only a few. Each artist's painting would be different, yet without too much difficulty one could identify the characteristics of the artists by
their paintings. In like manner, it seems to me, we all combine
the eight cognitive modes in our behavioral repertoire, yet
each of us does it in a characteristic way. Typology has its
ingredients, but each of us is different in the way we use them.

I have come to the conclusion that it is important to avoid
getting caught on the dilemma of whether the opposites are
really opposite. Jung left that question aside quite early in his
career. In his later work he was devoted to the possibility of
bringing together the opposites, to finding the harmony both
within and without that is consonant with seeing the person
as a whole, instead of as a collection of parts and pieces. The
process of analysis, almost by definition, is a taking apart and
looking at the pieces. But this must be done with the principle
in mind that the pieces, when examined separately, are like an
automobile when it is taken apart for repair. You might be
able to find out what is wrong with it, but that doesn't solve
the problem. Only when it is put back together again is it a
whole. It is more than the collection of its parts. It can do
what the parts separately cannot do. It runs.

In the framework of wholeness there is a harmony in
which everything is included. It is unconscious or undifferentiated at first. But with the beginning of consciousness comes
differentiation, first into opposites—myself and other—and
then fragmentation into the many. Typology began with the
separation into opposites—introversion and extraversion—
then it was broken down further into the functions which,
however, maintained their positions in opposition to each
other. But, with further differentiation, complexity set in and
it was no longer possible merely to think in terms of opposites
—there are all sorts of combinations. It is this that makes each
person unique.

Typology can be seen also as a spiritual practice. There is a
time for opposition that breeds antagonism, and there is a
time for embracing that is healing. Transcending the opposites

is the goal. Transcendence goes beyond categories of thought. Dualities exist only in the practical world of substance.

There is a quiet pool in which the moon is seen whole. When a stone is thrown into it, the image fragments. This is what consciousness does. The danger in typology is that, when we focus on the fragments, we tend to lose sight of the whole.

12

Psyche in the World

. . .

IN ANALYSIS sometimes there comes a precious moment when the analysand feels the power of a strong insight newly received and thanks the analyst most profusely for the gift. When this occurs in my practice I say to the analysand, "Please remember that what happens in this room is not nearly so important as what happens when you walk out of here. That is what really counts." All the self-examination that we do is valuable only as an introduction to our real selves as we live in the world. I firmly believe that none of us can be, or should be, so self-involved that the external world pales in importance in comparison with the inner world.

Yet depth psychology, which includes Jungian analysis, psychoanalysis and all their derivations, has been criticized as being solipsistic—and not without reason. Solipsism is nicely defined by Louis A. Sass in his book *The Paradoxes of Delusion* as "the doctrine in which the whole of reality, including the external world and other persons, is but a representation appearing to a single, individual self." Sass quotes Wittgenstein as saying that solipsism is an example of a philosophical disease born not of ignorance or carelessness but of abstraction, self-consciousness and disengagement from practical and social activity. This is a serious charge. For most people, most of the time, this is a distinctly undesirable habit of thought. But for others the kind of isolation that provokes this description may be as necessary for the psyche in deep distress as is an intensive care unit for a physical body in a life-threatening situation. During my own analytical training I lived in Zurich for four years without holding a job or having any other major responsibilities. I was intensely focused on my own analysis and on courses at the Jung Institute that only encouraged intense introversion. For me it was necessary to "disengage from practical and social activity" because at that time these had acquired such a negative tone for me and had been so firmly established in my own mind that there was little hope for a compromise between analysis and a "normal life." It was necessary for me to establish entirely different patterns of habit and direction if I was to undergo the inner transformation that would free me to live a more balanced and productive life.

I happened to be among the few fortunate people who could afford the luxury of taking a psychological "vacation" from the everyday world for a time and enter into unexplored realms of the psyche's activity. This luxury was bought at the price of selling my home and other assets to raise the necessary funds for an extended stay in Zurich. I believe that I was temperamentally suited for this particular path, having been deeply interested in the twists and turns of the psyche's labyrinthine ways since my early teens, but this extremely inward path is not something I would recommend for everyone. It is very strong medicine. In my own practice I usually encourage analysands to try to keep a balance between their inner processes and their lives in the world. I have come to be acutely aware that it is necessary for a person to have a relationship with the world that is compatible with the relationship between the different aspects of the individual psyche. I cannot forget the words of I Corinthians 13:2: "And though I have the gift of prophecy, and understand all mysteries, and all knowledge . . . and have not love—I am nothing."

There is some valid basis for the criticism that has been leveled against the isolation and self-absorption that intensive psychotherapy sometimes fosters. James Hillman, a Jungian analyst who has given up, or retired from, the practice of Jungian analysis, puts it succinctly in the title of his book, *We've Had a Hundred Years of Psychotherapy and the World's Getting Worse.* While I can appreciate his frustration, I must counter with the remark that this is not necessarily indicative of a cause-and-effect relationship; after all, we've had more than a hundred years of Western medicine, and the mortality rate in our population is still one hundred percent. And I am not so sure, in response to Hillman, that the world is getting worse. After all, the human race has come to its present condition as a result of its behavior over many thousands of years, and one hundred years is scarcely enough to cure its ills.

Psychotherapy, despite the relatively short period it has been on the scene and despite its limitations, has played an important role in some remarkable changes in human behavior, and its potential for the next century is most promising. However, before this promise can be fulfilled, the means for delivering psychotherapy will have to be adapted to meet the social, economic and political realities of the next decades.

The first century of depth psychology, of Jung, Freud and their followers, was a time in which it was seen as necessary for purposes of psychological health to disengage from the collective. Depth psychology was developing much as an individual person develops during the first half of life. Then the ego, or sense of identity, is just taking form and has to find its stance independent of what surrounds it. So depth psychology has had to make its way, to become known, and to earn respect as a special way of working with the psyche. Perhaps the next century will see a change similar to that which typically occurs during the second half of an individual's life when the person's values have become broader, when it is not enough for a person to do what is necessary for the individual but which takes into consideration the context in which the individual lives. It is not only the analytic way that must survive then, but what we have learned from analysis can be seen as a source of strength, insight and wisdom that can be injected into society to do its work. In the process analysis may even lose its own identity as a form of psychotherapy, but if the principles it embodies can continue to grow, develop and be fruitful, there is no real loss.

It is not only individuals who are today depressed, unfulfilled, or living without purpose or direction; much of this mood is abroad in the world. Unless consciousness changes, the world cannot change. For the most part, the uses of depth psychotherapy have been limited to a small proportion of the population, people with the economic means, the time, the temperament and the inclination to commit to a long-term project which temporarily may have an emotionally unsettling effect on them. For those who have undergone the process and stayed with it until some salutary results have been achieved, it has had a seminal effect. Most of these individuals have become empowered to live in the world in a different way than before—with greater insight, understanding and compassion for others, and with a perspective on life that goes beyond the satisfaction of their individual needs and desires. By and large, they are people who make valuable contributions to society. Their times of introspection and inner work have helped and continue to help make it possible for them to participate more fully, not less, in the affairs of the world. Change must begin with the individual, but can we any longer afford to heal the ills of the world person by person?

The individuation process, as Jung described it, was the product of a particular time in the history of the analytic process. Jung first defined individuation in 1913, in the initial version of his book on psychological types. He described individuation as "a person's becoming himself, whole, indivisible and distinct from other people or from collective psychology (although also in relation to these)."[1] Jung emphasized the attributes of the process as follows: "(1) the goal of the process is the development of the personality; (2) it presupposes and includes collective relationships, i.e., it does not occur in a state of isolation; (3) individuation involves a degree of opposition to social norms which have no absolute validity: The more a man's life is shaped by the collective norm, the greater is his individual immorality."[2]

This third point is just the issue with the world that analytical psychology must face today. Jung distrusted "the collective." He regarded collective norms and collective morality as contrary to the interests of the soul or psyche and believed that it was necessary in the process of psychological development for the individual to stand against "the collective." Writing just before the onset of World War I, with Switzerland as a neutral country keeping silent while preparations were being made on all sides for the imminent conflict, one could imagine his predicament. In those times, and for many years thereafter, most people—unless they were highly placed in official circles or else working people who were primarily concerned with the burdens of keeping bread on the table and caring for their families—were members of the collective, and were, as we would say today, "politically correct." They spoke in terms that were agreeable to the ruling classes, and they did not try to overthrow governments. So to advocate standing against the collective was to require a show of courage and conviction. One would have to be singularly devoted to one's own path to go against the conventional view.

During Jung's lifetime, analytical psychology was highly suspicious of all kinds of groups. The idea that groups of people reduced everyone down to the lowest common denominator prevailed in Jungian circles. Instead of submitting to the collective, psychological work was to be done in the privileged container of the consulting room between therapist and patient in strict confidentiality. There was no place in Jung's psychology for marital counseling, family counseling or group therapy. It was not until the 1970s that there could even be a discussion of working on dreams in a group at the Jung Institute in Zurich. This attitude has changed over the years in response to the changing spirit of the times. I know, because I was the first Jungian analyst to give a course on working with dreams in groups there. When I proposed the course a decade or more after Jung's death, there was a heated debate in the

Curatorium (the governing body) as to whether this should be permitted. The "experiment" was tried, with some reluctance on the part of the faculty, but met with an enthusiastic response from the students.

Over the past several decades people have become increasingly liberated from the dictates of the collective. To begin with, the collective no longer exists in the sense of the word as Jung used it. Most countries in the Western world today, and the United States perhaps more than others, have undergone population explosions due as much to immigration as to an increase in births. The result has been a burgeoning diversity in the population with respect to ethnicity, religion, race, sexual orientation, education and socioeconomic status. In the sixties, when we used to speak of "the counterculture," the image of radical young people who used psychedelics, lived in communes and never trusted anyone over thirty was conjured up. Today we can hardly speak of a counterculture, for our culture is so fragmented now that the majority of the people belong to the "minorities." And even among the so-called majority there are many political factions, each with enough power to challenge other political factions. The point of this is that there no longer exists anything like what Jung thought of as the collective. Consequently, there no longer exists a counterculture. We are all here together, we members of the motley crew of this spaceship Earth.

A major task of government, including that of the United States, in this last decade of the century seems to be to provide certain umbrella protections and services for its people. This sort of government is subject to and influenced by so many different interest groups, with all the checks and balances that implies, that it cannot be monolithic. Government today is and must be flexible and responsive to its people.

One imperative in the cultivation of this wide area is in the field of health care. The United States is the latest among the developed countries of the Western world to introduce a system which would guarantee basic health care to all its citizens. Mental health care must surely be included as a part of this program. This brings up the question, how is "mental health care" to be defined? Workers in the mental health field know that, in a program designed to provide universal health coverage, choices will have to be made as to who receives care and what kind. Surely the most seriously disturbed patients, people who would endanger themselves or others, will be the first to be included in the plan, followed by those who absolutely cannot manage to live outside of a protected environment. Next will come those whose functioning is sufficiently impaired to make it difficult for them to work or to attend school or to live with others or independently. Mental illness based on organicity and the treatment of addictions will surely be included. Treatment of the criminally insane must be a part of the package of covered services.

Near the end of the list will be short-term outpatient psychotherapy. This suggests that treatment will be available mostly to solve immediate problems or crisis situations. All mental health services will be "managed," that is, they will be subject to the approval of officials who have never seen the patient and whose decisions are largely based on protocols and economic considerations. Under such a program many people will receive affordable care that would not otherwise be available to them. But there will remain many people whose needs do not fall within the scope of the basic health care that is proposed or provided.

Long-term depth psychotherapy or analysis for people who are not seriously disturbed or dysfunctional may very well be considered to be outside the limits of the health care system. Analytic work does not focus primarily on immediate problems, but seeks to use the presenting symptoms as keys to understanding whole persons in the fullness of their beings. It does not simply try to remove or cover up the symptoms, but rather to discover their meaning and their message. The analytic process does not attempt to restore the individual to the former state that existed before the circumstance or condition that brought about the request for therapy. Rather, it seeks a more radical re-formation of the personality by integrating the different aspects of the psyche into a more harmonious whole. Body, mind and spirit are the realm of the analytic process. As with the remodeling of a building, it is usually necessary to go through a "demolition" phase before progress can be seen. In depth psychotherapy things may appear to get worse before they get better. The goal is not merely a restoration to "health," but a sense of wellness that surpasses anything that existed in this individual before. This comes about as the result of what Jung called a new *Weltanschauung* or "world view," which develops in the course of the analytic process.

The question must surely arise as to whether this kind of long-term depth psychotherapy, including analysis, can be considered "basic health care." How does a health care system define those of us who give this kind of care? How do we define ourselves? At this writing, it is not yet clear what the health care system will cover finally in the area of mental health but the likelihood is that other types of treatment will be given priority over depth psychology for some time to come. The practice of Jung's psychology may have to redefine itself if it is to survive in this climate.

Jung's psychology, and all psychology that seeks to probe the depth and meaning of human experience, make a contribution not only to the well-being of individuals, but to how they view the world and how they will influence it. There will always be those who seek the level of understanding toward which depth psychology strives. It has been said that this kind of work is elitist, available only to those who have the financial and educational resources to be able to enter fully into it. This is only partly true. Many people have sacrificed time and money and other activities they valued, to be able to do analytic work even if they did not have health care coverage for this. Yet many who have not been able to do this have an inner commitment to follow the path that leads toward greater consciousness in whatever way is possible for them.

I remember hearing my colleague Clarissa Pinkola Estés, author of *Women Who Run With the Wolves*, saying that she is a confirmed storyteller who supports her habit by doing Jungian analysis for a living. Perhaps some of us Jungian analysts will have to turn the tables and support our habit of practicing analysis with doing some other types of psychotherapy for a living. We can add many therapeutic skills to our repertoire that will serve purposes similar to the classical analysis, but will be more accessible to more people. I have discovered a few ways to do this over the years, and I would not be surprised to learn that many of my colleagues have done similar kinds of work, using the insights they have gleaned from analytic practice and applying them in other contexts. Often the adage "Necessity is the mother of invention" proves its worth.

My first opportunity to utilize this principle came about when I returned to Chicago from Zurich after finishing my analytic training. Since it would take time to build an analytic practice in a community where there had been no Jungian analyst before, it was necessary for me to take a paying job. The only position I could find that even remotely matched my qualifications was in a school for emotionally disturbed preschool children. To be honest, the job description called for a social worker, but I persuaded the director to change the title to psychologist. I imagined I would be doing in-depth work individually with the parents but this proved to be far from the case. I was told in no uncertain terms that this was a "family agency," and I would be obliged to work with the entire family, although I might later see one or another member of the family individually if that seemed appropriate. Having been trained to help the individual differentiate from the matrix of home and family and find his or her unique path, it went against everything I knew to see people in the context in which they lived. I expected people to come to my office, one at a time, and engage in dialogue with me. Can you imagine my feeling when I was told that I had to make a home visit on each case, spending time with the whole family, observing their interactions? Remember, this occurred in 1965, when family therapy was very new and few people had even heard of it. Because it was for me a matter of survival, I made that first home visit. What happened totally amazed me! Even if I had not spoken a word, to see before me the home with its decor that expressed the taste and interests of those who lived in it, the way the children's toys were scattered about, showing how strict or permissive the household was, the way the parents spoke to their children and vice versa, the relationship between the husband and the wife, the effort to make a good impression upon me or the lack of it, the ability on the part of everyone to deal with the unexpected—all this was sending messages to me that I never in a thousand years would have perceived from the analyst's chair in my office. I began to see that there were other ways. And still, with this first family, I discovered in the father a deep desire to understand his own nature, that included and went beyond his interest in developing a more harmonious relationship within the family. So, when I did have occasion later to work individually with the father, our interaction had more of the character of an analytic session. This did not interfere with my work with the mother or with the identified patient, who was the child in the school. I also learned there to do child therapy using small dolls and other figures to help children dramatize their own experiences with significant others in their lives. One result of this was that I later studied family therapy and learned how to use its methods to enhance the understanding I had of the structure of the psyche. Today, I have more choices as to how I will work with a person or family than I would have had otherwise.

Over the years my therapeutic tools have grown more numerous and varied as I have taught and given workshops in humanistic and transpersonal psychology using many approaches and techniques applicable to individuals and groups. I have found that certain principles learned from Jung's psychology are applicable to other methods of psychological work. I will mention just a few of these. The first principle is the importance of insight into the *projection* mechanism, whereby we project aspects of our own unconscious qualities onto others and behave as if the others who receive the projection are really what we imagine them to be. Analysis gives us the tools to recognize those projected aspects of ourselves and to reclaim them. This is particularly helpful, for example, for people who see themselves as being driven by someone to do something. This makes them feel helpless. In reality they drive themselves, but don't see it until they recognize that the slave driver is not outside so much as within, where it is subject to being transformed. Another principle has to do with taking personal responsibility—not for everything that happens to us, surely, but for the way we respond to events and circumstances. A third principle is the necessity of becoming aware of how we may be facilitating another person's negative behavior without realizing it. This is a principle that has been emphasized in the vast literature on co-dependence. The corollary to this, of course, is, how can we use consciousness to facilitate another person's *positive* behavior?

Still another principle has to do with avoiding the "victim" or scapegoat role. One thing I learned to accept early in my analysis is that the person who gets abused is the one who allows herself to be abused. This may seem like an overstatement, but it is probably true more often than not. And the last principle that I will note here, although there are many others that could be included, is the importance of ceasing to be reactive to external situations and to take instead a pro-active role in which the authentic person that you are is taking charge of your actions.

Let me cite an example of how some of these principles can be taken into the world and utilized outside of the analytic setting. Janet, an analysand of mine, had gone through certain experiences in her childhood and early adolescence that led her to feel victimized. These had been a source of ongoing pain for her. Being pro-active, she decided to do some research on how other women, similarly abused, had managed to recover sufficiently to lead successful and productive lives despite their early traumatic experiences. She assembled a small group of women and met weekly with them in a setting where they could tell their stories and share with one another their experiences of coping with their distress. In the course of these meetings the women developed a practical program for overcoming the "victim mentality." Janet then went on to teach the tested methods to other women.

Our society is replete with opportunities for the insights gained from depth psychology to be applied to social problems. The challenge to depth psychology is to find more ways to widen the area of its influence so that it permeates not only the field of health care, but also education, family life, the workplace, the economy, foreign policy and the ecology of nations. All these areas have a stake in achieving productive change, inasmuch as all are interrelated and interdependent parts of a whole. This is a large order. Long-term goals are easy to put aside when there are so many urgent needs crying for attention. To be sure, society needs people to put out the fires, but it also needs people to scan the entire terrain and see where the trouble spots are and how each one is related to or dependent upon another. The question that properly comes up next is, where do we find the resources to bring about the hoped-for change in consciousness? Who are the people who can help?

Let me suggest that we do not first call upon the people who have been the driving forces in the contemporary culture. We have already heard the voices of the arbiters of cultural consciousness. What we have heard far less are the voices of what we could call the cultural unconscious—or the less vocal parts of society. These people watch and listen, they observe and reflect. They know far more than most people give them credit for. It is time to ask them what they see, what they need and what they can contribute. We might begin by asking the ordinary person who is just struggling to get along in the world.

Immediately after the earthquake that rocked Los Angeles in January 1994, well-meaning social agencies prepared large buildings, schools, armories and the like to house the people who had been left homeless when the quake suddenly destroyed their homes at four thirty-one one Monday morning. Most of these people refused to go into the strong buildings, but insisted on sleeping out in the open. They were afraid that the buildings would collapse on them, and no amount of reasoning could reassure them otherwise. The relief workers listened to the people who knew what they needed, and set up canvas tents where they could feel safe in the open air with the ground underneath them and only a canvas shell between themselves and the sky. We learned from them that it is not useful to ignore the sensitivities of people.

Another resource is the elders of the community. Most younger people do not realize that elders, those who have cultivated their inner lives, are different from younger people in that they have less invested in their personal concerns. Having experienced losses of every kind in their lives, they realize that personally they have not much more left to lose and that the little that they have will also be gone before too long. They are interested not in sowing for a future harvest for themselves, but in making the most of what remains to them in time, in energy, in wisdom. They have seen eras of good fortune and eras of ill fortune come and go, and they know that everything changes, so they are not easily upset by the events of the moment. They may sometimes counsel just to wait, it will be different soon. They have watched history unfold, and they can foretell with uncanny sureness when the lesson we have not learned from history will present itself again in a slightly different form. The elders who have continued to enjoy a lively interest in the world around them have much to teach younger people.

Another resource: indigenous peoples. Almost everywhere in the days before colonial powers set forth into so-called primitive lands, including the land that has come to be the United States, people accepted life and death and the sometime violence of nature as quite natural. They did not attempt to exert control over nature. They lived as an integral part of their environment, drawing what they needed from it and no more, without trying to store up life's bounty for the future. Lands were not privately owned. The indigenous people did not exploit or deplete the land, but developed a reciprocal relationship with the environment. They taught their children what they needed to know to live in their world. They perceived the world as a spiritual existence embodied in the garments of nature—every tree and stone contained a spirit that was akin to the divine spirit. And so, guided by the spirit within, which we might call the voice of the unconscious, they trusted the ways of the world and shared its bounty with one another. Their respect has been for their ancestors and their concern is for the generations that will follow them. We can learn from these people, not by imitating their superficial representations, but by allowing them to be heard and listening closely to them while they tell us what they know.

Another resource is the immigrants who have recently arrived. Americans tend to forget that we are, by and large, the children and grandchildren of immigrants—the people who built this country with their own sweat and aspiration. A small boy in school was told by his teacher, "Now we are going to study native Americans." "Native Americans?" he cried out with some indignation. "Aren't I a native American? I was born here!" Yes, almost all natives of our land are the sons and daughters of those who came here as strangers. And others continue to come to our shores. It is the great variety of languages and customs and information that the strangers have brought that has grown into the eclectic mix of people we call Americans. Each ancestral tradition has taught its children something which they have carried to their new homeland. These are treasures and should be so regarded. Their very multiplicity underscores the psychological reality that we can and must retain our unique characteristics while blending harmoniously with the whole society.

Then there are the wisdom teachers, for example, the Tibetan masters. Forced out of their own country where they were isolated from the rest of the world, they fled, carrying with them the knowledge of things mysterious that are unknown here. Had it not been for their uprooting and their exile, we would not have access to their traditions concerning life and death, birth and rebirth. They give freely of their wisdom to those who will listen. There is much to be learned from these people, but even a little can be surprisingly enriching. The Dalai Lama once said, "My religion is very simple. Kindness." What a profound teaching!

The gay and lesbian community is another resource from which we can learn. I have asked myself, why is it that there are so many creative people in the arts among these men and women, far disproportionate to their numbers? My speculation has suggested at least two possible reasons. These are people who have distanced themselves from the straight and unyielding mores of a more conservative society, with all its sexual constraints and fears, to experience the reality of their own natures. In order to do this, they have had to defy convention. Their willingness to stand against the prejudices of people with closed minds was then extended beyond the realm of sexual preferences to preferences in the arts and in other areas where individuality was valued above conformity. Another contributing factor may be that many gay and lesbian people do not have families to support, and consequently they may have more freedom to pursue the careers and avocations of their choice. They can teach us much about creativity and its costs. Politically, these people have called our attention to the important principle of equal rights for all, something everyone professes to believe in but tends to forget from time to time. They can also teach us much about love and loss and pain, and how members of a community can support one another in the most difficult of times.

We might listen, too, to the many families who are deserting the cities with all their pressures and choosing life in small towns or rural settings. These are people who want to live in more natural surroundings. What are they seeking that life in our high-powered cities no longer offers them? What are they learning and what can they teach the rest of us?

Big businesses that want to improve their functioning are listening more and more to people in the rank and file of their organizations. It is the people whose hands are on the machinery who understand what is going on, what needs to be done to improve things, and how to go about making changes. "Management by walking around" is a good principle, because how can you know what to do unless you know what is being done? The efficiency of the hierarchical structures that characterized business organizations in the past is being seriously questioned now. Businesses are asking, how can we make the most of our human resources? Consultants with an understanding of depth psychology are being called in to "diagnose" the ills of the business and to help in developing "treatment plans."

There is one more frontier I want to mention in which the insights of psychology have been moving out of the consulting room and into the world. This is the area of illness and health. It is generally accepted today that almost all physical or organic diseases have psychological components. Physical and psychological problems are not separate entities, but are closely interrelated, for our emotional state affects the body and vice versa. Each person is a complex of body, mind and spirit (though the third aspect is not yet so widely recognized as a universal aspect of the human condition). The psyche, which is composed of mind and spirit, exerts a profound influence on the course of physical illness. We can will ourselves to die or we can surprise our doctors by the degree to which our own psychological practices can bring about "spontaneous" self-healing. This potential has been well known for many centuries by those engaged in healing professions. It has only been since the so-called scientific revolution—which began after the schism between faith and reason brought about by the seventeenth-century Enlightenment—that medical science turned away from the less rational means of healing and sought cures based on scientific methods of research and treatment. This development resulted in tremendous advances in knowledge about the body and in the technology and techniques of medical treatment. However, for quite some time, modern medicine's obsession with the treatment of the disease left little time or energy for attention to the treatment of the patient. The patient, too often, was "the appendicitis in

Room 304." Meanwhile, the care of the person—by which I
mean the suffering human soul—was left to those who minis-
tered specifically to the individual's own experience of disease, among them the priest, minister, rabbi, shaman, medicine man, herb doctor, faith healer and psychotherapist.
These were people skilled in the mysterious arts that have to
do with the invisible aspects of the human being as they interact with the invisible in the world: love and pain, purpose and
meaning—the list could go on and on.

More recently, members of the medical profession have
come to realize the importance of attending to these less tangible aspects of sickness and health. It is widely recognized in
medical circles now that the patient's attitude has much to do
with the progress of the illness and the efficacy of the treatment. Clergy do pastoral counseling and are members of the
hospital staff. Psychologists work in close cooperation with
physicians. Biological medicine has made great advances in
the use of psychoactive drugs. Most psychiatrists and other
physicians recognize that these medications, while often helpful in themselves, can serve mental patients more effectively
when combined with psychotherapy that seeks to support the
emotional experience of the patient, to uncover the root
causes of the distress and to help the individual come to terms
with these. On the other hand, today's psychologists recognize
the value of psychoactive medications in helping some patients become more accessible to psychotherapy than they
would be without them.

Prevention of illness and the quest for optimal wellness (or
peak performance) are related areas in which some of Jung's
insights can be helpful. Jung's psychology is, above all, optimistic. It is not so much oriented backward toward the cause
of dysfunction as it is oriented forward, toward what the
psyche can be when it is fully developed. It asks questions like,
Who am I? What am I meant to be? What is my potential? The
implication is that all that we can be is already present in us *in
potentia*, waiting to be awakened, like Sleeping Beauty awaiting her prince. It is the task of those who have been working

in the field of developing a wider consciousness to point out the path through the maze of brambles that is life; but it is the individual who must walk that path with courage, taking responsibility for his or her own journey. So the pursuit of wellness requires both knowledge and practice. The knowledge is both within the psyche in terms of a sense of what is right for us as individuals, and out in the world where we can learn from the experience of others. The practice lies in right living, in nutrition and exercise and self-understanding and a refusal to pursue a path that leads away from wholeness. For wholeness, health and healing all come from the same root—and essentially they are all one.

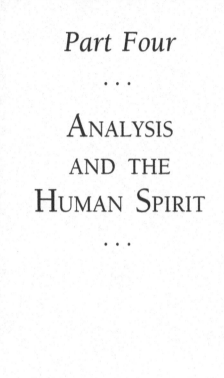

Part Four

. . .

ANALYSIS
AND THE
HUMAN SPIRIT

. . .

13

Religion, and Other Approaches to the Unknowable

. . .

WHEN THE EASY CONCEPT fails—that we are nothing but our own conscious personality—we are forced to face the proposition that "individual consciousness is based on and surrounded by an indefinitely extended unconscious psyche."[1] Jung's psychology, as we have seen, is based on the need he perceived to explore these indefinite extensities of the psyche, and to penetrate them—which he did, perhaps more deeply than any other psychologist or psychotherapist had done before. Since he regarded the unconscious as far more than a bundle of instincts plus the residues of individual consciousness, he could not imagine the unconscious as bound up in any single individual. As a psychotherapist he did not assign one unconscious to his patient and another to himself, with the possibility of connecting them through a chain of associations or bridging them by the transference. Rather, he saw that each person's consciousness emerges like an island from the great sea in which all find their base, with the rim of wet sand encircling each island corresponding to the "personal unconscious." But it is the collective unconscious—that sea—that is the birthplace of all consciousness, and from there the old ideas arise anew, and their connections with contemporary situations are initiated.

Realizations such as these were growing in Jung in the last years of his close association with Freud, and especially while he was pursuing his study of Miss Miller's fantasies, which he was to publish in his book *The Psychology of the Unconscious.*[2] In working on the amplification of these fantasies, Jung discovered their rootedness in non-personal experience. The themes of the fantasies paralleled themes of creation myths which Jung discovered through his research as having been manifested in various ancient civilizations in widely separated parts of the world. Everywhere people have yearned to know of their own psychic beginnings; and they have fashioned myths and legends, songs and rituals, to express their awareness of their individual littleness in a world of unimaginable magnitude. The study of comparative religion, legend and folklore, led Jung to reconsider the events of his own childhood and youth. They all had seemed so personal to him at the time, but now proved to be only ingenious new scenarios based on ageless archetypal plots.

While Jung was in his residency at Burghölzli at the turn of the century, his chief, the disciplined and demanding Professor Bleuler, had required that he concentrate on the psychiatric treatment of mental patients and on conducting the Word Association studies. During Jung's association with Freud, his desire to carry the new psychoanalytic theory into his own practice and research in order to validate it empirically took up most of his attention and thereby imposed limitations on his personal search. Whatever feelings Jung may have had during these years (1900–13) about the necessity of going beyond the province of the methodical researcher and theoretician, his responsibilities and loyalties held him in check. He directed his conscious efforts toward widening his experience and knowledge in areas to which he had committed himself both publicly and in the intimate circles of his professional associates.

The unconscious, however, did not fail to make its autonomous tendencies known to Jung whenever he turned his attention to it. I do not mean that he recognized the unconscious only in his patients, or in the clinical reports of others. The primary opening to the unconscious was through the aperture of his own consciousness, through his dreams and visions and the products of his imagination. Nevertheless, until his open break with Freud in 1913, Jung was firmly based in consciousness and, I believe, basically committed to the primary therapeutic goal of the growth and development of the ego personality. There were other voices calling him, and he listened, but he did not address himself fully to the confrontation with the unconscious until after he realized that he could never be as sure as he thought Freud was, that truth was truth, or that scientific investigation would sooner or later be able to expose the mysteries of the psyche.

After his separation from Freud and his withdrawal from the psychoanalytic circle, Jung found himself isolated from most of his former colleagues. He had no interest in justifying his position or winning adherents to it. The years from 1913 to 1917 were for Jung a period of inclining his ear toward his inner voices and allowing them opportunity for full expression. He voluntarily entered into the dimension of the nonrational, submitting himself to emotions over which he had little control. In the grip of strong affect, he suffered the experience of observing the contents of the unconscious as they formed themselves into images and as they became personified. Some of the figures that arose before him in his vision or imagination had their source in the history of ancient civilizations, some in myth and legend, some in epic poetry, and some in the Bible. Each being had its own symbolic import: for example, Salome appeared as the anima figure who was "blind because she does not see the meaning of things," and Elijah, "the figure of the wise old prophet represents the factor

of intelligence and knowledge."[3] Characters flooded into
awareness, often bringing confusion more than clarity.

A turning point came with the appearance of the figure
who was to become Jung's *psychagogue*, the instructor of his
soul in matters of the unconscious. The opening to the unconscious which preceded the appearance of the Philemon figure
came in a dream which he described as an epiphany:

> There was a blue sky, like the sea, covered not by clouds but
> by flat brown clods of earth. It looked as if the clods were
> breaking apart and the blue water of the sea were becoming
> visible between them. But the water was the blue sky. Sud-
> denly there appeared from the right a winged being sailing
> across the sky. I saw that it was an old man with the horns of
> a bull . . .[4]

Jung accepted this presence as a guiding spirit, at times as
real as a living personality. Jung wrote of Philemon:

> [He] brought home to me the crucial insight that there are
> things in the psyche which I do not produce, but which pro-
> duce themselves and have their own life. Philemon repre-
> sented a force which was not myself. In my fantasies I held
> conversations with him, and he said things which I had not
> consciously thought . . . He said I treated thoughts as if I
> generated them myself, but in his view thoughts were like
> animals in the forest, or people in a room, or birds in the air,
> and added, "If you see people in a room, you would not think
> that you had made those people, or that you were responsi-
> ble for them." It was he who taught me psychic objectivity,
> the reality of the psyche.[5]

The encounter with Philemon gave Jung the impetus to
continue with his experiment, and later, as he looked back
upon what had happened he was not quite sure whether he
had been doing the experimenting or whether the experiment
had been done *to him*. At any rate, he had committed himself
into the hands of the unknown, and his experiences filled him

with terror and wonder. He recorded the fantasies scrupulously, in order to be able to get some sort of grasp of them, to be able to face them in the clear light of reality and to try to understand what meaning might lie behind them.

At times during this period, Jung was so overcome with emotion that he feared that he might be in danger of losing his psychic balance altogether. Writing down the material helped him to keep it under control, since once it was objectified he could then turn his mind to other things, secure in the knowledge that the unconscious material was safe from loss or distortion. During this strained and difficult period of his life he never withdrew from his routine of active work and relatedness to his family. Life with his wife and children proved to be a stabilizing influence, as also was his psychiatric practice. He forced himself to move back and forth from the conscious position with its distinct, if temporal, demands—to the unconscious one. Gradually he attained a capacity for granting each position its important role in his life and, when it was necessary, to allow the interpenetration of the one by the other.

He had discovered the practice of active imagination. In principle, it was the same discovery that many people have made in the course of their struggle toward individuation. Only Jung was the pathfinder who introduced active imagination into the area of psychotherapy. He had the courage to state that psychotherapy cannot be defined altogether as a science. In making a science of her, he said, "the individual imagines that he has caught the psyche and holds her in the hollow of his hand. He is even making a science of her in the absurd supposition that the intellect, which is but a part and a function of the psyche, is sufficient to comprehend the much greater whole."[6]

The word "science" comes from the Latin *scientia*, which means knowledge, and therefore is identified with consciousness and with the intellectual effort to draw into consciousness as much knowledge as possible. But, with our psychological concept of the unconscious, and with all the evidence that has emerged to justify its reality, it is necessary to recognize·

that there is a very large area of human experience with which science cannot deal. It has to do with all that is neither finite nor measurable, with all that is neither distinct nor—potentially, at least—explicable. It is that which is not accessible to logic or to the "word." It begins at the outermost edge of knowledge. Despite the continuing expansion or even explosion of information, there will forever be limits beyond which the devices of science cannot lead a man.

It becomes a matter of seeing the "created world" in terms of a "creating principle." This is difficult when we conceive of ourselves as being among "the created" and hence being unable to comprehend that which was before we existed and which will continue after the ego-consciousness with which we identify ourselves no longer exists in the form in which we know it. We cannot, however much we strive, incorporate all of the unconscious into consciousness, because the first is illimitable and the second, limited. What is the way then, if there is a way, to gain some understanding of unconscious processes? It seemed to Jung, as it has to others who have set aside the ego to participate directly in the mystery, that if we cannot assimilate the whole of the unconscious, then the risk of entering into the unfathomable sphere of the unconscious must be taken.

It is not that Jung deliberately sought to dissolve the more or less permeable barrier between consciousness and the unconscious. It was, in effect, something that happened to him— sometimes in dreams, and sometimes in even more curious ways. Under the aegis of Philemon as guiding spirit, Jung submitted himself to the experience that was happening to him. He accepted the engagement as full participant; his ego remained to one side in a non-interfering role, a helper to the extent that observation and objectivity were required to record the phenomena that occurred. And what did occur shocked Jung profoundly. He realized that what he felt and saw resembled the hallucinations of his psychotic patients, with the difference only that he was able to move into that macabre half-world at will and again out of it when external necessity demanded that he do so. This required a strong ego, and an equally strong determination to step away from it in the direction of that super-ordinate focus of the total personality, the self.

However, we must remember that it was with no such clearly formulated goal that Jung in those days took up the challenge of the mysterious. This was uncharted territory. He was experiencing and working out his fantasies as they came to him. Alternately, he was living a normal family life and carrying on his therapeutic work with patients, which gave him a sense of active productivity.

Meanwhile, the shape of his inner experience was becoming more definite, more demanding. One day he found himself besieged from within by a great restlessness. He felt that the entire atmosphere around him was highly charged, as one sometimes senses it before an electrical storm. The tension in the air seemed even to affect the other members of the household; his children said and did odd things, which were most uncharacteristic of them. He himself was in a strange state, a mood of apprehension, as though he moved through the midst of a houseful of spirits. He had the sense of being surrounded by the clamor of voices—from without, from within—and there was no surcease for him until he took up his pen and began to write.

Then, during the course of three nights, there flowed out of him a mystifying and heretical document. It began: "The dead came back from Jerusalem, where they found not what they sought." Written in an archaic and stilted style, the manuscript was signed with the pseudonym of Basilides, a famous gnostic teacher of the second century after Christ. Basilides had belonged to that group of early Christians which was declared heretical by the Church because of its pretensions to mystic and esoteric insights and its emphasis on direct knowledge rather than faith. It was as though the orthodox Christian doctrine had been examined and found too perfect, and therefore incomplete, since the answers were given in that doctrine, but many of the questions were missing. Jung raised crucial questions in his *Seven Sermons of the Dead*. The blackness of the nether sky was dredged up and the paradoxes of faith and disbelief were laid side by side. Traces of the dark matter of the *Sermons* may be found throughout the works of Jung which followed, especially those which deal with religion and its infernal counterpoint, alchemy. All through these later writings it is as if Jung were struggling with the issues raised in the dialogues with the *"Dead,"* who are the spokesmen for that dark realm beyond human understanding; but it is in Jung's last great work, *Mysterium Coniunctionis*, on which he worked for ten years and completed only in his eightieth year, that the meaning of the *Sermons* finally finds its definition. Jung said that the voices of the *Dead* were the voices of the Unanswered, Unresolved and Unredeemed. Their true names became known to Jung only at the end of his life.

The words flow between the *Dead*, who are the questioners, and the archetypal wisdom which has its expression in the individual, who regards it as revelation. The *Sermons* deny that God spoke two thousand years ago and has been silent ever since, as is commonly supposed by many who call themselves religious. Paul, whose letters are sometimes referred to as "gnostic," supported this view in his Epistle to the Hebrews (1:1), "God who at sundry times and in divers manner spake in time past unto the fathers by thy prophets, hath in these last days spoken unto us by his Son . . ." Revelation occurs in every generation. When Jung spoke of a new way of understanding the hidden truths of the unconscious, his words were shaped by the same archetypes that in the past inspired the prophets and are operative in the present in the unconscious of modern man. Perhaps this is why he was able to say of the *Sermons:* "These conversations with the dead formed a kind of prelude to what I had to communicate to the world about the unconscious: a kind of pattern of order and interpretation of all its general contents."

I will not attempt here to interpret or explain the *Sermons*. They must stand as they are, and whoever can find meaning in them is free to do so; whoever cannot may pass over them. They belong to Jung's "initial experiences" from which derived all of his work, all of his creative activity. A few excerpts will offer some feeling for the "otherness" which Jung experienced at that time, and which was for him so germinal. The first *Sermon*, as he carefully lettered it in antique script in his Red Book, begins:

> The dead came back from Jerusalem where they found not what they sought. They prayed me let them in and besought my word, and thus I began my teaching.
>
> Hearken: I begin with nothingness. Nothingness is the same as fullness. In infinity full is no better than empty. Nothingness is both empty and full. As well might ye say anything else of nothingness, as for instance, white it is, or black, or again, it is not, or it is. A thing that is infinite and eternal hath no qualities, since it hath all qualities.
>
> This nothingness or fullness we name the pleroma.

All that I can say of the *pleroma* is that it goes beyond our capacity to conceive of it, for it is of another order than human consciousness. It is that infinite which can never be grasped, not even in imagination. But since we, as people, are not infinite, we are distinguished from the *pleroma*. The first *Sermon* continues:

> Creatura is not in the pleroma, but in itself. The pleroma is both beginning and end of created beings. It pervadeth them, as the light of the sun everywhere pervadeth the air. Although the pleroma pervadeth altogether, yet hath created body no share thereof, just as a wholly transparent body becometh neither light nor dark through the light which pervadeth it. We are, however, the pleroma itself, for we are a part of the eternal and the infinite. But we have no share thereof, as we are from the pleroma infinitely removed; not spiritually or temporally,

but essentially, since we are distinguished from the pleroma in our essence as creatura, which is confined within time and space.

The quality of human life, according to this teaching, lies in the degree to which each person distinguishes herself or himself from the totality of the unconscious. The wresting of consciousness, of self-awareness, from the tendency to become submerged in the mass, is one of the most important tasks of the individuated person. This is the implication of a later passage from the *Sermons:*

What is the harm, ye ask, in not distinguishing oneself?

If we do not distinguish, we get beyond our own nature, away from creatura. We fall into indistinctiveness . . . We fall into the pleroma itself and cease to be creatures. We are given over to dissolution in the nothingness. This is the death of the creature. Therefore we die in such measure as we do not distinguish. Hence the natural striving of the creature goeth towards distinctiveness, fighteth against primeval, perilous sameness. This is called the principium individuationis. *This principle is the essence of the creature.*

In the pleroma all opposites are said to be balanced and therefore they cancel each other out; there is no tension in the unconscious. Only in man's consciousness do these separations exist:

> *The Effective and the Ineffective.*
> *Fullness and Emptiness.*
> *Living and Dead.*
> *Difference and Sameness.*
> *Light and Darkness.*
> *The Hot and the Cold.*
> *Force and Matter.*
> *Time and Space.*
> *Good and Evil.*

Beauty and Ugliness.
The One and the Many . . .

These qualities are distinct and separate in us one from the other; therefore they are not balanced and void, but are effective. Thus are we the victims of the pairs of opposites. The pleroma is rent in us.

Dualism and monism are both products of consciousness. When consciousness begins to differentiate from the unconscious, its first step is to divide into dichotomies. It proceeds through all possible pairs until it arrives at the concept of the One and the Many. This implies a recognition that even the discriminating function of consciousness acknowledges that all opposites are contained within a whole, and that this whole contains both consciousness and that which is not conscious. Here lies the germ of the concept marking the necessity of ever looking to the unconscious for that compensating factor which can enable us to bring balance into the one-sided attitude of consciousness. Always, in the analytic process, we search the dreams, the fantasies, and the products of active imagination, for the elements that will balance: the shadow for persona-masked ego, the anima for the aggressively competitive man, the animus for the self-effacing woman, the old wise man for the *puer aeternus*, the deeply founded earth-mother for the impulsive young woman. We need to recognize the importance of not confusing ourselves with our qualities. *I* am not good *or* bad, wise *or* foolish—I am my "own being" and, being a whole person, I am capable of all manner of actions, good *and* bad, wise *and* foolish. The traditional Christian ideal of attempting to live out only the so-called higher values and eschewing the lower is proclaimed disastrous in this gnostic "heresy." The traditional Christian ideal is antithetical to the very nature of consciousness or awareness:

When we strive after the good or the beautiful, we thereby forget our own nature, which is distinctiveness, and we are deliv-

ered over to the qualities of the pleroma, which are pairs of opposites. We labour to attain to the good and the beautiful, yet at the same time we also lay hold of the evil and the ugly, since in the pleroma these are one with the good and the beautiful. When, however, we remain true to our own nature, which is distinctiveness, we distinguish ourselves from the good and the beautiful, and therefore, at the same time, from the evil and ugly. And thus we fall not into the pleroma, namely, into nothingness and dissolution.

Buried in these abstruse expressions is the very crux of Jung's approach to religion. He is deeply religious in the sense of pursuing his life task under the overwhelming awareness of the magnitude of an infinite God, yet he knows and accepts his limitations as a human being. This makes him reluctant to say with certainty anything about this "Numinosum," this totally "Other." In a filmed interview Jung was asked, "Do you believe in God?" He replied with an enigmatic smile, "I *know*. I don't need to believe. I know." Wherever the film has been shown an urgent debate inevitably follows as to what he meant by that statement. It seems to me that *believing* means to have a firm conviction about something that may or may not be debatable. It is an act of faith, that is, it requires some effort. Perhaps there is even the implication that faith is required because that which is believed in *seems* so preposterous. On the other hand, it is not necessary to acquire a conviction about something if you have experienced it. I do not *believe* I have just eaten dinner. If I have had the experience, I *know* it. And so with recognizing the difference between religious belief and religious experience. Whoever has experienced the divine presence has passed beyond the requirement of faith, and also of reason. Reasoning is a process of approximating truth. It leads to knowledge. But *knowing* is a direct recognition of truth, and it leads to wisdom. Thinking is a process of differentiation and discrimination. In our thoughts we make separations and enlist categories where in a wider view of reality they do not exist. The rainbow spectrum is not composed of six or seven colors; it is our thinking that determines how many colors there are and where red leaves off and orange begins. We need to make our differentiations in the finite world in order to deal expediently with the fragmented aspects of our temporal lives.

The *Sermons* remind us that our temporal lives, seen from the standpoint of eternity, may be illusory—as illusory as eternity seems when you are trying to catch a bus on a Monday morning. Either seems false when seen from the standpoint of the other. Addressed to the *Dead*, the words that follow are part of the dialogue with the unconscious, the pleroma, whose existence is not dependent on thinking or believing.

> *Ye must not forget that the pleroma hath no qualities. We create them through thinking. If, therefore, ye strive after difference or sameness, or any qualities whatsoever, ye pursue thoughts which flow to you out of the pleroma; thoughts, namely, concerning non-existing qualities of the pleroma. Inasmuch as ye run after these thoughts, ye fall again into the pleroma, and reach difference and sameness at the same time. Not your thinking, but your being, is distinctiveness. Therefore, not after difference, as ye think it, must ye strive; but after your own being. At bottom, therefore, there is only one striving, namely, the striving after your own being. If ye had this striving ye would not need to know anything about the pleroma and its qualities, and yet would come to your right goal by virtue of your own being.*

The passage propounds Jung's insight about the fruitlessness of pursuing philosophizing and theorizing for its own sake. Perhaps it suggests why he never systematized his own theory of psychotherapy, why he never prescribed techniques or methods to be followed. Nor did he stress the categorization of patients into disease entities based on differences or samenesses, except perhaps as a convenience for purposes of describing appearances, or for communicating with other therapists. The distinctiveness of individual men or women is not in what has happened to them, in this view, nor is it in what has been thought about them. It is in their own being, their essence. This is why a man or woman as therapist has only one "tool" with which to work, and that is the person of the therapist. What happens in therapy depends not so much upon what the therapist does, as upon who the therapist is.

The last sentence of the first *Sermon* provides the key to that hidden chamber which is at once the goal of individuation, and the abiding place of the religious spirit which can guide us from within our own depths:

> *Since, however, thought estrangeth from being, that knowledge must I teach you wherewith ye may be able to hold your thought in leash.*

Suddenly we know who the *Dead* are. *We* are the dead. We are psychologically dead if we live only in the world of consciousness, of science, of thought which "estrangeth from being." *Being* is being alive to the potency of the creative principle, translucent to the lightness and the darkness of the pleroma, porous to the flux of the collective unconscious. The message does not decry "thought," only a certain kind of thought, that which "estrangeth from being." Thought—logical deductive reasoning, objective scientific discrimination—must not be permitted to become the only vehicle through which we may approach the problematic of nature. Science, and most of all the "science of human behavior," must not be allowed to get away with saying "attitudes are not important, what is important is only the way in which we behave." For if our behavior is to be enucleated from our attitudes we must be hopelessly split in two, and the psyche, which is largely spirit, must surely die within us.

That knowledge . . . wherewith ye may be able to hold your thought in leash must, I believe, refer to knowledge which comes from those functions other than thinking. It consists of the knowledge that comes from sensation, from intuition, and from feeling. The knowledge which comes from sensation is the immediate and direct perception which arrives via the senses and has its reality independently of anything that we may think about it. The knowledge which comes from intuition is that which precedes thinking and also which suggests where thinking may go; it is the star which determines the adjustment of the telescope, the hunch which leads to the hypothesis. And finally, the knowledge which comes from feeling is the indisputable evaluative judgment; the thing happens to me in a certain way and incorporates my response to it; I may be drawn toward it or I may recoil from it, I love or I hate, I laugh or I weep, all irrespective of any intervening process of thinking about it.

It is not enough, as some of the currently popular anti-intellectual approaches to psychotherapy would have it, merely to lay aside the intellectual function. The commonly heard cries, "I don't care what you *think* about it, I want to know how you *feel* about it," are shallow and pointless; they miss the kernel while clinging to the husk. *To hold your thought in leash*, that seems to me the key, for all the knowledge so hard-won in the laboratory and in the field is valuable only in proportion to the way it is directed to the service of consciousness as it addresses itself to the unconscious, to the service of the created as it addresses itself to the creative principle, to the service of human needs as we address ourselves to God.

Jung's approach to religion is twofold, yet it is not dualistic. First, there is the approach of one person to God and, second, there is the approach of the scientist-psychologist to people's idea-of-God. The latter is subsumed under the former. Jung's own religious nature pervades all of his writing about religion; even when he writes as a psychotherapist he does not forget that he is a limited human being standing in the shade of the mystery he can never understand.

Nor is he alone in this. Margaret Mead has written, "We need a religious system with science at its very core, in which the traditional opposition between science and religion . . . can again be resolved, but in terms of the future instead of the past . . . Such a synthesis . . . would use the recognition that when man permitted himself to become alienated from part of himself, elevating rationality and often narrow purpose above those ancient intuitive properties of the mind that bind him to his biological past, he was in effect cutting himself off from the rest of the natural world."[7]

I have discovered in my analytic practice and also in my capacity as a teacher, that many people come to Jung knowing that he is one psychologist who takes seriously the need people have to find some correspondence between their rational thoughts and activities, and the dimensions of their lives to which the rational does not seem to apply: the areas of feelings, of love and of awe. How Jung's approach to these questions actually works in the lives of individuals may be illustrated by quoting from a paper titled "Potentials for the Application of Jungian Psychology to Religion," written by one of my students:

> I came into this class with a vague notion that Jungian psychology would be helpful in the task of relating psychology and religion. As the class progressed that expectation was richly fulfilled. My task in the Religion and Personality field is to discover what psychology and religion have to do with each other. Jung has offered one approach to that task which I find helpful and stimulating for my own thought.
>
> One of the reasons why there has not been to date a convincing psychology *of* religion (there has been an ample supply of modern attempts to do psychology *and* religion) is that both psychologists and theologians have ignored the important place of myth and symbol in the life of man and in religion. It is precisely here that Jung makes a unique and significant contribution.
>
> Once one accepts his theory of the archetypes, one must deal with myth and symbol. And once the cosmic and cultural dimensions of the archetypes are understood as well as their personal dimensions, we are immediately thrown into contact with the numinous aspects of life which many psychologists and historians of religion agree constitute religion. If we apply Jung's theory of archetypes to our understanding of religion, we are then forced to deal with the

structure of the psyche, and Jung's structural categories (e.g., the conscious, the unconscious, archetypes, shadow, anima, animus, self, etc.) are meaningless outside his theory of the dynamics of the psyche which includes such concepts as individuation, psychological typology, and the tension of opposites. Any of these structural or dynamic dimensions can not only throw light on how theologians understand individuals in relationship to God, but also can force them to re-evaluate the role and structure of the Church itself.

What Jung is attempting to understand and elucidate is, as the student quite correctly supposed, a psychology *of* religion. Jung puts the religious experience of the individual, which comes about often spontaneously and independently, into place with the religious systems that have been evolved and institutionalized in nearly every society throughout history.

In psychotherapy, the religious dimension of human experience often appears after the analytic process has proceeded to some depth. Initially, people come for help with some more or less specific problem. They may admit to a vague uneasiness that what is ailing may be a matter of personal issues, and that the "symptoms" or "problems" they face could be outcroppings of a deeper reality—the shape of which they do not comprehend. When, in analysis, they come face to face with the figurative representation of the self, they are often stunned and shocked by the recognition that the non-personal power, of which they have only the fuzziest conception, lives and manifests itself in them. Oh, yes, they have heard about this, and read about it, and have heard it preached from intricately carved pulpits, but now it is all different. It is the image in their own dreams, the voice in their own ears, the shivering in the night as the terror of all terrors bears down upon them, and the knowing that it is within them—arising there, finding its voice there, and being received there.

It is not in the least astonishing, [Jung tells us] that numinous experiences should occur in the course of psychologi-

cal treatment, and that they may even be expected with
some regularity, for they also occur very frequently in excep-
tional psychic states that are not treated, and may even
cause them. They do not belong exclusively to the domain of
psychopathology but can be observed in normal people as
well. Naturally, modern ignorance of and prejudice against
intimate psychic experiences dismiss them as psychic anom-
alies and put them in psychiatric pigeonholes without making the least attempt to understand them. But that neither
gets rid of the fact of the occurrence nor explains it.[8]

In our reading of Jung we find that in attempting to understand the numinous experience, people look to those earlier
and collective metaphysical ideas which have been associated
with religion, and more specifically, the religion into which
they happen to be born. They tend to develop a concept of
"God" based on the concept held by their parents, or their
educators, or their community. Jung says, "It seems to me at
least highly improbable that when a man says 'God' there
must in consequence exist a God such as he imagines, or that
he necessarily speaks of a real being. At any rate he can never
prove that there is something to correspond with his statement on the metaphysical side, just as it can never be proved
to him that he is wrong."[9]

Nor is there any more hope that the God-concept advanced by the various religions is any more demonstrable
than that expressed by the individual as "my own idea." The
various expressions that have been given voice about the nature of transcendental reality are so many and diverse that
there is no way of knowing absolutely who is right, even if
there were a single, simple answer to the question. Therefore,
as Jung saw it, the denominational religions long ago recognized that there was no way to defend the exclusivity of their
"truth" so, instead, they took the offensive position and proclaimed that their religion was the only true one, and the basis
for this, they claimed, was that the truth had been directly
revealed by God. "Every theologian speaks simply of 'God,' by

which he intends it to be understood that his 'god' is *the* God. But one speaks of the paradoxical God of the Old Testament, another of the incarnate God of Love, a third of the God who has a heavenly bride, and so on, and each criticizes the other but never himself."[10]

Such insights as this do not come only from reading the philosophers and the psychologists. They arise even more vividly out of the personal experience of the individual. Essentially this is where they find their true meaning—every other exposition of these ideas merely points in the direction of their meaning. I can illustrate this statement with an example from my practice. A young woman was studying theology, and was preparing to take her examination for the master's degree. A few nights before the exam she had the following dream: *I walk into the classroom to pick up my M.A. exam. They are printed on the backs of psychedelic posters. The exam question is, "Write a critical exposition of the play, 'Fools.'"*

Fools was the name of a play, she told me, that had been recently put on by the university faculty. It had flopped. As she gave her further associations to the dream, she said that while she had been preparing for the exams the phrase kept recurring in her mind, "The fool hath said in his heart that there is no God." She expressed her resistance to the *over-objectivity* that characterized the professors in her department. No personal religious experience was ever discussed in the classroom. She observed that the study of comparative religion—which seems to be a screen behind which can be established the one true faith—derives its rationale by purporting to determine what is valid and what is not, and ranking ideas in hierarchies.

The dream seems to be saying essentially that on one side she is being asked to look critically at the "play," the posturings of the theological faculty, who are acting the roles of fools. She has to deal with her recognition that they speak the lines which justify God, when God is not justified in their own experience. On the other side are the blazing colors of the psychedelic posters which express the breaking up of lightwaves into hues and forms to delight the eye—the ineffable is brought into the realm of human experience. She is faced with both; they both belong to the same sheet of paper, which is given to her as her task to make meaningful.

She can approach this task either with her intellectual function or with her spiritual function. Or, she can attempt to bring both to bear on the problem; she can at one time think and also "hold her thought in leash." If she chooses the second alternative, she will follow the example of Jung in his exposition of the religious side of the psyche, placing side by side the individual experience of the divine and the collective expression of it, with the many symbols and myths and rituals that attach to it.

A basic principle of Jung's approach to religion is that the spiritual element is an organic part of the psyche. It is the source of the search for meaning, and it is that element which lifts us above our concern for merely keeping our species alive by feeding our hunger and protecting ourselves from attack and copulating to preserve the race. We could live well enough on the basis of the instincts alone; the naked ape does not *need* books or churches. The spiritual element which urges us on the quest for the unknown and the unknowable is the organic part of the psyche, and it is this which is responsible for both science and religion. The spiritual element is expressed in symbols, for symbols are the language of the unconscious. Through consideration of the symbol, much that is problematic or only vaguely understood can become real and vitally effective in our lives.

The symbol attracts, and therefore leads individuals on the way of becoming what they are capable of becoming. That goal is wholeness, which is integration of the parts of the personality into a functioning totality. Here consciousness and the unconscious are united around the symbols of the self. The ways in which the self manifests are numerous beyond any attempt to name or describe them. I choose the mandala symbol as a starting point because its circular characteristics suggest the qualities of the self (the pleroma that hath no qualities). It is "smaller than small and bigger than big." In principle, the circle must have a center, but that point which we mark as a center is, of necessity, larger than the true center. However much we decrease the central point, the true center is at the center of that, and hence, smaller yet. The circumference is that line around the center which is at all points equidistant from it. But, since we do not know the length of the radius, it may be said of any circle we may imagine, that our mandala is larger than that. The mandala, then, as a symbol of the self, has the qualities of the circle, center and circumference, yet like the self of which it is an image, it has not these qualities.

Is it any wonder then, that the man who was not a man should be chosen as a symbol of the self and worshiped throughout the Christian world? Is it at all strange, when considered symbolically, that the belief arose that an infinite spirit which pervades the universe should have concentrated the omnipotence of his being into a speck so infinitesimal that it could enter the womb of a woman and be born as a divine child?

In his major writings on "Christ as a Symbol of the Self" Jung has stated it explicitly:

In the world of Christian ideas Christ undoubtedly represents the self. As the apotheosis of individuality, the self has the attributes of uniqueness and of occurring once only in time. But since the psychological self is a transcendent concept, expressing the totality of conscious and unconscious contents, it can only be described in antinomial terms; that is, the above attributes must be supplemented by their opposites if the transcendental situation is to be characterized correctly. We can do this most simply in the form of a quaternion of opposites:

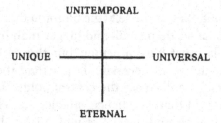

This formula expresses not only the psychological self but also the dogmatic figure of Christ. As an historical personage Christ is unitemporal and unique; as God, universal and eternal. . . . Now if theology describes Christ as simply "good" and "spiritual," something "evil" and "material" . . . is bound to arise on the other side . . . The resultant quaternion of opposites is united on the psychological plane by the fact that the self is not deemed exclusively "good" and "spiritual"; consequently its shadow turns out to be much less black. A further result is that the opposites of "good" and "spiritual" need no longer be separated from the whole:

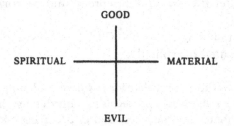

This *quaternio* characterizes the psychological self. Being a totality, it must by definition include the light and dark aspects, in the same way that the self embraces both masculine and feminine, and is therefore symbolized by the marriage *quaternio*.* Hence individuation is a "mysterium coniunctionis," the self being experienced by a nuptial union of opposite halves and depicted as a composite whole in mandalas that are drawn spontaneously by patients. [We recall

* See Chapter 7, "Anima and Animus."

how beautifully this was expressed in the active imagination
of the patient Charles and the ape-man.][11]

We have seen how, in analysis, the image of the self often
manifests very early and provides the impetus for the entire
process. It may come in a dream which is only partly understood, and remains in a prenascent state until its time has
come. This was the experience of Vincent, whose dream was
discussed in Chapter 8, "Circumambulating the Self." The
dream is repeated here, to show how the religious significance
of a dream sometimes only begins to emerge after it has been
carried to its maturity: *I am walking with a woman slightly
older than myself along a mountain path. It is a glacial idyllic
scene by moonlight. I am also somehow watching myself. We
come to some huge gray boulders. They are blocking our path.
We stop, and she turns to me and looks at me. We are engaged in
pleasant conversation. Suddenly she turns extremely ugly. Her
face takes on a greenish color and she gets very old. I realize
there is only one way to help the situation and that is to have
intercourse with her. My penis enters her vagina, then goes
through her body and into the rock behind her. Then she disappears and I am alone, having intercourse with the rock.*
The setting is surely referring to the aspect of the unconscious farthest from consciousness—the cold, colorless moonlight speaks of the mysterious side of life; the mountain, of the
heights of the spirit. The woman companion has two aspects,
the one "slightly older than myself" referring to the anima as
reflecting initially the experience of the personal mother and,
later on, the transference relationship with the analyst. In any
case it is this aspect of the anima that leads him to the boulders. Then, suddenly, the unique and unitemporal poles of the
quaternio shift into their opposites: The woman becomes old
and ugly; her face takes on a greenish color. She is ageless, yet
in being available for intercourse she offers youth to youth,
with the possibility of a creative union. The greenish color
that comes over her is the color of nature which, out of the
glacial stillness of the night, brings the shocking suggestion of

fertility and rebirth. The effect upon the man is to infuse him with a miraculous potency, so that his virile member is able to penetrate her and not only her, but through her and into the rock! "Hence, individuation is a 'mysterium coniunctionis,' the self being experienced as a nuptial union of opposite halves." Through the anima the individual has become united with his transpersonal self, as symbolized by the stone.

The stone, or the *lapis*, is a central symbol in the literature of alchemy. The search into the various aspects of its meaning occupied Jung in scholarly research throughout much of his life. He understood the alchemical opus as a process which at one time was an attempt to transform base materials into an incorruptible substance (gold, elixir, panacea, treasure hard to attain, pearl of great price, lapis), and to transform the original base nature of man into its spiritual potentiality in which it would find its union with the divine, which was called the *lapis philosophorum*, the philosopher's stone, and by many other names. The alchemical opus, understood symbolically as many of the medieval alchemists did understand it, was recognized by Jung as a striking parallel to the process of individuation.

The pre-form of this insight appeared in the first of the *Seven Sermons of the Dead* where it is said, "the striving of the creature goeth toward distinctiveness, fighteth against primeval, perilous sameness. This is called the *principium individuationis.*" We are caught in the struggle between the opposites; the stone is fixed and incorruptible. The individuation process is an *opus contra naturam;* it is a struggle against the natural, haphazard way of living in which we simply respond first to the demands made upon us by the circumstances of our environment and then to those of inner necessity, paying the most attention to the side that is most insistent at any given time. Individuation leads through the confrontation of the opposites until a gradual integration of the personality comes about, a oneness with oneself, with one's world, and with the divine presence as it makes itself known to us.

The beginning of the alchemical process parallels the legends of creation, the consolidation of a world out of formless chaos. In alchemy the opus starts out with a *massa confusa*, a teeming, disordered conglomeration of what is called *prima materia*. It goes through a series of transformations, all described in the most abstruse language, in a lore that predated Christianity and extended forward into the seventeenth century. We seldom get much of an idea of how the work was actually done, what materials were used and what results were achieved. Jung says, "The alchemist is quite aware that he writes obscurely. He admits that he veils his meaning on purpose, but nowhere,—so far as I know—does he say that he cannot write in any other way. He makes a virtue of necessity by maintaining either that mystification is forced on him for one reason or another, or that he really wants to make the truth as plain as possible, but that he cannot proclaim aloud just what the *prima materia* or the *lapis* is."[12] This is in a tradition of refusing to make easily available material that has been acquired only with great difficulty, on the grounds that the quest is at least as important as the goal, or that the importance of the goal rests on the energy and commitment that has been involved in the quest.

Jung cites one of the oldest alchemical tests, written in Arabic style: "This stone is below thee, as to obedience; above thee, as to dominion; therefore from thee, as to knowledge; about thee, as to equals." He comments on the passage:

[It] is somewhat obscure. Nevertheless, it can be elicited that the stone stands in an undoubted psychic relationship to man: the adept can expect obedience from it, but on the other hand the stone exercises dominion over him. Since the stone is a matter of "knowledge" or "science," it springs from man. But it is outside him, in his surroundings, among his "equals," i.e., those of like mind. This description fits the paradoxical situation of the self, as its symbolism shows. It is the smallest of the small, easily overlooked and pushed aside. Indeed, it is in need of help and must be perceived,

protected, and as it were built up by the conscious mind, just
as if it did not exist at all and were called into being only
through man's care and devotion. As against this, we know
from experience that it had long been there and is older than
the ego, and that it is actually the *spiritus rector* (guiding, or
controlling spirit) of our fate.[13]

The study of Jung's extensive writings on religion and alchemy, of which the above lines give only the merest suggestion, led Vincent into a consideration of his own potentiality
for realization of the promise of his dream. He was able to
apply the universal and transcendent themes, inherent in the
anima and the stone, to his personal life, and through them to
gain the broader perspective that was needed in order to face
the difficulties in his path with energy and equanimity.

One may well ask, Why did Jung become so involved with
the arcane material of alchemy with all of its pseudoscientific
pretensions, its inchoate philosophical speculations, its dubious conclusions? Why did he not utilize more the symbolic
presentations of the orthodox religions, the well-ordered logic
of the Church Fathers and the disciplined precepts of the non-
Christian religions? To be sure he did not overlook these latter,
but however well versed in the "establishment philosophies"
he may have been, there is no doubt that the subject of alchemy held him fascinated. What was it that managed to draw
his attention from the academic or conventionally accepted
intellectual position to the opposing one, at which people
tended to look askance? What was it that had long ago pried
him away from his medical studies to attend the séances
where S.W. fell into trance states and described her visions?
What was it that had him spending his nights at Burghölzli,
after a full day of research and psychotherapy, poring over the
possible meaning behind S.W.'s apparently hysterical performances? What led Jung to jeopardize his psychiatric career
just as it was beginning, in order to join forces with the doctor
from Vienna whose radical theories were bringing down the

criticism of practically every prominent European psychiatrist? And again, when Freud was well established and regarded, what was it that led Jung to leave the group, and to pursue an analytical approach that intensified the roles of religion and myth in the field of psychology just as the field of psychology was struggling to enter the arena of the sciences as a respected junior member?

Perhaps the answer to these questions is intimated in Jung's writing concerning the Sacrament of the Mass. In his account of "Transformation Symbolism in the Mass"[14] Jung described the acts in detail and commented on the symbolic significance of the sequence of the transformation rite: the oblation of the bread, the preparation of the chalice, the elevation of the chalice, the censing of the substances and the altar, the epiclesis, the consecration, the greater elevation, the post-consecration, end of the canon, breaking of the host, consignatio, commixtio and conclusion. He tells us: "the uttering of the words of the consecration signifies Christ himself speaking in the first person, his living presence in the *corpus mysticum* of the priest, congregation, bread, wine, and incense, which together form the mystical unity offered for sacrifice. At this moment the eternal character of the one divine sacrifice is made evident: it is experienced at a particular time and in a particular place, as if a window or a door had been opened upon that which lies beyond space and time."[15] "The Mass thus contains, as its essential core, the mystery and miracle of God's transformation taking place in the human sphere, his becoming Man, and his return to his absolute existence in and for himself."[16]

Jung then makes the statement that although the Mass is a unique phenomenon in the history of comparative religion, its symbolic content is rooted in the human psyche. Therefore, it may be expected that we would find similar patterns of symbolism both in the history of earlier peoples and in the contemporary non-Christian world. He does, indeed, find examples of religious rites which come very close to Christian practices, and he describes those of the Aztecs, in particular, that of the *teoqualo*, "god-eating," as recorded by a missionary in the early sixteenth century. He then reviews in alchemical literature some parallel rites of transformations as depicted in visions and practices, in myths and rituals and in allegorical legends. He deals at length with the visions of Zosimos, a natural philosopher and alchemist of the third century, whose works have been preserved, though in a corrupt state. He relates a number of Zosimos's dream-visions, all of which, Jung says, appear to go back to the same dream—in which Zosimos observes a priest who becomes split into the figures of the sacrificer and the one who is sacrificed. As the sacrificed, he submits voluntarily to the torture through which he is transformed. But as sacrificer he is pierced through with his own sword and is ritually dismembered. As the priest stands before him high on an altar, Zosimos hears a voice from above say to him, "Behold, . . . I have completed the ascent up the steps of light. And he who renews me is the priest, for he cast away the density of the body and by compelling necessity I am sanctified and now stand in perfection as a spirit *(pneuma)*."[17]

Jung studiously compares in all details the visions of Zosimos with the sacrifice of the Mass, the crucifixion and the resurrection. At last he comes to this interpretation:

> Looked at from the psychological standpoint, Christ . . . represents a totality which surpasses and includes ordinary man, and which corresponds to the total personality that transcends consciousness. We have called this personality the "self." Just as, on the more archaic level of the Zosimos vision, the homunculus [a mannikin that is produced by an alchemist in a vessel or flask] is transformed into *pneuma* and exalted, so the mystery of the Eucharist transforms the soul of the empirical man, who is only a part of himself, into his totality, symbolically expressed by Christ. In this sense, therefore, we can speak of the Mass as the *rite of the individuation process.*[18]

It seems to me that in his essay, "The Lapis-Christus Parallel," in *Psychology and Alchemy*, the true position of Jung vis-à-vis the opposition between orthodox Christianity and alchemy is made clear. There is Christ; and there is the stone. Christ comes to earth, is born and lives for man, dies and is sacrificed for the sake of man's salvation. The stone, the precious body, is concealed in the *prima materia*, the confused mass; and it is man, symbolically represented as the alchemist and the soror, who must save the stone from dissolution in matter. The Christians received the spiritual benefits of the Mass for themselves personally, to improve the circumstances of their existence in the widest sense. But the alchemists performed their labors for the perfection of the precious substance, not merely for themselves, but more importantly for the King (which is Jung's symbol for God), or for the King's Son. As he points out, the alchemist "may play a part in the *perfectio*, which brings them health, riches, illumination, and salvation; but since they are the redeemers of God and not the ones to be redeemed, they are more concerned to perfect the substance than themselves."

Now we begin to discover where, in Jung, there comes the parting of the ways. As a religious man he can say "I don't need to believe in God, I *know*." He can accept Christ and the meaning of Christ in his personal life as the One through whom he is redeemed. This is given to him, through the grace of God, and he does not question it. For him Christ is truly a symbol of the self, the most congruent symbol of the self for him, in terms of his rootedness in the Christianity of his fathers. For a Jew, or a Hindu, for example, the self would be expressed in different symbols.

As a psychotherapist, however, Jung approaches his patient with an open attitude, an attitude that says, "Here is a person before me whose nature is unknown to me. The nature of the contract to which we will commit ourselves is also unknown to me. And the goal, the end of the process, is equally unknown." Therefore the alchemist becomes a guiding symbol for Jung as he takes up the task of tinkering with the human soul. The consulting room is symbolically represented by the alchemist's laboratory. From this it can be seen how the alchemical opus parallels the individuation process.

Although Jung recognized the possibility of projecting his own unconscious contents into the symbolism of alchemy, he was careful to make it clear in speaking of the alchemist: "One should not suppose for a moment that he presumes to the role of redeemer from religious megalomania. He does so even less than the officiating priest who figuratively sacrifices Christ. The alchemist always stresses his humility and begins his treatises with invocations to God. He does not dream of identifying himself with Christ; on the contrary, it is the coveted substance, the *lapis*, that alchemy likens to Christ."[19]

Jung's alchemical studies, drawing as they did from the fields of archaeology and comparative religions, led him time and time again to face the importance of the role of astrology in the history of human consciousness. It was characteristic of Jung, when he became interested in a subject to pursue his research with thoroughness and zeal, and the lore of astrology was no exception. If Jung's interest in alchemy had led to misunderstanding on the part of the general public, his interest in astrology has had an even more confusing effect. Hard-nosed scientists asserted that Jung's scientific respectability was called into question when he investigated a field such as this, which lies outside the area of what is considered by them to be proper subject matter for experimental research. On the other side, many people who wanted to give an air of authenticity to their assertions about the validity of astrological predictions have tried to persuade an unwitting public that Jung was a "true believer" in astrology as a predictive instrument. I am quite convinced that he was not, and I would not even raise the question in this book, except for the fact that it has often come up in my practice. Here is another instance of people hearing a half-truth or a patently fraudulent statement about Jung, and then coming to a Jungian analyst because they think she will understand such things, or that she will support their beliefs.

When the question does come up—and it usually comes up in the form, "What did Jung *really* think about astrology?" —I do not dismiss it lightly. I believe that the query belongs to the questioner's search for meaning in his life, and that probably he has gotten lost between the world of the senses and the world of symbols, and needs to find a workable reorientation. Perhaps, in a wider sense, a similar subjective condition inspired Jung to study the astrological symbols and their relationship to psychological and religious history. Since I could not speak directly with Jung about this, I can only base my conclusions on my reading of his extensive writing on the subject. In his chapter on "The Sign of the Fishes," in *Aion*, he amplified and interpreted the astrological symbolism connected with the theme of Christ as the fish (pisces). He dealt with the archetypal basis for the development of and belief in astrology in his essay, "Synchronicity: An Acausal Connecting Principle," in *The Structure and Dynamics of the Psyche*. This essay also contains a report on a research project directed by Jung for the purpose of testing certain astrological hypotheses. A personal and subjective view of astrology, its uses and abuses, may be found in Jung's *Memories, Dreams, Reflections*. Other references to the subject of astrology are scattered throughout the speculative-philosophical portions of Jung's writings.

I believe that by quoting a passage from Jung here, we may get the flavor of his objective scientific investigations into the tenets and folklore of astrology as a historical phenomenon. Appreciating this open and inquiring attitude on the part of Jung will prepare us for an understanding of his psychological observations concerning the belief in the power of the stars to influence our lives. Jung writes in *Aion:*

> A direct astrological aspect of Christ's birth is given us in Matthew 2:1 ff. The Magi from the East were star-gazers who, beholding an extraordinary constellation, inferred an

equally extraordinary birth. This anecdote proves that
Christ, possibly even at the time of the apostles, was viewed
from the astrological standpoint or was at least brought into
connection with astrological myths . . . Since this exceedingly complex question has been discussed by those who are
more qualified than I, we can support our argument on the
well-attested fact that glimpses of astrological mythology
may be caught behind the stories of the worldly and other-
worldly life of the Redeemer.

Above all, it is the connections with the age of the Fishes
which are attested by the fish symbolism, either contemporaneous with the gospels themselves ("fishers of men," fish-
ermen as the first disciples, miracle of loaves and fishes), or
immediately afterwards in the post-apostolic era. The symbolism shows Christ and those who believe in him as fishes,
fish as the food eaten at the Agape, baptism as immersion in
a fish-pond, etc. At first sight, all this points to no more than
the fact that the fish symbols which had always existed had
assimilated the figure of the Redeemer; in other words, it
was a symptom of Christ's assimilation into the world of
ideas prevailing at that time. But to the extent that Christ
was regarded as the new aeon, it would be clear to anyone
acquainted with astrology that he was born as the first fish of
the Pisces era.[20]

It is clear from this passage that Jung was acquainted with
the history of the primitive science or pseudo-science of astrology as it was long before the appearance of Jesus. Astrology is principally the ancient art or science of divining the fate
and future of human beings from indications given by the positions of the stars, sun, moon and planets. The belief in a
connection between the heavenly bodies and human life has
played an important part in history. From the earliest written
records recovered from the sands or caves of Babylonia,
through the studies and speculations of Greece and Rome,
from which it spread into Jewish, Arabic and Christian lore in
the West, and Chinese and Indian culture in the East, astrology has had an uninterrupted history of five thousand years.

In earlier days, as much as now, people have always wanted to "predict and control" their environment. Always we have used what we believed to be the best means available to accomplish this end, and always people have believed that the knowledge and techniques of their own day were based upon the authority of all previous knowledge, and incorporated current discoveries and observations, hence were "true," while the beliefs of an earlier day were "myths" in the sense of having been primitive or naïve.

In Babylonia, as well as in Assyria as a direct offshoot of the Babylonian culture, astrology had taken its place in the official cult as one means the priests had for ascertaining the will and intention of the gods. At its base is the indisputable fact that people's lives and welfare were largely dependent on phenomena in the heavens: the fertility of the soil depends upon the sun shining in the heavens and the rain that comes from the heavens. Likewise, the disasters caused by storm and inundation were seen as originating in the heavens. From this, the conclusion was drawn that the great gods had their seats in the heavens. It was a natural step for the priests, who corresponded to the scientists of a later day, to perfect a theory of accord between the phenomena observed in the heavens and occurrences on earth. The movements of the sun, moon and planets conveyed to the more intelligent mind the conception of a rule of law and order in the universe as against the more popular notion of chance and caprice. The sun, moon and planets became identified with the gods, and the concepts of ruling gods and ruling planets became hopelessly indistinguishable.

The predictive element in astrology grew out of a belief that the stars and planets did indeed rule not only the abstract nature, but also the lives of human beings. Therefore, it was important to people's control of their fate to discover ways of foreseeing what these ruling bodies were likely to do next. The only way of dealing with the unknown and the unknowable is to project the contents of the unconscious, in terms of a person's own hopes and fears, upon the incomprehensible object of concern. By ascribing human tendencies and human characteristics to the various planet-gods, people were able to account for the vagaries of fate. The character of the ruling bodies and the relations between them would then be seen as characterizing or influencing events taking place on earth. It is a matter of simple observation to recognize that the moment of a child's birth corresponds in time with a specific configuration of heavenly bodies. In a time when little was known about the many and diverse factors contributing to the development of the individual temperament, it was believed that the ruling constellations determined the dimensions of the nascent personality.

Modern science has shown that the correspondence of the stars and other natural elements and forces with events and human personality are not related in the simple, causalistic way that the ancients believed they were. But, as we all know, and as ecologists are constantly pointing out, there is a correspondence, there is a very evident relationship between people and their larger environment. The more we discover about this relationship, the more we are able to withdraw our projections of unconscious contents. The process of projection, that is, making subjectively determined, yet reasonable, suppositions about the unknown, is the first step toward going ahead to test the suppositions, the hypotheses, and eventually to withdraw those suppositions that are proved to be basically projections.

In his essay on *Synchronicity* (Jung's term for meaningful coincidences of events separated in space and/or in time),[21] Jung examined some of the beliefs surrounding apparently related incidents which seem to have no causal connection. These incidents could be, for example, the coincidence of a person's dream with an actual event that occurs at the same time some distance away; it could be ESP (extra-sensory perception) of phenomena that appears as a response to a situation that the individual could not have learned about through any ordinary means of sense perception or transfer of information; it could be a horoscope reading which corresponds to the observed character of the individual or his self-image, or an astrological prediction which seems to be borne out in subsequent events. The possibility of finding meaning in these correspondences had tantalized Jung for many years. The beginning of his serious study goes back to the days when Albert Einstein was developing his first theory of relativity. During this time Einstein was a guest on several occasions for dinner in Jung's home. In a letter on Einstein and synchronicity, Jung wrote: "It was Einstein who first started me off thinking about a possible relativity of time as well as space, and their psychic synchronicity."[22]

The study of meaningful coincidences could not be complete for him without a careful scrutiny of astrology. Since there was a lack of legitimate scientific data either validating or invalidating the correspondence of predictions based on horoscopes with subsequent events, Jung undertook an astrological experiment in the hope of finding out for himself something about the accuracy of such predictions. The proposition to be tested was the astrological assumption that certain individuals, as characterized by their horoscopes, will be predisposed to marry certain other individuals. The experiment is described in detail, and carefully worked out with statistical analysis comparing the horoscopes of married couples with those of non-married couples. The results of the experiment greatly abbreviated, were given by Jung as follows: "Although our best results . . . are fairly improbable in practice, they are theoretically so probable that there is little justification for regarding the immediate results of our statistics as anything more than chance . . . From the scientific point of view the result of our investigation is in some respects not encouraging for astrology . . . there is little hope of proving that astrological correspondence is something that conforms to law."[23]

Astrology has never been proved to be a valid means for predicting events or characterizing an individual. Nor did alchemy ever succeed in transforming base metals into gold. Yet these two precursors of modern science provide us with a wealth of data concerning the psychological nature of people and their symbols. Taken literally, astrology and alchemy have little meaning for most people today; for they belong to a world in which beliefs were based on the appearances of things, and the appearances of things have changed. What was believed to be true in those days is no longer believed. But taken symbolically, they provide us with a history of the development of consciousness through an ever changing panoply of archetypal images. These images point backwards to the unknown and unknowable, to the archetypes of the collective unconscious. The symbolic representations that we construct, in astrology and elsewhere, connect us with our roots in the past, from which we can draw the strength for growth.

Ever since Alan Watts exchanged his starched clerical collar for a Japanese silk kimono and found wisdom in insecurity —if not for life everlasting, then long enough to influence a younger generation—Americans have been turned on to the mysterious East. A rediscovery of ancient truth has led many of these people into fads and fantasies inspired by the pilgrims from the Orient, and a smaller number to the serious study of Hinduism, Taoism and Zen Buddhism. In their reading, they often discover that Jung had taken a similar path many years before, and had learned a great deal about Eastern religions and philosophy both through study and through his travels in India. If they have read his essays on Eastern religion in *Psychology and Religion*[24] they have some feeling for the great respect Jung held for much of the sacred teaching of the Orient. Also, they will have some understanding of his views on the potential effects of certain traditional Eastern ways of thinking upon the Western mind. All too frequently, however, Jung's writings have been misunderstood or only partially understood. His interest in Eastern religious thought and certain practices associated with it—like his interest in séances, in alchemy, or in astrology—have been incorrectly construed as a wholehearted and literal endorsement for use by Westerners today.

During the period of greatest fascination with psychedelic

drugs among college students and college drop-outs in the late 1960s, Tibetan mysticism was seized upon as a model or ideal to be sought within the psychedelic experience. Cecelia, whose case was discussed in Chapter 2, was one of these. *The Tibetan Book of the Dead*[25] had been available to the English-speaking reader since it was compiled and edited by W. Y. Evans-Wentz in 1927. It only became a best-seller on campuses from Harvard to Berkeley when Leary, Metzner and Alpert publicized it in their efforts to provide instant illumination for American youth through LSD. Their book, *The Psychedelic Experience: A Manual Based on the Tibetan Book of the Dead*, contains in its introductory section, "A Tribute to Carl G. Jung." Jung is presented, quite correctly, as one who understood that the unconscious could, and in extraordinary states did, manifest itself in hallucinations such as have been called "The Magic Theatre," and "The Retinal Circus," where energy is transformed into strangely frightening bodily sensations, "wrathful visions" of monsters and demons, visions of the earth-mother, boundless waters, or fertile earth, broad-breasted hills, visions of great beauty in which nature flowers with an intense brilliance that is not known to ordinary consciousness. Messrs. Leary et al. suggest that *The Tibetan Book of the Dead*—in which these images are described in exquisite detail so that the living may recite the text (or oral tradition) to the dying or newly dead person in order to guide him on his path into the realm of Spirit—is not a book of the dead after all. It is, they assert, "a book of the dying; which is to say a book of the living; it is a book of life and how to live. The concept of actual physical death was an exoteric façade adopted to fit the prejudices of the Bonist tradition in Tibet . . . the manual is a detailed account of how to lose the ego; how to break out of personality into new realms of consciousness; and how to avoid the involuntary limiting processes of the ego . . ."[26] In this sense, they identify "personality" with the conscious ego state, a state which in their view must be put aside in order to break into new realms of consciousness. They suggest that Jung did not appreciate the necessity for this leap into the unknown, since, in their words, "He had nothing in his conceptual framework which could make practical sense out of the ego-loss experience."[27]

But here these purveyors of imitation psychosis by the microgram (which occasionally, unfortunately, turns into the real thing) are the ones who miss the point, who misread Jung completely. Jung did know what it was like to come to the edge of ego-loss experience. His commitment had long been to the inner vision, but however close he came to total immersion in it, he felt that it was important, for Westerners at least, to maintain some contact with the ego position. To lose this entirely, it seemed to Jung, would be unconsciousness, madness or death. For him it was impossible to conceive of that state, described in *The Tibetan Book of the Dead* as the attainment of the Clear Light of the Highest Wisdom, in which one is merged with the supreme spiritual power, without the paradoxical conclusion that there is something left outside to experience the "conceiving." That something is ego-consciousness, which of course is not present in an unconscious state, in psychosis or after death, because ego-consciousness is by definition a term which describes our awareness of our nature and identity vis-à-vis that which "we" are not.

Jung explains his own difficulty, which is perhaps the difficulty of the Westerner, to realize what the Tibetan Buddhist calls *One Mind*. The realization of the *One Mind* (according to Jung's reading of *The Tibetan Book of the Great Liberation*) creates "at-one-ment" or complete union, psychologically, with the non-ego. In doing so, *One Mind* becomes for Jung an analogue of the collective unconscious or, more properly, it is the same as the collective unconscious. Jung writes:

> The statement "Nor is one's own mind separable from other minds," is another way of expressing the fact of "all-contamination." Since all distinctions vanish in the unconscious condition, it is only logical that the distinction between separate minds should disappear too . . . But we are unable to imagine how such a realization ["at-one-ment"] could ever

be complete in any human individual. There must always be somebody or something left over to experience the realization, to say "I know at-one-ment, I know there is no distinction." The very fact of the realization proves its inevitable incompleteness. . . . Even when I say "I know myself," an infinitesimal ego—the knowing "I"—is still distinct from "myself." In this as it were atomic ego, which is completely ignored by the essentially non-dualist standpoint of the East, there nevertheless lies hidden the whole unabolished pluralistic universe and its unconquered reality.[28]

When Jung says of *The Tibetan Book of the Dead* "it is a book that will only open itself to spiritual understanding, and this is a capacity which no man is born with, but which he can only acquire through special training and experience," his statement rests on an incomplete understanding of the spiritual teaching of the East, and most particularly of the deeper meaning and guidance in this profound book. During Jung's lifetime there was little opportunity for Westerners to learn directly from leading exponents of Tibetan Buddhism, hidden away as they were in their mountain fastnesses. But today, many great spiritual teachers who were expelled from their native land have come to the West, and have helped to clarify their beliefs with respect to dualism and "at-one-ment." As an example, I quote from Sogyal Rinpoche's *The Tibetan Book of Living and Dying:*

There are many aspects of the mind, but two stand out. The first is ordinary mind, called by the Tibetans *sem.* One master defines it: "That which possesses discriminating awareness, that which possesses a sense of duality—which grasps or recognizes something external;—that is mind. Fundamentally it is that which can associate with an 'other' —with any 'something' that is perceived as different from the perceiver." *Sem* is the discursive, dualistic thinking mind, which can only function in relation to a projected and falsely perceived external reference point . . .

Then there is the very nature of mind, its innermost es-

sence, which is absolutely and always untouched by change
or death. At present it is hidden within our own mind, our
sem, enveloped and obscured by the mental scurry of our
thoughts and emotions. Just as clouds can be shifted by a
strong gust of wind to reveal the shining sun and wide-open
sky, so, under special circumstances, some inspiration may
uncover for us glimpses of this nature of mind . . .

Do not make the mistake of imagining that the nature of
mind is exclusive to our mind only. It is, in fact, the nature
of everything. It can never be said too often that to realize
the nature of mind is to realize the nature of all things.[29]

We need to remember that Jung, for all his metaphysical
speculations, was in the first place and the last essentially a
psychotherapist, and his life was devoted to discovering the
means through which he could help individuals to know their
lives as rich in meaning in this world, namely, the world of
consciousness. This world may be immeasurably deepened
and enhanced as we have seen throughout our reading of
Jung, by the data of the unconscious. Of utmost importance is
it that the unconscious material flow into consciousness, and
furthermore, that material from consciousness flow into the
unconscious, adding new elements which dissolve, transform
and renew what has been present all along. But the most important thing, from the Jungian point of view is that the ego
may not *fall into* the unconscious and become completely submerged, overwhelmed. There must always be an "I" to observe
what is occurring in the encounter with the "Not-I."[30]

This was why he favored the method of "active imagination" for his own patients, and why this method is widely used
by analytical psychologists today. Admittedly, it is a slow process, this establishing of an ongoing dialogue with the unconscious, but we accept that. Confronting the unconscious for us
is not an "event," but rather a "condition" in which we live. It
is serious business, it is play; it is art and it is science. We
confront the unknown at every turn, except when we lose the
sense of ourselves (ego) or the sense of the other (the unconscious).

In my work with analysands, questions often come up about the relationship of active imagination to the practices of yoga and Eastern meditation. Students and analysands come to recognize that the dialogue between the ego and the unconscious, through the agency of the transcendent function in all its symbolic expressions, bears a certain resemblance to the symbolism of Tantric yoga in India and Tibet, lamaism, and Taoistic yoga in China. Yet Jung, who had studied these traditions for over half a century, beginning when they were quite unknown in the West except to a few scholars, did not advocate the adoption of these methods as a whole in the West, nor even their adaptation to our occidental modes and culture. The reason for this, as I have come to believe through study of Jung's writing, is that a psychotherapy based upon a psychology of the unconscious, a psychotherapy which is the "cure of souls" is, indeed, the "yoga" of the West.

Jung has pointed out that an uninterrupted tradition of four thousand years has created the necessary spiritual conditions for yoga in the East. There, he says, yoga is

the perfect and appropriate method of fusing body and mind together so that they form a unity . . . a psychological disposition . . . that transcends consciousness. The Indian mentality has no difficulty in operating intelligently with a concept like *prāna*. The West, on the contrary, with its bad habit of wanting to believe on the one hand, and its highly developed scientific and philosophical critique on the other, finds itself in a real dilemma. Either it falls into the trap of faith and swallows concepts like *prāna, atman, chakra, samādhi*, etc., without giving them a thought, or its scientific critique repudiates them one and all as "pure mysticism." The split in the Western mind therefore makes it impossible at the outset for the intentions of yoga to be realized in any adequate way. It becomes either a strictly religious matter, or else a kind of training . . . and not a trace is to be found of the unity and wholeness of nature which is characteristic of yoga. The Indian can forget neither the body nor the mind, while the European is always forgetting either the one or the other . . . The Indian . . . not only knows his own nature, but he knows also how much he himself is nature. The European, on the other hand, has a science of nature and knows astonishingly little of his own nature, the nature within him. For the Indian, it comes as a blessing to know of a method which helps him to control the supreme power of nature within and without. For the European, it is sheer poison to suppress his nature, which is warped enough as it is, and to make out of it a willing robot . . .[31]

He concludes his discussion with the warning:

Western man has no need of more superiority over nature, whether outside or inside. He has both in almost devilish perfection. What he lacks is conscious recognition of his inferiority to the nature around and within him. He must learn that he may not do exactly as he wills. If he does not learn this, his own nature will destroy him.[32]

The reasonable question at this point would be, "How do we learn this?" Perhaps I can approach it by telling about a brilliant young psychotherapist. Hannah worked in a university setting, treating student-patients. She was also attending graduate school and expected to get her degree "some day," but had never seemed in too much of a hurry about it. When Hannah came into analysis, she was immersed in some intense relationships with close men and women friends, in the Women's Liberation movement, and more than one demanding campus activity. She was feeling increasingly fragmented, expending herself in every direction, attempting to bring her knowledge and will to bear, first on this problem, then on that. As she felt under more and more pressure, she became increasingly assiduous about seeking out various new ways of dealing with the situations and conflicts that arose in her personal life and her work.

One "panacea" followed another. For a while there was yoga. But only by the hour, for there was always someplace to rush off to, someone who needed her, or some obligation she had promised to fulfill. The need she felt to socialize expressed itself in a round with encounter groups. Then she would feel too extraverted, so she would try meditation for a while. The passivity she came to in meditation turned her attention to her body—there was where the problems were impressed, encapsulated, she came to believe. A course of bio-energetics would follow, giving her an opportunity to attack physically each part of the body in which the impress of the psychic pain was being experienced, and to have it pounded or stretched or pushed or pulled into submission. Other techniques, ranging from attempts to control alpha waves in the brain through bio-feedback training, all the way to the scheduled rewards of behavior modification therapy, were attempted by Hannah in the attack on her own nature. In the race to gain control over herself she had failed to learn that she could not do exactly as she willed, and consequently her own nature was destroying her.

In the course of our analytic work, I did not tell her that her own nature, if she continued to heed it so little, would destroy her. I watched with her, the experiences she brought to the analytic sessions, and the effects that these experiences were having upon her. We talked about the high hopes with which she was accustomed to approach each new method or technique. She was interested in analyzing the results of her activities, but always impatient to go on to something else, always wanting to try a new way. For a while she was nearly hysterical between her enthusiasms and disappointments. It was just at this time that Hannah announced her desire to establish and organize a "crisis center" on campus where people who were suicidal, or in some other way desperate, could come for immediate help. The whole proposition was so untimely in view of her own tenuous situation, her own near desperation, that it was not difficult for me to help her come to the realization that the first "crisis patient" would be, or indeed, already was, herself. It was then that she began to become aware of the necessity to look at the crisis within herself, to see what was disturbed there.

But looking within was not so easy. That which was within was so cluttered by all the appurtenances, the many personas she was used to putting on for various occasions, that it was difficult to find out who the "who" was behind all its guises. This involved looking at her behavior, and also at her attitudes, not as something she initiated in order to create an effect, but in a different way. Strange to say, because she had never thought of it in just that way, she had to discover that her ego was not the center of the universe! But it was far more than a new way of thinking. Thinking, in fact, scarcely entered into it. Perhaps it came to her just because necessity made her shift her perspective, and perhaps a factor was the analytic transference itself, through which she observed and experienced the therapist as one who resisted using her own ego to enforce change upon the patient. It was a slow process, the process of change, and mostly it went on under the surface, below the matters that were actually discussed in the session. Occasionally hints of it emerged in dreams; sometimes they were acknowledged, sometimes that did not seem necessary.

Then there was a vacation for Hannah, a chance to get away from external pressures and to hike in the mountains and sleep under the open sky. Returning, at the beginning of the semester, Hannah announced that she was going to spend a little more time studying, that she was going to limit her other activities to those she could carry on without feeling overburdened. During the past two years, she admitted, she had coasted through graduate school without reflecting on her activities, without seeing what she was experiencing under the wider aspect of the history of human experience. Now she wanted to learn, and to do it at a relaxed and unhurried pace.

In the next weeks I noticed a growing calm in Hannah. At last the day came when it could be expressed. She came into my study, sat down, and was silent for a few moments, and she then told me: "Something important happened to me this week. I discovered what 'the hubris of consciousness' means. Oh, I had read many times that the intellectual answers are not necessarily the right answers, but this is not what it is. It is on a much different level than that. It means—one can hardly say it, for if I do I will spoil it, and I don't want to do that. The striving after awareness—as though awareness were something you could 'get' or 'have,' and then 'use' is pointless. You don't seek awareness, you simply *are* aware, you allow yourself to be—by not cluttering up your mind. To be arrogant about consciousness, to feel you are better than someone else because you are more conscious, means that in a similar degree you are unconscious about your unconsciousness."

Hannah had dreamed that she was in a small boat, being carried down a canal, in which there were crossroads of concrete, which would have seemed like obstacles in her way. But the boat was amphibious, and when it came to the concrete portions it could navigate them by means of retractable wheels.

She took the dream to portray her situation—she was equipped for the journey on which she was embarked, and she was being guided along, within certain limitations, in a direction the end of which she did not foresee. It was not necessary for her to make the vehicle go; all she had to do was to be there and go with it, and she would have time to spare to observe the scenery and learn what she could from everything around her. She was a part of all that, and not any longer one young woman out to save the world, or even a part of it. She *was* a part of it, and she did not even have to save herself. As she became able to hear with her inner ear the harmony of nature, and to see it with her inner eye, she could begin participating with it and so cease fighting against nature.

She was now experiencing the sense of "flowing along" as a bodily experience, in a body that was not separate from the psychic processes that experienced it. But she would never have known the smoothness, the ease, the utter delight of "flowing along" unless she had come to it as she did, through the confrontation with its opposite, the futile exercise of beating herself against insuperable obstacles.

Obviously, this particular way of coming to a harmonious

ego-self relationship is not appropriate or even possible for everyone. People must find their own individual ways, depending on many inner and outer circumstances. Hannah's case is important, however, in that it exemplifies a certain sickness of the Western world, which seems to affect the ambitious, the energetic, the aggressive, and the people who achieve "success," in the popular sense of the word. These are also the people who, more frequently than not, become weary, depressed, frustrated, dependent on medications, alcohol and illicit drugs to handle their moods, sexually unfulfilled, and who sometimes even admit to being "neurotic." Unlikely as it may seem, their problem is essentially a religious one; for it has to do with that "hubris of consciousness" which prevents us from looking beyond ourselves for the solution to our problems and for the meaning that lies hidden in all that we do, and see, and are.

Fortunately for us, in the years since Jung's death, the world has grown smaller and the intellectual intercourse between East and West has increased manyfold. The stream of human beings emigrating from Asia to the West has brought with it the treasures of Taoism and Buddhism. Taoism teaches the joy that derives from blending with the natural forces in the universe, rather than contending with them. The most beautiful metaphor for the path of the Taoist is "the water-course way," in which one flows, like water, over and under and through every obstacle, with a yielding softness that even wears away rock, on the way to the ultimate destination, the sea. No tortuous tension here, for the one who practices this way finds harmony within and without. Buddhist teachings, on the other hand, provide a complete and specific guide for the conduct of life. The Dalai Lama has expressed the essence of this philosophy as the active practice of compassion toward everything that lives.

Let us hope that the wisdom of the East may prove good medicine for the "sickness of the Western World."

14

We Were Born Dying

. . .

WHEN THE LATE-WINTER SUN burns the snow off tree branches and buds begin to swell, we anticipate that in due time there will be tiny yellow green leaflets, then pale leaves greening as summer progresses, which will turn red or golden in autumn, and that before the winter returns they will become dry and brittle and subject to the merciless wind which tears them off and blows them away. Nor are we surprised, though, when some leaves drop before they are fully grown, nor when some are blown off or chewed up by insects when they are fully ripe and strong-looking, nor that there are always a few that, shriveled and brown, cling tightly to the twig in the face of autumn storms and winter winds, until the new buds gently nudge them aside.

I have observed in the course of my work, and also in the events in my personal life, that nature has an inexorable way of proceeding that is, at the same time, unpredictable as to details. We enter into life, but despite the actuarial tables and the learned doctors' prognoses there is no way of knowing whether we shall die in the spring or the summer of life or cling to our last breath in the icy cold of winter. Only one thing is certain, individual lives proceed onward toward their goal, which is death, and it is the knowledge of that fact which determines much that we do, and the choices that we make. I heard a television announcement the other day asking for contributions to aid research on a fatal children's disease. The sentence that caught my attention was, "Did you know that some children are born dying?" I started for a moment and then I knew why the words had stabbed me—I know that *all* children are born dying, *we are all born dying!* This is the central fact of life, of analysis; it is the core of the individuation process.

In the beginning we lie curled up, unconscious, in the maternal womb. We grow there until it is time to be born, and then emerge to begin the circular journey which takes us through childhood and youth upward to the mid-point of life, then slowly, softly downward through the years of maturity, toward a gradual or sudden surrender of the ego to the unknowable—to the darkness in the womb of earth, the matrix of the unconscious. At every stage of life, the individuation process is going on. In some people it is pure nature expressing herself spontaneously, while in others it is highly cultivated. Since in every life the same goal is reached, and what lies beyond remains a mystery, the process is the only thing that matters. The sooner we realize it, the sooner we identify with the flowing stream (or any other metaphor of process which presents itself), the more likely we are to be able to become free of pointless struggles and fruitless conflicts. Thus, we liberate our energies for that collaboration with nature, which is self-realization in the highest sense. And yet, wanting self-realization is a modest desire, saving us from the exhaustion which comes from the effort of striving itself—no matter what we are striving for.

Jung, in his old age, was able to look back and reflect: "My life as I lived it had often seemed to me like a story that has no beginning and no end. I had the feeling that I was a historical fragment, an excerpt for which the preceding and succeeding text was missing."[1]

Hannah, the analysand who discovered the capacity in her to flow with life, was consciously involved in individuation while she was still young, on the very edge of her career. She had come to an attitude not so very different from the one Jung expressed, an attitude which would support her through the exigencies of her life—and they would be many, because she was curious and adventurous and unafraid.

Engaged in this same ubiquitous search was Byron, an analysand of mine. He was a social worker who had at one time intended to become a minister, but had left the seminary just before ordination. He gave as his reason his perception that the life of a cleric necessitated a rigid patterning and adherence to a creedal structure which he did not believe was possible for him. In the course of his battling inwardly against the traditional doctrines, he had lost the sense of his own personal contact with God. So then he had to ask, what is the battle all about? Are we fighting over the color of the Emperor's New Clothes?

In his daily work, Byron struggled over the practical problems of food, clothing and shelter for low-income families. The task was discouraging; he could never provide enough of whatever was needed in material things, and in matters of the spirit they asked nothing and he offered nothing. He became depressed and gradually withdrew from his casual friendships, maintaining only one or two close relationships. For the most part he felt very much alone, and especially as he was approaching his thirty-third birthday.

The time was of great symbolic importance for him. Thirty-three was the age at which Jesus died, having accomplished all that he could during his earthly life. Byron reflected on his own life: what had he done in his thirty-three years? What if he were to die now, what would have been the meaning of his life? The idea of death began to haunt him. More and more he thought about the possibility of dying—at times it was appealing, at other times ghastly and horrifying.

On the eve of his birthday Byron decided to confront his fear and fascination with death, with the help of as much marijuana as he could manage to smoke. He had used marijuana occasionally in the past, but only a few puffs, and this time he determined that it would be different—he wanted to go into the feelings that had frightened him, and he would loose the barriers that had until this time prevented his doing so. He would go into the feelings and come out again, and he would then deal with what he had experienced. To make sure of this he would write down everything he saw and heard and felt.

He related, afterward, how he did this, stoned on grass, holding onto his pen with all his strength, forcing the letters, the words, to flow out of it like a thin stream of blood from his fingers, and with all the pressure and all the pain. Under the influence of the drug, he had begun to write:

> DEATH IS AN ORGASM
> the final one.
> Is the death-wish nothing more than a giant fuck pretasted?
> So too the sacrament of the altar
> a pre-taste of bliss, of glorious bliss?
> What is so gorgeous as ORGASM? COSMIC ORGASM?
> The final fuck-up is a fuck-out of existence

Clutching the pen to direct its vibrations, he set forth his experience:

> I finally held it to the breaking-point—until I collapsed—
> A foretaste of the real, the GOD-DAMNED real (!!!!) thing.

Then in carefully lettered words, the letters growing larger as they progressed down the page:

> To have gone there and come back is to have a call,
> I suppose . . .
> But to say WHAT!!???
> Not just that one was there!!!
> Is there an answer!!!!??????

Words from the rock opera floated up at him:

JESUS CHRIST SUPERSTAR said
that to learn how to die one only has to die.

The poem of life and death took shape in a hazy way as the blue smoke thickened:

It all began tonight by picturing myself underwater
as I was holding the smoke . . .
Swimming, swimming, holding my breath . . . YES, that's
*   where*
I began to taste of death and liked it . . .
begin the orgasmic experience of life . . .
downing the half (or more)—dying . . .
this repeats itself as one dies in orgasm—now with a
woman, a thought, a friend, a vision . . . then in the final
*   one.*

                    • • •

ANXIETY experienced to pt. of panic—
Then acceptance of it overcoming it.
Getting beyond ego and ego-loss.

                • • •

The period of the mystics co-incides
with that of ars moriendi,[2]
whether they coincide or not.

                • • •

When the heat of death burns the insides of your veins,
you're beginning to see glory.
To learn HOW to die (in glory) you only have
to die (willingly) . . .
You give yourself back to God . . . What could be more
*   sexual*
in the spiritual sense than to return from whence we came?

                    • • •

33 was experienced
orgasmically—
Now starts the second half—a half that is already
beyond death (a little), willing to die and from thence
beginning to transcend death (a little).

                    • • •

Able to get back to Holy of Holies . . .
to see the problems of wearers of the cloth . . .

Kept from their orgasm with the world, forced to fuck
the Church, which became
for them the Real Presence of Death . . .
fuck the Church, die to death . . .
that you may die to life and capture willingly
the life that willing death has to offer.

                              .   .   .

Learn to die that you may live again.

                    .   .   .

Death is the ultimate assurance of a tranquil end . . .
the everlasting extension of the utterly embracing silence
that follows one's intercourse . . .
think then of the depth of bliss in the silence following
one's intercourse with death.

                         .   .   .

He who penetrates through beyond death . . .
begins to taste of a life that can know no end.
ONE EXISTS in the afterglow of death, NO MORE:
one LIVES (and creatively!)

                         .   .   .

What message can I bring from beyond death . . .
If I'm called to preach that. . . .
Then WHAT (!) am I to say?
A vision of light at depth, of the darkness,
at the deep end of the shaft . . .
It opens up—

Here a sketched circle, within it a great burst of light, ex-
ploding, shooting out in all directions.

                    JESUS CHRIST superstar MESSAGE:
                    TO CONQUER death, you only have to die . . .
                    He then proceeded to do just that . . .
                    TO DIE . . .
                    and by doing so
                    conquer it . . .
                    commending Himself to the Father . . .
                    that should have ended orgasmically—on a
                    high (or RISING) tone,

> *not on a spirit trailing*
> *off to the depths.*

. . .

At the end Byron had felt exhilarated, as though the long tense quiet search for the mystery of death were ended. The tone of the cry at the crucifixion should not be weak and resigned, he averred, but forthright and courageous. This death, the death of Jesus Christ incarnate in him, in his contemporary life, in "Jesus Christ Superstar," was the death of his own spiritual frustration, leaving as residue the jaded, dejected, unfruitful ego-part, encapsulated in ennui, disorientation, anxiety and isolation. The way was made open for rebirth, into the second half of life.

"Writing the notes under the influence of pot," he said later, "I was feeling that this was the most important thing I would ever do—to capture these ecstatic moments for all time . . . the sense of eternity must not fly away, I must get them down . . . the pen was a strong, electric, resistant thing, I was hanging on to it for dear life. The feeling of falling and falling . . . the panic that goes with every muscle tensing up in the fear of falling . . . then at some point the fear turns into an acceptance of falling. So let me fall, and then the body can go limp and it doesn't feel bad anymore."

He said, "The point is not to solve the problems of the world, nor even to resolve them; what seems to be right is to dissolve the problem, break it down into tiny particles as a detergent breaks down grease, and then assimilate the substance of the problem. The individual must become able to do that."

Continuing, "You have to let the inner voice tell you what to do. The New Testament says, the Holy Spirit will give you the words. If you let yourself fall into your own resources, then the kinds of conflicts you feel on the conscious level are transcended."

What can the analyst do in the face of the powerful matter surging up out of the depths? I could only be there, be there and let him know that he was not mad but had tapped the source of the archetypal vision, which is timeless, and in which death is not an end, but merely an incident.

During the few months following the experience just related, Byron's work on himself had fully begun. He felt that his ego boundaries were more permeable, and insisted that he was no longer bound by his daily chores and responsibilities. Outside, in the world, it didn't appear that he had changed very much. No objective measure would have picked up what was happening (except, perhaps, a chemical analysis for marijuana). But Byron knew, as I knew, that everything was different. Death and resurrection for him had only belonged to a concept before. After, he said that there was no longer any need for him to *believe* in death and resurrection. He said it was his reality, and that every cell in his body bore witness to that. I warned him that it was not all that simple, that he might be going through a period of inflation, of pseudo-enlightenment. I suggested to him that ego boundaries need not enslave a person, but could provide a safe space from which to view the wider and deeper dimensions of reality. I urged him to examine his experience from a clear-eyed perspective, unclouded by any mind-altering substance. He was not willing, perhaps not able, to do this and, shortly after his plunge into the depths of the unconscious, he left analysis. I was not in favor of it, but finally it was his choice to make.

Much later, after I had lost contact with Byron, I learned that he had led a troubled life. He was in difficulty with the law at various times, not only about his use of drugs, but also about some unethical behavior associated with his work. It seems, as a friend of his told me, that Byron always felt that laws and moral codes did not apply to him. In the end he had to pay a terrible price for his dissociation from the ego world and its necessary restraints. I can only hope that his innate creativity may have helped him find the lost ego-self relationship and cherish it.

Psychological death and rebirth was experienced by another man in my practice, an older man, Julian, who is well into the second half of life. It manifested itself in two dreams.

Here is the first: *Our way of getting there at all is full of difficulties. It is furtive, sub-legal, via boats, smuggling, sneaking, avoiding authorities, being chased—somehow I feel on the side of the officers, yet I help the hoods. After climbing through intricate alleys, rushing up stairs, leaping rooftops, we find ourselves in the labyrinthine, plush-carpeted and gilt interiors of a nineteenth-century-style opera house like La Scala. We are always being rushed about from this to that loge for a glimpse of this or that elaborately dressed person. I am trying to arrange a secret rendezvous—is it Lola?—of complicated proportions. Everywhere are glimpses of luxury—in architecture, interiors and dress.*

Then, suddenly, it all begins to fall apart—columns and walls split and disintegrate before my eyes. The rich decorations and costumed people all collapse and melt away in clouds and showers of paste, chalk, plaster. It is as though all had been made of chalk masks, a pretense of overwhelming proportions. How could I ever have taken it all for real? Pillars, balconies, ornate frescoes crumble and fall into total ruin and final catastrophe. I, too, fall with a thunderous clatter. I awake with fear and trembling.

Although the reality of Julian's precarious position remained relatively unconscious to him, the dream accurately depicted it. He was a successful business executive, as measured by conventional standards—he had made a lot of money and lived in a fine house; he did all the proper things like dressing his wife elegantly and inviting the right people to his parties. He pretended to be interested in social reforms, and spoke a good deal about morality and justice. But it had all been a front, a persona which did not fit the person behind it. That person had been an exploiter of the weak, an opportunist of sorts. He had carried on shoddy romantic affairs which had been damaging both to the women involved and to his wife. Inside of all the splendor and artistry that his appearance displayed—the opera house of the dream—was decay and dust. "Gilt" covered it all, could this have been a play on the word? For all his savoir-faire, Julian was feeling the overwhelming burden of having lived a false and mean life. And, suddenly, when he looked in the mirror, the years of dissolution stared back at him and he knew that he was sick inside. This was what had brought him into analysis. All that he had struggled to attain over the years seemed empty and unimportant. If only he could feel like a decent person, if only he could get free of the burden of the bad deals and chicanery and lies and infidelity.

And yet, he had not faced the real truth until this dream. The real truth is, of course, the fact of death. The fact is that he must now look around himself and see the hollow splendor that he had built up while in the process of sacrificing his own integrity, and ask himself, "Is this all there is?"

In his youth, Julian had wanted to be an artist. Early he had become discouraged—for one thing, he was convinced that he wasn't sufficiently talented to become outstanding, for another he was unwilling to struggle financially when there was a chance that he could follow a more lucrative profession. But always he had told himself, "Someday when I have enough money I'll buy a small house by the seashore and take vacations and long weekends off to go there and paint." There had never been enough time for that and there had never been enough money.

Now, at fifty, time was getting ever shorter; he could expect at best another twenty years or so. On the other hand, tomorrow or today might be his last. Panic was setting in— there had to be another way to live, there had to be a way to get out of the way things were now.

I thought of what Jung had said in his essay on "The Stages of Life":

Thoroughly unprepared, we take the step into the afternoon of life; worse still, we take this step with the false assumption that our truths and ideals will serve us as hitherto. But we cannot live the afternoon of life according to the programme of life's morning; for what was great in the morning will be little at evening, and what in the morning was true will at evening have become a lie. I have given psychological treatment to too many people of advancing years, and have looked too often into the secret chambers of their souls, not to be moved by this fundamental truth.[3]

Before the advent of Julian's dream of destruction, he had been aware that his life internally was a shambles, but he felt that there was little hope of accomplishing any radical change. The problems seemed insurmountable, he was enmeshed in the complicated structure of his own construction, there was no way of getting out. "Labyrinthine" was the word the dream supplied, and it was well chosen. The dream showed him that it could collapse, all and all, suddenly and completely. In his own soul the event had already been foreseen.

We talked about the meaning of the dream, but said nothing about how life could change in practical terms. Transformation occurs only when the inner situation is right for it. The dream had indicated that the inner situation was clearly bound to change now—we needed to observe it and to be ready to follow the lead of the unconscious. In a way, Julian had come to the same point which Byron had reached: the point of having to let himself fall, to simply let go and fall, fall into his own resources, and let go of the conflicts that he had been grappling with on the conscious level.

A few days after the dream of destruction, Julian had another dream: *I am at some kind of double funeral. Two women are dead. I say to Bill that the mothers (deceased) looked nice—in a kind of conventional funeral remark. He is angry because one of the women was not his mother, the other was. He wanted all the compliments. I walk up to the woman who was not Bill's mother to look at her, and she turns, rises up, looks fresh and exceedingly healthy, and gives a tremendous, defecating blast. Two doctors come in and remark that she has soiled the sheets. The deceased now lives in a kind of vigorous exuberant health.*

Julian had some associations to the dream. He told me: "I had read before of Martin Luther's moment of great transformation: it had happened on the monk's toilet, and he who had been chronically constipated suddenly experienced this tremendous defecating blast; at the same time his psyche experienced a renewal, he no longer spoke and wrote in a stilted way, but in a vigorous, expressive German."

The double funeral, the two women, puzzled him. One was known, but the one who was restored to life was unknown. The latter must mean then, the soul-woman, the anima who represents the life of the unconscious and its guiding spirit. It is she who is apparently dead, and yet the dream tells the dreamer very clearly that she is only blocked and *apparently* dead, the excrement of her life—his soul's life—has been contained too long, it has putrefied, it has poisoned her, it has brought on the appearance of death. Still, in its very putrefaction the micro-organisms come powerfully alive and create the explosive situation within. Either the foul stuff has to be expelled, or the corpse is really a corpse. The unconscious shows what must happen and furthermore, by presenting the whole image in the funeral scene, it becomes clear that now there is really nothing to lose. This re-emphasizes the scene of the previous dream, when the building collapses and consequently is seen to have been nothing but a decayed shell anyway.

The "doubling" motif appears again, with the two doctors who come in. We conjecture that this may refer to the analytic process, and that seems right. I am not the one who heals, nor is the patient—the two of us belong to the healing moment—but we are there, basically, to note what occurs. Perhaps this scene also suggests that we are not supposed to congratulate ourselves. That theme came up earlier when the shadow-figure, Bill, "wanted all the compliments." It is clear from the role of the doctors—just being there and paying attention to what has happened—that they do not *do* anything. The situation has been recognized, it has been faced. And from the very depths of the unconscious, the change has come, and burst into the world. When it comes out there is much noise and it is ugly and it stinks, but it is possible for the dead woman, now rid of her rotting feces, to live anew. Perhaps she will guide Julian in returning to some of his earlier interests, painting, for instance, when the time is right. The other dead woman, pristine and properly peaceful, is dead for all time.

The death-in-life experiences which we call *psychological death*—in contrast to *organic death*—have been described in two men, one in his thirties and one in his fifties. For both of these, the specter of organic death was somewhat distant; each felt the inevitability of it, but neither felt it pressing so close that he was without hope. They were ill-prepared for death, both of them, but they were prepared to prepare.

It would be possible to relate many cases in which death is feared or denied, or where there is protest against the fact of death, by an individual for himself or on behalf of someone close to him. We all know such cases, and we are well enough acquainted with their pitiable nature.

I will bring to a close this discussion of analysis in the Jungian mode with a report on the case of a man approaching seventy years of age, who has lived his life in knowing awareness of the fact we have posited here: *We were born dying.*

Abraham is a judge, a Roman Catholic, and a philosopher. Reared in the tradition of the Church, he has spent much time on and off during his lifetime in the study of the writings of the Church Fathers and mystics. Also, contemplative "infused" prayer has been for him at certain periods a direct meeting with the *spiritus rector*, the divine guide within. But at other times, he had been tempted to involve himself in various schemes and projects that clashed with his personal idealism, and he had given in to the proffered temptations on many occasions. He made and lost several modest fortunes, made them through questionable dealings and lost them through greed. There were also some inconsequential love affairs which made him feel slight in his own eyes. Always, when he went through a period of reverses, he had found his way back to himself through withdrawal from his more extraverted activities and the practice of meditation. He would be able to get himself into better order and begin to function again in a more integrated way, with his philosophical grounding and his activities of the day finding a closer harmony. But it was life full of distraction and allurements, with which he had constantly to come to terms in one way or another.

At the time he came into analysis he was preparing to retire. There would be a modest pension, little money had been saved otherwise. His wife had been urging him to go back into the private practice of law, but he had made the decision not to do so. He was interested now in composing his thoughts, reading, writing, taking long walks and enjoying his small garden. Life was like a flower that has stood the heat of the sun throughout the long day and now, at evening, he was willing to see the petals begin gently to draw up as dusk approached.

He had been ill for a week with one of the chronic complaints that afflict the aging, and had stayed home in bed. By Friday he was feeling better and several friends had come in over the weekend to visit.

On Monday when Abraham came to analysis, he told me that he had felt that his visitors over the weekend had been mainly "business friends." "They totally dried me up—maybe it was partly the medicine I was taking. We were having conversations about certain judicial matters. When they left I wanted to get back to the quiet mood of the sickness, the thoughts I had had then, the meditation. So, after a short rest, I began to organize my thoughts, and I would like to relate them to you."

He then proceeded, and I will try to put down the gist of what he said from my recollection and from the notes I made after the session was over. Here is the essence of it:

"I am feeling less uptight. I'm not trying specifically to cling to insight or meaning. I have felt in a double bind—the temptation to expand, to capitalize on my efforts all these years, or to withdraw, into a smaller and yet—in an inner sense—an infinitely wider existence.

"I had an insight. Part of the meaning of the double bind is that I have been trying consciously to loosen up—to put myself through a regimen of inner discipline. Now it seems to me that the more you consciously try to interfere with natural behavior, the more you tighten up. It is not 'let go'—*that* is too active; what is necessary is just to 'let be'—let *myself* be, principally, as well as the world.

"I remember when I was engaged on a day-to-day pursuit of detachment. My goal was to loosen the grip of my desires. It required a certain amount of will, this detachment—it was like using a stiff wire scrubbing brush on my psyche.

"I've always been goal-directed. I think basically that is where the real desert of my life has been. As I look back on it, living in the present moment—in *fact*, practicing the sacrament of the present moment—was an illusion, a *fiction* to conceal the unconscious motivations that obsessed me. I was no less goal-directed, no freer nor less bound than before; it was, in fact, purely spurious.

"I'm reminded—some one of the great spiritual voices (St. Teresa?) was speaking of the ascent of the ladder, La Scala,[4] saying, the soul is like an infant constantly demanding the mother's breast, and peevish and irritable if it is deprived of it. St. Teresa said that we try to *do* too much—like children we constantly want to love, to crave, spiritual experience.

"Our thinking in terms of past events, field events, are futile things; we become blinded with historicism and overlook the fact that the purely historic events may be futile—because the event occurring in the field was perceived improperly— therefore we may have derived a false meaning. Thus only through this mysterious organ in the psyche that we call intuition are we at all able to arrive at a meaning of what we have lived through, and the extent to which we have, in participating in it, falsified it.

"Examining ourselves from an internal viewpoint and not from a standpoint that is culturally determined, we are able to work out meanings to relate what we then were to what we are now. Even Heraclitus[5] never believed altogether in the flux, since he thought there was a persistence in 'becoming.'

"I feel that the real meaning of my life is to find a freedom from fear and the 'false anxieties' that have obsessed me since childhood."

Here I asked Abraham what he meant by "false anxieties."

He continued: "If an anxiety does not equate in some form of causal relationship to some contemporaneous aspect of life —if, in fact, its structure is almost fetishistic, I say it is 'false.' I am not referring to *Angst*, to which we are all subject, but to the shames and fugues that have beset me all my life.

"For the first time in my life I have confronted my own ambiguity. [Here he referred to some writing he is doing in an attempt to clarify these matters.] I think everyone somewhere knows that the real source of *Angst* is not the existential *Angst*, but a coming to awareness of a basic ambiguity, an ambiguity that lies behind the appearances.

"The great paradox is ambiguity and freedom—the ambiguity that lies between the polarities of determinism and free will—and it is within these polarities that we have to choose our standards, our ethos, both as relates to our personal lives and our view of the world.

"So you see, I have had an insight."

We could stop here, and leave the matter of Abraham with the assumption that he was able to live out his days holding in his psyche the tension of the opposites, polarities in balance, as he proceeded on the path to the inevitable final goal. But somehow life is not like that; just when one thinks one has acquired knowledge and understanding, the spiral of individuation takes another turn, and there are new problems, new difficulties. A person seems to be in much the same place as before, but looks upon the situation from another level, with more distance, more perspective, and so there is a difference from the way it was.

The events in Abraham's life were such that he did not take the rest he had anticipated. A few months after the experiences related above, a very important political position was offered to him. It promised to make use of all his talents, his lifetime of acquired skills and knowledge. He had been reluctant to take on the new responsibility just at the time he was preparing to retire, but he was urged and pressed by those who said he was the only man for the job, and that he was badly needed. At last he gave in.

The responsibilities of his new position were indeed demanding. He missed a couple of analytic sessions, saying that something important had come up. Then he suspended his analysis for a while, telling me that the work he had gotten into was just too much, and that during the period of adjusting to the additional requirements that were placed upon him he was feeling that he simply could not give adequate attention to his analysis. He stayed away for a few weeks, then telephoned and asked to return to me for regular sessions.

The first few sessions after he came back were frightful and discouraging. He had lost most of the calm which had characterized the last sessions before he had taken the new position, and especially the one which I have described. He was tense, nervous, fidgety, chain-smoking—anything but composed. He complained about the pressures of work, about his physical health, his aches and pains. He expressed a longing for the deeply grounded peace he had known only a few months before, but which now seemed out of reach. Even his dreams had been affected; he described them as "drenched in grays, blacks, and the soapy colors of street lights seen through a slight fog."

I noted that Abraham would now come into each session in an agitated state, sometimes with trembling hands, obviously suffering. There was little I could do for him except to feel his feelings with him, and to let him know that I was as much a participant in his suffering as another human being could be, while at the same time maintaining the objectivity that would be necessary if I were to help make it possible for clarity to enter his situation. By the end of each session his level of anxiety would be greatly reduced and he would have, if nothing more, the courage to face a few more days of stress and disquietude.

Then one day he came in more vibrant than I had seen him in a long time, saying he had had an experience which began as a dream, but was more than a dream, for it encompassed a strange and powerful vision. He began with the dreaming part: *I am in a building, looking out over a parapet. The building starts to move—the movement is toward the East. Streets with pedestrians and cars are passed. The building functions like a train.*

Then, he told me, he became suddenly aware that he was no longer dreaming. The light in his room had changed, from the usual twilight or half-lit night, to full daylight. This is how he said it was:

With the light, suddenly the numinosity appears. I am no longer on the other side, the dreaming-ego side, the side that belongs to "my" unconscious. I have left this behind. I have crossed over. I am in another world.

"What strikes me as not only significant, but also stupefying, is that I lost consciousness of the dreaming-I. Phenomenologically, there was no longer an *I* to perceive, on this side of the dream screen. I recall rubbing my hands, my face; engaging in those traditional reassurances of a personal substance and saying quite distinctly—'I am awake, I am really here.'

"There was a real division between the two sides of the screen. First, I was here, this side in the reality of the unconscious; then I was there, fully conscious, but with no screen in front of me, no sense of awareness of the dreaming-I looking. I was conscious and I was engaged in another world. Still, there persisted the ego sensation: perception was organized; the other world in which I so briefly found myself was multivalued, yet at the same time I perceived a difference in the energy gradients; there was unity and multiplicity. They existed together and they did not exist together. I was conscious of no change, either before or after. I was in one place, then the other, by a sort of quantum leap."

From this new state, which was not dreaming, but another

sort of consciousness from that which we experience as a shallow skin on the surface of the unconscious, the vision of light faded and darkness returned. Then the dream continued:

The building of the earlier part of the dream now becomes a train. The train is shunted at a siding. I walk into another building. It is a courthouse, but it has a small chapel on the first floor as you go in. [He later realized, upon reflecting, that it was similar in arrangement to the courthouse into which he was planning to move the next week.] *The chapel was Catholic. There was a center aisle and rows of benches sharply descending on either side of the aisle. The chapel would not seat forty people. I genuflect. I have an armful of umbrellas, suitcases, and a topcoat. I attempt to sit down and I find the bench occupied by another person; she has packages of her own strewn around, but helps me arrange mine. I say that I will sit on the next bench below. I turn and look at the woman. She has a long crooked nose like a certain opera star, which I had always felt was unfortunate, a narrow razor-edge face and beautiful kind eyes, lovely hair, and a magnificent, full-breasted body. I am sexually attracted to her and realize at once and fully that I could wind up in bed with her.*

There is another fragment to the dream—a moment when I realize that in the back of the chapel someone has stolen my topcoat.

We analyzed the dream, or rather he analyzed the greater part of it, for his understanding of himself over the long years of search and contemplation had made it possible for him to draw meaning out of the seemingly meaningless symbols of the unconscious. I give you basically what he said about the dream, expressed as it was in the atmosphere of intense dialogue, questioning, wondering, answering, absorbing. My own contributions are present also, but the process has been so much a mutual endeavor all along that it is not easy to sort it out in terms of whether the material originated with him or with me. This mutuality had been evidenced in a long series of synchronistic events that had occurred between us—we both would think of the same book at the same time, or he would telephone me just when I was pondering one of his dreams—so that it seems fully believable that we were connected on an unconscious level by some archetype which was constellated in our way of being with one another.

To return to the dream—Abraham remembered that the dream of the moving building was a recurrent theme. He experienced it as a structure, an internal structure that carried him along. He said, "The building seems to me to be the space-time continuum congruent with the perceiving ego. I am moving through historical time. I notice that I am being transported. I have not placed this mechanism in motion. This is a streaming motion over which I have no control, that does not frighten me, which I tolerate fully, which I do not question. This is very different when compared to my inching-progress in 'real' time, when every circumstance seems to 'gall my kibe.' I am assured of something extraordinary about this movement."

I asked him about "the East."

"I am moving toward the East. The building is carrying me. The East evokes thought of Spirit, of William Blake and the gnostics, the alchemists, the direction in which men turn in prayer—Mecca, Jerusalem, the rising sun."

So this is the direction into which the unconscious guided him at this important moment in his life! And, when he turned toward the East, being moved from within, he had a sudden experience of the Holy. He described this so I could nearly see and feel it.

"Suddenly the dream becomes numinous, I mean to say, filled with a sense of the presence of divinity. I realized, while within the core of sleep, that I had not had a numinous dream. Now the numinosity was signified by the appearance of light.

"What really startled me about the dream," Abraham continued, "was that, when I made the effort of recall, the faint hum of the body disappeared. Sometimes I can almost sense my body's recumbency as a recollected secondary factor after the dream content is recalled. I have often had the impression that the body was a stage upon which the dream was enacted. Direction, in terms of dream movements, seems to result in an orientation so precise, in terms of the four quadrants, that the direction or the understanding of it must have a very ancient archetypal organization."

Looking back over the records of his dreams over the past few months he saw that over and over again the action upon the inner screen was oriented with precise reference to the cardinal points of the compass without fail. Abraham, as dreamer, always knew the direction, whether East, West, North or South, which he assumed in the dream. With reference to this dream, he explored the symbolism of the East for the deeper meaning it would provide through the process of amplification:

"In Blake, the East is the seat of the emotions. If the movement is toward the West, the East becomes the seat of Ulro, Hell; the West is the location of the spirit. Yet other and contrary values have been assigned in astrological and gnostic literature to these compass points. Perhaps they can only be interpreted within the context of the actual present of the individual. I mean all this in terms of a system of symbols neither absolute nor random. I must apply to them that homespun system of probability theory—common sense. This is coupled with intuition, which leads me more surely. Emotions are, in a sense, the spirit of the body, the pervasive odor of sacrificial meats, rendered upon the coals of the altar to the utterly other, whether it be the other self, or God."

As Abraham accepted this interpretation provisionally, a great deal of meaning emerged from the matrix of the unconscious events. He was able to see the unconscious (the building) carrying him toward an antinomy of emotional balance (eastward) against the stream of the rational westward movement which might have seemed to overwhelm him in this particular moment in time and space in which he was engaged as he moved into a new phase of endeavor. He could now see that the non-rational in his life was opposed to the rational; the movement toward the East was the opposition of the unconscious, a corrective maneuver to allay a headlong flight into the rigid frame of work and obligation.

Halfway between the sections of the dream came the moment of light—the identification with a balanced world of light and color. The ensuing dream section spoke clearly of the balance of opposites, in showing to Abraham's dreaming mind that neither the one extreme nor the other was wholly satisfactory. The *being-there* experience was a prefiguration of individuation, the actual attainment and, also, the indication of the path that lay between the polarities. This was the meaning of the experience of the moment of awakening: the attainment of a new state; the placement of this experience within the linear, therefore rational and dreamlike experience.

Abraham described how his sudden break with this world was recaptured from the frozen depths of the dream, at the time that he made the active effort of recall. There was a remarkable and totally inexplicable break between one part of the dream and the other; and again, when he returned to the dream state. He said, "I immediately had the impression of being in another framework; not of time or space, but something totally altered. Nor was there any rejection or nausea or anxiety. It was a state that I accepted totally, calmly, as though it were predestined."

It was impossible not to attribute this complete capacity for acceptance of the unknowable to some prognostic element; probably deeply rooted biologically, related to the dissolution of organic systems. It is necessary to interpret these rare experiences on different levels at the same time, particularly with persons well past mid-life.

To return to the text of the dream: The building which seems to be a train, or like a train, brought up several associations. One, especially, dipped unexpectedly into the dreamer's childhood, to a recollection of his father's last days. His father had been ill in the hospital, and when he was recovering from an injection of morphine he had begun to talk about riding a freight train (moving from west to east) and how he was going to jump off at the place where the tracks came close to his house. The hospital was the train, the freight train; he was wanting to get out of bed in order to go home. He was obviously hallucinating, and yet he was *there*. He died not long after.

Abraham commented on a quite other use of the word "train," the French use—*en train*—which means to set to work, to get going, to start, to put in hand, to begin, to throw into gear, to make ready . . . as, *mettre en train*.

Putting it all together, he saw that there were coincidences at different levels and within different segments of the dream, spaced linearly, so that the whole might be seen as a totality: the emotions, balance, yielding to the will of God, work, the reminder from his father's hallucination—that the bottom is all hallucination, in a normal sense, or a universal sense of Maya; that the visionary light was a partial experience of individuation—perhaps an unconscious satori. This latter was reinforced by the loss of the topcoat—perhaps one of the layers of the ego.

The woman was also present in the small and sacred place. When Abraham came in he was heavily laden with all sorts of impedimenta. She helped him, with great good humor, to arrange the various articles. He was totally paralyzed by the multitude of the burdens—a typical response to his complicated life situation. He described the other figure as a representation of the analyst, and his reactions to her as follows:

"The woman herself was divided into two parts: one part, her face, was very unpleasant—ugly and distorted. [He emphasized the word *distorted*.] The eyes, the hair, were transcendently beautiful; the face, in all its crooked, mean distortions with its crooked, long nose, seemed not so much like an absolute block, but like a dam posited between the upper and the lower parts of her. Nothing impeded my sexual response to the body. My immediate reaction to this on awakening was that the ugliness was only a mask, and that this served as a psychological deterrent, splitting the analyst in a very realistic way between the upper and the lower poles. Concealed behind this mask must be the repressions which had been rejected by the conscious mind.

"I do not believe in the *censor* of Freud," Abraham continued, "nor in a lot that flows from it. Nevertheless, I do feel that much that he has interpreted and ascribed to this automation is a result of factors that arise elsewhere, as is the case in this dream. The dream itself obviously has reference to the transference of patient to analyst. I cannot see the transference as a neurosis, nor shall I ever. I further believe that if you have a male-female relationship, you can only have a male-female reaction."

The distortion in the image of the woman was very sensible. The analyst had been idealized by the patient. She had received the projection of the anima of the patient, she reflected beauty and wisdom, and her expressiveness, which meant so much to him was symbolized by the opera star, a singer, which is, of course, a homonym for the analyst's name: Singer. But the analyst was also a person, a very human person, who was in reality unable to measure up to the image in the psyche of the patient. The dream apprised him of this, by diminishing the overvalued physical appearance and the attraction of the woman for him. This was the way the dream denied to the patient and the analyst a full resolution of their relationship. The patient was responsive to the analyst on an unconscious level, as the dream showed, but the patient and the analyst were separated in terms of the aesthetic value—the distortion of the analyst's face. The analyst had to be decapitated to reach the patient; the patient had to be blinded to reach the analyst. Thus, it was clear that the transference was meant to be an inner relationship, assimilated to the patient, and not to be lived out in an objective relationship, as a love affair.

Working through this dream became a profound experience for Abraham. It was no less so for me, for it deepened my understanding of the process and brought me closer to the experience of living toward death as I moved slowly through the experience with my patient.

In the weeks that followed, Abraham regained the calm that he had known before, but this time it was deeply grounded in its archetypal basis and would not easily be moved. In the sessions that followed, the insights and feelings became as friends; Abraham could reach into them and take hold of them, even in the midst of his busy days and his worldly responsibilities.

Little by little his attitude toward his work changed. He found that he could do what was necessary without always feeling that what he accomplished was insufficient. He was content with expending his best efforts, and he had come to realize that those efforts would naturally be forthcoming as he also took time for his work on himself, his dreams, and his contemplative practices. Gradually he began to delegate portions of his work to other people. He sought out younger men who would be able to assume the tasks which he himself had been doing and who would be able, when the time came, to relieve him of his responsibility. His analytic work became increasingly important to him. Much of it was done without the analyst's help, although he continued to come in and discuss some of the events of his inner life which he felt needed clarification.

Then one day he brought a dream which he did not understand, and which troubled him deeply. This is the dream: *I am married. I have one child, about eighteen months old, barely walking. I take him by the hand and tell him that we will have an adventure. We find ourselves by a gigantic concrete sewer pipe. A small boat is at the landing. We get into the boat and take off, beginning to descend. We go deeper and deeper. I am paddling, steering the boat. We finally emerge in clear water. Someone tells us to get out, that the water is clear, it is rainwater, not sewage. We walk through the shallows to the shore. We are suddenly in a busy arcade. There are many stores. Much business is being transacted. A woman tells me that the business is finished. I can go back up. I take the child in my one arm and pull the blanket over his head and begin to swim upstream. I am not aware of any cold. I feel quite warm. We arrive in a room far*

*above. Another woman takes the child from me and I disrobe to
my shorts and dry myself. Shortly another woman comes to me
and tells me the child is dead. I exclaim that it is impossible. She
says that he has died through exposure to the cold in the water. I
am horrified and grief-stricken. I fall to my knees and ask God to
give him back to me. I pray.*

Feelings of grief and loss pervaded the days between the
dream and Abraham's coming to analysis. It seemed incomprehensible to him—after all his suffering and struggling to
come to consciousness—that this child, this gift of God,
should be taken from him. What was the symbolism of the
child, the symbolism of the rest of the dream?

It had been about eighteen months since Abraham's sickness, when he had found the time to reflect upon his life as he
had lived it in the past, goal-directed in his professional work
and even goal-directed in his spiritual pursuits. During this
period came insights which had their fruition in his change of
commitment—from goal to process. Also, during this time
there had been the swing away from the inner life, and the
many distractions that brought the opposite pole into the foreground of his attention. And then the movement turned back
to the other direction, but in a less violent, more tenable way.
And now there is a child of eighteen months, the child who
has grown from that time of new beginnings until this.

The concrete sewer pipe is a conduit of sorts through
which he must go with the child, through the filth and debris
which has been in his life and has sloughed off from his life, to
the place where the water is pure rain water. The past has
been clarified, through his working on it and his willingness to
look at it carefully and see the meaning in it. But again he
finds himself in the hustle and bustle of the marketplace—this
refers to his intensification of his professional life. In time he
is told that the business is finished. This can be nothing else
than a prefiguration of the end of life, his life. He can go back
up. There is to be another transformation, but this time there
is no vessel to carry him, he must swim through the waters.
And, in those waters he is not aware of any cold. The waters

are the waters of the unconscious, the final journey to the room "far above," which to the Roman Catholic would signify the eternal abode. Upon arriving here he is told that the child is dead; and he cannot believe it, he cannot accept it.

Throughout this dream there has been a woman near him. In the beginning of the dream it is said that he is "married." There has been in his life the experience of the *coniunctio oppositorum,* the meeting of the opposites. He has come to terms with his feeling side as well as his intellectual side. Over the long years Eros has come to rest beside Logos, so that the sacred marriage, called by the ancients the *hieros-gamos,* has occurred. The women whom he meets at various stages of his journey are guides through the mysterious regions of the unconscious; as such they are manifestations of the anima, the vessel of the soul.

But the child, who is the child whom he must give up in the end? We have learned that historically the appearance of a divine child heralds a new development, or an era of important change. In most legends and myths the advent of the child is hailed with joy and celebration. Not so in Abraham's dream. When the dream became fully articulate upon waking, Abraham was overwhelmed by the recollected grief and yet at the same time he was shocked into intense attention. That attention had not wavered very long, he kept returning and returning to the dream.

As we talked about the dream, the meaning of the child emerged out of the shade of sorrow. In the end a person must lose that which is most precious, that to which one's whole life has been devoted. The treasure is consciousness; it is the ego's final sacrifice to the self. This sacrifice must be offered before the ultimate moment when the individual merges with the unconscious and stands before God.

Abraham falls to his knees and asks God to give him back the child. He prays.

It is the prayer that may not or may be answered.

It belongs to the unknowable.

Notes

Introduction

1. C. G. Jung, *Memories, Dreams, Reflections.*
2. Ibid., p. 4.
3. Ibid., p. 84.
4. Ibid., p. 45.
5. Ibid., p. 32.
6. *Lehrbuch der Psychiatrie*, 4th Edition, 1890.
7. *Structure and Dynamics of the Psyche*, C. W. 8, p. 353.
8. Werner Heisenberg, *Physics and Philosophy*, p. 31.
9. Ibid., pp. 55–56.
10. *Memories, Dreams, Reflections*, p. 147.
11. *Psychiatric Studies*, C. W. 1, p. 3.

CHAPTER 1
Analyst and Analysand

1. *The Practice of Psychotherapy*, C. W. 16, pp. 53, 54.
2. Adapted from *Structure and Dynamics of the Psyche*, C. W. 8, p. 377.
3. James Hillman, *Suicide and the Soul*, p. 101.
4. See Chapter 7, "Anima and Animus: The Opposites Within."
5. Gerhard Adler, "Methods of Treatment in Analytical

Psychology," in *Psychoanalytic Techniques*, Benjamin B. Wolman, ed., p. 340.

6. Horace B. English and Ava C. English, *A Comprehensive Dictionary of Psychological and Psychoanalytical Terms*.
7. *The Practice of Psychotherapy*, C. W. 16, p. 164.
8. Gerhard Adler, op. cit., p. 344.
9. "Psychology of the Transference," in *The Practice of Psychotherapy*, C. W. 16, p. 178.

Chapter 2
Complexes by Day and Demons by Night

1. Sigmund Freud, *The Psychopathology of Everyday Life*.
2. *The Archetypes and the Collective Unconscious*, C. W. 9, i.
3. *The Structure and Dynamics of the Psyche*, C. W. 8, p. 315.
4. *Psychiatric Studies*, C. W. 1.
5. Ibid., p. 24.
6. Ibid., p. 39.
7. Ibid., p. 56.
8. Eugen Bleuler's article "Upon the Significance of Association Experiments," in C. G. Jung, *Studies in Word Association*, pp. 1–7, passim.
9. Ibid.
10. *Psychogenesis in Mental Disease*, C. W. 3, p. 41.
11. "A Review of the Complex Theory," in *The Structure and Dynamics of the Psyche*, C. W. 8, p. 92.
12. Ibid., p. 93.
13. Ibid.
14. Ibid., p. 96.
15. J. E. Cirlot, *A Dictionary of Symbols*, pp. 328–29.
16. Exodus 15:25.
17. Mircea Eliade, *Images and Symbols*, pp. 37–38.
18. In *Civilization in Transition*, C. W. 10.
19. Ibid., p. 50.
20. Ibid., p. 72.
21. "The Psychological Foundations of the Belief in Spirits," in *The Structure and Dynamics of the Psyche*, C. W. 8, p. 311.
22. Ibid., pp. 311–12.
23. Ibid., p. 312.

CHAPTER 3
From Associations to Archetypes

1. *Memories, Dreams, Reflections*, p. 148.
2. Ibid., p. 150.
3. Letter quoted in *Two Essays on Freud and Jung*, by Jolande Jacobi, p. 25.
4. *The Archetypes and the Collective Unconscious*, C. W. 9, i, "Concerning the Archetypes with Special Reference to the Anima Concept," p. 58.
5. Sigmund Freud, "Leonardo da Vinci and a Memory of His Childhood." Referred to by Jung in "The Concept of the Collective Unconscious," *The Archetypes and the Collective Unconscious*, pp. 44–49.
6. *Der Mythus von Der Geburt des Helden*, published in the series, *Schriften zur angewandten Seelenkunde*, Vienna: F. Deuticke, Heft 5, quoted in Freud, *Moses and Monotheism*, p. 7.
7. Sigmund Freud, *Moses and Monotheism*, pp. 7–11.
8. C. G. Jung, "The Psychology of the Child Archetype," in *The Archetypes and the Collective Unconscious*, C. W. 9, i, p. 152.
9. Ibid., p. 153.
10. "The Psychological Aspects of the Kore," in *The Archetypes and the Collective Unconscious*, C. W. 9, i, p. 183.
11. See also *Psychological Types*, Part II, Def. 26; "The Archetypes of the Collective Unconscious," "Concerning the Archetypes with Special Reference to the Anima Concept," "Psychological Aspects of the Mother Archetype," "The Psychology of the Child Archetype," and "The Psychological Aspects of the Kore," all in *The Archetypes and the Collective Unconscious*, C. W. 9, i; Commentary on *The Secret of the Golden Flower*, in *Alchemical Studies*, C. W. 13. For alternate sources see the complete list of Jung's *Collected Works* at the end of this volume.
12. Glover, *Freud or Jung*, pp. 21–22.
13. "The Personal and Collective Unconscious," in *Two Essays in Analytical Psychology*, C. W. 7, p. 65.
14. Ibid.

CHAPTER 4
Are Archetypes Necessary?

1. Jolande Jacobi, *Complex, Archetype, Symbol,* p. 31.
2. William Blake, *Visions of the Daughters of Albion,* p. 191.
3. Jones, *The Life and Works of Sigmund Freud,* Vol. 1, p. 29.
4. *Memories, Dreams, Reflections,* p. 168.
5. Alfred Lord Tennyson, *De Profundis,* in *Victorian and Later English Poets,* James Stephens, Edwin L. Beck and Royall H. Snow, eds., p. 187.
6. *Memories, Dreams, Reflections,* p. 167.
7. "The Sacrifice," in *Symbols of Transformation, C. W.* 5, pp. 416–17.
8. Ibid.
9. Ibid., pp. 417–18.
10. *Roche Report: Frontiers of Clinical Psychiatry,* March 12, 1969.
11. Ibid.
12. "Archetypes of the Collective Unconscious," in *The Archetypes of the Collective Unconscious, C. W.* 9, i, p. 5.
13. Ibid.
14. Ibid., pp. 4–5.
15. Joseph Campbell, *The Masks of God: Primitive Mythology,* p. 30.
16. N. Tinbergen, *The Study of Instinct,* pp. 7–8.
17. Campbell, loc. cit.

CHAPTER 5
Individuation: The Process of Becoming Whole

1. *Two Essays in Analytical Psychology, C. W.* 7, p. 171.
2. *The Secret of the Golden Flower,* p. 83.
3. Ibid., p. 160.
4. James M. Robinson, ed., *The Nag Hammadi Library,* p. 47.
5. Jolande Jacobi, *The Way of Individuation,* p. 19.

CHAPTER 6
Persona and Shadow

1. *Two Essays in Analytical Psychology, C. W.* 7, pp. 155–56.
2. Ibid., p. 156.
3. *Aion, C. W.* 9, ii, p. 8.

4. *Two Essays in Analytical Psychology*, C. W. 7, pp. 158–59.
5. Ibid., p. 159.
6. Ibid., p. 161.
7. Ibid., p. 162.
8. *Über die Energetik der Seele und andere psychologische Abhandlungen*, Zurich: Rascher, 1928, p. 158.

Chapter 7
Anima and Animus: The Opposites Within

1. C. W. 7.
2. In *The Archetypes and the Collective Unconscious*, C. W. 9, i.
3. Jung, *Contributions to Analytical Psychology*. New York: Harcourt, Brace, 1928. Cited in Phyllis Chesler, *Women and Madness*. New York: Doubleday, 1972. p. 77.
4. Jung, *Two Essays in Analytical Psychology*, C. W. 7, p. 205.
5. Ibid.
6. Jung, "The Stages of Life," in *The Structure and Dynamics of the Psyche*, C. W. 8, p. 399.
7. Jung, *Two Essays in Analytical Psychology*, C. W. 7, p. 186.
8. *The Feminine Mystique*, p. 304.
9. Ibid.
10. Ibid., p. 378.

Chapter 8
Circumambulating the Self

1. Edward C. Whitmont, *The Symbolic Quest*, p. 216.
2. *The "I" and the "Not-I."*
3. *Psychology and Alchemy*, C. W. 12, p. 304. For further study of alchemy in Jung's works, see the entire book, *Psychology and Alchemy*, also see *Alchemical Studies*, C. W. 13; *Mysterium Coniunctionis*, C. W. 14; *The Secret of the Golden Flower*, and "The Psychology of the Transference" in *The Practice of Psychotherapy*, C. W. 16. Also see Chapter 13, below.
4. *The Perennial Philosophy*, pp. 3–4.
5. William Blake, *A Song of Liberty*.
6. The archetype of the divine child is discussed by Jung in his essay "The Psychology of the Child Archetype," in *The Archetypes and the Collective Unconscious*, C. W. 9, i.

7. Cf. also Bacchus, Dionysus.
8. Marie-Louise von Franz, *The Problem of the Puer Aeternus.*
9. Ibid.
10. A full discussion of this archetype and the preceding one appears in James Hillman's essay, "Senex and Puer: An Aspect of the Historical and Psychological Present," in *Eranos-Jahrbuch* XXXVI/1967, Zurich: Rhein-Verlag, 1968.
11. *The Archetypes and the Collective Unconscious,* C. W. 9, i, p. 263.
12. William Blake, "Proverbs of Hell," from *The Marriage of Heaven and Hell.*
13. *Two Essays in Analytical Psychology,* C. W. 7, p. 225.
14. Cf. *Aion,* C. W. 9, ii, p. 22 and "The Psychology of the Transference" in *The Practice of Psychotherapy,* C. W. 16.
15. *Aion,* loc. cit.
16. Ibid., p. 23.
17. The reader is referred especially to the following volumes of the *Collected Works:* the entire book *Two Essays in Analytical Psychology,* C. W. 7; the last three essays in *The Archetypes and the Collective Unconscious,* C. W. 9, i; all of *Aion,* C. W. 9, ii; sections throughout *Psychology and Religion: West and East,* C. W. 11; *Psychology and Alchemy,* C. W. 12; *Alchemical Studies,* C. W. 13; *Mysterium Coniunctionis,* C. W. 14; and "The Psychology of the Transference" in *The Practice of Psychotherapy,* C. W. 16.
18. Cf. Jung, *The Secret of the Golden Flower,* p. 99f.

CHAPTER 9
Understanding Our Dreams

1. *Freud and Psychoanalysis,* C. W. 4, pp. 25ff.
2. *Memories, Dreams, Reflections,* p. 158.
3. Ibid., p. 161.
4. Ibid.
5. "The Practical Use of Dream Analysis," in *The Practice of Psychotherapy,* C. W. 16.
6. "General Aspects of Dream Psychology," in *The Structure and Dynamics of the Psyche,* C. W. 8, pp. 263–64.
7. "The Practical Use of Dream Analysis," in *The Practice of Psychotherapy,* C. W. 16, p. 149.
8. Ibid., p. 147.

9. "General Aspects of Dream Psychology," in *The Structure and Dynamics of the Psyche, C. W.* 8, p. 241.

10. Gershom Scholem, *Major Trends in Jewish Mysticism*, p. 44.

11. Jung, *The Secret of the Golden Flower*, pp. 91–92.

12. Jung, "General Aspects of Dream Psychology," in *The Structure and Dynamics of the Psyche, C. W.* 8, pp. 266ff.

13. Cf. Jung's essays, "General Aspects of Dream Psychology," and "On the Nature of Dreams," in *The Structure and Dynamics of the Psyche, C. W.* 8.

CHAPTER 10
Dreaming the Dream Onward: Active Imagination

1. Gerhard Adler, *Studies in Analytical Psychology*, pp. 60–61. For a fuller treatment of active imagination, see Gerhard Adler, *The Living Symbol*, and C. G. Jung, "The Transcendent Function," in *The Structure and Dynamics of the Psyche, C. W.* 8.

CHAPTER 11
Psychological Types: Key to Communication

1. *Two Essays in Analytical Psychology*, p. 18.

2. Ibid., p. 24.

3. Ibid., p. 26.

4. Ibid., p. 27.

5. Ibid., p. 31.

6. Ibid.

7. Ibid., pp. 34f.

8. Ibid., p. 39.

9. Ibid., p. 40.

10. Jung's analysis of their differences are to be found in the first of the *Two Essays in Analytical Psychology*.

11. Cited in *Psychological Types*, p. 9.

12. The following descriptions of cognitive modes are adapted from the *Interpretive Guide for the Singer-Loomis Inventory of Personality*, pp. 11–18.

CHAPTER 12
Psyche in the World

1. Jung, *Psychological Types,* C. W. 6.
2. Ibid.

CHAPTER 13
Religion: and Other Approaches to the Unknowable

1. Jung, *Psychology and Religion: West and East,* C. W. 11.
2. Revised and later published in the *Collected Works as Symbols of Transformation,* C. W. 5.
3. *Memories, Dreams, Reflections,* p. 182.
4. Ibid., pp. 182–83.
5. Ibid., p. 183.
6. *Psychology and Religion,* C. W. 11, p. 84.
7. "Five Who Care," *Look* magazine, April 21, 1970.
8. *Mysterium Coniunctionis,* C. W. 14, p. 547.
9. Ibid., p. 548.
10. Ibid.
11. *Aion, Researches into the Phenomenology of the Self,* C. W. 9, ii, p. 62 f.
12. *Psychology and Alchemy,* C. W. 12, p. 277.
13. *Aion,* C. W. 9, ii, p. 167.
14. *Psychology and Religion: West and East,* C. W. 11, pp. 201–96.
15. Ibid., p. 214.
16. Ibid., p. 221.
17. Ibid., pp. 226–27.
18. Ibid., p. 273.
19. *Psychology and Alchemy,* C. W. 12, pp. 338–39.
20. *Aion,* C. W. 9, ii, pp. 89–90.
21. In *The Structure and Dynamics of the Psyche,* C. W. 8, pp. 417–531.
22. Letter to Dr. Selig dated 25 February, 1953, in *Spring,* 1971, p. 127.
23. *The Structure and Dynamics of the Psyche,* C. W. 8, p. 475.
24. *Psychology and Religion: West and East,* C. W. 11, contains psychological commentaries on *The Tibetan Book of the Great Liberation* and *The Tibetan Book of the Dead;* "Yoga and the West," the "Foreword to Suzuki's Introduction to Zen

Buddhism," "The Psychology of Eastern Meditation," "The
Holy Men of India: Introduction to Zimmer's *Der Weg zum
Selbst*," "Foreword to the *I Ching*" and his "Commentary on
The Secret of the Golden Flower: a Chinese Book of Life."

25. W. Y. Evans-Wentz (compiler and editor), *The Tibetan Book of
the Dead*, with a psychological commentary by Dr. C. G. Jung.
26. Timothy Leary, Ralph Metzner, and Richard Alpert, *The
Psychedelic Experience: A Manual Based on the Tibetan Book of
the Dead*, p. 22.
27. Ibid.
28. "Psychological Commentary on *The Tibetan Book of the Great
Liberation*," in *Psychology and Religion*, C. W. 11, pp. 504–5.
29. Sogyal Rinpoche, *The Tibetan Book of Living and Dying*,
pp. 46–47.
30. Cf. M. Esther Harding, *The "I" and the "Not-I."*
31. *Psychology and Religion*, C. W. 11, p. 533.
32. Ibid., p. 535.

Chapter 14
We Were Born Dying

1. *Memories, Dreams, Reflections*, p. 291.
2. *Ars moriendi*, the art of dying, was one of the favorite subjects
of philosophers and theologians during the Renaissance. Many
treatises were written to instruct the soul in the manner of
dying. An oriental example would be *The Tibetan Book of the
Dead*, which was referred to in Chapter 13.
3. *The Structure and Dynamics of the Psyche*, C. W. 8, p. 399.
4. How different the meaning of the same symbol when it
appears to two different people! (Cf. Julian's dream, p. 427.) A
patient once told me, "I have been doing some thinking about
the Freudian apparatus: the choice and insistence upon
arbitrary meanings is, on the whole, and with the whole
person observed, something like treating the patient with a
gypsy dream book. So little comes from the patient and so
much from the analyst. I suspect the long silences and the
apparent blocking are unconscious ploys to divert the
conscious mind from those meanings which surface from the
unconscious dream experience to a system of references which
accords with the symbolic dictionary."

5. Heraclitus (c. 540–475 B.C.) was said to be in a real sense the
   founder of metaphysics. He believed that the fundamental
   uniform fact in nature is constant change. He thus arrived at
   the principle of relativity: harmony and unity consist in
   diversity and multiplicity. The senses are "bad witnesses"; only
   the wise man can obtain knowledge. This attitude is implicit in
   the *Seven Sermons of the Dead* (cf. Chapter 13).

List of
Works Cited

BOOKS

ADLER, GERHARD: *Studies in Analytical Psychology*. New York: G. P. Putnam's Sons (1966).

——: *The Living Symbol*. New York: Pantheon Books (1961). Bollingen Series 63.

BAKAN, DAVID: *Sigmund Freud and the Jewish Mystical Tradition*. New York: D. Van Nostrand Co. (1958).

BERTINE, ELEANOR: *Human Relationships*. New York: Longmans, Green and Company (1958).

——: *Jung's Contributions to Our Times*. New York: G. P. Putnam's Sons (1967).

BLAKE, WILLIAM: *The Complete Writings of William Blake, with all the Variant Readings*, edited by Geoffrey Keynes. London: The Nonesuch Press (1957).

BLY, ROBERT: *Iron John: A Book about Men*. Redding, MA: Addison Wesley (1990).

CAMPBELL, JOSEPH: *Hero with a Thousand Faces*. New York: Pantheon Books, Bollingen Series 17 (1949).

——: *The Masks of God: Primitive Mythology*. New York: Viking Press (1959).

CHESLER, PHYLLIS: *Women and Madness.* New York: Doubleday (1972).

CHINEN, ALLAN B.: *Beyond the Hero: Classic Stories of Men in Search of Soul.* New York: Jeremy P. Tarcher/Putnam (1993).

CIRLOT, J. E.: *A Dictionary of Symbols.* New York: Philosophical Library (1962).

ELIADE, MIRCEA: *From Primitives to Zen.* New York: Harper & Row (1967).

———: *Images and Symbols,* translated by Philip Mairet, from the Librairie Gallimard, 1952, London: Harvill Press (1961).

ENGLISH, HORACE B., and AVA C.: *A Comprehensive Dictionary of Psychological and Psychoanalytical Terms.* New York: Longmans, Green and Company (1961).

ESTÉS, CLARISSA P.: *Women Who Run With the Wolves.* New York: Ballantine (1992).

EVANS-WENTZ, W. Y., compiler and editor: *The Tibetan Book of the Dead.* Oxford: A Galaxy Book; Oxford University Press (1969).

FRANKL, VIKTOR: *Man's Search for Meaning.* New York: Washington Square Press (1969).

FREUD, SIGMUND: The Standard Edition of the *Complete Psychological Works,* translated from the German under the General Editorship of James Strachey, in collaboration with Anna Freud, assisted by Alix Strachey and Alan Tyson. London: The Hogarth Press and the Institute of Psycho-Analysis (1968).

Vol. IV: *The Interpretation of Dreams.*

Vol. VI: *The Psychopathology of Everyday Life.*

Vol. XXIII: *An Outline of Psycho-Analysis.*

Vol. XXIII: *Moses and Monotheism.*

———: *Moses and Monotheism.* New York: A Vintage Book (1939).

FRIEDAN, BETTY: *The Feminine Mystique.* New York: W. W. Norton (1963).

GLOVER, EDWARD: *Freud or Jung.* Cleveland, Ohio: A Meridian Book, World Publishing Co. (1963).

HARDING, M. ESTHER: *The "I" and the "Not-I."* New York: Pantheon Books, Random House, Bollingen Series 79 (1965).

———: *The Parental Image, Its Injury and Reconstruction.* New York: G. P. Putnam's Sons for the C. G. Jung Foundation (1965).

———: *The Way of All Women.* New York: G. P. Putnam's Sons (1970).

———: *Women's Mysteries.* New York: G. P. Putnam's Sons (1971).

HEISENBERG, WERNER: *Physics and Philosophy.* New York: Harper and Brothers (1958).

HILLMAN, JAMES: *Suicide and the Soul.* New York: Harper & Row (1964).

———: *We've Had a Hundred Years of Psychotherapy and the World's Getting Worse.* San Francisco: HarperSanFrancisco (1993).

HUXLEY, ALDOUS: *The Perennial Philosophy.* New York: Harper Colophon Books (1970).

JACOBI, JOLANDE: *Complex/Archetype/Symbol in the Psychology of C. G. Jung.* New York: Pantheon Books, Bollingen Series 57 (1959).

———: *The Way of Individuation.* New York: Harcourt, Brace & World (1967).

JANOV, ARTHUR: *The Primal Scream, Primal Therapy: The Cure for Neurosis.* New York: G. P. Putnam's Sons, 1970.

JONES, ERNEST: *The Life and Work of Sigmund Freud,* 3 vols. New York: Basic Books (1953).

JUNG, CARL G.: *Collected Works.* Princeton: Princeton University Press, Bollingen Series XX. Edited by Sir Herbert Read, Michael Fordham, M.D., M.R.C.P., and Gerhard Adler, Ph.D. Translated by R. F. C. Hull.

Vol. 1: *Psychiatric Studies* (1957).

Vol. 3: *Psychogenesis in Mental Disease* (1960).

Vol. 4: *Freud and Psychoanalysis* (1961).

Vol. 5: *Symbols of Transformation* (1956).

Vol. 6: *Psychological Types* (1971).

Vol. 7: *Two Essays on Analytical Psychology* (1953).

Vol. 8: *The Structure and Dynamics of the Psyche* (1960).

Vol. 9, i: *The Archetypes and the Collective Unconscious* (1959).

Vol. 9, ii: *Aion: Researches into the Phenomenology of the Self* (1959).

Vol. 10: *Civilization in Transition* (1964).

Vol. 11: *Psychology and Religion: West and East* (1958).

Vol. 12: *Psychology and Alchemy* (1953).

Vol. 13: *Alchemical Studies* (1967).

Vol. 14: *Mysterium Coniunctionis* (1963).

Vol. 16: *The Practice of Psychotherapy* (1954).

———: *Contributions to Analytical Psychology.* New York: Harcourt, Brace (1928).

———: *Memories, Dreams, Reflections,* recorded and edited by Aniela

Jaffé. New York: Pantheon Books, a division of Random House (1963).

———: *Modern Man in Search of a Soul.* New York: A Harvest Book, Harcourt Brace & Co. (1933).

———: *Psychological Reflections*, selections edited by Jolande Jacobi. New York: Harper Torchbooks (1961).

———: *Psychological Types.* London: Routledge & Kegan Paul (1959). (Now available in the *Collected Works* as Volume 6.)

———: *Psychology of the Unconscious.* London: Kegan Paul, Trench, Trubner (1922).

——— et al.: *Studies in Word Association*, authorized translation by Dr. M. D. Eder. New York: Russell and Russell (1969).

———: *The Secret of the Golden Flower: A Chinese Book of Life*, translated and explained by Richard Wilhelm with a Commentary by C. G. Jung. New York: Harcourt, Brace & World (1965).

———: *Über die Energetik der Seele und andere psychologische Abhandlungen.* Zurich: Rascher (1928).

JUNG, EMMA: *Animus and Anima.* New York: The Analytical Psychology Club of New York (1957).

KEEN, SAM: *Fire in the Belly: On Being a Man.* New York: Bantam (1991).

KRAFFT-EBING: *Lehrbuch der Psychiatrie.* 4th Edition (1890), cited in Jung, *Memories, Dreams, Reflections.*

LEARY, TIMOTHY; RALPH METZNER; and RICHARD ALPERT: *The Psychedelic Experience, A Manual Based on the Tibetan Book of the Dead.* New Hyde Park, New York: University Books (1964).

LEVI, EDWARD H.: *Points of View.* Chicago: A Phoenix Book, University of Chicago Press (1969).

McGLASHAN, ALAN: *A Savage and Beautiful Country.* Boston: Houghton, Mifflin (1967).

MEYER, V., and EDWARD S. CHESSER: *Behavior Therapy in Clinical Psychiatry.* New York: Science House, 1970.

MOORE, ROBERT L., and DOUGLAS GILLETTE: *King, Warrior, Magician, Lover.* San Francisco: HarperSanFrancisco (1990).

MYERS, ISABELLE B.: *The Myers-Briggs Type Indicator.* Palo Alto, CA: Consulting Psychologists Press (1962).

NEUMANN, ERICH: *Amor and Psyche: The Psychic Development of the Feminine*, translated by Ralph Manheim. New York: Pantheon Books (1956). Bollingen Series 54.

————: *The Great Mother*, translated by Ralph Manheim. New York: Pantheon Books (1955). Bollingen Series 47.

PLATO: *The Republic*. Chicago: Encyclopedia Britannica, Great Books of the Western World, Vol. 7 (1955).

RANK, OTTO: *The Myth of the Birth of the Hero*. Vienna: F. Deuticke, Heft 5 (1909).

ROBINSON, JAMES A. (ed.): *The Nag Hammadi Library*. San Francisco: Harper & Row (1988).

ROSZAK, THEODORE: *The Making of a Counter-Culture*. Garden City, New York: Doubleday & Company, Inc., Anchor Books (1969).

SASS, LOUIS A. *The Paradoxes of Delusion: Wittgenstein, Schreber and the Schizophrenic Mind*. Ithaca, NY: Cornell University Press (1993).

SCHOLEM, GERSHOM G.: *Major Trends in Jewish Mysticism*. New York: Schocken (1961).

SINGER, JUNE: *Androgyny: The Opposites Within*. Boston: Sigo Press (1989).

————, and MARY LOOMIS: *The Singer-Loomis Inventory of Personality*. Palo Alto, CA: Consulting Psychologists Press (1984).

SOGYAL RINPOCHE. *The Tibetan Book of Living and Dying*. San Francisco: HarperCollins (1992).

STEPHENS, JAMES; EDWIN L. BECK; and ROYALL H. SNOW: *Victorian and Later English Poets*. New York: American Book Company (1937).

TINBERGEN, N.: *The Study of Instinct*. London: Oxford University Press (1951).

VON FRANZ, MARIE-LOUISE: *The Problem of the Puer Aeternus*. New York: Spring Publications (1970). A private limited edition.

WHEELWRIGHT, JOSEPH B., JANE WHEELWRIGHT, and J. H. BUEHLER: *Jungian Type Survey* (the Gray-Wheelwright Test). San Francisco: Society of Jungian Analysts of Northern California (1964).

WHITMONT, EDWARD C.: *The Symbolic Quest*. New York: G. P. Putnam's Sons (1969).

WOLMAN, BENJAMIN B., editor, *Psychoanalytical Techniques*. New York: Basic Books, Gerhard Adler article, "Methods of Treatment in Analytical Psychology" (1967).

PERIODICALS

Behavior Today, June 22, 1970.
Chicago *Sun-Times*, August 12, 1970, p. 64.

GREELEY, ANDREW M.: "There's a New Time Religion on Campus," The New York *Times* Magazine, June 1, 1969.

HILLMAN, JAMES: "Senex and Puer: An Aspect of the Historical and Psychological Present," *Eranos-Jahrbuch* XXXVI/1967, Zurich: Rhein-Verlag (1968).

JUNG, CARL G.: "Letter to Dr. Selig dated 25 February, 1953," *Spring*, 1971.

MEAD, MARGARET: "Five Who Care," *Look*, April 21, 1970.

OTTO, HERBERT A.: "Has Monogamy Failed?" *Saturday Review*, April 25, 1970.

Roche Report: Frontiers of Clinical Psychiatry, March 12, 1969.

OTHER SOURCES

JACOBI, JOLANDE: *Two Essays on Freud and Jung*, Zurich: C. G. Jung Institute (1958). A pamphlet privately printed.

JUNG, CARL G.: *Seven Sermons of the Dead*, an unpublished manuscript privately circulated by Dr. Jung.

Women in the University of Chicago, Report of the Committee on University Women (May 1, 1970). Prepared for the Committee of the Council of the University Senate.

Index

Health care
  "managed," 124, 358
  mental, 18–19, 357–59
  and psychological components
    of disease, 367–69
Heine, Heinrich, *Deutschland,* 326
Heisenberg, Werner, xxxiv
Helios, 232
Hephaestus, 334
Heracles, 99
Hermes, 179
Hermes Trismegistus, 134
Hero (archetype), 128, 220
Hero's quest, 220
Hesse, Hermann, xv
Hillel, Rabbi, 12–13
Hinduism, xxiv, 117, 138, 408
  See also Yoga
Hitler, Adolf, 179
Homosexuality, 34–35, 37, 206
Hormones, male and female, 186–
  87
Hubert, H., 127
Huxley, Aldous, xv, 213
Hypnagogic visions, 71
Hysterical people, 328

Icarus, 233
Id, 95, 96
Imagination
  active. *See* Active imagination
  as universal quality, 87–88
Imago Dei, 126
Immigrants, 365
Impotence, 167, 235
Incest, Jung's conception of, 116–
  18
Incest barrier, 117–18
Incest wish, 97
Indigenous peoples, 364–65
Individual Psychology, 320, 322
Individuation (individuation
    process), 12–14, 133–57
  actualization of unconscious
    needed for, 79

in analysis, 143–44
  an analysand's poem, 155–57
  archetypal journey, 220–31
  dreams, 139–43, 145–52
  reason for crisis, 160
can continue into old age, 191
definition of, 137
freeing of ego as result of, 231
Jung on, 355–56
the Mass as rite of, 400
as natural process, 137
psychic energy as thrust for,
  209–10
self as instigator of, 218–19,
  395–96
in *Seven Sermons of the Dead,*
  382, 396
as "way of individuation," 6, 12,
  136–37
Inferiority complex, 46
Innate releasing mechanism
    (IRM), 127, 128
Instinct, 95, 96, 106, 322
International Association of
    Analytical Psychologists, xiv
Interpretation of Dreams, The
    (Freud), xxxv, 51, 91, 243
Introversion, 324–29, 345–46
  as Platonic, 326–27
  popular knowledge of, 319–20
Introverted feeling, 332–33
Introverted intuition, Plato as
    example of, 331–32
Introverted sensation, 334, 337–38
Introverted thinking, 333, 346
Intuition, 329, 330, 346
  in *Seven Sermons of the Dead,*
    387
Irenaeus, 126
IRM (innate releasing
    mechanism), 127, 128
Iron John (Bly), 205
Isolated psychic processes, as
    impossible, 69
"Ivenes," 58, 60

The Collected Works of C. G. Jung

BOLLINGEN SERIES XX.
PUBLISHED BY PRINCETON UNIVERSITY PRESS.
PRINCETON, NEW JERSEY

* Published 1957; 2nd edn., 1970.

*2. Experimental Researches

Translated by Leopold Stein in collaboration with Diana Riviere

STUDIES IN WORD ASSOCIATION (1904–7)

The Associations of Normal Subjects (by Jung and F. Riklin)
An Analysis of the Associations of an Epileptic
The Reaction-Time Ratio in the Association Experiment
Experimental Observations on the Faculty of Memory
Psychoanalysis and Association Experiments
The Psychological Diagnosis of Evidence
Association, Dream, and Hysterical Symptom
The Psychopathological Significance of the Association Experiment
Disturbances in Reproduction in the Association Experiment
The Association Method
The Family Constellation

PSYCHOPHYSICAL RESEARCHES (1907–8)

On the Psychophysical Relations of the Association Experiment
Psychophysical Investigations with the Galvanometer and
    Pneumograph in Normal and Insane Individuals (by F.
    Peterson and Jung)
Further Investigations on the Galvanic Phenomenon and Respiration
    in Normal and Insane Individuals (by C. Ricksher and Jung)
Appendix: Statistical Details of Enlistment (1906); New Aspects of
    Criminal Psychology (1908); The Psychological Methods of
    Investigation Used in the Psychiatric Clinic of the University of
    Zurich (1910); On the Doctrine of Complexes ([1911] 1913); On
    the Psychological Diagnosis of Evidence (1937)

†3. The Psychogenesis of Mental Disease

The Psychology of Dementia Praecox (1907)
The Content of the Psychoses (1908/1914)
On Psychological Understanding (1914)
A Criticism of Bleuler's Theory of Schizophrenic Negativism (1911)

* Published 1973.
† Published 1960.

On the Importance of the Unconscious in Psychopathology (1914)
On the Problem of Psychogenesis in Mental Disease (1919)
Mental Disease and the Psyche (1928)
On the Psychogenesis of Schizophrenia (1939)
Recent Thoughts on Schizophrenia (1957)
Schizophrenia (1958)

*4. Freud and Psychoanalysis

Freud's Theory of Hysteria: A Reply to Aschaffenburg (1906)
The Freudian Theory of Hysteria (1908)
The Analysis of Dreams (1909)
A Contribution to the Psychology of Rumour (1910–11)
On the Significance of Number Dreams (1910–11)
Morton Prince, "The Mechanism and Interpretation of Dreams": A
    Critical Review (1911)
On the Criticism of Psychoanalysis (1910)
Concerning Psychoanalysis (1912)
The Theory of Psychoanalysis (1913)
General Aspects of Psychoanalysis (1913)
Psychoanalysis and Neurosis (1916)
Some Crucial Points in Psychoanalysis: A Correspondence between
    Dr. Jung and Dr. Loÿ (1914)
Prefaces to "Collected Papers on Analytical Psychology" (1916, 1917)
The Significance of the Father in the Destiny of the Individual (1909/
    1949)
Introduction to Kranefeldt's "Secret Ways of the Mind" (1930)
Freud and Jung: Contrasts (1929)

†5. Symbols of Transformation (1911–12/1952)

PART I

Introduction
Two Kinds of Thinking
The Miller Fantasies: Anamnesis
The Hymn of Creation
The Song of the Moth

* Published 1961.
† Published 1956; 2nd edn., 1967. (65 plates, 43 text figures.)

PART II

*6. Psychological Types (1921)

†7. Two Essays in Analytical Psychology

* Published 1971.
† Published 1953; 2nd edn., 1966.

*8. The Structure and Dynamics of the Psyche

On Psychic Energy (1928)
The Transcendent Function ([1916]/1957)
A Review of the Complex Theory (1934)
The Significance of Constitution and Heredity in Psychology (1929)
Psychological Factors Determining Human Behavior (1937)
Instinct and the Unconscious (1919)
The Structure of the Psyche (1927/1931)
On the Nature of the Psyche (1947/1954)
General Aspects of Dream Psychology (1916/1948)
On the Nature of Dreams (1945/1948)
The Psychological Foundations of Belief in Spirits (1920/1948)
Spirit and Life (1926)
Basic Postulates of Analytical Psychology (1931)
Analytical Psychology and *Weltanschauung* (1928/1931)
The Real and the Surreal (1933)
The Stages of Life (1930–1931)
The Soul and Death (1934)
Synchronicity: An Acausal Connecting Principle (1952)
Appendix: On Synchronicity (1951)

†9. The Archetypes and the Collective Unconscious

PART I

Archetypes of the Collective Unconscious (1934/1954)
The Concept of the Collective Unconscious (1936)
Concerning the Archetypes, with Special Reference to the Anima
    Concept (1936/1954)
Psychological Aspects of the Mother Archetype (1938/1954)
Concerning Rebirth (1940/1950)
The Psychology of the Child Archetype (1940)
The Psychological Aspects of the Kore (1941)
The Phenomenology of the Spirit in Fairytales (1945/1948)
On the Psychology of the Trickster-Figure (1954)
Conscious, Unconscious, and Individuation (1939)
A Study in the Process of Individuation (1934/1950)

* Published 1960; 2nd edn., 1969.
† Published 1959; 2nd edn., 1968. (Part I: 79 plates, with 29 in color.)

* Published 1959; 2nd edn., 1968. (Part I: 79 plates, with 29 in color.)
† Published 1964; 2nd edn., 1970. (8 plates.)

The Undiscovered Self (Present and Future) (1957)
Flying Saucers: A Modern Myth (1958)
A Psychological View of Conscience (1958)
Good and Evil in Analytical Psychology (1959)
Introduction to Wolff's "Studies in Jungian Psychology" (1959)
The Swiss Line in the European Spectrum (1928)
Reviews of Keyserling's "America Set Free" (1930) and
    "La Révolution Mondiale" (1934)
The Complications of American Psychology (1930)
The Dreamlike World of India (1939)
What India Can Teach Us (1939)
Appendix: Documents (1933–38)

*11. Psychology and Religion: West and East

WESTERN RELIGION

Psychology and Religion (The Terry Lectures) (1938/1940)
A Psychological Approach to the Dogma of the Trinity (1942/1948)
Transformation Symbolism in the Mass (1942/1954)
Forewords to White's "God and the Unconscious" and Werblowsky's
    "Lucifer and Prometheus" (1952)
Brother Klaus (1933)
Psychotherapists or the Clergy (1932)
Psychoanalysis and the Cure of Souls (1928)
Answer to Job (1952)

EASTERN RELIGION

Psychological Commentaries on "The Tibetan Book of the Great
    Liberation" (1939/1954) and "The Tibetan Book of the Dead"
    (1935/1953)
Yoga and the West (1936)
Foreword to Suzuki's "Introduction to Zen Buddhism" (1939)
The Psychology of Eastern Meditation (1943)
The Holy Men of India: Introduction to Zimmer's "Der Weg zum
    Selbst" (1944)
Foreword to the "I Ching" (1950)

* Published 1958; 2nd edn., 1969.

*12. Psychology and Alchemy (1944)

Prefatory note to the English Edition ([1951?] added 1967)
Introduction to the Religious and Psychological Problems of
    Alchemy
Individual Dream Symbolism in Relation to Alchemy (1936)
Religious Ideas in Alchemy (1937)
Epilogue

†13. Alchemical Studies

Commentary on "The Secret of the Golden Flower" (1929)
The Visions of Zosimos (1938/1954)
Paracelsus as a Spiritual Phenomenon (1942)
The Spirit Mercurius (1943/1948)
The Philosophical Tree (1945/1954)

‡14. Mysterium Coniunctionis (1955–56)

AN INQUIRY INTO THE SEPARATION AND SYNTHESIS OF PSYCHIC
OPPOSITES IN ALCHEMY

The Components of the Coniunctio
The Paradoxa
The Personification of the Opposites
Rex and Regina
Adam and Eve
The Conjunction

**15. The Spirit in Man, Art, and Literature

Paracelsus (1929)
Paracelsus the Physician (1941)
Sigmund Freud in His Historical Setting (1932)
In Memory of Sigmund Freud (1939)
Richard Wilhelm: In Memoriam (1930)

* Published 1953; 2nd edn., completely revised, 1968. (270 illustrations.)
† Published 1968. (50 plates, 4 text figures.)
‡ Published 1963; 2nd edn., 1970. (10 plates.)
** Published 1966.

On the Relation of Analytical Psychology to Poetry (1922)
Psychology and Literature (1930/1950)
"Ulysses": A Monologue (1932)
Picasso (1932)

*16. The Practice of Psychotherapy

GENERAL PROBLEMS OF PSYCHOTHERAPY

Principles of Practical Psychotherapy (1935)
What Is Psychotherapy? (1935)
Some Aspects of Modern Psychotherapy (1930)
The Aims of Psychotherapy (1931)
Problems of Modern Psychotherapy (1929)
Psychotherapy and a Philosophy of Life (1943)
Medicine and Psychotherapy (1945)
Psychotherapy Today (1945)
Fundamental Questions of Psychotherapy (1951)

SPECIFIC PROBLEMS OF PSYCHOTHERAPY

The Therapeutic Value of Abreaction (1921/1928)
The Practical Use of Dream-Analysis (1934)
The Psychology of the Transference (1946)
Appendix: The Realities of Practical Psychotherapy ([1937] added, 1966)

†17. The Development of Personality

Psychic Conflicts in a Child (1910/1946)
Introduction to Wickes's "Analyse der Kinderseele" (1927/1931)
Child Development and Education (1928)
Analytical Psychology and Education: Three Lectures (1926/1946)
The Gifted Child (1943)
The Significance of the Unconscious in Individual Education (1928)
The Development of Personality (1934)
Marriage as a Psychological Relationship (1925)

* Published 1954; 2nd edn., revised and augmented, 1966. (13 illustrations.)
† Published 1954.

*18. The Symbolic Life

Miscellaneous Writings

†19. General Bibliography of C. G. Jung's Writings

‡20. General Index to the Collected Works

See also:

C. G. JUNG: LETTERS
Selected and edited by Gerhard Adler, in collaboration with
    Aniela Jaffé.
Translations from the German by R. F. C. Hull.
  vol. 1: 1906–1950
  vol. 2: 1951–1961

THE FREUD/JUNG LETTERS
Edited by William McGuire,
translated by Ralph Manheim and R. F. C. Hull

C. G. JUNG SPEAKING: INTERVIEWS AND ENCOUNTERS
Edited by William McGuire and R. F. C. Hull

---

* Published 1976.
† Published 1979.
‡ Published 1979.

About the Author

JUNE SINGER is a Jungian analyst who has practiced and taught for over thirty years. She holds a Diploma in Analytical Psychology from the C. G. Jung Institute in Zurich and a Ph.D. from Northwestern University. Dr. Singer was a founder of the C. G. Jung Institute of Chicago and of the Inter-Regional Society of Jungian analysts. She is the author of *A Gnostic Book of Hours: Keys to Inner Wisdom; Seeing Through the Visible World: Jung, Gnosis and Chaos; Love's Energies; Androgyny: The Opposites Within;* and *The Unholy Bible: Blake, Jung and the Collective Unconscious.*

June Singer lives in Palo Alto, California.